JEREMIAH 26-52
A Commentary in the Wesleyan Tradition

*New Beacon Bible Commentary

JEREMIAH 26-52
A Commentary in the Wesleyan Tradition

Alex Varughese
Mitchel Modine

BEACON HILL PRESS
OF KANSAS CITY

Copyright 2010
by Alex Varughese, Mitchel Modine, and Beacon Hill Press of Kansas City

ISBN 978-0-8341-2406-6

Printed in the United States of America

Unless otherwise indicated all Scripture quotations are from the *Holy Bible, New International Version*® (NIV®). Copyright © 1973, 1978, 1984 by International Bible Society. Used by permission of Zondervan Publishing House. All rights reserved.

King James Version (KJV).

The following have been used by permission:

The *New American Standard Bible*® (NASB®), © copyright The Lockman Foundation 1960, 1962, 1963, 1968, 1971, 1972, 1973, 1975, 1977, 1995.

The New English Bible (NEB). Copyright © by the Delegates of the Oxford University Press and the Syndics of the Cambridge University Press, 1961, 1970.

The *New King James Version* (NKJV). Copyright © 1979, 1980, 1982 Thomas Nelson, Inc.

The *New Revised Standard Version* (NRSV) of the Bible, copyright 1989 by the Division of Christian Education of the National Council of the Churches of Christ in the USA. Used by permission. All rights reserved.

The *Revised Standard Version* (RSV) of the Bible, copyright 1946, 1952, 1971 by the Division of Christian Education of the National Council of the Churches of Christ in the USA.

Library of Congress Cataloging-in-Publication Data

Varughese, Alex, 1945-
   Jeremiah 26-52 / Alex Varughese, Mitchel Modine.
     p. cm. — (New Beacon Bible commentary)
   Includes bibliographical references.
   ISBN 978-0-8341-2406-6 (pbk.)
  1. Bible. O.T. Jeremiah XXVI-LII—Commentaries. I. Modine, Mitchel. II. Title.

   BS1525.53.V37 2010
   224'.207—dc22

                                                  2009042740

DEDICATION

To the loving memory of my parents, who lived a life
of devotion to God and trust in his promises
—Alex Varughese

To Mike and Lisa: you helped more than you knew
—Mitchel Modine

COMMENTARY EDITORS

General Editors

Alex Varughese
    Ph.D., Drew University
    Professor of Biblical Literature
    Mount Vernon Nazarene University
    Mount Vernon, Ohio

George Lyons
    Ph.D., Emory University
    Professor of New Testament
    Northwest Nazarene University
    Nampa, Idaho

Roger Hahn
    Ph.D., Duke University
    Dean of the Faculty
    Professor of New Testament
    Nazarene Theological Seminary
    Kansas City, Missouri

Section Editors

Joseph Coleson
    Ph.D., Brandeis University
    Professor of Old Testament
    Nazarene Theological Seminary
    Kansas City, Missouri

Kent Brower
    Ph.D., The University of Manchester
    Vice Principal
    Senior Lecturer in Biblical Studies
    Nazarene Theological College
    Manchester, England

Robert Branson
    Ph.D., Boston University
    Professor of Biblical Literature Emeritus
    Olivet Nazarene University
    Bourbonnais, Illinois

George Lyons
    Ph.D., Emory University
    Professor of New Testament
    Northwest Nazarene University
    Nampa, Idaho

Alex Varughese
    Ph.D., Drew University
    Professor of Biblical Literature
    Mount Vernon Nazarene University
    Mount Vernon, Ohio

Frank G. Carver
    Ph.D., New College, University of Edinburgh
    Professor Emeritus of Religion
    Point Loma Nazarene University
    San Diego, California

Jim Edlin
    Ph.D., Southern Baptist Theological Seminary
    Professor of Biblical Literature and Languages
    Chair, Division of Religion and Philosophy
    MidAmerica Nazarene University
    Olathe, Kansas

CONTENTS

General Editors' Preface	11
Acknowledgments	13
Abbreviations	15
Bibliography	17

INTRODUCTION	21
A. The Importance of the Book of Jeremiah	21
B. Historical Setting	22
C. Jeremiah the Prophet	24
D. Content, Genre, and Structure	26
E. Hebrew Text Traditions of Jeremiah	31
F. Theological Themes	31
1. The Incomparable Creator	32
2. The Sovereign God's Special Relationship to Israel	32
3. The Sovereign God of the Nations	33
4. The Sovereign Judge of Judah	34
5. The Sovereign God's Promise of Israel's Healing and Restoration	35
6. God's Sovereignty and Freedom	36
7. The Sovereign God's Sovereign Word	37

COMMENTARY	39
"Build and Plant": A New Phase in the Prophet's Ministry (26:1-24)	39
1. The Temple Sermon (26:1-6)	43
2. The Trial (26:7-16)	46
3. Support for the Verdict (26:17-19)	51
4. The Unlucky Uriah (26:20-23)	53
5. Jeremiah's Escape from Death (26:24)	55
"Build and Plant": The Judean Question About the Yoke of Babylon (27:1—29:32)	60
A. Submit to Babylon (27:1-22)	61
1. Yahweh's Command to Jeremiah (27:1-4)	62
2. Yahweh's Message to the Kings (27:5-11)	64
3. Yahweh's Word to Zedekiah (27:12-15)	67
4. Yahweh's Word to the Priests and the People (27:16-18)	69
5. Yahweh's Word About Pillars, Fixed Objects, and the Remaining Vessels (27:19-22)	70

B. The Prophet Encounters the Prophet (28:1-17)	73
1. The Prophet vs. the Prophet—Round One (28:1-4)	74
2. The Prophet vs. the Prophet—Round Two (28:5-9)	76
3. The Prophet vs. the Prophet—Round Three (28:10-11)	78
4. The Prophet vs. the Prophet—Round Four (28:12-17)	79
C. An Unwelcome Letter (29:1-32)	83
1. Unpack and Settle Down in Babylon (29:1-14)	86
2. Another Word to the Bad Figs (29:15-19)	93
3. Because They Have Committed Folly (29:20-23)	94
4. Aren't You in Charge? (29:24-28)	95
5. He Will Not See the Good (29:29-32)	97
"Build and Plant": The Promise of Restoration (30:1—33:26)	**102**
A. Yahweh Promises to Restore Judah and Israel (30:1—31:40)	103
1. Write in a Book (30:1-3)	105
2. Comfort to Those Who Mourn (30:4-7, 8-11)	107
3. I Will Heal You (30:12-17)	114
4. A City Shall Be Built on Its Mound (30:18-22)	118
5. The Tempest of Yahweh (30:23-24)	122
6. The Promise of Grace in the Wilderness (31:1-6)	124
7. With Weeping and Rejoicing They Shall Return (31:7-14)	128
8. Yahweh Comforts Rachel and Ephraim (31:15-22)	136
9. A Pleasant Dream (31:23-26)	144
10. All Shall Die for Their Own Sins (31:27-30)	146
11. The New Covenant (31:31-34)	150
12. Yahweh's Enduring Relationship with Israel (31:35-37)	161
13. The Rebuilding of Jerusalem (31:38-40)	163
B. Jeremiah's Confident Hope in the Future of Judah (32:1-44)	166
1. Jeremiah's Arrest and Imprisonment (32:1-5)	167
2. Jeremiah Purchases Hanamel's Field (32:6-15)	168
3. Jeremiah's Prayer (32:16-25)	171
4. Yahweh's Response (32:26-44)	173
C. The Full Restoration of Israel (33:1-26)	178
1. The Promise of Healing, Prosperity, and Security (33:1-13)	179
a. Yahweh's Promise to Jeremiah (33:1-3)	179
b. The Restoration of Jerusalem (33:4-9)	179
c. A Place of Joy and Thanksgiving (33:10-11)	181
d. The Restoration of Pastoral Life (33:12-13)	182
2. Yahweh's Faithfulness to His Covenants (33:14-26)	182
a. A Righteous Branch for David (33:14-16)	182
b. Davidic Kings and Levitical Priests (33:17-18)	183
c. Yahweh's Eternal Covenants (33:19-22)	184
d. God's Fidelity to Israel (33:23-26)	185
"Build and Plant": Destruction Before Restoration (34:1-22)	**188**
1. A Tragic but Hopeful Word to Zedekiah (34:1-7)	190
2. The Consequence of Covenant Breaking (34:8-22)	191

"Build and Plant": Fidelity in Relationship (35:1-19)	196
1. A Symbolic Act (35:1-11)	198
2. The Message to Judah (35:12-17)	199
3. The Message to the Recabites (35:18-19)	201
"Build and Plant": A Defiant King and the Indestructible Word (36:1-32)	203
1. Production of the First Scroll (36:1-7)	205
2. Baruch's First Reading (36:8-13)	207
3. Baruch's Second Reading (36:14-19)	207
4. Third Reading and Destruction of the First Scroll (36:20-26)	208
5. Production of the Second Scroll (36:27-32)	209
"Build and Plant": The Death of a Nation (37:1—44:30)	212
A. Zedekiah-Jeremiah Encounters with Interludes (37:1—38:28a)	213
1. Prelude: Introduction of King Zedekiah (37:1-2)	213
2. Zedekiah Sends Officials to Jeremiah (37:3-10)	214
3. Interlude: Jeremiah Accused of Treason (37:11-16)	215
4. Jeremiah Meets Zedekiah in the Palace (37:17-21)	216
5. Interlude: Jeremiah Accused of Treason Again (38:1-13)	217
6. Jeremiah Meets Zedekiah at the Temple (38:14-28a)	220
B. The Fall of Jerusalem (38:28b—39:18)	224
1. Summary Statement (38:28b—39:3)	224
2. Zedekiah After the Fall (39:4-10)	226
3. Jeremiah After the Fall (39:11-14)	229
4. Oracle of Comfort to Ebed-Melech (39:15-18)	232
C. Judah Becomes a Province of Babylon (40:1—41:18)	235
1. Jeremiah's Support of Gedaliah (40:1-6)	235
2. Gedaliah as Governor (40:7-12)	237
3. The Rebellion of Ishmael (40:13—41:18)	238
D. The "End" of Life in Judah (42:1—43:7)	243
1. Request for an Oracle (42:1-6)	244
2. Oracle: Do Not Go to Egypt (42:7-22)	246
3. Response: Jeremiah Is Lying (43:1-7)	249
E. A Sign-Act and the First Two Oracles in Tahpanhes (43:8-13; 44:1-14)	251
F. Debate with the Devotees of the Queen of Heaven (44:15-30)	256
"Build and Plant": Yahweh's Word to Baruch (45:1-5)	263
"Build and Plant": Oracles Against the Nations (46:1—51:64)	268
1. Against Egypt (46:1-28)	271
2. Against Philistia (47:1-7)	277
3. Against Moab (48:1-47)	279
4. Against Ammon (49:1-6)	283
5. Against Edom (49:7-22)	285
6. Against Damascus (49:23-27)	286

7. Against Kedar and Hazor (49:28-33)	287
8. Against Elam (49:34-39)	288
9. Against Babylon (50:1—51:64)	289

"Build and Plant": The Fall of Jerusalem—Reprise (52:1-34)   305

1. (Re-)Introduction of Zedekiah (52:1-3)	306
2. Siege, Fall, and Destruction of Jerusalem (52:4-27)	307
3. Counting the Cost (52:28-30)	311
4. The Ending That Does Not End (52:31-34)	314

GENERAL EDITORS' PREFACE

The purpose of the New Beacon Bible Commentary is to make available to pastors and students in the twenty-first century a biblical commentary that reflects the best scholarship in the Wesleyan theological tradition. The commentary project aims to make this scholarship accessible to a wider audience to assist them in their understanding and proclamation of Scripture as God's Word.

Writers of the volumes in this series not only are scholars within the Wesleyan theological tradition and experts in their field but also have special interest in the books assigned to them. Their task is to communicate clearly the critical consensus and the full range of other credible voices who have commented on the Scriptures. Though scholarship and scholarly contribution to the understanding of the Scriptures are key concerns of this series, it is not intended as an academic dialogue within the scholarly community. Commentators of this series constantly aim to demonstrate in their work the significance of the Bible as the church's book and the contemporary relevance and application of the biblical message. The project's overall goal is to make available to the church and for her service the fruits of the labors of scholars who are committed to their Christian faith.

The *New International Version* (NIV) is the reference version of the Bible used in this series; however, the focus of exegetical study and comments is the biblical text in its original language. When the commentary uses the NIV, it is printed in bold. The text printed in bold italics is the translation of the author. Commentators also refer to other translations where the text may be difficult or ambiguous.

The structure and organization of the commentaries in this series seeks to facilitate the study of the biblical text in a systematic and methodical way. Study of each biblical book begins with an **Introduction** section that gives an overview of authorship, date, provenance, audience, occasion, purpose, sociological/cultural issues, textual history, literary features, hermeneutical issues, and theological themes necessary to understand the book. This section also includes a brief outline of the book and a list of general works and standard commentaries.

The commentary section for each biblical book follows the outline of the book presented in the introduction. In some volumes, readers will find section ***overviews*** of large portions of scripture with general comments on their overall literary structure and other literary features. A consistent feature of the commentary is the paragraph-by-paragraph study of biblical texts. This section has three parts: **Behind the Text, In the Text**, and **From the Text**.

The goal of the **Behind the Text** section is to provide the reader with all the relevant information necessary to understand the text. This includes specific historical situations reflected in the text, the literary context of the text, sociological and cultural issues, and literary features of the text.

In the Text explores what the text says, following its verse-by-verse structure. This section includes a discussion of grammatical details, word studies, and the connectedness of the text to other biblical books/passages or other parts of the book being studied (the canonical relationship). This section provides transliterations of key words in Hebrew and Greek and their literal meanings. The goal here is to explain what the author would have meant and/or what the audience would have understood as the meaning of the text. This is the largest section of the commentary.

The ***From the Text*** section examines the text in relation to the following areas: theological significance, intertextuality, the history of interpretation, use of the Old Testament scriptures in the New Testament, interpretation in later church history, actualization, and application.

The commentary provides ***sidebars*** on topics of interest that are important but not necessarily part of an explanation of the biblical text. These topics are informational items and may cover archaeological, historical, literary, cultural, and theological matters that have relevance to the biblical text. Occasionally, longer detailed discussions of special topics are included as ***excurses.***

We offer this series with our hope and prayer that readers will find it a valuable resource for their understanding of God's Word and an indispensable tool for their critical engagement with the biblical texts.

Roger Hahn, Centennial Initiative General Editor
Alex Varughese, General Editor (Old Testament)
George Lyons, General Editor (New Testament)

ACKNOWLEDGMENTS

This volume completes the commentary on the Book of Jeremiah in the New Beacon Bible Commentary project. Jeremiah 1-25, written by Alex Varughese, was published by Beacon Hill Press of Kansas City in 2008.

We are pleased that God's providential grace has brought us together to work on this volume. Both of us were privileged to have Professor Herbert B. Huffmon as our mentor and dissertation adviser at Drew University. The Book of Jeremiah was the focus of our respective Ph.D. dissertations at Drew University (Varughese 1984, "The Hebrew *Vorlage* Underlying the Old Greek Translation of Jeremiah 1-20"; Modine 2006, "'Everything Written in This Book': The Perceptions of the Exile in the Book of Jeremiah"). We express our gratitude to Professor Huffmon for his continued friendship and interest in our personal and professional lives.

Our respective educational institutions where we currently serve as professors deserve our special gratitude and recognition. Mount Vernon Nazarene University provided Varughese with a reduced teaching load to work on this volume. Asia-Pacific Nazarene Theological Seminary helped Modine learn how to fit the demands of writing into a tightly packed academic schedule.

We are thankful to Beacon Hill Press of Kansas City for its vision, planning, and commitment to produce the New Beacon Bible Commentary series. We want to express our deep appreciation to Bonnie Perry, director of Beacon Hill Press of Kansas City, for her words of encouragement and the faithful support we have received during the course of our writing.

We are grateful to our families for their support and love that made it possible for us to find the time and energy needed to complete this volume.

Finally, and most importantly, thanks be to God for his gracious presence and the guidance of his Holy Spirit that strengthened and instructed us during our journey through his Word.

—Alex Varughese
—Mitchel Modine

ABBREVIATIONS

With a few exceptions, these abbreviations follow those in *The SBL Handbook of Style* (Alexander 1999).

General

A.D.	anno Domini (precedes date) (equivalent to C.E.)
B.C.	before Christ (follows date) (equivalent to B.C.E.)
B.C.E.	before the Common Era
BDB	*Hebrew and English Lexicon of the Old Testament*
BHS	*Biblia Hebraica Stuttgartensia*
C.E.	Common Era
cf.	compare
ch	chapter
chs	chapters
e.g.	*exempli gratia*, for example
esp.	especially
etc.	*et cetera*, and the rest
f(f).	and the following one(s)
i.e.	*id est*, that is
lit.	literally
LXX	Septuagint
MS	manuscript
MSS	manuscripts
MT	Masoretic Text (of the OT)
n.	note
n.d.	no date
n.p.	no place; no publisher; no page
nn.	notes
NT	New Testament
OT	Old Testament
s.v.	*sub verbo*, under the word
v	verse
vv	verses

Modern English Versions

KJV	King James Version
NASB	New American Standard Version
NEB	New English Bible
NIV	New International Version
NKJV	New King James Version
NRSV	New Revised Standard Version
RSV	Revised Standard Version

Print Conventions for Translations

Bold font	NIV (bold without quotation marks in the text under study; elsewhere in the regular font, with quotation marks and no further identification)
Bold italic font	Author's translation (without quotation marks)

Behind the Text:	Literary or historical background information average readers might not know from reading the biblical text alone
In the Text:	Comments on the biblical text, words, phrases, grammar, and so forth
From the Text:	The use of the text by later interpreters, contemporary relevance, theological and ethical implications of the text, with particular emphasis on Wesleyan concerns

Old Testament

Gen	Genesis	Dan	Daniel		
Exod	Exodus	Hos	Hosea		
Lev	Leviticus	Joel	Joel		
Num	Numbers	Amos	Amos		
Deut	Deuteronomy	Obad	Obadiah		
Josh	Joshua	Jonah	Jonah		
Judg	Judges	Mic	Micah		
Ruth	Ruth	Nah	Nahum		
1—2 Sam	1—2 Samuel	Hab	Habakkuk		
1—2 Kgs	1—2 Kings	Zeph	Zephaniah		
1—2 Chr	1—2 Chronicles	Hag	Haggai		
Ezra	Ezra	Zech	Zechariah		
Neh	Nehemiah	Mal	Malachi		
Esth	Esther				
Job	Job				
Ps/Pss	Psalms				
Prov	Proverbs				
Eccl	Ecclesiastes				
Song	Song of Songs / Song of Solomon				
Isa	Isaiah				
Jer	Jeremiah				
Lam	Lamentations				
Ezek	Ezekiel				

(Note: Chapter and verse numbering in the MT and LXX often differ compared to those in English Bibles. To avoid confusion, all biblical references follow the chapter and verse numbering in English translations, even when the text in the MT and LXX is under discussion.)

New Testament

Matt	Matthew
Mark	Mark
Luke	Luke
John	John
Acts	Acts
Rom	Romans
1—2 Cor	1—2 Corinthians
Gal	Galatians
Eph	Ephesians
Phil	Philippians
Col	Colossians
1—2 Thess	1—2 Thessalonians
1—2 Tim	1—2 Timothy
Titus	Titus
Phlm	Philemon
Heb	Hebrews
Jas	James
1—2 Pet	1—2 Peter
1—2—3 John	1—2—3 John
Jude	Jude
Rev	Revelation

Greek Transliteration

Greek	Letter	English
α	alpha	a
β	bēta	b
γ	gamma	g
γ	gamma nasal	n (before γ, κ, ξ, χ)
δ	delta	d
ε	epsilon	e
ζ	zēta	z
η	ēta	ē
θ	thēta	th
ι	iōta	i
κ	kappa	k
λ	lambda	l
μ	my	m
ν	ny	n
ξ	xi	x
ο	omicron	o
π	pi	p
ρ	rhō	r
ρ	initial rhō	rh
σ/ς	sigma	s
τ	tau	t
υ	upsilon	y
υ	upsilon	u (in diphthongs: au, eu, ēu, ou, ui)
φ	phi	ph
χ	chi	ch
ψ	psi	ps
ω	ōmega	ō
ʽ	rough breathing	h (before initial vowels or diphthongs)

Hebrew Consonant Transliteration

Hebrew/Aramaic	Letter	English
א	alef	ʼ
ב	bet	b
ג	gimel	g
ד	dalet	d
ה	he	h
ו	vav	v or w
ז	zayin	z
ח	khet	ḥ
ט	tet	ṭ
י	yod	y
כ/ך	kaf	k
ל	lamed	l
מ/ם	mem	m
נ/ן	nun	n
ס	samek	s
ע	ayin	ʻ
פ/ף	pe	p
צ/ץ	tsade	ṣ
ק	qof	q
ר	resh	r
שׂ	sin	ś
שׁ	shin	š
ת	tav	t

BIBLIOGRAPHY

Albertz, Rainer. 2003. *Israel in Exile: The History and Literature of the Sixth Century B.C.E.* Trans. David Green. Atlanta: Society of Biblical Literature.
Bauer, Angela. 1999. *Gender in the Book of Jeremiah: A Feminist-Literary Reading.* Studies in Biblical Literature 5. New York: Peter Lang.
Blackwood, Andrew W., Jr. 1977. *Commentary on Jeremiah.* Waco, Tex.: Word Books.
Bonhoeffer, Dietrich. 1971. *Letters and Papers from Prison.* Ed. Eberhard Bethge. New York: Macmillan.
Bozak, Barbara. 1991. Life "Anew": A Literary–Theological Study of Jer 30-31. Analecta Biblica 122. Roma: Pontificio Instituto Biblico.
Bracke, John M. 2000a. *Jeremiah 1-29.* Louisville, Ky.: Westminster/John Knox.
_____. 2000b. *Jeremiah 30-52 and Lamentations.* Louisville, Ky.: Westminster/John Knox.
Bright, John. 1965. *Jeremiah: A New Translation with Introduction and Commentary.* Anchor Bible 21. Garden City, N.Y.: Doubleday.
_____. 2000. *A History of Israel.* Fourth Ed. Louisville, Ky.: Westminster/John Knox.
Brueggemann, Walter. 1983. "The Book of Jeremiah: Portrait of the Prophet." *Interpretation* 37:130-45.
_____. 1991. *To Build, to Plant: Jeremiah 26-52.* International Theological Commentary. Grand Rapids: Eerdmans.
_____. 1998. *A Commentary on Jeremiah: Exile and Homecoming.* Grand Rapids: Eerdmans.
_____. 2002. "Editor's foreword." In Daniel L. Smith-Christopher, *A Biblical Theology of Exile.* Overtures to Biblical Theology. Minneapolis: Fortress. Pp. vii-ix.
_____. 2007. *Old Testament Theology: The Theology of the Book of Jeremiah.* Cambridge: Cambridge University Press.
Carroll, Robert P. 1981. *From Chaos to Covenant: Uses of Prophecy in the Book of Jeremiah.* London: SCM.
_____. 1986. *The Book of Jeremiah.* Old Testament Library. Philadelphia: Westminster.
Chazan, Robert, William W. Hallo, and Lawrence H. Schiffmann, eds. 1999. *Ki Baruch Hu: Ancient Near Eastern, Biblical and Judaic Studies in Honor of Baruch A. Levine.* Winona Lake, Ind.: Eisenbrauns.
Christensen, Duane L. 1975. *Transformations of the War Oracle in Old Testament Prophecy.* Missoula, Mont.: Scholars Press.
Clarke, Adam. 1823. *The Book of the Prophet Jeremiah. The Holy Bible: A Commentary and Critical Notes* IV. New York: Abingdon-Cokesbury Press. Pp. 249-396.
Clements, Ronald E. 1988. *Jeremiah.* Interpretation. Atlanta: John Knox.
Craigie, Peter C., Page Kelley, Joel F. Drinkard Jr. 1991. *Jeremiah 1-25.* Word Biblical Commentary 26. Dallas: Word.
Dever, William G. 1990. *Recent Archaeological Discoveries and Biblical Research.* Seattle: University of Washington Press.
Dick, Michael B., ed. 1999. *Born in Heaven, Made on Earth: The Creation of the Cult Image in the Ancient Near East.* Winona Lake, Ind.: Eisenbrauns.
Duckat, Walter. 1968. *Beggar to King: All the Occupations of Biblical Times.* New York: Doubleday.
Duhm, B. 1901. *Das Buch Jeremia.* Tubingen: J.C.B. Mohr (P. Siebeck).
Finkelstein, Israel, and Neil Asher Silberman. 2001. *The Bible Unearthed: Archaeology's New Vision of Ancient Israel and the Origin of Its Sacred Texts.* New York: Free Press.
Fretheim, T. E. 2002. *Jeremiah.* Macon, Ga.: Smyth & Helwys.
Gottwald, Norman K. 1964. *All the Kingdoms of the Earth: Israelite Prophecy and International Relations in the Ancient Near East.* New York: Harper and Row.
Grayson, A. K., ed. 1970. *Assyrian and Babylonian Chronicles.* Locust Valley, N.Y.: J. J. Augustin.
Habel, Norman. 1965. "The Form and Significance of the Call Narratives." *Zeitschrift fur die alttestamentliche Wissenschaft* 77:297-323.
Harrison, Roland K. 1973. *Jeremiah and Lamentations.* Ed. D. J. Wiseman. Tyndale Old Testament Commentaries. Downers Grove, Ill.: InterVarsity.
Heschel, Abraham J. 2001. *The Prophets.* New York: HarperPerennial.
Hill, John. 1999. *Friend or Foe? The Figure of Babylon in the Book of Jeremiah MT.* Leiden: Brill.

Holladay, William L. 1986. *Jeremiah 1: A Commentary on the Book of the Prophet Jeremiah, Chapters 1-25*. Hermeneia. Philadelphia: Fortress.

———. 1989. *Jeremiah 2: A Commentary on the Book of the Prophet Jeremiah, Chapters 26-52*. Hermeneia. Philadelphia: Fortress.

Huffmon, Herbert. 1959. "The Covenant Lawsuit in the Prophets." *Journal of Biblical Literature* 78:290-95.

———. 1999a. "Jeremiah of Anathoth: A Prophet for All Israel." In Robert Chazan, William W. Hallo, and Lawrence H. Schiffmann, eds. *Ki Baruch Hu: Ancient Near Eastern, Biblical and Judaic Studies in Honor of Baruch A. Levine*. Winona Lake, Ind.: Eisenbrauns. Pp. 261-71.

———. 1999b. "The Impossible: God's Words of Assurance in Jeremiah 31:35-37" in *On the Way to Nineveh*. Ed. Stephen L. Cook and S. C. Winter. Atlanta: American Schools of Oriental Research.

Hyatt, James P. 1956. *Jeremiah*. The Interpreter's Bible, vol. V. Nashville: Abingdon.

Jackson Sharp, Carolyn. 2003. *Prophecy and Ideology in Jeremiah: Struggles for Authority in the Deutero-Jeremianic Prose*. London: T & T Clark.

Jones, Douglas Rawlinson. 1992. *Jeremiah*. New Century Bible Commentary. Grand Rapids: Eerdmans Publishing Co.

Keel, Othmar, and Christoph Uehlinger. 1998. *Gods, Goddesses, and Images of God in Ancient Israel*. Trans. Thomas H. Trapp. Minneapolis: Fortress.

Keown, Gerald L., Pamela J. Scalise, and Thomas G. Smothers. 1995. *Jeremiah 26-52*. Word Biblical Commentary, vol. 27. Dallas: Word Books.

Lipschits, Oded. 2005. *The Fall and Rise of Jerusalem: Judah Under Babylonian Rule*. Winona Lake, Ind.: Eisenbrauns.

Lundbom, Jack R. 1999. *Jeremiah 1-20: A New Translation with Introduction and Commentary*. Anchor Bible 21A. New York: Doubleday.

———. 2004a. *Jeremiah 21-36: A New Translation with Introduction and Commentary*. Anchor Bible 21B. New York: Doubleday.

———. 2004b. *Jeremiah 37-52: A New Translation with Introduction and Commentary*. Anchor Bible 21C. New York: Doubleday.

Mays, James Luther. 1969. *Amos: A Commentary*. The Old Testament Library. Philadelphia: Westminster Press.

McKane, W. 1986. *A Critical and Exegetical Commentary on Jeremiah*. 2 vols. International Critical Commentary. Edinburgh: T & T Clark.

Miller, Patrick D. 2001. *The Book of Jeremiah*. New Interpreter's Bible 6. Nashville: Abingdon. Pp. 555-926.

Mowinckel, Sigmund. 1914. *Zur Komposition des Buches Jeremia*. Kristiania: J. Dybwad.

Nicholson, Ernest W. 1970. *Preaching to the Exiles: A Study of the Prose Traditions in the Book of Jeremiah*. Oxford: Blackwell.

O'Connor, Kathleen M. 1988. *The Confessions of Jeremiah: Their Interpretation and Role in Chapters 1-25*. Society of Biblical Literature Dissertation Series 94. Atlanta: Scholars.

Oppenheim, A. Leo, ed. 1969. "Varia." In James B. Pritchard, ed., *Ancient Near Eastern Texts Relating to the Old Testament [ANET]*, 3rd ed. Princeton: Princeton University Press.

Outler, Albert C., ed. 1984. *The Works of John Wesley. Volume 1. Sermons I:1-33*. Nashville: Abingdon Press.

Parke-Taylor, Geoffrey H. 2000. *The Formation of the Book of Jeremiah: Doublets and Recurring Phrases*. Society of Biblical Literature Manuscript Series 51. Atlanta: Society of Biblical Literature.

Potter, H. D. 1983. "The New Covenant in Jeremiah XXXI 31-34." *Vetus Testamentum* XXXIII: 347-57.

Pritchard, James B., ed. 1969. *Ancient Near Eastern Texts Relating to the Old Testament [ANET]*, 3rd ed. Princeton: Princeton University Press.

von Rad, Gerhard. 1965. *Old Testament Theology*. Vol. 2. New York: Harper.

Rawlinson Jones, Douglas. 1992. *Jeremiah*. New Century Bible Commentary. Grand Rapids: Eerdmans.

Robinson, Bernard P. 2001. "Jeremiah's New Covenant: Jer 31, 31-34." *Scandinavian Journal of the Old Testament* 15:181-204.

Shanks, Hershel, ed. 2005. "The Other Shoe: Five Accused of Antiquities Fraud," *Biblical Archaeology Review* (March/April 2005).

Skinner, John. 1922 (repr. 1963). *Prophecy and Religion: Studies in the Life of Jeremiah*. Cambridge: Cambridge University Press.

Smith-Christopher, Daniel L. 2002. *A Biblical Theology of Exile*. Overtures to Biblical Theology. Minneapolis: Fortress.

Stager, Lawrence E. 1995. "The Impact of the Sea Peoples (1185-1050 BCE)." In Thomas F. Levy, ed., *The Archaeology of Society in the Holy Land*. London: Leicester University Press. Pp. 332-48.

Stulman, Louis. 1998. *Order Amid Chaos: Jeremiah as Symbolic Tapestry*. Sheffield: Sheffield Academic Press.

_____. 2005. *Jeremiah*. Abingdon Old Testament Commentaries. Nashville: Abingdon.

Swetnam, James. 1974. "Why Was Jeremiah's New Covenant New?" Studies on Prophecy: A Collection of Twelve Papers. Supplement to Vetus Testamentum XXVI. Leiden: E. J. Brill.

Terblanche, M. D. 2000. "No Need for a Prophet Like Jeremiah: The Absence of the Prophet Jeremiah in Kings" in *Past, Present, Future: The Deuteronomistic History and the Prophets*. Ed. Johannes C. De Moor and Harry F. Van Rooy, Oudtestamentische Studiën XLIV. Leiden, Holland: Brill. Pp. 306-14.

Thompson, J. A. 1980. *The Book of Jeremiah*. New International Commentary on the Old Testament. Grand Rapids: Eerdmans.

Trible, Phyllis. 1978. *God and the Rhetoric of Sexuality*. Philadelphia: Fortress.

Varughese, Alex. 2004. "The Royal Family in the Jeremiah Tradition" in *Inspired Speech: Prophecy in the Ancient Near East. Essays in honor of Herbert B. Huffmon*. Ed. John Kaltner and Louis Stulman. London: T & T Clark International. Pp. 319-28.

_____. 2008. *Jeremiah 1-25*. New Beacon Bible Commentary. Kansas City: Beacon Hill Press of Kansas City.

De Vaux, Roland. 1965. *Ancient Israel: Religious Institutions*. New York: McGraw-Hill.

Wenthe, Dean O., ed. 2009. *Ancient Christian Commentary on Scripture: Jeremiah, Lamentations*. Downers Grove, Ill.: InterVarsity Press.

Wesley, John. 1975 (repr.). *Explanatory Notes upon the Old Testament*. Salem, Ohio: Schmul Publishers.

Wilson, Robert R. 1999. "Poetry and Prose in the Book of Jeremiah." In Robert Chazan, William W. Hallo, and Lawrence H. Schiffmann, eds. *Ki Baruch Hu: Ancient Near Eastern, Biblical and Judaic Studies in honor of Baruch A. Levine*. Winona Lake, Ind.: Eisenbrauns. Pp. 413-27.

Wolff, Hans Walter. 1974. *Anthropology of the Old Testament*. Philadelphia: Fortress Press.

INTRODUCTION

A. The Importance of the Book of Jeremiah

The book of Jeremiah occupies a prominent place in the OT canon on at least three counts: (1) its massive size (the second longest book in the Bible and the longest prophetic book); (2) the complexity of its content and message; and (3) the towering prophetic figure behind the book that stands shoulder to shoulder with other great prophets such as Isaiah and Ezekiel. The tradition has placed this book between the scrolls of Isaiah and Ezekiel to highlight its significance as a major prophetic book. The theology of the book of Jeremiah is in direct contact with other OT books such as Hosea and Deuteronomy, and it intersects with theological themes and ideas found in a number of other OT books, most notably Genesis, Exodus, Psalms, Job, Proverbs, Isaiah, and Ezekiel.

Jeremiah's influence is found in several NT books, particularly in the Gospel of Matthew, Acts, several Pauline writings, Hebrews, and Revelation. Only the Gospel of Matthew preserves the name of Jeremiah in the response of the disciples to Jesus' question, "Who do people say the Son of Man is?" (Matt 16:13). Matthew also indicates that the massacre of infants in Bethlehem ordered by King Herod was a direct fulfillment of Jer 31:15 (Matt 2:17-18). All the Synoptic Gospels preserve Jeremiah's words "den of robbers" in Jesus' charge against the money changers and traders in the temple (Matt 21:13; Mark 11:17; Luke 19:46; see Jer 7:11). Jeremiah's new covenant message (31:31-34) is quoted almost verbatim in Heb 8:8-12.

B. Historical Setting

The opening statement of the book of Jeremiah (1:1-3) indicates that God's word came to Jeremiah in the thirteenth year of Josiah's reign (627 B.C.) and that it continued until the end of the eleventh year of Zedekiah's reign (587 B.C.). This statement thus locates the prophet's ministry during the late seventh and early sixth centuries B.C., a period that witnessed tumultuous change in the history of the ancient Near East (the political events outlined below follow the history of this period in Bright 2000, 313-47).

In 627 B.C. (the year of Jeremiah's call) Ashurbanipal (669-627 B.C.), the Assyrian king, died, leaving the already weakening empire in the hands of rival political leaders. Judah was under the rule of a young king named Josiah (640-609 B.C.) who was placed on the throne at the age of eight. Josiah inherited a kingdom that was politically and religiously a vassal state of Assyria. His father Amon (642-640 B.C.) and his grandfather Manasseh (687-642 B.C.) promoted Assyrian forms of worship and other pagan religious practices in the land (2 Kgs 21:1-26). At the age of sixteen, Josiah "began to seek the God of his father David," and at the age of twenty (628 B.C.), "he began to purge Judah and Jerusalem of high places, Asherah poles, carved idols and cast images" (2 Chr 34:3; see vv 4-7). This religious reformation was aimed at restoring to Judah its national faith in God and liberating the nation from its political and religious loyalty to Assyria. Josiah's reform activities may have been prompted by the weakening of the Assyrian Empire during the final years of Ashurbanipal. During this religious reformation, the Book of the Law was found in the temple, which led Josiah to call the nation for the renewal of the covenant with God; the Book of the Law gave further impetus to Josiah to continue his reform activities (622 B.C.; 2 Kgs 22:3—23:14).

The Assyrian Empire continued to crumble in the next two decades. Babylon, led by Nabopolassar (626-605 B.C.), defeated Assyria and gained freedom in 626 B.C. A coalition of Babylonians and Medes brought Nineveh, the capital of the Assyrian Empire, to its end in 612 B.C. The coalition forces then moved to capture Haran, Assyria's last stronghold. In the meantime, Egypt decided to help its longtime rival Assyria recapture Haran from the Babylonian-Mede forces. As the Egyptian army led by Pharaoh Neco II was marching northward through Palestine, Josiah decided to stop them at Megiddo. In the battle that followed, Josiah was killed (609 B.C.). The Egyptians continued their march to Haran, but their attempt to help the Assyrians failed. The Babylonians established themselves as the new power broker in the ancient Near East.

It is not clear what prompted Josiah to get involved in international politics. Egypt's effort was clearly an attempt to exert its power during this critical period of geopolitical changes. Josiah may have foreseen the Egyptian ambition and perhaps decided to show support for Babylon, the emerging new world power. Whatever may have been Josiah's intentions, the tragic outcome of his effort to stop the Egyptians was Judah's loss of independence to Egypt. After Josiah's death, the Judeans placed his son Jehoahaz on the throne (609 B.C.). But Pharaoh Neco deposed him and deported him to Egypt and placed his older brother, Eliakim, on the throne with the regnal name Jehoiakim. Jehoiakim remained a vassal of Egypt for the next four years (609-605 B.C.) and paid heavy tribute to Egypt with money and silver and gold he collected as taxes from the people (2 Kgs 23:31-35).

In the meantime, Egypt continued its attempt to gain control of the Syria-Palestine region. This led to a series of confrontations between the Egyptians and the Babylonians resulting in a decisive victory of Babylon over Egypt at Carchemish in 605 B.C. Nebuchadnezzar, who later took the throne of Babylon after the death of Nabopolassar in 605 B.C., led the Babylonian army in this battle. The Babylonian offensive continued southward into Palestine, which brought the Babylonian army to the Philistine Plain (604 B.C.). In that year, Jehoiakim decided to change his allegiance to Nebuchadnezzar, the new master of the region. Three years later in 601 B.C., Jehoiakim rebelled against Babylon (24:1); this may have been prompted by the withdrawal of the Babylonian army and its return home from the Egyptian border after suffering temporary setback in the battle against Egypt. In retaliation, the Babylonians sent bands of Syrians, Moabites, and Ammonites to destroy Judah (v 2). Second Kings reports the death of Jehoiakim (v 6), but the cause of death is not stated. According to the Chronicler's account, Nebuchadnezzar bound him in fetters to take him to Babylon (2 Chr 36:6). Scholars assume that he was assassinated during a palace revolt or that he died on his way to Babylon as a prisoner in 598 B.C. His son Jehoiachin took the throne and ruled for three months. In 597 B.C. he surrendered to Nebuchadnezzar, who came to Jerusalem with his army. The Babylonian army took Jehoiachin, his mother, royal family members, high-ranking officials, and skilled workers to Babylon as prisoners along with treasures from the palace and the temple. Nebuchadnezzar placed on the throne Mattaniah, Jehoiachin's uncle, and gave him the regnal name Zedekiah (2 Kgs 24:8-17).

Zedekiah's rule lasted for eleven years (597-587 B.C.). He made a trip to Babylon in the fourth year of his reign (Jer 51:59), perhaps to assure Nebuchadnezzar of his loyalty to Babylon. For reasons not clearly known, he rebelled against Babylon (2 Kgs 24:20). This may have been prompted by the message of the false prophets that God will soon bring Jehoiachin and the exiled people back to Judah and that God will break the yoke of Babylon (Jer 29:1-4). Nebuchadnezzar brought his army to Judah to put an end to Judah's rebellion. The Babylonians laid a siege against the city of Jerusalem; in 587 B.C., the city was taken by the Babylonians. Zedekiah, who attempted to escape, was captured and brought before Nebuchadnezzar at Riblah. He was blinded and taken as a prisoner to Babylon. The Babylonians destroyed the city and burned down the houses in the city, including the temple, and deported the population to Babylon. Only some of the poorest people were left in the land (2 Kgs 25:1-21).

Nebuchadnezzar appointed Gedaliah as governor over the population that was left in Judah. Under Gedaliah's leadership, those who were left in the land regrouped and Gedaliah challenged them to stay in the land and submit to Babylonian rule. Even those Jews who escaped to Transjordan states returned to Judah, and there seems to have been a very brief period of peaceful life in the land (Jer 40:7-12). This came to an end and the nation was in turmoil again when a resistant group led by Ishmael, a royal family member, murdered Gedaliah around 582 B.C. Gedaliah's friends, led by Johanan, pursued Ishmael and the rebels, and the rebels escaped to the Ammonite territory. Fearing reprisal from Babylon, Johanan and his followers decided to leave Judah and escape to Egypt. They took with them Jeremiah as their hostage, without paying attention to his warning against going to Egypt (chs 41—43).

Jeremiah's ministry took place during this politically volatile period, which witnessed the rise and fall of major empires in the ancient Near East in the late seventh and early sixth centuries B.C. As the above outline of history indicates, Judah was caught in the middle of these geopolitical changes, and the impact of these events on Judah's political existence was disastrous. The book of Jeremiah gives witness to the crumbling political, social, moral, and religious conditions of Judah during this period. More than that, it gives witness to God's sovereign involvement in the historical process of this period. As God's spokesperson during this critical moment in the history of Judah and the nations of the world, it was Jeremiah's task to remind the covenant people of God that God's judgment on them for breaking their covenant with him was taking place through these historical events. The book indicates to us that his message to Judah, however, fell upon deaf ears.

C. Jeremiah the Prophet

The name Jeremiah, which is not an unusual name in the OT, more commonly appears in the book in the long form *yirmĕyāhû*, and nine times in the short form *yirmĕyâ* in 27:1—29:3 (Holladay 1986, 15). The meaning of the name is uncertain. Scholars suggest several possible meanings: "Yahweh exalts or lifts up" or "Yahweh casts or hurls" or "Yahweh loosens."

The book of Jeremiah does not contain any lengthy account of the personal life of the prophet. The biographical accounts in the book mostly sum up the prophet's actions and words. In the introductory statement of the book (1:1), Jeremiah is mentioned as the son of Hilkiah, a priestly resident in the village of Anathoth in the tribal territory of Benjamin. Hilkiah's identity is not known to us. An individual by the name Hilkiah served as high priest during the days of Josiah (2 Kgs 22:3-20). There is little evidence in the book that connects Jeremiah with Hilkiah the high priest of Josiah. Jeremiah's family association with Anathoth suggests that he may have been a descendent of Abiathar the priest, who in turn descended from the house of Eli (see 1 Sam 14:3; 22:20). He served as priest alongside Zadok during the days of David (2 Sam 15:24-29). Solomon exiled Abiathar to his family estate in Anathoth for giving support to Adonijah's claim to the throne after David's death. Solomon also made Zadok, who supported his kingship, as the priest in the place of Abiathar (1 Kgs 2:26-27, 35). It is very likely that the influential priests in Jerusalem who presided over the affairs of the temple belonged to the family of Zadok.

Jeremiah's prophetic ministry began in the thirteenth year of Josiah, in 627 B.C. (Jer 1:2). His call came while he was a young boy; his young age may have been the reason for his resistance to God's call (v 6). However, upon divine compulsion and reassurance, he accepted the task of the prophetic office (vv 7-10). His subsequent actions and words indicate that he constantly lived under this divine constraint to be Yahweh's spokesman to Judah.

Perhaps due to the conviction that Judah's destruction was near, and at the specific command of Yahweh, Jeremiah was never married (16:1-4). Yahweh's words, which Jeremiah spoke, made him more of an enemy than a friend of his nation. He was often denounced, pursued, and ostracized by his enemies. Even men of his own hometown of Anathoth wanted to put an end to his life (11:21-23). He was once barred from entering the temple (36:5), and a temple official had him beaten and put in stocks (20:2). The temple officials argued unsuccessfully before the royal officials that Jeremiah deserved the death penalty for announcing the destruction of the temple (26:1-9; cf. 7:1-15). His frequent calls to surrender to Babylon would have prompted the nation to view him as a traitor. After the Babylonian attack and deportation of the Judean citizens in 597 B.C., Jeremiah was thrown into a dungeon on charges of deserting to the enemy. Later he was transferred to a guardhouse where he remained until the destruction of Jerusalem in 587 B.C. (chs 37—38). The Babylonian army released him from the guardhouse and gave him the option either to stay in Judah or to go to Babylon as a royal guest, but he opted to stay in Judah (ch 40). Though Jeremiah was determined to stay in his ruined homeland, Johanan and his friends took him to Tahpanhes, a town within the Egyptian border (ch 43).

The last known utterance of Jeremiah comes from this Egyptian locale (43:8—44:30), where presumably his life came to an end.

Recent scholarly assessment of the portrayal of Jeremiah in the book as a literary and theological product of the Deuteronomic traditions that gave shape to the book in the exilic/postexilic period greatly diminish and discount or even suppress the voice of the historical person of Jeremiah. Thus Carroll claims that the person of Jeremiah in the book is not a "real person" but the product of "various levels of tradition" making up the book (1986, 64). Brueggemann is more conciliatory than Carroll in his assessment of the person of Jeremiah. He does not think the book presents a "descriptive, biographical report" of the person of Jeremiah. He argues for the possibility that Jeremiah in the book is an "imaginative" and "theologically intentional" literary reconstruction of the "portrait" of the prophet governed by "a powerful person of memory." He also thinks that "the prophet himself was fully resonant" with the later portrayals of the prophet by the Deuteronomic tradition (1983, 131-32; also 2007, 27-28).

This commentary follows the trustworthiness of the historical reportage of Jeremiah in the book. The historical and biographical narratives in the book present the prophet as a person who was deeply aware of his calling to be a prophet of Yahweh at a critical time in Judah's history. He struggled with this call because it made him a person of intense conflict and dispute in the land, but he saw in the historical process the overwhelming display of Yahweh's sovereignty, which gave him the courage to speak with integrity about the coming death of Judah as well its resurrection. The rejection of his message by the nation did not persuade him to withdraw from his ministry, but he remained a stubborn spokesperson for Yahweh. With stunning poetic imagination, he conveys in the book his (and Yahweh's) grief, agony, and suffering over a people who have stubbornly chosen for themselves the path of self-destruction. The book also portrays Jeremiah as a prophet of intense hope, who with passion and eloquence communicated to the nation Yahweh's gracious plans for its restoration and resettlement in the land after the days of its death and exile in a foreign land.

D. Content, Genre, and Structure

Materials in the book of Jeremiah seem to be organized into several literary blocks around the theme of judgment and salvation. However, the arrangement of these materials does not show any discernible chronological order or literary and theological coherence. Commentators generally divide the materials in the book into two sections: the first section (chs 1—25) centers on the message of judgment on Judah and Jerusalem and the second section (chs 26—52) centers on the theme of hope and salvation for Judah and Jerusalem. Most of the first section is in poetry; scattered here and there are prose materials mostly in the form of sermons. This section contains words of indictment against the social, political, and religious corruption of Judah and repeated threats and warnings of the nation's destruction through the agency of Babylon. This section also includes numerous calls for national repentance; these calls imply that the nation may avoid the impending judgment by giving heed to God's call for repentance. The theme of salvation is sparsely found in a few isolated places in chs 1—25.

Biographical and historical narratives constitute the major part of the second section (chs 26—52). Chapter 26 narrates the events that followed Jeremiah's sermon in the temple (ch 7). This section also has large blocks of poetry (chs 30—33; 46—51). The theme of judgment is also found in chs 26—52 but is overshadowed by words of hope and salvation. Biographical materials are mostly accounts of events that happened during the reign of King Jehoiakim (chs 26, 35, 36) and King Zedekiah (chs 27—29, 34, 37—39) given without any chronological order. Judgment theme with repeated warnings of the coming exile appears in these chapters. The final days of Judah, the fall of Jerusalem, and the tragic fate of the Judeans are summarized in the biographical accounts in chs 40—44. An oracle addressed to Baruch constitutes chapter 45. Death of the nation, which is anticipated in chs 1—25, is taking place in these chapters as a historical reality. Scholars think that the biographical materials in chs 36—45 reflect the scribal activity of Baruch and hence describe these chapters as Baruch Narrative.

The book of consolation (chs 30—33), which contains hopeful words about restoration, is found before the narrative that deals with the destruction of Jerusalem and the exile of Judah to Babylon. Chapters 46—51, the oracles against the nations, announce Yahweh's judgment of the surrounding nations. The book ends with an epilogue (ch 52), which corresponds to a great extent with the historical account of 2 Kgs 24:18—25:30.

The book of Jeremiah shows a variety of genre utilized by the prophet to convey Yahweh's message. Messenger-style speech is the most common genre in these chapters. Other genres include sermons, lawsuit, dialogue, symbolic acts, torah instruction, proverbial sayings, vision accounts, laments, prayers, and biographical reports. Scattered throughout chs 1—25 are recurring emotional outbursts of Jeremiah in the form complaints, laments, and prayers ("confessions").

The book of Jeremiah has generated considerable interest and speculation concerning its content and composition in the last one hundred years. Modern attempts to understand the book are usually traced to the studies of Duhm (1901) and Mowinckel (1914), who have identified in the book several literary strands or sources. Mowinckel described these as poetic oracles (source A), historical narratives (source B), and prose speeches (source C). He concluded that (1) the poetic oracles in chs 1—25 reflect Jeremiah's authentic words; (2) source B makes up the biographical materials in chs 26—44; and

(3) prose sermons that are scattered throughout the book share the theological concerns and language of the book of Deuteronomy (1914, 21-38).

Though most recent scholars seldom describe the book in the categories employed by Duhm and Mowinckel, the debate over the content and composition of the book is alive and well. Two dominant and divergent views persist today. The first approach seeks to place the words of Jeremiah in the historical setting of the late seventh and early sixth centuries B.C. This view attributes all the poetic oracles and prose discourses to the prophet himself. The prose discourses may or may not contain theological expressions of later editors. This view attributes much of the so-called Deuteronomic words and phrases to the prophet himself. The historical and biographical materials come from Baruch the scribe, who was a trusted friend of the prophet. This view, with some variations, is reflected in the commentaries of William Holladay (1986, 1989) and Jack Lundbom (1999, 2004a, 2004b).

The second approach understands the book as a whole, particularly the prose sermons, the result of the Deuteronomistic editing of the book (editors who were influenced by the theological concerns and language of Deuteronomy). Opinions of scholars on the extent of the Deuteronomic influence range from an overall editing of the book to an extensive Deuteronomistic redaction of the entire book. Carroll has suggested in his commentary that the book in its present form is the end product of the activities of various "redactional circles and levels of tradition" representing different social groups vying for power and position after the fall of Jerusalem. He suggests a long period for the formation of the book in its present form extending from the fall of Jerusalem into the Persian period (1986, 55-82). McKane also reaches a similar conclusion. He notices in the book a "long and complicated process of growth," "extending over a very long period . . . to which many people have contributed" (1986, xlviii).

This commentary approaches the study of the book of Jeremiah from the perspective that the book for the most part is made up of the words of Jeremiah, put together in the present form by compilers and editors of the words of Jeremiah during the Babylonian exile. As a book that has been through editorial hands during the exile, it is likely that the book in its present form may contain some of the theological perspectives and concerns of the community that gave the book its final shape. Nonetheless, it is difficult to isolate these additions from the original words of Jeremiah because the book lacks clear expressions of the conditions and the realities of the exile. There is no clear voice of the exilic community speaking in the book, as in Isa 40—55. Moreover, the exile of 587 B.C. is portrayed in chs 1—25 as an impending event; only in the historical accounts of chs 39—40 do we find references to the events of 587 B.C. Therefore, this commentary takes the seventh and sixth century B.C. historical context reflected in the book for its face value. Further, this commentary takes the view that the community that gave shape to the book's final form preserved the historical context of the late seventh and early sixth centuries B.C. and the voice of Jeremiah during this period to give recognition to the reality that its present suffering (the Babylonian exile) is the outcome of its rejection of God's words spoken through the prophet. From this perspective, one can also imagine that this community found the hope for its future in the words of the prophet who also spoke of its restoration and rebuilding.

Though there are two divergent positions on the content and composition of the book, modern commentators in general have followed the view that materials in the book lack a clear structure and organization and that the book shows no chronological order or literary and theological coherence. In response to this prevailing view, Stulman has recently shown theological and literary unity to the book from his perspective of the book as "a symbolic tapestry with narrative seams" in his *Order Amid Chaos: Jeremiah as Symbolic Tapestry* (1998, 17; 2005, 13). He finds five major units in each of the two sections of the book; the first section (chs 2—6; 7—10; 11—17; 18—20; 21—24) deals with the theme of "dismantling" and the second section (chs 27—29; 30—33; 34—35; 36—45; 46—51) deals with the theme of "rebuilding." Each section has an introduction and conclusion (chs 1, 25 and chs 26, 52 respectively). Stulman argues that the prose sermons "provide important rhetorical, literary, and theological clues for understanding the text" of Jeremiah (2005, 15).

The conventional division of the book into two major sections (chs 1—25 and 26—52) is based on the assumption of some thematic continuity within these sections. The common assumption is that chs 1—25 follow the theme of uprooting and chs 26—52 follow the theme of rebuilding. This is for the most part a reasonable understanding of the book and its content. However, we will see later as we work through the text that this line is not that clearly evident in the book; words of rebuilding are found in chs 1—25, and God's activity of uprooting is found in chs 26—52.

Approaching the book from a traditional historical perspective (an approach quite different from that of Stulman; see Stulman 1998, 2005 for his methodological and interpretive approach to the study of Jeremiah), this commentary aims to show that within these two major sections, there are smaller and larger literary blocks and that the various literary units within these blocks are linked together by common theological themes or some literary features. This commentary also aims to show that these smaller and larger literary blocks contribute to the overall structure of the book. In spite of the overall untidiness of the book, the book is thus readable; the common themes and literary features within these smaller and larger literary blocks contribute to the readability of the book. Thus we arrive at the same conclusion made by Stulman (i.e., that Jeremiah in its final form is readable and that it has literary and theological unity) from a different methodological and interpretive approach to the understanding of the book. In volume one of this commentary (see Varughese 2008, 26), the reader will find discussion on the structure of chs 1—25. The following discussion focuses on the structure of chs 26—52.

The various larger and smaller literary blocks in chs 26—52 deal with two key issues. On the one hand, these literary blocks show that Yahweh's words of judgment on Judah are being fulfilled in the history of the nation. The narrative units chs 26—52, for the most part, focus on events that have taken place during the reign of Zedekiah (597-587 B.C.; see chs 27, 28, 29, 32, 33, 34, 37, 38, 39) and perhaps during the five or six years after the fall of Jerusalem in 587 B.C. (see chs 40, 41, 42, 43, 44). In this section, we also find judgment as a reality unfolding also on the neighboring nations of Judah. Judgment in these chapters is either happening or will soon happen. On the other hand, these chapters also focus on Yahweh's work of restoration of Judah and Israel. The days of uprooting and tearing down will be followed by days of building and planting. The building and planting theme dominates chs 29—33. The prophet gives hope about the building and planting of not only the exiled community that lives in Babylon and in other parts of the world (chs 29—33) but also the Judean remnant that is left in the land after the destruction of Jerusalem by the Babylonians in 587 B.C. (42:9-12). Even in the oracles against the nations, we find here and there the promise of Israel's restoration (46:27-28; 50:4-5, 17-20, 33-34; 51:5-6).

In the present literary arrangement of the book, the oracles of hope (chs 30—33) are placed before the narratives that deal with the unfolding of Yahweh's judgment (chs 37—44). This seems to serve a key theological function intended by the editors of the book. The readers come across words of comfort and consolation—hope in the building and planting of the nation—before the stories of the end of Judah's history. As the outline of chs 26—52 given below indicates, various literary blocks within this section are organized around Yahweh's promises of restoration—the building and planting activities of Yahweh—which overshadows the narratives that deal with the Babylonian invasion of Judah and the subsequent history of Judah. This arrangement of the content of chs 26—52 serves to highlight the dominant concern of this section—Yahweh's promise of the rebuilding of Judah and Israel. This theme provides an overall unity to the various literary blocks in chs 26—52.

In the commentary that follows later in this volume, an overview of each literary block is provided to show the literary and theological coherence of various literary units within these literary blocks. This does not, however, mean that the literary blocks themselves are arranged in any coherent order. Chapters 26—52 continue to have the appearance of an anthology of smaller blocks of materials arranged without any particular order.

"Build and Plant": A New Phase in the Prophet's Ministry (26:1-24)
"Build and Plant": The Judean Question About the Yoke of Babylon (27:1—29:32)
"Build and Plant": The Promise of Restoration (30:1—33:26)
"Build and Plant": Destruction Before Restoration (34:1-22)
"Build and Plant": Fidelity in Relationship (35:1-19)

"Build and Plant": A Defiant King and the Indestructible Word (36:1-32)
"Build and Plant": The Death of a Nation (37:1—44:30)
"Build and Plant": Yahweh's Word to Baruch (45:1-5)
"Build and Plant": Oracles Against the Nations (46:1—51:64)
"Build and Plant": The Fall of Jerusalem—Reprise (52:1-34)

E. Hebrew Text Traditions of Jeremiah

There is a substantial difference between the text preserved in the Hebrew Bible (MT) and the Greek translation (LXX) of the book of Jeremiah. Recent studies have shown that the LXX is a translation of a shorter Hebrew edition of the book of Jeremiah, which had about 3,000 fewer words than the text tradition preserved in the MT. This shorter Hebrew text of Jeremiah is not available to us, but it is believed to be the textual source for the Greek translation. Scholars regard the MT as an expanded edition of the book. Fragments of both of these Hebrew text traditions of Jeremiah have been found among the Dead Sea scrolls. A significant variation between the two text traditions (in addition to numerous missing words, phrases, or verses in the shorter edition) is the placement of the oracles against the nations. In the MT these are placed in chs 46—51. In the LXX these oracles are placed in 25:14—31:44.

How and when the two divergent Hebrew text traditions of the book of Jeremiah were developed is not known. Scholarly speculation is that these two editions derive from a common source and that these two editions were nurtured and read as "scripture" by two separate Jewish communities. The MT is associated with the Jewish communities in Babylon or Palestine; the shorter text that underlies the LXX is associated with the Jewish communities in Egypt. The tradition assigns Tahpanhes in Egypt as the location of Jeremiah's last known oracles (43:8—44:14, 20-30). This leads to the possibility of tracing the shorter text to Jeremiah and/or Baruch, who were taken to Egypt against their will by the Jewish group that escaped to Egypt (43:1-7).

F. Theological Themes

The theology of the book of Jeremiah is born out of the intense and painful historical crisis that Judah/Jerusalem experienced during the violent geopolitical power shift in the Euphrates-Tigris-Nile region in the late seventh and early sixth centuries B.C. The task of the theology of this book is essentially to make sense of the harsh and difficult historical realities of this period. The theology of this book addresses the historical, political, social, and religious conditions of Judah before the tragic events of 587 B.C.; it also speaks about Judah's future beyond the days of its tragic end. The book accomplishes this task by its portrait of God as the sovereign Lord of history and particularly by linking contemporary historical events with God's purposive actions in history that display his sovereignty over Judah and the kingdoms of the world.

This understanding of God provides the general theological framework for the vision of reality communicated through the various types of materials in the book. This theological framework is not developed in any systematic way in the book; however, it is possible to pull out various expressions of this unifying theology of the book through a careful reading of the book. In this volume, we will limit our observations to the theological expressions of God's sovereignty over Judah and the nations in the world found in Jer 26—52 (see Varughese 2008, 27-33, for theological issues in chs 1—25).

1. The Incomparable Creator

Jeremiah's claim of the sovereignty of God is linked essentially to his understanding of God as the incomparable Creator of the earth and the heavens (see 51:15-19; this is a duplicate of 10:12-16). He is sovereign because he is the Creator. God's sovereignty is first and foremost evident in his creative power and wisdom through which he brought the earth and the heavens into existence. He "made the earth" and "stretched out the heavens"; he preserves and sustains his creation by giving it rain (51:15-16; see also 27:5; 32:17; 33:2). Day and night come at their appointed time because he has established a covenant with them and the "fixed laws of heaven and earth" (33:25, 20). Creation, in all of its aspects, belongs to the sovereign power of God. As the Creator of the universe, God's sovereignty extends over everything in the universe. The frequently found epithet for God "Yahweh of hosts" (*Yhwh Sebaoth*) in this book (total eighty-two times; fifty-four times in chs 26—52) is a consistent reminder of the sovereignty and dominion of Yahweh over all the powers of the universe.

There is no comparison between this living God and the worthless idols of the nations, the work of human hands (51:15-19). As the sovereign Creator, he alone is the object of worship and fear (v 19). The prophet mockingly characterizes the idols of the nations as "worthless, a work of delusion" (v 18 NRSV) and idol worshippers as "senseless and without knowledge" (v 17). In response to the claim of the Jewish exiles in Egypt that they enjoyed prosperity when they were faithful in their worship of the "Queen of Heaven," the prophet tells them to go ahead with their vows to this pagan goddess and reminds them that the prosperity they seek will not come because ultimately it is Yahweh's "word [that] will stand" (44:28). Moreover, this incomparable "God of all flesh" (32:27 NRSV), who made all "the people and animals that are on the earth" (27:5) is an all-powerful God and there is nothing that is too difficult for him (32:17, 27). He is also "great in counsel" and "mighty in deed" and his "eyes are open to all the ways of mortals" (32:19 NRSV).

2. The Sovereign God's Special Relationship to Israel

In the midst of a mocking and sarcastic rejection of idols, the book portrays God the Creator as "the Portion of Jacob," to whom belongs Israel, "the tribe of his inheritance" (51:19). The relationship between God and Israel is a covenant relationship; God has entered into a covenant with Israel and Israel is his special possession. This relationship and God's undying faithfulness to Israel that attends to this relationship is the underlying theological basis for God's frequent assurance to Israel that he is their God and they are his people (see the covenant formula "your God" and "my people" in 30:22; 31:1; 32:38). God's faithfulness to Israel continues even in the midst of Israel's covenant breaking and God's judgment on Israel's sin. This covenant relationship is eternal and is the basis for Israel's hope in its continued existence as a people in the world (31:35-37). God promises not to reject Israel; this promise is grounded solely on God's faithfulness to the covenant with its ancestors Abraham, Isaac, and Jacob (31:36-37). Israel is a people who "found grace," a people who are recipients of God's "everlasting love" and "faithfulness" (31:2-3 NRSV). God's faithfulness to Israel motivates him to offer a new covenant to the house of Israel and the house of Judah (31:31-34).

3. The Sovereign God of the Nations

The sovereign Creator of the universe who has a special relationship with Israel is also the sovereign God of the nations. He determines and directs the destiny of the nations and uses them as agents of his sovereign plans and purposes. Both the nations of the world and the nation Israel with whom Yahweh has entered into a special covenantal relationship must acknowledge God's sovereignty over the universe and his moral order for the world. This acknowledgment or lack thereof is the basis of God's shaping of the destiny of nations in the world.

This theological conviction of Jeremiah is unpacked in chs 27—29 and chs 46—51. In chs 27—28, the prophet makes the bold assertion that Nebuchadnezzar, king of Babylon, is Yahweh's servant and that he has given to this pagan king power and authority over all the nations; this dominion of Babylon is moreover extended to three generations of rulers (27:6-7). It is Yahweh's plan that all nations shall serve Babylon during the period allotted to its political domination over the world (27:7; 29:10). Since the Babylonian king is Yahweh's chosen servant to carry out his plans and purposes in the world, particularly for the people of Judah, it is imperative that the nations and Judah submit to the "yoke" of Babylon (27:8). Submission to Babylon means submission to Yahweh's will; refusal to submit to Babylon means refusal to submit to Yahweh, the consequence of which will be severe judgment that will come in the form of sword, famine, and pestilence. These will be the tragic effects of Babylon's ruthless attack on the nations that resist the imperial program of military expansion and domination of the world. On the other hand, submission to the yoke of Babylon—obedience to Yahweh's will—means life; those who obey Yahweh will be spared from destruction (27:12, 17).

The oracles against the nations (chs 46—51) vividly portray the sovereignty of Yahweh over the nation. Jeremiah, Yahweh's prophet to the nations (see 1:5, 10), announces Yahweh's judgment, not only Israel's immediate neighbors (Egypt, Philistia, Moab, Ammon, Edom, Syria, Kedar, and Hazor) but also faraway nations (Elam, Babylon). Yahweh brings judgment not only on these nations but also on their gods (46:25; 48:7; 49:3; 50:2; 51:44, 47). Pride, arrogance, and idolatry are frequently mentioned sins of the nations. Though Yahweh sent Babylon as an "enemy from the north" to punish Judah (see 6:22-23), it is now time for the punishment of Babylon (chs 50—51). Yahweh will send destroyer nations against the destroyer nation and they shall come from the north (51:48). Babylon was once a weapon in the hands of Yahweh for his punishment of Judah; now it is the object of his wrath. The rise of Babylon is Yahweh's work; its fall also is Yahweh's work.

The prophet perceives Yahweh as the sovereign Lord of history who exercises his sovereignty over the affairs of the world. Geopolitical changes and political domination one nation over other nations do not happen because of massive military machinery or superior conquest strategies of kings and emperors. Political changes in the world are brought about by Yahweh. Babylon's destruction that the kings of the Medes will accomplish is Yahweh's "purposes against Babylon" (51:29). Moreover, it is part of Yahweh's plan to restore the exiles of Israel to their homeland. In that sense the destruction of Babylon means salvation to the exiled people of Yahweh.

4. The Sovereign Judge of Judah

The prophet gives clear warning to Judah about the impending Babylonian invasion of Judah as Yahweh's punishment of the nation for its continued resistance to Yahweh's will (see the narratives in chs 27, 28, 34, 37, 38). The narratives that deal with the destruction of Jerusalem and Judah in chs 39—40, however, do not mention Yahweh or Jeremiah's words to Judah in its darkest hour. The silence of Yahweh and his prophet in these chapters means that the hour has come for Judah to suffer the consequence of its persistent sins against Yahweh. Jeremiah has warned persistently about the tragic consequences of covenant breaking and Judah's stubborn resistance to Yahweh's will. What he has spoken so clearly is being fulfilled in Judah's contemporary history and there is no further word of warning, but only a silence—perhaps the sign of Yahweh's grief over the destruction of his people and the land he gave them as a gift. However, this silence is broken in the rest of chs 26—52, and particularly in chs 30—33, with grand promises of restoration and renewal of relationship between Yahweh and his people. These chapters indicate that judgment is not final and does not determine the end of Yahweh's relationship with Israel. In the end Yahweh's compassion for his people and his faithfulness to the covenant prevails over Israel's sins and Yahweh's punishment of sin.

5. The Sovereign God's Promise of Israel's Healing and Restoration

In the book of Jeremiah, the theme of restoration is not an afterthought, an idea that the editors of the book came up with in the final stages of the production of the book. This theme is at the core of Jeremiah's preaching. Yahweh called Jeremiah to announce destruction and rebuilding, uprooting and tearing down and building and planting, and judgment and salvation (1:10). So it is not surprising that we find a heavy emphasis on the theme of restoration and rebuilding in the preaching of Jeremiah in the years that immediately precede the fall of Jerusalem in 587 B.C. The editors of the book place this core conviction of Jeremiah (see chs 30—33) before the narratives that deal with Jerusalem's destruction (chs 39—40) to show the importance of this theme in Jeremiah's preaching. What this means is that hope comes even before tragedy happens. The nation that walks through the valley of death in 587 B.C. walks with hope in the days of its restoration.

The preaching of Jeremiah in chs 26—52 reflect the prophet's stubborn hope in the future of Israel, the return of the exiles of Israel to their homeland, the reunification of the two divided kingdoms, return of normal life conditions in the land, and the faithful leadership of Davidic kings and Levitical priesthood. His purchase of the land while he was in prison is the most incredible and outrageous display of hope in the return of normal life in the land (ch 32).

The program of restoration in chs 26—52 is elaborate. The letter to the exiles of 597 B.C. clearly conveys Yahweh's plan to bring them back to their homeland (29:10-14). Like a shepherd, Yahweh will keep Israel his flock and lead them to their homeland (31:10). The theme is reiterated in 31:8-14, 17; 32:37; 50:19. Yahweh will restore the fortunes of Israel (30:3, 18; 32:42-44; 33:7). The restoration of the exiles means their salvation (30:10-11; 31:7), and this promise of salvation is clearly announced in 30:11. In 50:33, the exile of Israel is compared to the bondage of the nation by oppressive powers that refuse to let them go (the Babylonian exile as parallel to Israel's bondage in Egypt). Salvation from Babylon will be brought about by Yahweh the Redeemer, Yahweh of Hosts, the strong and mighty God of Israel (50:34; see also 31:11). This means the end of the yoke of Babylon, the end of Israel's servitude to Babylon (30:8).

Though Israel is experiencing Yahweh's judgment because of its numerous sins and great guilt, Yahweh promises to bring healing and health to the nation that is afflicted with an incurable wound for which there is no medicine (30:12-17; 33:6). Yahweh also promises to forgive and pardon the nation and cleanse it from its sin and guilt (33:8; 50:20). Yahweh will also enter into a new covenant with the restored, forgiven, and cleansed nation; the laws of the new covenant will be written on the heart of individuals (31:31-34). The new covenant also promises Yahweh's forgiveness of Israel; he will remember Israel's sin no more (31:34). In the restored community, all will know Yahweh and all will enjoy the gift of the singleness of heart to live in obedience and fear of Yahweh (31:34; 32:39-40). Moreover, the covenant with Israel will be an eternal covenant (32:40).

Yahweh's plan of restoration of Israel also includes the rebuilding of Israel as a unified nation (31:27-28; 33:7, 14-15, 23-26) with increase in its population (30:19). The people will enjoy normal life activities; sounds of joy will be heard in the streets and in the land again (31:4-5, 24; 33:10-13). The rebuilding of Jerusalem is another part of the program of restoration (31:38-40; 33:9, 16). The prophet anticipates the return of all Israel to worship Yahweh in Zion/Jerusalem (31:6, 12; 50:4-5).

The restored people will live under the faithful leadership of Davidic kings who will diligently administer justice and righteousness in the land (30:9; 33:15). The prophet describes Yahweh's covenant with David as a covenant that cannot be broken; this means there will always be someone on the throne of David (33:17-22). This same promise is also given to the Levitical priests in 33:17-22. The restored nation receives in these verses the promise of perpetual political and religious leadership.

The final chapter of Jeremiah reflects the prophet's hope in the restoration of Israel in a more concrete way (ch 52). The book ends with a note about the hope being realized in a small measure; the release of Jehoiachin from prison by the Babylonian king is most likely a sign of hope in the impending freedom of the exiles from Babylon (52:31-34). The restoration is thus not simply a promise but a reality that the people will soon experience in their lives.

6. God's Sovereignty and Freedom

In several places in chs 26—52, the book holds God's sovereignty and his freedom in proper balance. These chapters make clear that God who determines the course of history is also open to changing his plans and purposes and that he indeed changes his mind according to human response. The decisions he makes are not inflexible and final. In the opening chapter of this section, the prophet, while announcing judgment, also expresses Yahweh's willingness to suspend his judgment and spare the nation from the disaster he intends to bring upon them (26:3; see also 36:3). In the same way, though he has chosen Babylon as the instrument of his judgment, Judah and the nations are given the opportunity to live, if they should choose to submit to the yoke of Babylon (ch 27). Yahweh gives the city and King Zedekiah into the hands of the Babylonians but offers a peaceful death and normal burial to Zedekiah (34:2-5). The prophet counsels the Judeans who are determined to go to Egypt to seek refuge there that they will be planted and built up if they remained in the land of Judah. However, if they reject this counsel and go ahead with their plans, then death and destruction will follow them in the land of their self-imposed exile (42:7-17). These texts show that God who is sovereign and free to change his mind also permits human beings to respond either positively or negatively to his demands. These texts also show that God's word of judgment on Judah became a reality not because this word was spoken as an unalterable decree but precisely because Judah refused to give heed to God's repeated calls to change from their self-centered ways of thinking and follow Yahweh's plans and purposes for them.

7. The Sovereign God's Sovereign Word

Throughout the book of Jeremiah there is a focused attention on God's sovereign word. The introduction presents the words of Jeremiah as the "word of the LORD" (*děbar yhwh*) (1:1-2). The prophet's message is often introduced by phrases such as "the word of the LORD came to me," "the LORD said to me," "thus says the LORD," "oracle of the LORD," and "the word that came to Jeremiah from the LORD." The book is replete with the phrase "oracle of Yahweh" (168 times; Holladay 1986, 35). The Hebrew word *dābār* ("word") is found over ninety times, far more than any other OT book (Stulman 2005, 28).

The book, from the beginning to the end, aims to show how God's sovereign word is at work in Judah's national life, including the life of the prophet, as well as in the international scene. It is this sovereign word that calls and appoints Jeremiah to be a prophet to the nations (1:4-10). This word authorizes the uprooting and tearing down of Judah and the nations; it is also this word that authorizes the building and planting of Judah and the nations (v 10). The word about the uprooting of Judah dominates chs 1—25. Chapters 26—52 demonstrate the powerful effect of Yahweh's word. The word spoken about Judah's destruction is fulfilled in this section. However, it is also the word that brings about restoration and rebuilding, covenant renewal, faithful leadership, and secure life in the land. The exiled community would also have found in this word about its future, the theological rationale for its present condition of exile. In the end, what remains for Judah is the word about its restoration; this word comes to the exiled nation as the hope-filled word, graciously spoken by a compassionate God who is the source of comfort for the hurting and grieving people of Judah and Israel.

The book also acknowledges the reality that God's word is often distorted and contradicted by (false) prophets who claim to have their authority to deliver the word from God. The story of Jeremiah's confrontation with Hananiah the prophet—perhaps the leader of the false prophets in Jerusalem—shows how Jeremiah might have been confused by the forceful delivery of an oracle by Hananiah in Yahweh's name that totally contradicted the oracle of Jeremiah (ch 28). In his response to Hananiah, Jeremiah indicates that the test of the authenticity of a prophetic word is in the content of the word. Often the content of Yahweh's word has to do with admonitions and discipline and even threat of judgment. This is especially true in the context of sin and disobedience. Jeremiah's speech to Hananiah implies that Yahweh seldom speaks peace (*shalom*) to a people who live in disobedience to his commands. However, the nature of the people is such that they prefer to hear words of peace and prosperity rather than words of judgment. Hananiah represents those who reject Yahweh's true words and ridicule Yahweh's true prophets. God's sovereign word ultimately triumphs and reveals Hananiah as a fraud who has spoken presumptuously in Yahweh's name (28:15-17).

Finally, Yahweh's word is not a casual word spoken to a particular group of people. The story of the writing of the scroll (ch 36) illustrates how Yahweh's spoken word survives in the written form for generations to hear and respond to his admonitions in a positive way. King Jehoiakim who has the ultimate responsibility to hear the word and lead the nation in a covenant living not only disregards the word but also destroys it. The king's burning of the scroll—the shredding of documents that reveal the king's culpability for the nations' impending disaster—does not mean the end of Yahweh's word. The key issue in this story is that the king cannot succeed in silencing Yahweh's word. He may destroy a scroll, but he cannot silence the voice of Yahweh. The survival of the book for Israel's ancient readers and its readers over the last two thousand years is a remarkable testimony to the power of Yahweh's word.

COMMENTARY

"BUILD AND PLANT"

A NEW PHASE IN THE PROPHET'S MINISTRY (26:1-24)

Overview

Except for its lack of poetic oracles, ch 26 mirrors the complex character of the book of Jeremiah. In the words of Fretheim, this chapter is "incoherent" whether we approach it "from a literary or historical perspective" (2002, 367). Carroll describes it as a "fictional story" made up of a "complex of different strands of redaction which has developed an original story about a public procedure for establishing Jeremiah's authenticity in a number of different ways" (1986, 515). If Carroll's assessment of ch 26 is accepted, then one would expect to find in the narrative some artificial cohesiveness, which is woefully lacking in the narrative. Stulman describes ch 26 as the introduction to the second half of Jeremiah with its focus on the intense opposition to Jeremiah's message, the culpability of the opposition to the destruction of Jerusalem and the temple, and the emergence of a community of faithful who are receptive to the prophetic message (26:16-19), which shows up at certain critical points to save the life of Jeremiah (26:24; 36:19; 38:7-13). This chapter, according to Stulman, introduces hope for Judah's future and its new beginning, in spite of its impending exile and the destruction of the city and the temple (2005, 233-42). Some who see this chapter as the trial that followed the temple sermon (see in ch 26) also find in this narrative the influence of Deuteronomic ideas and language (in vv 3-5, 12-15) and place it in the exilic period (Nicholson 1970, 52-56).

Chapter 26, though it has the appearance of a unified story, has gaps at several critical points. These gaps suggest the possibility that we have before us a loosely constructed biographical narrative that seeks to accomplish multiple goals; this means that there are multiple ways of reading this narrative. The usual explanation is that ch 26 provides the account of the trial that followed Jeremiah's temple sermon (7:1-15). However, there is no sufficient explanation for its placement in ch 26. Why didn't the editors place this narrative immediately following the sermon in 7:1-15? This question does not have a good answer. It is also not clear when this narrative was added to the book, though the likelihood is that there is an interval between the date of the delivery of the sermon and the trial, and the date of the composition of the narrative and its addition to the book. It is likely that the sermon and the trial took place in 609 B.C., the first year of Jehoiakim's reign. There is sufficient evidence in the book that serious threat to Jeremiah's life and intense opposition to his message, however, developed only after Jehoiakim's burning of the scroll (36:1; the fourth year of Jehoiakim). Thus a date following Jehoiakim's burning of the scroll in 605 B.C. is a good possibility (ch 36) for the composition of this narrative. This may further explain the general, rather than specific, historical reference in 26:1 ("at the beginning of the reign of King Jehoiakim," v 1 NRSV; compare with specific dates in 25:1; 36:1; 45:1). Stulman's view that ch 26 introduces the second half of the book with focus on opposition to the prophet's ministry thus provides a reasonable explanation for its present location in the book. It can even be said that the general historical reference provides a link between the sermon and the trial, and perhaps a second phase of Jeremiah's ministry, a period of conflict, opposition, and death threat that will continue for the rest of the prophet's life.

A cursory examination of the parallels between the call and commission of the prophet in 1:4-19 and ch 26 yields some support for the view that the editors may have intentionally placed this narrative in ch 26 to introduce a new phase in the career of the prophet. The prophet's personal life experiences narrated here are intimately linked to his call and commission, and his message and the experience of the nation described in chs 27—45. In 1:4 and 26:1, Yahweh's word comes to the prophet (following the historical reference). Yahweh commissions Jeremiah to speak whatever Yahweh commands him to speak (1:7). In 26:2 Yahweh commands the prophet to speak **all the words** that he commands him to say to the people of Judah. In chs 2—25, the focus of Jeremiah's message was on judgment. However, the message of restoration dominates the prophet's message in chs 27—52.

There is a clear warning about opposition to the prophet in 1:18-19; the narrator focuses on opposition to Jeremiah in 26:7-9. In ch 1, the opponents are powerful political and religious leaders and the people of the land. In ch 26, Jeremiah's opposition comes from the priests, the prophets, and the people. In chs 27—29, the opposition to Jeremiah's message comes from false prophets. King Jehoiakim remains in the background in ch 26, but the incident about Jehoiakim's murder of Uriah (26:20-23) clearly indicates the royal opposition to the prophet's message, which is taken up in ch 36, where the king is the leading antagonist of the prophet. In chs 37—38 royal officials and even Zedekiah stand opposed to the prophet's message.

Yahweh warns Jeremiah not to be afraid in 1:7-8; in ch 26, the prophet speaks with courage and defends his message in spite of the demand for his death by religious leaders (vv 8, 12-15). This courageous stand of the prophet continues at every critical point in the second half of the book (see his words to Zedekiah in chs 37—38, words to Johanan and his associates and the Jewish exiles in Egypt in chs 42—44).

The content of the message Yahweh gives to Jeremiah in ch 1 includes Yahweh's work of uprooting and tearing down (1:10); Jeremiah speaks of the destruction of the city and the temple (26:6). Chapter 39 focuses on the destruction of Jerusalem and the exile of Judah. The theme of building and planting (1:10) is taken up in detail in chs 30—33.

Yahweh promises to be with Jeremiah to rescue him from his opposition (1:8, 19). Jeremiah is saved from the death sentence by the verdict of the court by the officials; he also receives the support of the elders who spoke in favor of a verdict of innocence, and his life is spared by Ahikam son of Shaphan (26:16, 17-19, 24). Threat against his life is intensified, but Yahweh preserves the life of the prophet through help that comes from some unexpected sources (see 36:19; 37:7-13; 39:11-14; 40:1-6). Yahweh himself hides the prophet from the associates of King Jehoiakim (36:26). Even King Zedekiah acts at a critical time to save the prophet's life by keeping him in the court of the guard rather than sending him to the prison in the house of Jonathan (37:20-21). Moreover, Yahweh also promises to protect those who demonstrated loyalty to the prophet (see 39:15-18; 45:1-5).

The above analysis provides some justification for viewing ch 26 as the beginning of a new section in the book of Jeremiah, and the introduction to a new phase in the ministry of the prophet. The survival of the prophet from the hands of those who seek to kill him signals hope for the survival of Judah beyond the days of its impending destruction. Both the prophet and the nations survive solely because of Yahweh's gracious intervention. This is a key issue in chs 26—52.

BEHIND THE TEXT

Chapter 26 contains the biographical account of a key incident in the life of the prophet. In the LXX, this narrative is located in 33:1-24. The narrative begins with a historical reference that places the event reported here to the beginning year of the reign of Jehoiakim. This narrative is most likely the report of the events that happened after Jeremiah's temple sermon (Bright

1965, 171; Holladay 1989, 101-3; Lundbom 2004a, 284-85). The narrative contains a summary of 7:1-15 in 26:4-6. The narrative focuses on the consequence of preaching the temple sermon, and hence only a brief summary of the sermon is given in this narrative. Holladay considers this narrative as the work of Baruch (1989, 103). Others find in this narrative the influence of Deuteronomistic ideas and language and place it in the exilic period (Nicholson 1970, 52-56). This is the earliest dated event in Jeremiah's career aside from the reference to "the thirteenth year of Josiah" in 1:2, and its historical value cannot be underestimated. The Uriah incident (26:20-23) and the strong biographical orientation of the narrative lend further support to the authenticity of the historical reference in v 1. This narrative places the ministry of Jeremiah in an intensely hostile setting, and the hostility reflected in this narrative will follow him throughout his prophetic career.

This biographical narrative follows the pattern of a detailed trial. It aims to tell the story of a critical incident in the life of the prophet; it also functions to authenticate Jeremiah as a true prophet who courageously proclaimed Yahweh's word in the midst of intense opposition from powerful religious authorities.

This narrative unit has three parts: part 1 (vv 1-6) begins with Yahweh's instructions to Jeremiah to speak his words in the temple courtyard (vv 1-3); it is followed by a summary of Jeremiah's sermon (vv 4-6). Verses 1-6 together thus present the crime, which is instigated by Yahweh and committed by the prophet. The crime of the prophet is that he truthfully and obediently proclaimed the word given to him by Yahweh.

Part 2 narrates the actual trial itself (vv 7-16). This trial section opens with the indictment of the prophet by the people, the priests, and the prophets and their verdict of death to the prophet (vv 7-9). The priests and the prophets and the people thus assume the role of prosecution, judge, and jury. This is followed by the report of the arrival of the princes of Judah who together with "all the people," assume the judicial role in this narrative. The priests and the prophets officially bring the charges against Jeremiah and argue for the death penalty (vv 10-11). In the next section, the prophet makes his defense before the princes and the people in which he reiterates his message and claims that he is a true prophet of Yahweh. Any punishment imposed upon him will incur blood guilt upon the people and the city (vv 12-15). The trial section ends with a verdict from the officials and the people (v 16). They find the prophet not guilty of the charges against him, but as a true prophet who does not deserve the death sentence.

In part 3, the narrator adds to the trial account two additional elements. In vv 17-19, some of the elders of the land speak in favor of the prophet, almost as if they take the role of witnesses for the defendant. Ironically, this defense follows the verdict in v 16, and so it seems out of place in the narrative structure. In its present location, this defense seems to serve as a defense of the verdict, and not of the prophet himself. The second element of this section is a report about another prophet who was put to death by Jehoiakim for preaching the same words of judgment that Jeremiah preached (vv 20-23). It is likely that the incident of Uriah took place not too long after the trial of Jeremiah. The intent of this additional story is probably to show the dangerous consequences of prophetic preaching during the reign of Jehoiakim. The trial narrative ends with the report that Jeremiah's life was saved by the intervention of Ahikam son of Shaphan (v 24). This last part (vv 17-24) also serves to contrast Hezekiah the penitent king with Jehoiakim the defiant king. The purpose of the entire narrative is clear. Jerusalem's future depends on the penitent response of the people to God's word of judgment; continued defiance will only lead to death and destruction.

IN THE TEXT

1. The Temple Sermon (26:1-6)

■ 1 This unit introduces the year, the setting, and an abbreviated version of Jeremiah's temple sermon. Some scholars regard "the beginning of the reign" (NRSV) as Jehoiakim's accession year or the period between his accession to the throne and his first New Year's Day (v 1). Bright dates this to a period between September 609, the year of Jehoiakim's accession, and April 608, his first New Year's Day, assuming that the Nisan calendar was in use in Judah during this time (Bright 1965, 169). Verse 1 assumes that the recipient of ***this word from Yahweh*** was Jeremiah.

■ 2 Verse 2 states the command from Yahweh to Jeremiah. This command seems to be a paraphrase of 7:2. The command in 7:2 is to stand in the "gate" of the temple and speak, whereas here the command is to stand in the ***court*** of the temple and **speak.** In 7:2 the location is perhaps the gate to the inner courtyard of the temple. **Courtyard** in 26:2 is most likely the inner courtyard where the people assembled daily and on festival days. The temple court is also the location of Jeremiah's preaching in 19:14. The general location of Jeremiah's preaching is thus the same in both 7:2 and 26:2.

The message is addressed to **all *the cities* of Judah** (v 2). The intended audience is the people of the cities of Judah. This corresponds to "all . . . Judah" in 7:2. Verse 2 also makes clear that worship was the context in which Jeremiah was to deliver Yahweh's word. The occasion was most likely a festival or some other special time when all the people of Judah came to Jerusalem to worship in the temple. Yahweh's command also insists on the full delivery of the content of his message ("do not hold back a word" [NRSV]). This additional command, which is lacking in 7:2, is parallel to Moses' command to Israel to not subtract or take away anything from what he commands them to do (Deut 4:2; 12:32). Jeremiah must not submit to pressure from his opponents and reduce or diminish Yahweh's words out of fear of consequences. Lundbom states, "Prophets of Yahweh must 'speak the word, the whole word, and nothing but the word'" (2004a, 287).

■ **3** Verse 3 makes clear the goal of the prophet's preaching. Yahweh's purpose is to give warning to his people through Jeremiah concerning the judgment he is planning against them, in the hope that the people will pay attention to his warning and consequently **repent** (*šub*) of their **evil way**. The repentance of the people will in turn prompt Yahweh to cancel the judgment he has planned against them. The people's repentance will lead Yahweh to **relent** (*nḥm*). The people's response to Yahweh's word anticipates contriteness and recognition of wrongdoing. Yahweh's response, on the other hand, is a change in his plan, which does not imply feeling of remorse or contriteness (see 18:8). It is also important to note here that what Yahweh hopes to see take place is individual decision and response (**each will turn from his evil way**). Though the people as a whole is intended here, emphasis is given in this verse to each individual's response to Yahweh's word.

■ **4** Verses 4-6 contain Yahweh's word that Jeremiah was commanded to speak. The worshipping community is the recipient of the message (**you shall say to them**). The message conveys two demands from Yahweh: listen to Yahweh's word and walk in his law, and listen to the words of Yahweh's prophets (vv 4-5). The issue of listening to Yahweh and walking in his law sums up Yahweh's explicit demands outlined in 7:3-10. The temple sermon touches on the subject of Yahweh speaking persistently (7:13; see 7:25 on Yahweh sending his servants the prophets).

Yahweh's demands are introduced with a conditional clause (*protasis*) in the negative in 26:4 (**if you do not . . .**), which strongly implies dire consequences for disobedience. This negative conditional clause deals with two issues—the worshipping community's failure to listen to and live by the demands of Yahweh's Torah (v 4) and its failure to pay attention to the words of the prophets (v 5). The consequence (*apodosis*) is stated in v 6. The conditional formula appears in 7:5 in the positive, which is stated there as a challenge to obey Yahweh's word in order to enjoy the benefits and blessings of obedience (see 7:7).

The negative conditional clause in 26:4 implies that the worshipping community exists without any regard for Yahweh's Torah (**my law**) that he has **set before** them at Mount Sinai. Listening to Yahweh's word and walking in his law exemplify covenant relationship. Yahweh's speech is a strong denunciation of the nation's breaking of the Sinai covenant. The temple sermon deals with this issue more explicitly by giving detailed listing of covenant-breaking activities by the worshipping community (7:8-9).

■ **5** In vv 4 and 5, keeping of the Sinai covenant laws and listening to the words of the prophets receive equal importance. Israel received Yahweh's Torah through Moses, Yahweh's servant ("my servant," Num 12:7). Later in Israel's history, Yahweh's prophets (**my servants the prophets**) have occupied the office that Yahweh established through Moses. An important task of the prophets was to remind the covenant people to live the Torah obedient life. The phrase ***constantly I am sending*** implies Yahweh's continued efforts in the past and the present to bring the people back to the covenant way of life though the people **have not listened** to the prophetic message (v 5). The Torah obedience here is not the cultic and ritual observances of the law. The people being addressed here are worshippers in the temple, which imply that they keep the legal requirements of the Torah. The Torah obedience here in this text, as in 7:5-10, is the fulfillment of the ethical and moral requirements of the Torah—living out the demands of the Torah in social and communal relations.

■ **6** The consequence of persistent rejection of the Torah and the prophetic word is stated in v 6. If the people continue to pay no attention to Yahweh's demands, then certainly the temple will suffer the fate of **Shiloh.** In 7:12 the sermon directs the people to see for themselves the impact of Yahweh's judgment on the place where the tabernacle was located in the early history of Israel in Canaan. The mention of the ruined Shiloh and linking it with the fate that awaits the temple would have been sufficient reasons for the priests to become angry and hostile toward the prophet.

A further consequence of the rejection of the Torah and the prophetic word is that the city of Jerusalem will become "a curse for all the nations of the earth" (v 6 NRSV). "Curse" (*qĕlālâ*) is a word found often in Jeremiah and in Deuteronomy to convey the idea of a person or a nation as the object of contempt and ridicule. The text here indicates that the city will be the object of contempt for all the nations of the earth. The threat in 7:12-15 lacks specific and explicit words about the fate of the city. The narrator understands and interprets the implications of the threat against the temple on the city in which it is located. Stulman finds in this curse word against the city echoes of the ancestral promises in Gen 12:3 and points out that here we have the threat of the reversal of "the promise of life to intimate the death of Israel" (2005, 238). The city is the symbol of the vocational calling of Israel to be a source of blessing to all the families of the earth. Its death means that no blessing will flow from the city to the nations of the earth. The nations that were to become participants in Israel's ancestral blessings will curse the city because of its failure to bring them a blessing. This threat is a powerful challenge to the people to take the necessary action to avoid this grave calamity that awaits the city.

The sermon in its summary form implicitly invites the worshipping community to respond positively to the demands of Yahweh, which is essential to the continued existence of the temple and the city, the symbols of Yahweh's presence and protection of his people. The judgment of the exile of the nation in 7:15 does not receive any mention in this text. What is strongly implied is the hope that positive response to Yahweh's demand will result in his change of plans.

2. The Trial (26:7-16)

■ **7** Verses 7-9 report the crowd's initial response to Jeremiah's sermon. Those who have heard the message included **the priests, the prophets and all the people**—the religious leaders and the laity who were present in the temple court in the context of worship (v 7). The priests have vested interest in the temple as the custodians of the national center of worship. The continued existence of the temple was a key concern of the priests because it guaranteed their own survival. The prophets may have been either temple prophets (Holladay 1989, 105) or false prophets who have been promoting a city-temple ideology and preaching the message of peace to the people.

■ **8** In v 8 the narrator reports the response of the audience when the prophet finished saying *all that Yahweh commanded* him to say to **all the people**. This suggests that the prophet's primary concern was to address the people, though the priests and the prophets were in the audience. The prophet faithfully carries out his task without holding anything back. However, the message touches a raw nerve and it brings an instant negative reaction from the audience. Jeremiah's opponents include **the priests, the prophets and all the people** (v 8). **The people** also join in the pronouncement of death to the prophet who brings Yahweh's judgment words against the temple-city structures. They **seized** the prophet and pronounced the verdict *you shall surely die* (v 8). The verdict is pronounced before bringing an actual charge against the prophet. The actual charge itself is stated in v 9.

Commentators find the reference to **all the people** as problematic since later the narrator reports that "all the people" crowded around Jeremiah in the temple (v 9) and the priests and the prophets present their charge against the prophet to the officials and to "all the people" (v 11). Later "all the people" along with the princes find the prophet not guilty of the charges against him (v 16). Some scholars think that the reference in v 8 is a secondary addition based on v 7. The LXX supports the MT reading here. It is possible that the people changed their mind about the prophet (v 16) after hearing his defense before them and the princes (vv 12-15). Perhaps the narrator attempts to show here the fickleness of the people; they are easily swayed by differing voices and are unable to make up their minds about the prophet's guilt or innocence. They begin as a hostile crowd but change their minds when they hear his defense, but in the end it is from the hand of "the people" that Jeremiah needs protection (v 24).

■ **9** Verse 9 outlines the charge against Jeremiah, which begins with the question, *Why have you prophesied in Yahweh's name?* This is the central issue in the charge against Jeremiah. He is speaking in the name of Yahweh, but his words contradict the commonly perceived ideas about the temple-city structures. The temple crowd could not conceive of the idea that Yahweh would allow his temple to be destroyed and that he would abandon his promises concerning the city (Ps 132:13-14). In the temple-city ideology, **this house** and

this city are eternal and inviolable structures. These are secure structures and their security lies in the eternal promises of Yahweh to his people. To say that the temple will suffer the fate of **Shiloh** and that the city of Jerusalem will become a **desolate and deserted** place is blasphemy, particularly when it is said in Yahweh's name. It is a lie spoken in Yahweh's name. ***Why have you prophesied in Yahweh's name?*** is thus not a question that seeks an answer from the prophet but an accusation that he is a blasphemer and a lying prophet. The punishment for such crime is death. Verse 9 ends with the note that the people **crowded** up to Jeremiah in the temple, perhaps incited by the charge against him. The crowd is angry and upset and is about to take action against the blasphemer-prophet.

It is important to note, as Holladay does, the omission of the conditional formula "if you do not listen to me" in the accusers' paraphrase of Jeremiah's sermon. He notes that Jeremiah's accusers transform the prophet's covenant speech into an announcement of punishment (1989, 105). By giving attention to the words about the destruction of the temple and the city, the audience thus effectively exempt themselves from the covenant responsibility to respond to Yahweh's words. They do not hear the explicit call for repentance and transformation (7:5-7), but only the provocative words of punishment, words in their thinking would not have come from Yahweh. Their interpretive framework is not the covenant theology but the temple-city ideology, whereas the narrator works within the framework of the Sinai covenant theology that calls for covenant obedience and a repentant way of life. The people crowd around the prophet in the house of Yahweh, not to hear him speak Yahweh's words but to express their hostility and hatred. The house of Yahweh has become not only "a den of robbers" (7:11) but also a place where the true prophet's life is in danger.

■ **10** Verse 10 introduces a legal proceeding. **These things** perhaps refer to the words of the prophet and the verdict of death against the prophet by the priests, the prophets, and the people and the uproar in the temple court (v 10). How the news arrived in the palace is not clear; it is likely that the priests might have sent the word to the palace. The news prompted the **officials** (*sārîm*) **of Judah** to go up from the palace to the temple area. This group may have included both royal family members and nonroyal officials with military and civil authority (Lundbom 2004a, 291; Holladay 1989, 106). They **took their places at the entrance of the New Gate** of the temple, which indicates that they arrived there to initiate an official hearing of this case against Jeremiah. Verse 10 thus implies the role of this group as officers of the court or judicial administrators with authority to pronounce judgment in the setting of a court. Court was held in ancient Israel at the city gate (see Amos 5:10, 12, 15). Here the court setting is the **New Gate** in the temple area. The MT lacks reference to the temple but simply refers to ***the entrance of the New Gate of Yahweh*** as the place where the princes ***sat*** to hear the case. The precise location of this gate is not known; it is also mentioned in 36:10 as in the "upper courtyard" area.

■ 11 Verse 11 sums up the charge brought against the prophet by **the priests and the prophets**. They function here as the prosecution. They present the charge before **the officials and all the people**. In v 8, the prophet's accusers include "all the people." In the narrative the people (mentioned eight times in vv 7-18) play various roles (see comment on v 8). Here they do not have judicial authority but simply form the crowd that listens to the charges.

The case against the prophet does not begin with the indictment but with the demand for the verdict of death. ***Death sentence to this man*** (lit., "a sentence of death to this man") conveys the seriousness with which the priests and the prophets handle any attempt to contradict the popular beliefs about the temple and the city (v 11). Those who challenge the temple-city ideology do not deserve to live. The guardians of the status quo do not refer to Jeremiah as a prophet, but simply as **this man**. They refuse to acknowledge him as a prophet, because calling him a prophet would mean implicit acknowledgment of the authority of Jeremiah to speak on behalf of Yahweh.

In v 9 the charge includes the prophet's words of threat against the temple. In v 11 the reason for the demand of the verdict of death is that the prophet spoke **against this city** (Jerusalem). It is possible that the accusers focus on Jeremiah's words against the city to incite the officials and to turn them against Jeremiah. They know that the officials have vested interest in the political stability and the continued existence of the city. They omit any reference to the prophet's words against the temple perhaps to show that their charge against Jeremiah does not have any self-interest or self-preservation in mind. Then again, the destruction of the city means the destruction of the temple. Speaking against the city is speaking against Yahweh who promised to dwell in the city and to protect and defend the city. The charge is thus treason, blasphemy, and false prophecy all bundled together. Ironically, the accusation against the prophet conveniently omits any reference to the prophet's call for reform/repentance (see 7:5-7). As in the pretrial charge in v 9, the ground for the prosecution's charge against Jeremiah is its own self-serving political and religious ideology. It is clear that the prophet's opponents are working outside the framework of the covenant theology, which calls for Torah obedience and a repentant way of life.

The demand for the death sentence is consistent with the punishment prescribed for blasphemy and false prophecy in the law of Moses (Lev 24:16; Deut 18:20). The prophet's accusers also remind the officials that they (the officials) have **heard . . . with** their **own ears** Jeremiah's prophecy **against this city**. Though the officials were not present in the temple when Jeremiah spoke to the people, the priests and the prophets may have sent messengers to the palace with the complaint that contained only the words spoken against the city.

■ **12** Verses 12-15 present Jeremiah's defense. The defense speech is also addressed to the **officials** and to **all the people** (v 12). Jeremiah begins his defense with the claim that ***Yahweh has sent*** him ***to prophesy*** against the temple (**this house**) and **this city**. He thus establishes himself as a true prophet and counters the charge of false prophecy and blasphemy. His opening statement also shows that there is no falsehood in his words. The prosecution's charge omitted the words he spoke against the temple, but Jeremiah gives a true version of his words and includes both the temple and the city as the focus of his prophecy. He also acknowledges that what they have heard is true. If there is falsehood, it lies with the people who have brought the charges. They are not telling the whole truth. This admission of the whole truth of what he has said is clearly intended to establish his credibility as a trustworthy prophet and his prophetic authority.

■ **13** Jeremiah's defense includes another reiteration of his message. This time the message is addressed to all who are present at this hearing. The officials who have not heard his original message now hear Yahweh's message directly from the mouth of the prophet. The opening particle (***and now***, v 13) turns the attention to the present (Lundbom 2004a, 292), thus inviting the officials and the people to pay attention to the prophetic words. This speech repeats the call to **reform** (lit., "make good") the **ways** and ***doings*** of the people. The narrator's paraphrased version of the temple sermon lacks this call to reform (26:4-6). Here we have a repetition of the call to reform in the original sermon (see 7:3, 5).

Yahweh's primary concern is the transformation of the covenant community. He insists on the commitment of the people to the covenant way of life. A clear evidence of this commitment to reform is the integrity of the court. This speech thus implicitly instructs the officials and the people to be impartial in their judgment on this case against the prophet. The prophet also urges his audience to **obey *Yahweh* your God,** the One who is calling his people to change their ways and actions (v 13). Your God is the One with whom the people have made a covenant, the stipulations of which included the requirement of obedience and listening to the voice of the covenant maker (Exod 19:5). Jeremiah reminds the officials and the people that he is speaking on behalf of their covenant maker.

Jeremiah includes in his defense Yahweh's words to him that he will relent and will not bring ***the evil which he has spoken against*** the people if they reformed their ways and actions (v 13; see 26:3). The temple sermon itself does not refer to Yahweh relenting or changing his mind. The goal of the prophet's preaching is not to announce the inescapable reality of judgment but to invite the people to reform, which in turn will lead to a change in Yahweh's plan against them.

■ **14** Jeremiah, in his defense speech, reminds the court of its moral and ethical responsibility to do that which is proper according to the standards of the covenant community (v 14). Jeremiah's statement, **I am in your hands,** indicates a clever but powerful strategy. On the one hand, though he speaks with authority as Yahweh's spokesperson, he also humbles himself and surrenders to the power of the court rather than surrendering to the power of Yahweh to save him. On the other hand, this surrender to the court places on the court the burden of moral and ethical responsibility to give an impartial judgment. ***Do to me as seems good and right in your eyes*** is another reminder to the court of its covenant obligation to do that which is just and right. The court should not yield to the unjust and unrighteous demand of the powerful religious authorities and impose the death penalty on an innocent person who spoke Yahweh's words truthfully to the people.

■ **15** Though the prophet surrenders himself to the power of the court, he concludes his speech with the strong reminder of the consequence of an unjust verdict by the court (v 15). If the court puts him to death and thus carries out the wishes of the priests and the prophets, it will then incur **guilt of innocent blood** on the officials (**yourselves**), **on this city and on those who live in it** (v 15). The death of an innocent prophet will indeed provoke Yahweh's wrath, and it will have grave consequence on the whole city. In the original sermon the prophet called the people to put an end to shedding innocent blood (7:6). Here the prophet warns the court that the future of the city and its inhabitants is inextricably bound to the fate of the prophet (Stulman 2005, 239). If the court finds the prophet guilty, then the city has no future. Conversely, the future of the city rests on the court's acquittal of the prophet.

Jeremiah concludes his defense by his claim that **in truth *Yahweh* has sent** him **to speak all these words** (v 15). He is the one who is speaking truthfully, and he is the one whom Yahweh has sent to speak the truth to the members of the court and the people. He has spoken **all these words** that Yahweh has given him to speak; these words contain the call to reform as well as words of judgment. If there is any falsehood, it is in the charges that are made against him by his opponents. Jeremiah here compellingly makes the case for Yahweh's sovereign authority over the temple, the city, and its inhabitants. No religious or political power can silence Yahweh's sovereign words or his messenger. It is now up to the court to decide the case here between the contested claims of true and false prophecy.

■ **16** The verdict of the court in v 16 comes as a surprise to the readers of this narrative. **The officials and all the people** determine that **this man should not be sentenced to death.** The court decides not to yield to the demand of the priests and the prophets. The court concurs with the prophet's claim that he has spoken **in the name of *Yahweh* our God.** The people now come to the support of the prophet, perhaps moved by the prophet's passionate and bold speech.

What prompted the officials and the people to rule in favor of the prophet is not clear in v 16. Lundbom thinks that the verdict acknowledges the call to reform (2004a, 293). However, the narrative does not report any action taken by the court or the repentance of the people. Brueggemann sees in the verdict the court's recognition of the right of the prophet to speak and the community's responsibility to take seriously the prophetic voice (1998, 236). It seems that here the court followed the Deuteronomic criteria as the basis for its verdict (see Deut 18:21-22). Jeremiah's claim that he has spoken in Yahweh's name (his self-defense) has been accepted by the court (see Deut 18:18). However, Deuteronomic criteria also make clear that the true test of the authenticity of a prophet is the fulfillment of his words spoken in Yahweh's name. An unfulfilled word means an illegitimate prophecy and an illegitimate prophet. The Deuteronomic standards of true and false prophecy prohibit a person from presumptively speaking in Yahweh's name. These standards also implicitly caution against prematurely determining a prophetic word as true or false prophecy. Ultimately it is the fulfillment of the word that gives credibility to the prophet, but prophecy seldom comes with specific reference to the time of its fulfillment. (See exceptions in 28:3; 29:10. It was Yahweh's further revelation to Jeremiah that gave Jeremiah the confidence that Hananiah spoke falsely in Yahweh's name.) That means that the community must live with certain ambiguity about a prophetic word. The court's ruling here is a call to wait and not to make a premature judgment about the authenticity or the falsity of Jeremiah's words.

3. Support for the Verdict (26:17-19)

■ **17** In the setting of the court proceedings, what follows (vv 17-19) could be understood as the statement of witnesses. However, if this is so, then the witnesses speak after the verdict is given. It is preferable to understand the speech of the elders as support given to the court's decision by citing a previous incident. **Men from the elders** (*zĕqēnîm*) **of the land** (v 17) are those who have age and experience. They are people who have experience in legal matters (Deut 21:2). They also know historical and legal precedents. They are presented here as those who remember past events. Some among the elders present at this hearing come forward and give a historical precedent to this incident and tell how a previous Judean king responded to a prophet's harsh words against Zion/Jerusalem. The speech of the elders is directed to **the entire assembly of people** (v 17).

■ **18** The elders' statement begins with an introduction of **Micah of Moresheth** as a prophet during the reign of **Hezekiah king of Judah** followed by a quotation of Micah's words about Zion addressed to **the people of Judah** (v 18). Micah's ministry is traditionally dated to 742-687 B.C. Moresheth (Mic 1:1), also known as Moresheth Gath (Mic 1:14) is a village in the Shephelah region about 25 miles southwest of Jerusalem.

Yahweh Sebaoth in Jeremiah

Jeremiah uses the title "Sebaoth" (*ṣĕbāʾôt*, meaning "hosts") to the divine name Yahweh eighty-two times in the book. A majority of the occurrences of this title is in chs 26—52 (fifty-four times). The LXX usually omits the title except eleven times in the book. Nine times the LXX translates it as *pantokratōr* ("Almighty"); one time each as *tōn dunameōn* ("the Power") and *sabaōth* ("Hosts"). Yahweh Sebaoth or Yahweh of Hosts ("the LORD Almighty" in the NIV) conveys the idea of Yahweh's sovereignty and power over the whole universe. All the powers of heaven, and kings and kingdoms of this world are subject to the authority. This understanding of God is critical to the prophet's perception and evaluation of contemporary historical events, particularly the role of Babylon as his instrument of judgment on Judah in the sixth century B.C.

The elders introduce Micah's words with the introductory formula, **Thus says Yahweh Sebaoth,** and then quote the words of the prophet found in Mic 3:12. This introductory formula is lacking in Mic 3:12 (see "This is what the LORD says" in Mic 3:5). The elders introduce this formula to authenticate Micah's words as Yahweh's words. This instance of quoting an earlier prophet is unique in the OT. We do not know if this statement was available to the elders in the written form or if they were quoting an authoritative oral tradition that preserved Micah's prophecies. Micah made this statement perhaps during the early part of the reign of Hezekiah (715-687 B.C.), about a hundred years prior to Jeremiah's temple sermon and the subsequent trial.

The elders remind the audience that Jeremiah is not the first prophet to pronounce harsh words against **Zion/Jerusalem**. The capital city where power resides has been critiqued and challenged by previous prophetic tradition. Micah's words, **Zion shall be ploughed like a field and Jerusalem shall become a ruin,** imply the total devastation and ruin of the capital city. Micah's words focus also on the destruction of "the mountain of the house" (NRSV) or the Temple Mount. Micah also said that the Temple Mount will become forested **high places** (*bāmôt* also refers to high mountains that have become places of worship). The place of Yahweh's worship will become like a pagan worship site. Micah's words imply the destruction of the city and the desecration of the Temple Mount. It is worth noting here that Jeremiah's pronouncements against the temple and the city included a call for repentance and the possibility of escaping Yahweh's judgment, whereas Micah offered no possibility for the future of the temple and the city.

■ 19 The primary focus of the elders' speech is not Micah's words but the response of King Hezekiah and the people of Judah to the prophetic word. The first two rhetorical questions in v 19 forcefully assert what the appropriate response should be to a prophetic word spoken in Yahweh's name. Answer to the elder's first question (**Did Hezekiah king of Judah *and all Judah* indeed put him to death?**) is clear. Certainly, the prophet who spoke in Yahweh's name was not put to death by Hezekiah or anyone else in Judah. This question may have been intended as a reprimand to those who demand the death of Jeremiah. In the second question, the elders assert the positive response of the king (***Did he not fear Yahweh and entreat the face of Yahweh?***). Though the MT indicates the response of only Hezekiah, the LXX reading shows that both the king and the people feared and made supplication to Yahweh. We do not have any historical records that indicate Hezekiah's supplication before Yahweh, though the king made supplications during the Assyrian crisis and during his illness that threatened his life (see 2 Kgs 19:14-19; 20:1-3). However, the tradition maintains the memory of the king's supplication before Yahweh in response to Micah's prophecy against Zion/Jerusalem. The elders' speech thus not only supports the acquittal of Jeremiah by the officials and the people but also offers the missing element in the court's verdict. This speech implicitly calls the ruling king (Jehoiakim) and all Judah to reform and amend their ways and doings following the model of Hezekiah. The third rhetorical question in v 19 shows the response of Yahweh to the king's prayer and supplication. Yahweh indeed relented or changed his mind (*nḥm*) and did not **bring the evil** he has spoken against Zion/Jerusalem. The city was spared because of the appropriate response to the prophetic word. This is precisely what Jeremiah said would happen if the people would respond to his message of judgment against the temple and the city (v 13).

The elders' speech concludes with the words that they ***are doing a great evil against*** themselves. The elders count themselves among the people who are now faced with the reality of Yahweh's judgment. It is likely that this last statement is a warning to the people that the trial should end here with the verdict pronounced by the court and that the priests and the prophets and the people should not press for an appeal or take further action against the prophet. Any such action would bring disaster upon the nation. It is also possible to read this final statement as the elders' strong warning to the political and religious leaders and the nation as a whole that by their continued rejection of the prophetic call to reform and amend their ways they are bringing upon themselves the disaster spoken by the prophet. This statement thus completes what is lacking (i.e., the call to respond to the prophetic word) in the verdict of acquittal by the court. The elders thus come not only to rescue the prophet from the death threat but also to support and sanction the prophetic word. If this assumption is correct, then the exilic readers of this narrative would have seen the exile as the consequence of rejecting not only the prophetic word but also the voice of the elders.

4. The Unlucky Uriah (26:20-23)

■ **20** The narrator supplements the story of Jeremiah's trial with the story of the fate of **Uriah son of Shemaiah from Keriath Jearim,** ***a man who was prophesying in Yahweh's name,*** during Jeremiah's time (vv 20-23). Most likely the martyrdom of Uriah took place sometime after the trial of Jeremiah but still in the early days of Jehoiakim's reign when he was a loyal vassal of Egypt (Holladay 1989, 103, 109). Nothing more is known about Uriah. **Keriath Jearim** was located about eight miles north and northwest of Jerusalem. The ark of the covenant was housed here after the destruction of Shiloh (1 Sam 7:1-2). Uriah thus comes from a town with ancient covenant traditions. The Hebrew form of the verb (*mitnabbē'* from *nb'* means "prophesy with zeal") indicates the intensity of Uriah's prophecy against Jerusalem and Judah. What he precisely said about the city and the land is not given; the implication (***like all the words of Jeremiah***) is that he also prophesied the destruction of Jerusalem and Judah. Uriah receives a status equal to that of Jeremiah as a faithful spokesperson of Yahweh.

■ **21** The story places the prophesying of Uriah during the reign of **Jehoiakim** (v 21). The king and **all his officers and officials** heard the words of Uriah. Jehoiakim is not involved in the trial of Jeremiah but remains in the background. Here in the Uriah incident, he is at the forefront and seeks to ***kill*** the prophet. Later in ch 36 (which narrates the incidents that happened in 604 B.C.), the king orders his men to seize Baruch and Jeremiah (possibly to put them to death). This suggests that the Uriah incident is added to the narrative here to show a drastic shift in Jehoiakim's attitude toward the prophets.

The Uriah narrative includes reference to his **fear** for his life and his escape to **Egypt** when he heard about the king's plan to kill him (v 21). It is likely that the narrator is simply narrating the story without any hidden agenda of comparing and contrasting the two prophets. However, in the end, the one who remains in the land and courageously faces the opposition is the one who survives. The one who escapes is brought back and without trial, he is put to death by the ruthless Jehoiakim.

■ **22** The identity of **Elnathan son of Acbor,** the leader of the king's posse, is not clearly known (v 22). In ch 36, Elnathan son of Acbor is among those to whom Micaiah son of Gemariah reports about Baruch's reading of Jeremiah's scroll in 604 B.C. (36:12). Elnathan is among those who urge Jehoiakim not to burn the scroll of Jeremiah (36:25). Acbor is listed among the advisers of King Josiah (2 Kgs 22:12, 14). Elnathan thus belongs to a family of royal advisers and officials. Lundbom (2004a, 297) suggests the possibility that Elnathan in this narrative may have been Elnathan of Jerusalem, Jehoiakim's father-in-law (2 Kgs 24:8). If this narrative and ch 36 refer to the same Elnathan, what brought about the change in his attitude to the prophetic word spoken by Jeremiah is not clear. If we are dealing with the same individual, then this narrative seems to suggest that those who were sympathetic to Jeremiah's message included some powerful officials who belonged to the palace.

■ **23 Egypt** was probably not the safest place for Uriah to escape Jehoiakim's wrath (v 23). The political alliance between Jehoiakim and Pharaoh Neco, who placed him on the Judean throne in 609 B.C., would have made it easier for Elnathan to get the support of Egyptian officials to arrest Uriah and bring him back to Jerusalem. This event could have happened before 604 B.C., before Jehoiakim broke off his loyalty to Neco and made alliance with Nebuchadnezzar.

Verse 23 implies that Uriah did not get the trial that Jeremiah received. The lack of mention of Uriah's trial in the narrative indicates the serious deterioration of the judicial process shortly after Jeremiah's trial and the king's direct involvement in silencing those who opposed him and his policies. The king himself ***struck him down with the sword.***

Jehoiakim's total contempt for Uriah (and for all prophets, for that matter) is further highlighted in the description of the treatment of Uriah's dead body. The king simply dumps or casts (*šālak*) the dead body of the martyred prophet **into the *graves* of the common people.** The burial place for the common people or ordinary people was most likely located in the Kidron Valley, between the Temple Mount and the Mount of Olives (see 2 Kgs 23:6; Lundbom 2004a, 298). Jeremiah's curse on Jehoiakim announced that the corpse of the king who despised Yahweh's word and ruled with violence and injustice shall be "cast out" (*šālak*) (36:30 NRSV) and that his corpse shall be "thrown out [*šālak*] beyond the gates of Jerusalem" (22:19 NRSV). It may be that this curse language was provoked by the manner in which Jehoiakim treated Uriah (see Holladay 1989, 110).

Martyrdom of the Prophets

Conflict between political powers and prophets is a common theme in the OT, the history of which goes back to the days of Samuel and Saul. Samuel had an upper hand as the one who installed Saul, on behalf of God, as king, but later prophets did not have much political clout and so often suffered violent retaliation and even death by the hand of rulers who saw the prophets as a threat to their power. The Elijah stories mention the killing of prophets by Jezebel in Israel in the mid-ninth century (1 Kgs 18:4, 13; 19:10). In Judah in the late ninth century, King Joash ordered the death of Zechariah who prophesied that Yahweh has forsaken the king because the king has forsaken Yahweh and transgressed his commandments (2 Chr 24:20-22). The OT pseudepigraphical work, *The Martyrdom and Ascension of Isaiah*, preserves the legend about the martyrdom of Isaiah during the reign of Manasseh in the seventh century. Uriah's death by the hand of Jehoiakim between 608 and 604 B.C. shows the continued trend in the killing of the prophets in ancient Israel. The Christian tradition also preserves the memory of the martyrdom of Israel's prophets (Matt 23:37; Acts 7:52; see also a possible allusion to the legend about Isaiah's martyrdom in Heb 11:37).

5. Jeremiah's Escape from Death (26:24)

■ **24** In the final verse of the trial narrative, the narrator returns to the story of

Jeremiah (v 24). In this verse, Jeremiah's antagonist is not the king, but **the people**. This is further evidence of the intrusive nature of the Uriah story in ch 26.

The Shaphan Family in Jeremiah

Ahikam son of Shaphan, along with his father Shaphan, is listed among the royal advisers to King Josiah in 2 Kgs 22:12 and 14. Shaphan played a prominent role in the finding of the book of the law in the temple (2 Kgs 22:3-20). The Shaphan family was an influential family that served the royal house during the days of Josiah, Jehoiakim, and Zedekiah (Lundbom 2004a, 298-99). Ahikam's brother Gemariah was among those who urged Jehoiakim not to burn Jeremiah's scroll (36:10, 12, 25). Elasah son of Shaphan was one of the two royal officials whom Zedekiah sent to Nebuchadnezzar (and one of the two individuals whom Jeremiah entrusted his letter to the exiles) (29:3). After the destruction of Jerusalem in 587 B.C. the Babylonians appointed Ahikam's son Gedaliah as governor of Judah, and they entrusted Jeremiah to Gedaliah (39:14; 40:5-6). The Shaphan family's intervention to protect the prophet at critical times suggests that this family was a powerful political ally of Jeremiah. It is not clear that this family's involvement in the life of Jeremiah was motivated by its support for the prophet's particular theological perspectives. Brueggemann suggests that the Shaphan family and perhaps other powerful people in Jerusalem saw the prophet as a representative of their particular perspective, and that their support for the prophet thus meant that they were taking a dangerous and risky stand against the king (2007, 31-32).

26:24

Verse 24 indicates that Jeremiah was saved from the people who wanted to put him to death because of the intervention of **Ahikam son of Shaphan.** There is no other mention of Ahikam in the book though other members of the Shaphan family appear in the book as influential members of the royal court (29:3; 36:10, 12, 25; 39:14; 40:5-6). Ahikam may have been a member of the court that pronounced the not guilty verdict at the trial of Jeremiah. We do not know why the people still wanted to put Jeremiah to death. **The people** here could mean those who were influenced by the priests and the prophets, and not "all the people." If the reference means "all the people," then we see here a fickle crowd that once agreed with the court that Jeremiah spoke in Yahweh's name, but remain unresponsive to the call to amend their ways and thus resistant to Yahweh's word and his spokesperson.

FROM THE TEXT

God commanded Jeremiah that he must speak all the words that he received from God and not withhold anything. The authority of God's word demands faithful proclamation of the whole testimony of the Scriptures. When scripture is selectively preached or consulted, we hear only what we want to hear and preach only what others want to hear. Just as fear of opposition may drive us to reduce and diminish God's word, our desire for success and popularity may also prompt us to reduce and diminish God's word. Our preaching that focuses only on one issue without balancing it with the opposite issue (faith/works, heaven/hell, life/death, prosperity/misfortune, suffering/healing, peace/war, justice/injustice, etc.) runs the risk of holding back the full witness of the Bible. God commanded Jeremiah to speak both judgment and the possibility of salvation through reform and change. God's concern expressed in this text is that salvation of his people can come only through their decision to reform and change. This kind of handling of God's word is what conveys the whole truth about God and his word. Any holding back of God's word in the end means misconceptions about God and the way in which he relates to humanity. The text urges us to speak the truth, the whole truth, and nothing but the truth about God.

God's speech to Jeremiah indicates his strong desire to change his mind or change his decision of judgment on the people of Judah. This is his righteous response to those who listen to his words and change their evil ways. God reveals his righteousness in both his judgment on sinners and in the salvation of those who repent of their sin. Judgment and salvation in this text are not some fated events by some eternal and unchangeable decree of God. The text clearly portrays God as a merciful and gracious God who takes no pleasure in the death of sinners (see Ezek 18:32).

Jeremiah preached listening to God, walking according to his Torah, and paying attention to the prophetic word as the conditions for God's continued relationship with his people and for the future of the temple and the city. These conditions call for a life that is lived in constant listening and obedience to God's Torah or instruction. God's instructions come to us through the Scriptures. We read scripture, we hear it proclaimed, and claim to know it. However, that knowledge cannot be equated with obedience. A call to listen is also a call to obedience. This positive response indicates commitment to live on God's terms. Lives that are shaped by God's word constantly pay attention to God's word, seek his guidance for everyday life, and follow the way of life taught in the Scriptures. The truly listening community of faith is where one will find faithful living, where the demands of God's righteousness are fulfilled in the everyday activities and interactions of its members.

God's warning that the city of Jerusalem, by its rejection of the prophetic call to repent and reform, would become a curse for all the people of the earth has implications for the contemporary readers of this text. The city that was called to be a source of blessing to the world through the ancestral promises (Gen 12:3) is threatened with the nullification of its blessing and promises from God. This comes as a warning in the text, but the readers of this story in the exile would have experienced this as a reality. God's call to us to live in relationship with him, though it is a privilege granted to us by his grace, is also a call to live as a source of blessing to others in the world, to our social and communal responsibility. Our relationship with God is not a private affair with implications only for our lives. Through obedience we receive God's blessings and become a source of blessing to others. Conversely, through disobedience we may become a curse, cursed by God and cursed by the world. This text is an urgent reminder to the community of faith to be "the salt of the earth" and "the light of the world" (Matt 5:13-17).

The reaction of the priests and the prophets and the people to Jeremiah's sermon shows the usual ways of human response to God's word. We find in the response of the priests and the prophets and the people a total rejection of the word, attempt to describe the prophetic voice as a lie, hearing only half of what the prophet said, and finally, attempt to silence the prophetic voice. What is obvious here is the lack of response to the prophet's call to Torah obedience and faithful living. The audience hears only what it wants to hear and violently reacts to the words of the prophet that threaten its established religious ideology and its perception of reality. Opposition to faithful preaching of God's word, then and now, happens when people perceive it as a threat to their settled ways of life and conduct and to their ill-conceived and false notions of reality. Jesus' preaching also produced a similar response because of his constant challenge to see things different from the established ways of thinking promoted by the religious and political establishment of his day (Mk 3:6; 14:1). Jesus said and did things that threatened the secure existence of the religious leaders of his day. He also faced a similar trial for speaking against the temple (see Lundbom for parallels between Jer 26 and Mk 13—14; 2004a, 301-2). This text reminds us of two things: first, faithful preaching of God's word seldom affirms us in our comfortable ways of life but often calls into question the way we think, act, and live our lives. The proper response to God's faithful word, when we find it unacceptable because it challenges and critiques our set ways of living and acting, is to pause and listen and reflect on the word in an earnest attempt to hear God speak to us. The Spirit of God can work in our hearts only when we pay attention to the voice of God, even though we may find in it words that are difficult for us to hear and obey.

Though there is no mention of God saving Jeremiah from his enemies, we could without doubt surmise this as a report of God's intervention through human agencies. In 36:26, where a similar life-threatening situation in the life of the prophet is narrated, he escapes the threat because God hides him from his enemies. In ch 38, it is Ebed-Melech, an Ethiopian eunuch, who initiates the prophet's rescue from the cistern where he was left to die by the officials (38:4-13). The narrative in ch 26 mentions the officials, the people, the elders, and Ahikam all involved in the rescue of the prophet. Brueggemann sees the protection of Jeremiah in this story strictly as "human and political" (1998, 239 note). We cannot deny the human involvement in this story, but in the end, it is the story of a faithful prophet of God who goes on with his fearless speaking on behalf of his God who called him and promised to protect him from his enemies (1:4-19). The story is thus not simply the story of a successful outcome of a human attempt to save the life of the prophet. Officials acquit the prophet in this story but in 38:4 demand his death. There is no clear indication in this story that the crowd was fully sympathetic to the message of the prophet. The story begins and ends with a word about the hostility of the people toward the prophet. Thus life-and-death issues are not ultimately determined by human agencies in this story. The prophet lives on, and he continues to proclaim God's word because God is with the prophet to deliver him from the hand of his enemies (1:19).

From this story we learn that just as God remained faithful to his promises to the prophet, we need to raise our voices in defense of those whose voices are seldom heard—those who face violence and death at the hands of cruel and unjust political regimes and violent social, ethnic, and religious groups in our world. Our silence to these issues means our silent complicity to injustice in the world and our own silent death. "Our lives begin to end the day we become silent about things that matter" (Martin Luther King Jr.). Those in this narrative who listen to truth, speak truth, and act on behalf of truth are examples of courage and risk-taking. They give hope to Jeremiah and to all who are victimized in the world. They refuse to remain silent but speak out on behalf of the one who is being threatened with the death sentence. The text reminds us that it is in our joining with these fearless defenders of the innocent that we become participants with God in bringing hope to those whose lives are in jeopardy in our world. This is where we find true life, life with the one who came "to serve, and to give his life as a ransom for many" (Mk 10:45).

"BUILD AND PLANT"

THE JUDEAN QUESTION ABOUT THE YOKE OF BABYLON (27:1—29:32)

Overview

Jeremiah chs 27—29 belong to the period shortly after the events of 597 B.C. in the early part of the reign of Zedekiah. The Babylonian invasion and the deportation of Jehoiachin and the prominent officials of Judah have shaken Judah's long-held beliefs about the temple, the city of Jerusalem, and the Davidic house as stable and secure religious and political establishments, the permanence of which was guaranteed by Yahweh. These chapters reflect the political and theological crisis of Judah in the years between 597 and 587 B.C.

Chapters 27—29 are linked together by the critical question about the nature and extent of the Babylonian hegemony over Judah. Answers to this question come from competing theological circles and give conflicting perspectives on the current theological and political crisis of Judah. Jeremiah, Yahweh's authorized prophet, sees in the historical events Yahweh's active involvement through the agency of Babylon; so he declares that the Babylonian hegemony over Judah will last for a while. What Judah faces now is the judgment of Yahweh. He gives hope and speaks of a future for the nation "when seventy years are completed for Babylon" (29:10). The hope expressed here by the prophet is the focus of chs 30—33. The optimistic but false prophets of Judah give a positive spin on the current political crisis and maintain the view that the effect of the Babylonian invasion of 597 B.C. is short-term and that soon life will return to normal in Judah. The content of chs 27—29 has continuity with the vision of the baskets of figs in ch 24, which also belongs to the period between 597 and 587 B.C. Chapters 27 and 28 are placed in the fourth year of Zedekiah (594/3 B.C.; 27:1; 28:1). Chapter 29 belongs to a period not too long after the deportation of 597 B.C.

Chapter 27 is in autobiographical form, whereas third person narration characterizes the content of chs 28—29. Chapter 27 contains the prophet's symbolic act of wearing a yoke, and ch 28 contains the account of Hananiah performing a symbolic act by breaking the yoke that Jeremiah put on his neck. These symbolic acts convey conflicting words from Yahweh, but the tradition that preserved these stories clearly recognizes Jeremiah as Yahweh's true prophet. Chapter 29 contains the content of a letter that Jeremiah sent to the Judeans who were taken as captives to Babylon in 597 B.C. as well as the content of a letter written by Shemaiah, a false prophet among the exiles in Babylon, to the priests in Jerusalem.

Lundbom cites a number of linguistic peculiarities that are frequently found in these chapters, particularly the ending of names compounded with the divine name Yahweh, such as Jeremiah, Zedekiah, etc., with *yâ* rather than *yāhû* spelling. Most notably, the spelling of Jeremiah's name as *yirmĕyâ* instead of *yirmĕyāhû* is found only in these chapters in the book. In chs 27—29, Nebuchadnezzar's name is spelled with an "n" (except in 29:21); in the rest of the book the name is spelled with "r" (Nebuchadrezzar) (2004a, 304). (Note: In this volume, the common spelling of the name with "n" will be followed [Nebuchadnezzar].)

The Hebrew text of chs 27—29 (MT) shows numerous additions that are not found in the Greek translation (LXX). In addition to numerous minor omissions in the LXX, this version lacks 27:1, 7, 12-14*a*, 17; 29:16-20, and portions of 27:8, 10, 19, 20*b*-22; 28:3, 4, 14; 29:1, 6, 11, 12, 14, 25.

A. Submit to Babylon (27:1-22)

BEHIND THE TEXT

The date of the events narrated in ch 27 has been a subject of discussion among scholars. In the MT, v 1 begins as follows: **in the beginning of the reign of Jehoiakim,** but then in vv 3 and 12 it is Zedekiah who receives attention. Jeremiah 28:1 identifies the same year as the "fourth year" of King Zedekiah. The LXX omits 27:1. Most modern versions and commentators correct the MT and replace the name Jehoiakim with Zedekiah. It is also a common assumption among scholars that **the beginning of the reign** does not mean the accession year of Zedekiah, but the early period of his reign, which is further identified in 28:1 as "the fifth month" of "the fourth year" of Zedekiah, which would place the events around 594 to 593 B.C.

Verse 3 indicates that ambassadors of Edom, Moab, Ammon, Tyre, and Sidon came to Jerusalem for a meeting with King Zedekiah. The purpose of the meeting is not explicitly stated; however, Yahweh's message in vv 5-11 implies that its purpose was to form a coalition to resist the political domination of Babylon over these nations. Commentators agree that there was an internal rebellion against Nebuchadnezzar in Babylon in December 595 and January

594 B.C. Holladay speculates that the Jerusalem meeting of envoys from Judah's neighboring states occurred around spring or summer of 594 B.C., when the news of internal rebellion in Babylon reached the vassal states in the west (1989, 118).

Chapter 27 begins with an introductory note on the historical setting of Yahweh's word that came to Jeremiah (v 1), followed by Yahweh's command to the prophet (vv 2-4). Verses 5-11 contain Yahweh's word to the kings of the neighboring nations that sent ambassadors to Jerusalem. Yahweh's word addressed to Zedekiah is found in vv 12-15, followed by his word to the priests and the people (vv 16-18). The chapter ends with a word concerning the pillars and vessels of the temple (vv 19-22).

IN THE TEXT

1. Yahweh's Command to Jeremiah (27:1-4)

■ 1 Verse 1 establishes the historical setting of the incident reported in ch 27. We follow the scholarly consensus and read v 1 as follows: **in the beginning of the reign of Zedekiah son of Josiah king of Judah, this word came to Jeremiah from Yahweh. In the beginning of** the reign (*běrēʾšît mamleket*) is identified in 28:1 as the "fourth year" of Zedekiah. The likely setting of this incident is thus 594 to 593 B.C. The NIV **early in the reign** conveys the intent of the text. **This word** refers to Yahweh's command to Jeremiah (vv 2-4), the words to the envoys from other nations (vv 5-11), the word to Zedekiah (vv 12-15), and the word to the priests and the people (vv 16-22). Verse 1 is lacking in the LXX.

■ 2 Verse 2 begins Yahweh's command to Jeremiah, which is continued in vv 3-4. The command here is to perform a symbolic act that involves the making of **straps and bars of yoke** and wearing them on the neck of the prophet. The Hebrew word *môsērôt* means leather straps or bands used to secure the oxen in the yoke at the neck. **Bars of yoke** (*môṭôt*) are wooden crossbars used in the construction of a yoke. The usual word for yoke in Hebrew (*ʿōl*) is not found here; however, bars of yoke conveys the idea. The plural form here suggests the making of more than one yoke. The command in v 3 (**send them**) suggests the sending of the bars of yoke with the envoys from other nations to their respective kings. Thus this command involves the making of multiple yokes, one for the prophet to put on his neck and the rest to be given to the envoys.

Holladay suggests that the **bars of yoke** here are not the full crossbar of a yoke but rather just "yoke pegs" that are inserted vertically on the crossbar and secured at the bottom end with ropes. The wooden pegs and the ropes together make up a collar around the neck of an animal. He sees here "collars" made of wooden pegs and ropes that would have been easy for the prophet to put on his neck and to be sent with the envoys, rather than the whole yoke

(Holladay 1989, 119-20). This collar-yoke idea does not convey the full intent of the symbolic act. If the intent of this act is to powerfully and forcefully convey the idea of servitude, bondage, and hardship, then the interpretation of the bars of yoke as whole yokes is necessary. Then again, as a yoke on the neck of a human being, one could expect here a smaller yoke than the full size yoke on the neck of animals used by farmers in ancient Palestine. Yahweh is asking the prophet to experience bondage and servitude in his own life to visibly represent the hardship the people must face under the yoke of Babylon. A yoke collar would have hardly met this objective. It is precisely the heaviness and the cumbersomeness of this act that drives home its intended message. If we assume that Jeremiah's yoke was like the typical yoke in the ancient times intended for two oxen, then one side of his yoke would have been empty. It may have been his intent to invite his listeners to "occupy the empty place on the other side of the yoke" (Keown, Scalise, Smothers 1995, 48).

■ **3** Verse 3 continues Yahweh's command to Jeremiah. Commentators are not certain about the meaning of **send *them* to the kings of Edom . . .** The Hebrew verb here (*wĕšillaḥtām*) has a third plural suffix and literally means ***send them.*** The NIV reading omits this suffix (as do most modern translations), assuming that Yahweh was not asking the prophet to send yokes but his message to the kingdoms mentioned in this verse. The MT and most ancient versions preserve "them," meaning yokes. We prefer to keep the MT reading. Yahweh is thus commanding Jeremiah to perform another symbolic act; the accompanying message is stated in vv 8-11.

The rest of v 3 indicates a visit of the **envoys** of the kings of Edom, Moab, Ammon, Tyre, and Sidon to **Jerusalem** to meet with **Zedekiah.** Jeremiah was commanded to send the yokes with these messengers to their respective kings. It is not clear whether these envoys are already in Jerusalem or that they will arrive soon. The purpose of the visit is not stated; most commentators see this as a meeting of the nations to discuss resistance against Nebuchadnezzar. It is also not clear who has called this meeting. If it was initiated by Zedekiah, then it was certainly an act of rebellion against Nebuchadnezzar (see Ezek 17:15 for a similar rebellion on the part of Zedekiah by sending ambassadors to Egypt in 589/8 B.C.). However, the fact that envoys are coming to Jerusalem means that rebellion against Babylon has already been planned by the kings of Edom, Moab, Ammon, and Tyre and that this coalition is sending envoys to Jerusalem to enlist Zedekiah's support. At this early stage in his career as a puppet king installed by Babylon, it is unlikely that Zedekiah would have the courage or the will to initiate a rebellion against Nebuchadnezzar.

■ **4** Verse 4 contains Yahweh's command to Jeremiah to give the envoys his **message** and the command to the envoys to deliver that message to their **masters.** The message comes from **Yahweh of hosts, the God of Israel.** The One who sends this message is the God of Israel, the sovereign Creator of the universe, the One who commands all the earthly and heavenly powers. The titles utilized here implicitly call the kings to pay attention to what the sovereign God of the universe has to say to them through his prophet.

2. Yahweh's Message to the Kings (27:5-11)

■ **5** Yahweh's message to the kings of Edom, Moab, Ammon, Tyre, and Sidon begins with his self-identification as the One who **made the earth and *human beings*** and the animals that are on *the face of the earth.* The LXX omits ***human beings*** and the animals that are on *the face of the earth.* He made the earth and its human and animal inhabitants by his **great power and outstretched arm.** Here Jeremiah makes clear the basic tenet of Israel's creation faith. Israel's God is the Creator of the universe and all human and animal life (see 10:12-16; 32:17, 27). Yahweh's work of creation is a demonstration of his **great power and outstretched arm** (see 32:17). This is the same power that Yahweh manifested when he brought Israel out of Egypt (Deut 9:29). The Israelite readers would have understood Yahweh as Creator and Redeemer; the intent here is to convince the non-Israelite nations that believe in a creator that Israel's God is indeed the Creator God. **I give it to *whoever is right in my eyes*** further emphasizes Yahweh's sovereign power and claim over the whole world as its Creator. The Creator is not subject to what he created, but rather creation is subject to the Creator. The focus here is on Yahweh's freedom to do what seems best to him or what pleases him to do. This action of Yahweh is not arbitrary or whimsical, but in full conformity to his character as a just and righteous Creator. His actions always have the end purpose of accomplishing his will and purpose for his creation.

■ **6** Following the claim of his sovereignty and freedom, Yahweh makes known what he has done to demonstrate his power over the world. Verse 6 begins with the phrase ***and now,*** which indicates transitions to divine action with an emphatic **I** (**I *have given***). Yahweh's message to the envoys from the countries in the Transjordan and Phoenician region is that he has given their lands (***all these lands***) in to **the hand of** his **servant Nebuchadnezzar king of Babylon.** The phrase ***all these lands*** (*hāʾărāṣôt hāʾēlleh*) allows no claim on the part of these nations that these lands belong to the nations, but it implies that they belong to Yahweh (the NIV's **your countries** permits such a claim). This is not a future action on the part of Yahweh, as the NIV suggests, but an action that has already been undertaken by him. This is Yahweh's gift to the Babylonian king, which includes not only these lands but also ***the beast of the field.*** Yahweh who created the earth and the beast of the field (Gen 1) freely gives dominion over these lands and the animals that live upon them to Nebuchadnezzar. This means everything in these lands have already become subject to the power of Nebuchadnezzar by Yahweh's action.

The Babylonian king is designated in v 6 as Yahweh's **servant** (see also 25:9 and 43:10). Nebuchadnezzar is called Yahweh's servant not because of any relationship of loyalty to and worship of Yahweh on the part of Nebuchadnezzar, but because of his task given to him by Yahweh as the one who will carry out the will and purpose of Yahweh. Yahweh's plan is that these lands and its peoples, including its animal life, *serve* the king of Babylon. Political subjugation of these nations to Babylon is clearly the idea here. The text makes clear that geopolitical events that are taking place in the world of Jeremiah are no accidental events or events planned and executed by the king of Babylon, but part of the plans of Yahweh, the God of Israel and the Creator of the universe. Nebuchadnezzar is only Yahweh's human agent, a servant under Yahweh's authority. This relationship is only temporary and its only goal is the fulfillment of Yahweh's plans at this time in human history.

■ **7** Verse 7, which is lacking in the LXX, indicates an indefinite period of the Babylonian domination of the nations. **All nations** here most likely means the nations mentioned in v 3 including Judah. Servitude to Babylon by these nations will last for three generations. Rulers who came after Nebuchadnezzar were his son Amel-Marduk or Evil-Merodach (562-560 B.C.), and Neriglissar (560-556 B.C.) and Nabonidus (556-539 B.C.). Both Neriglissar and Nabonidus had no blood relation to Nebuchadnezzar. Therefore, reference to **grandson** does not need to be understood literally; the phrase son and his grandson may simply mean three generations of rulers (Lundbom 2004a, 316).

After three generations of political domination over these lands, Babylon itself will receive Yahweh's judgment. The phrase **until comes the time of even his own land** indicates that there is a time limit for the Babylonian domination. **The time of even his own land** is the time of Yahweh's visitation of Babylon in judgment. This **time** is not given; it implies a time after the political domination of Babylon for three generations. Yahweh's plan to bring judgment on Babylon means that at the present time it is simply an instrument in Yahweh's hand as the agency through which he will bring judgment on other nations including Judah. When the time comes, tables will be turned; the nations that serve the king of Babylon will have their day. They will rise up and make Nebuchadnezzar their servant (see 25:14). The Babylonian power will come to an end. The phrase **many nations and great kings** anticipates the rise of other world powers after the decline of the Babylonian Empire. The judgment word should be understood as a word about Yahweh's judgment on Babylon in the days to come, though in this verse refers to Nebuchadnezzar's servitude to the nations (**make him serve**). As history shows, Nebuchadnezzar was long gone from the historical scene when the Persians took control of Babylon in 539 B.C. Later readers would have understood from this text that Babylon's destruction happened according to Yahweh's will revealed to the nations more than four decades before it happened.

■ **8** Yahweh's message to the kings of the nations continues in v 8. This verse deals with the outcome of the nation's resistance to Nebuchadnezzar. Since the Babylonian king is Yahweh's designated servant, servitude to Babylon means servitude to Yahweh. Conversely, resistance against Babylon is resistance to Yahweh's will. Any **nation or kingdom** that refuses to **serve Nebuchadnezzar king of Babylon** will receive punishment from Yahweh. The next clause *who will not give his neck to the yoke of the king of Babylon* clarifies what serving Nebuchadnezzar means in this verse. This verse further expresses the significance of the yoke that Jeremiah sends with the envoys to their kings. The nations that sent their envoys to Jerusalem to plan rebellion against Babylon receive from the prophet a yoke, which symbolically conveys to them their proper course of action at this critical time in history. This is not time to rebel but to surrender. Disregarding or rejecting Yahweh's word about their political servitude to Babylon will have grave consequence. Any attempt to rebel against Babylon is rebellion against Yahweh.

The outcome of rebellion against Yahweh/Babylon will be **sword, famine and plague,** the means with which Yahweh will bring his judgment on those who defy his word. Yahweh will consume them **by his hand**—by the hand of the king of Babylon. Sword, famine, and plague all convey the outcome of invasion and ruthless military activities that the Babylonians will undertake to subjugate the nations that rebel against its political domination. The implicit warning here is that these nations will be besieged by Babylon, which will lead to famine and plague and to subsequent destruction of human lives. This will come as punishment from Yahweh for rejecting his warning.

■ **9** Verses 9-10 contain a warning to the kings that they should not listen to the political counsel given by the **prophets, diviners,** *dreamers* ("dreams" in the MT), **mediums,** and **sorcerers** in their countries. **Diviners** are those who predict the future by various methods of divination, such as casting lots, examining livers, shaking arrows, etc. *Dreamers* (most commentators revocalize the MT *ḥălōmōtêkem* ["your dreams"] to *ḥōlĕmōtêkem* ["your dreamers"]) are those who claim revelation through dreams (see Jeremiah's harsh words against prophets who claimed revelation through dreams in 23:25-32). **Mediums** (the meaning of the Hebrew word used here is not certain; see "soothsayers" NRSV) are probably those who practice the art of fortune telling by observing natural phenomena (Lundbom 2004a, 318). **Sorcerers** are those who cast evil spells or practice magic. In pagan nations, divination, soothsaying, magic, sorcery, and consulting the spirits of the dead were customary ways of seeking the will of deities. However, these practices were strictly forbidden in ancient Israel, where the traditional faith upheld belief in one true and living God (Yahweh) and prophecy and prophets as the legitimate channels of divine-human communication (Deut 18:10-11, 18-19). Verse 9 indicates that the kings of the nations mentioned in v 3 were receiving political counsel as a directive from their gods through various methods of divination that they should **not serve the king of Babylon.** The directive from Yahweh the God of Israel, the sovereign Creator of the universe, however, implies his sovereign control over the affairs of human history. Current political events are part of his plan and will for these nations and Babylon. Therefore they should pay attention to Yahweh's words and not to the words of their local gods.

■ 10 Verse 10 asserts that the words of prophecy given to the kings by the local diviners are indeed a great *lie* (*šeqer*). Jeremiah considers here and elsewhere in the book that words that do not originate with Yahweh are lies, words that do not contain truth. These false prophecies result in only one thing, and that is the removal of the recipients of these lies from their land. That means false prophecy accomplishes the opposite result of what it claims to accomplish. It does not result in security and welfare, but in destruction and dispersion. This is Yahweh's judgment on those who listen to false prophecies. **I will banish you and you will perish** (omitted in the LXX) is Yahweh's judgment word.

■ 11 In v 11 the prophet announces the positive outcome of obedience to Yahweh's words. Nations that pay attention to the warning given by Yahweh and submit themselves to **the yoke of the king of Babylon** will receive Yahweh's favor. He will spare them from exile and they will live in their own lands. Yahweh will permit those who **serve** (ʽ*bd*) the king of Babylon to stay in their own land and **till** it (ʽ*bd*) and enjoy the prosperity of their land. Disruption of life is not Yahweh's plan for these nations. Life in the land, however, also means political bondage to Babylon. But this is also Yahweh's will for these nations, including his own people Judah.

3. Yahweh's Word to Zedekiah (27:12-15)

■ 12 Jeremiah's message to **Zedekiah** essentially repeats the call to the nations to surrender to Babylon and be spared from the outcome of rebellion to Babylon. One could assume that the word to Zedekiah is also a word to the people of Judah. This message comes as a command from Yahweh. Zedekiah receives the word from Yahweh that, if he wishes to live, then it is imperative that he submit to the yoke of the king of Babylon. The command from Yahweh is *bring your necks;* both the verb in the imperative and the noun are in plural, which suggests that the command is given here to Zedekiah and to the nation as a whole. Moreover, submission being demanded from Zedekiah and Judah is not submission to Nebuchadnezzar alone, but submission to **his people**—his officials and perhaps the Babylonians as a whole. The LXX ends this verse with "bring your (pl.) neck" and omits the rest of vv 12 and 13, and continues with the words "and serve the king of Babylon" in v 14. Verse 12 ends with the imperative **live,** a command from Yahweh as well as his promise of life to Judah. Yahweh has no desire for the destruction and exile of his people. The possibility for life and the realization of Yahweh's promise, however, depends on Judah's submission to the demands of Yahweh and to the political power of Babylon.

Psalm 2 and Jeremiah 27

Yahweh's words to Zedekiah in 27:12-15 convey an ideology that challenges the notion of universal authority that Yahweh has granted to the Davidic kings and Yahweh's patronage of the Davidic kings claimed in Ps 2. Psalm 2, a psalm that was most likely used in the liturgy of coronation of the Davidic kings, speaks of the futile attempt of the nations to rebel against Yahweh and his "anointed" (Davidic kings who rule in Jerusalem). This psalm also upholds the traditional notion of a Davidic king as Yahweh's "son" whom Yahweh has established as his appointed ruler in Jerusalem over the nations. The challenge and invitation of Ps 2 to the pagan nations is to submit to the authority of the Davidic kings, which in turn means submission to Yahweh's sovereign kingship over the world. In Jer 27, this religious-political ideology takes a backseat. In the particular religious, historical, and political context of Israel, it is not a Davidic king (Zedekiah) who receives universal authority from Yahweh, but a pagan king—the king of Babylon—who is also called Yahweh's "servant." This shift is not to be understood as Yahweh's breaking of his covenant with David (2 Sam 7:12-16), but as another indication of Yahweh's sovereignty over world affairs and his freedom to use any nation in the world to accomplish his plans and purposes at any time in human history.

■ **13** Verse 13 reissues the question of life and death. Yahweh has given the king the conditions for life and death and his promise of life as a reward for obedience to Yahweh. Now it is up to Zedekiah to make the right choice—the choice of life. Yahweh's question, **Why should you die, you, and your people,** reiterates the warning that the outcome of making the wrong choice would be death. Not only the king, but also his people will die by **the sword, famine and plague.** This is the destiny of all the nations that refuse to **serve the king of Babylon.** Yahweh's question also suggests that the choice of death on the part of the king of Judah would be an incomprehensible act, and more than that, an explicit act of rebellion against Yahweh's will.

■ **14** Verse 14 contains essentially the same message given to the kings of the nations in vv 9-10. This verse refers only to **the words of the prophets**; diviners, dreamers, mediums, and sorcerers most likely were not among the royal counselors in Judah. The warning to the king is that he should not pay attention to or be influenced in his life-and-death decision making by the words of the optimistic prophets in the land. The words of the prophets of Jerusalem are the same as the words of the prophets, diviners, dreamers, mediums, and sorcerers of the nations. Their words, **You will not serve the king of Babylon,** contradict Yahweh's words. Zedekiah is being warned here that he should not listen to these words because this prophecy is ***falsehood*** (šeqer). The agreement of the prophets of Judah/Jerusalem with the words of the oracle givers of the nations puts them both in the same group. These prophets do not speak Yahweh's true words.

■ **15** Verse 15 makes clear that the prophets who advocate an anti-Babylonian policy to Zedekiah are not prophets sent by Yahweh. They are neither called by Yahweh nor sent by him as his prophets. **I have not sent them** is an emphatic denial of any association Yahweh has with these prophets. Though they do not stand in any relation to Yahweh, they audaciously claim prophetic authority and their relation to Yahweh, and thus claim the privilege to speak in his **name**. What they speak in Yahweh's **name** as prophecy is ***falsehood.*** The only thing that can happen when prophets speak falsehood in Yahweh's name is the hastening of Yahweh's judgment. They think they are speaking words that would bring welfare and peace to the nation. But their words have the opposite effect. Yahweh's true words spoken by Jeremiah offer the promise of life, but the falsehood spoken by the optimistic prophets would lead only to exile and destruction. This is the destiny that awaits both the king and the optimistic prophets. This is the same judgment word given to the kings of the nations in v 10.

4. Yahweh's Word to the Priests and the People (27:16-18)

■ **16** The addressees of Yahweh's words and the focus of the message change in vv 16-18. The **priests** and the **people** are addressed in these verses. The subject of the message is ***the vessels of Yahweh's house*** that Nebuchadnezzar took to Babylon in 597 B.C. According to 2 Kgs 24:10-13, Nebuchadnezzar "carried off all the treasures of the house of the LORD" and "cut in pieces all the vessels of gold in the temple" (NRSV). The prophets are promising to the people the immediate return of these vessels taken to Babylon. Priests would have had a vested interest in seeing the return of the temple vessels because they were an integral part of their priestly vocation. For the people, the vessels were not only part of the national treasure but also symbols of Yahweh's holy presence in the temple. These vessels had been part of their history since the days of Solomon. The message of the return of the vessels would have given the people a sense of optimism that Yahweh is working again in their history on their behalf as their delivering God.

Yahweh's message to the priests and the people begins with an admonition not to **listen to *the words of your* prophets who *are prophesying to you*.** The admonition **Do not listen** disallows any claim on the part of the prophets as Yahweh's authentic spokespersons and their words as Yahweh's words. Moreover, they are ***your prophets;*** they are not Yahweh's prophets but the people's prophets. The people wholeheartedly subscribe to the illegitimate claim of these prophets and listen to their optimistic words as Yahweh's true words to them, while rejecting Jeremiah the true prophet of Yahweh. Their optimistic message is that ***in a very short time the vessels of Yahweh's house will be returned*** from **Babylon**. What gave them confidence in preaching this message is not clear. This message is clearly in line with the temple-city ideology and the notion of Yahweh's binding relation to the temple and the city. This message conveys hope in an immediate reversal of the misfortune that happened to the temple vessels as a theological necessity. It is possible that the optimistic prophets anticipated a successful outcome of the plot against Babylon by the nations that met in Jerusalem. Yahweh announces to the priests and the people that this message is ***falsehood*** (*šeqer*) and they should not hold their hopes high on an immediate return of the temple vessels from Babylon. If they had been Yahweh's prophets, they would have known his plans and spoken the truth to the people.

■ 17 Verse 17 (the LXX omits the entire verse) begins with the repetition of the command **Do not listen** as in v 16. These prophets are not trustworthy sources of Yahweh's word to his people. Their message about an imminent return of the temple vessels is not from Yahweh. Yahweh's word comes as a command to the priests and the prophets that they should **serve the king of Babylon *and live*.** This is the same message given to Zedekiah (see v 12). Previously, Yahweh raised the question about the futility of the death of the people by war-related atrocities (v 13). Here in v 17, in a similar way Yahweh questions the futility of the city becoming a ruined place. The priests and the people could avoid this tragedy by serving the king of Babylon.

■ 18 Verse 18 could be understood in two ways. On the one hand, this verse seems to be saying to the audience that these prophets should be making intercessions with Yahweh to prevent further loss of the temple vessels and the vessels of the royal house to Babylon. Intercession with Yahweh is a legitimate role of true prophets. If these individuals have prophetic authority, then they need to validate their claim and persuade Yahweh through their intercession to change the course of events already set in motion by him. In that sense this verse seems to be a challenge issued to the prophets. On the other hand, this verse also implies that these prophets neither have any legitimate relationship with Yahweh nor have the prophetic authority and the intercessory capacity to change the course of events. Lundbom thinks that Jeremiah is "mocking" the false prophets (2004a, 322). They can intercede or cry out all they want, but Yahweh will not hear them because they are not his prophets. Yahweh's plan is to deliver the vessels remaining in the temple and the palace into the hands of the king of Babylon. Verses 19-22 seem to support this latter reading of this verse.

5. Yahweh's Word About Pillars, Fixed Objects, and the Remaining Vessels (27:19-22)

■ 19-21 Verses 19-21 introduce Yahweh's speech concerning the vessels that are left in the temple and the palace. This long introduction is repetitious. It begins with the typical introductory formula, ***For thus said Yahweh Sebaoth,*** which is repeated again in v 21 (***For thus said Yahweh Sebaoth,*** **the God of Israel**). The introduction makes clear that the subject of the message is **the pil-**

lars, and **the Sea** and the **stands** and ***the rest of the vessels remaining*** in Jerusalem (**in this city**). The LXX makes no reference to the pillars, the Sea, and the stands. Also, it lacks the phrase ***remaining* in this city**. See 1 Kgs 7:15-37 for a detailed description of the two freestanding bronze pillars called Jachin and Boaz, the molten sea, a large vessel made of bronze that was filled with water, and the ten stands of bronze. Verse 20 further identifies these vessels as those that Nebuchadnezzar left in the temple when he deported Jehoiachin and the aristocratic members of the city in 597 B.C. The LXX omits **along with all the nobles of Judah and Jerusalem.** Verse 21 repeats v 19; the focus of Yahweh's word is on the vessels that remain in the temple. In this verse, Yahweh's word also is about the vessels remaining ***in the house of*** **the king of Judah and in Jerusalem.** The LXX omits v 21.

■ **22** Verse 22 sums up the fate of the vessels mentioned in vv 19-21. Yahweh's plan is to deliver them into the hands of the Babylonians. **They will be taken to Babylon** is his judgment word. However, there will be an end to this displacement of the temple vessels and other vessels taken from the city. Yahweh's promise is that he will ***visit*** them (*pqd*). Now these vessels are faced with his visitation in judgment. But he will visit them again, to **bring them back** and to **restore them** to the place where they belong—in his house in Jerusalem. This verse is rather short in the LXX; it simply reads: "To Babylon it shall be taken, says the Lord." This future visitation of Yahweh is the hope given to Zedekiah and the people of Judah. The urgent appeal is to surrender to Babylon, but this judgment is only for a short period. God's plan is to restore them just as he has promised to restore the remaining vessels that will be taken to Babylon. The word that **they will be taken to Babylon** was fulfilled in 587 B.C.

FROM THE TEXT

Jeremiah's task during his encounter with the ambassadors of other nations, King Zedekiah, and the people of Judah in particular is to convey a historical reality based on his particular conviction of what the creator God is doing at the present moment in human history. The prophet who speaks here is a person who has thorough knowledge of current political events. Political wisdom communicated by individuals who claim to have access to channels of divine-human communication in the neighboring nations and by the prophets of Judah is resistance to the power of the king of Babylon. That political wisdom is grounded in the social ideals of collective strength and standing together as a group to resist an oppressive political regime. This would have been the most prudent way to handle the current crisis, according to most Judeans of Jeremiah's day. The prophets of Judah who were telling Zedekiah not to serve the king of Babylon most likely were confident that Yahweh would want his people to resist an evil power. Their urgent appeal to Zedekiah indicates a firm belief that their God who liberated them from the power of Pharaoh would not want them to be under bondage to any power in the world.

But Jeremiah reads historical realities differently. He is also confident in God's power. God is the Creator of the universe; he is also the sovereign God of nations and human history. God's will for his people and for the surrounding nations at this time in history is to submit to the imperial power of Babylon. Submission to Babylon means submission to God's will. Judging from modern standards, Jeremiah's pro-Babylon stand during this critical period of national security threat from Babylon would have been the worst possible political embarrassment for Zedekiah and the people of Judah. But Jeremiah arrives at this stance from his theological discernment of history and his sharp reading of political realities of his day. On the one hand, he recognizes the sin of the covenant nation as the root cause of their perilous condition. Submission to Babylon is therefore submission to the judgment of God. Judah's resistance to Babylon is in turn resistance to God's judgment. At this most critical time in the history of the nation, as a religious leader, he tells the truth rather than painting a rosy picture based on a distorted view of historical and political realities. Judah's salvation from the current crisis depends on acknowledging that truth about God's will for his people. On the other hand, his political wisdom also gives him the deep awareness that Judah's resistance to Babylon, an imperial power with massive military resources, would result in massive loss of everything that is near and dear to the people of Judah.

Modern readers of this text will find God's call to Judah, his covenant people, to submit to Babylon, a ruthless and evil political power, a difficult problem. We are troubled by this call to submit to evil that comes from God who hates evil, God who is good, loving, and compassionate. Jeremiah makes clear in this chapter that what God does at this time in world history is a manifestation of God's sovereignty and power as the Creator of the world and that he is free to act according to his pleasure (27:5). Miller reminds us that what God does as "right" in his eyes is not always manifested in what human beings perceive as "right" in a particular moment (2001, 787). The call to submit to Babylon needs to be understood in its historical, political, and theological context. One should understand it also in the context of God's judgment word against Babylon in v 7. This ruthless power that serves the purpose of God will have its end. This end of Babylon should be kept in mind when we read about its beginning, both of which Jeremiah understands as manifestations of God's creative power at work in human history.

Jeremiah is a model of courageous preaching to the twenty-first century. He may not have been absolutely sure about the outcome of Judah's surrender to Babylon and the precise way it would come out of this dangerous period, but he was convinced of the disastrous consequence of Judah's resistance. He describes the words of the prophets who urge resistance as lie or a product of their imagination. His theological discernment of history and the announcement of the course of its direction originate in his faith in God as the Creator and the Lord of history; the only things he claims here as certitudes are the fact of God's absolute sovereignty and the reality of the judgment of sin. Armed with these certitudes, he proclaims the course of events to come. He does not remain silent and let events dictate his faith, but rather he exercises faith and sees the coming events through the eye of faith. One might say with Brueggemann that Jeremiah in this chapter takes an "enormous political risk" when he renders his theological judgment of events to come (1998, 247). One might also say that contemporary preaching that engages in theological discernment of historical realities without ideological and political bias, but with strong faith in God who acts in history in his just and righteous ways, follows the footsteps of Jeremiah and models faithful proclamation of God's enduring Word to its twenty-first-century listeners.

B. The Prophet Encounters the Prophet (28:1-17)

BEHIND THE TEXT

Chapter 28 has historical continuity with the narrative in ch 27. The phrase **in that year** connects the narrative to the incident reported in ch 27; the MT incorrectly names Jehoiakim as the king in 27:1 (see discussion of 27:1). Also in 27:2, we find the report of Yahweh's command to Jeremiah to perform a symbolic act. In 28:10, the narrator reports the prophet Hananiah's symbolic act.

Though this chapter begins with a first person narrative (**Hananiah . . . said to me;** v 1), in v 5 the narrative shifts to the third person. The narrative as a whole is a third person account and most scholars attribute this biographical narrative to Baruch. Carroll describes ch 28 as a story rather than a historical event (1986, 541), but most commentators see this as a historically authentic account (for example, see Holladay 1989, 127; Lundbom 2004a, 326). This narrative is part of the biography of Jeremiah in which the focus is on opposition to Jeremiah's message coming from another person who also spoke with prophetic authority.

The opening verse places the incident reported in this narrative in the fifth month of the fourth year of Zedekiah. Holladay identifies the fifth month of the fourth year of Zedekiah (v 1) as July/August 594; Hananiah died in the seventh month of that year (September/October 594) (1989, 127). Commentators who support the historicity of this narrative place the event in 594-593 B.C.

This chapter has four main sections. In the first section, the focus is on Hananiah and his oracle (vv 1-4). This is followed by a response from Jeremiah (vv 5-9). Hananiah breaks the yoke and then gives another short oracle in the third section (vv 10-11). In the final section, Jeremiah speaks Yahweh's word to Hananiah, which was fulfilled two months later (vv 12-17).

IN THE TEXT

1. The Prophet vs. the Prophet—Round One (28:1-4)

■ 1 Verse 1 introduces the date and the setting of the initial encounter between Jeremiah and Hananiah. The event took place in the early part of the reign of King Zedekiah. The **fifth month** and the **fourth year** give the precise date of this incident. The fifth month in the Jewish calendar is the month of Ab (July/August). The fourth year of Zedekiah was 594-593 B.C. Jeremiah's symbolic act of wearing the bars of yoke and his appeal to Judah and to the neighboring nations to submit to the imperial power of Babylon (see ch 27) is the immediate context of the incidents reported in ch 28.

In ch 27 Jeremiah strongly warned against listening to the words of prophets or any diviners who promote rebellion against Babylon. No doubt this would have infuriated the prophets in Jerusalem who were among the counselors and advisers of Zedekiah. **Hananiah son of Azzur,** a **prophet** from **Gibeon,** perhaps the leader of this group of prophets, steps forward and speaks and acts on behalf of this group. Hananiah, a common name in the OT, means "Yahweh is gracious." He came from the village of Gibeon, a Benjaminite city, about five miles north of Jerusalem, in proximity to Anathoth, the hometown of Jeremiah. Inscription of the name Hananiah on twenty-two jar handles found at Gibeon (Lundbom 2004a, 330) seems to indicate that this name was either a popular name in that area or that Hananiah the prophet was a prominent and wealthy citizen of that village. The MT labels him as a **prophet,** but the LXX adds to the title the adjective "false." He also utilizes the traditional messenger formula and thus claims Yahweh as the source of his message (see vv 2, 11). The Hebrew text thus seems to present this whole episode as an encounter between two prophets; both prophets speak on behalf of Yahweh. At the end of the narrative, Jeremiah clearly emerges as the prophet who truthfully speaks for Yahweh, and he discredits Hananiah's claim of prophetic authority. Jeremiah charges that Hananiah misled the nation with his lying words.

Verse 1 presents Hananiah's words directly addressed to Jeremiah. The setting of this encounter is the temple and **the priests and all the people** are the general audience. The presence of the people in the temple suggests that the context of worship or some other religious occasion required the people to be in the temple area. As the narrative progresses, it becomes clear that the narrative focuses more on the issue of true and false prophecy. Who has insight into Judah's future and Yahweh's immediate actions on behalf of his people? Who speaks for Yahweh? Whose words have true prophetic authority? Whose words should Judah listen to? These questions are at the heart of this narrative.

■ **2** Hananiah introduces his words with the messenger style formula: ***thus said Yahweh of hosts,*** God of Israel. There is a bold claim here that the source of his message is Yahweh and that he is a true messenger sent by Yahweh. His words presented as Yahweh's words are bold and emphatic. ***I have broken*** the yoke of the king of Babylon is Yahweh's word, according to Hananiah. The verb ***I have broken*** (*šābartî*) suggests that Yahweh has already taken the decisive action to put an end to the Babylonian power over Judah. Hananiah may have made this bold claim based on the assertions of Isaiah that Yahweh will liberate his people from the yoke of foreign oppressors (see Isa 9:4; 10:27; 14:25). If this is true, Yahweh's word spoken in the context of a previous historical crisis is the basis of his judgment on current political realities. Jeremiah has made clear that at this point in history it is Yahweh's intent to place Judah under the yoke of Babylon. Hananiah not only contradicts the word Yahweh has spoken through Jeremiah in ch 27 but also raises the question of the credibility of Jeremiah as a true prophet.

■ **3-4** Hananiah then proceeds to give a prediction of two clear events that will soon happen as a result of Yahweh's breaking of **the yoke of the king of Babylon** (v 4). Yahweh's actions are stated in the first person form (**I will bring back;** vv 3, 4). The first event will be the return of ***all the vessels of Yahweh's house*** that were carried away by Nebuchadnezzar to Babylon, and the second will be the return of king **Jehoiachin** and all the people exiled to Babylon in 597 B.C. Yahweh's zealousness for his house and his property and his people underlies this optimistic message. The LXX omits the second part of v 3 (**that Nebuchadnezzar king of Babylon removed from here and took to Babylon**). In 22:26-27 Jeremiah predicted that Jehoiachin will die in the land of his captivity. Hananiah contradicts that message with an optimistic view that Yahweh will bring back Jehoiachin and all the exiles of Judah (v 4 in the LXX omits the phrases **I will also bring back to this place . . . son of Jehoiakim king of Judah . . . , who went to Babylon, declares the LORD,** and simply reads as "and Jehoiachin and the exiles of Judah"). Hananiah is confident that these events will happen because Yahweh has ***broken*** **the yoke of the king of Babylon.** Yahweh has already undertaken this decisive action to restore his property that was forcefully taken to Babylon by Nebuchadnezzar.

We do not know if Hananiah represented a pro-Jehoiachin party opposed to the rule of Zedekiah, a puppet king placed on the Judean throne by Nebuchadnezzar. Jehoiachin's return would mean a change in the regime in Judah. The political overtones of this message cannot be underestimated. Hananiah's prediction that these events will happen **within two years** is a strong refutation of Jeremiah's warning to the people in 27:16. Jeremiah sees the current crisis ending with Yahweh's visit of his people (see 27:22; also "seventy years" in 29:10), whereas Hananiah sees Yahweh already at work to restore normal religious and political life in Judah.

2. The Prophet vs. the Prophet—Round Two (28:5-9)

■ **5** The narrator introduces Jeremiah's response to Hananiah. The **prophet Jeremiah** now speaks directly to the **prophet Hananiah.** In both cases the title is lacking in the LXX. The title **prophet** for both individuals in the MT may be intentional. The MT titles give equal status to both individuals as legitimate prophets and thus build up the intensity of Jeremiah's response to Hananiah as a confrontation between two prophets of Yahweh. The narrator is clearly aware of the fact that Hananiah is not a true prophet; but the reader will have to wait until this confrontation is over to recognize who indeed is speaking as Yahweh's authorized prophet. The witness of this confrontation is the same as in v 1; Jeremiah also speaks before the priests and the people who are present in the temple.

■ **6** Jeremiah opens his response to Hananiah with an unexpected **"Amen! May the LORD do so!"** Is he agreeing with Hananiah's words? Or, is he making fun of the audacity of Hananiah's ill-founded hope? Or, is he expressing doubt in his own words and the revelation he received from Yahweh concerning the fate of the vessels of the temple and the exiles? Could he have been wrong? Or, is he simply expressing his deep-seated desire for the immediate return of the vessels and the exiles even though he knows that it will not happen for a while? Holladay suggests that Jeremiah might be mocking Hananiah (1989, 127-28). Lundbom thinks it unlikely that Jeremiah is expressing his agreement with Hananiah's words and says, "Jeremiah is pretending to wish a successful outcome to Hananiah's words" (Lundbom 2004a, 334). However, it is possible that Jeremiah was shocked by the bold and overconfident speech of Hananiah and perhaps felt a bit uncertain about his own previously spoken words concerning the fate of the temple vessels and the exiles in Babylon. The language of Jeremiah's response here is not confrontational; the real confrontation takes place in vv 13-16. The speech that follows in vv 8-9 seems to set the standard with which to distinguish true prophecy from false prophecy. Though Jeremiah is not agreeing with Hananiah's words, he begins his speech with an expressed desire for the immediate return of the temple vessels and the exiles. However, he does not revise or modify his previously spoken words about the temple vessels and the exiles.

True and False Prophecy

Jeremiah's confrontation with Hananiah in 28:1-9 illustrates the ambiguity and uncertainty about the claims of a prophet who speaks in Yahweh's name. In this narrative, Jeremiah expresses uncertainty about the authenticity of his opponent's claim. He neither affirms nor rejects the words of Hananiah but simply hopes for the end of the Babylonian crisis though he himself called for Judah's submission to Babylon. He uses the Deuteronomic criteria and reminds the people and Hananiah that they will have to wait and see the fulfillment of Hananiah's claim of peace before recognizing his claim as Yahweh's true prophet (see Deut 18:21-22).

■ **7** In v 7, Jeremiah appeals to Hananiah and the people to give attention to his words (***Only listen now this word which I speak***). Though Hananiah is addressed directly in v 8, by including **all the people** as the audience of his response, Jeremiah makes clear that the discourse that follows on true and false prophecy (vv 8-9) is primarily for the benefit of the people who are influenced by the optimistic words of Hananiah. It is then possible that Jeremiah's words in v 6 may have been a clever strategy to appease the crowd so that they may be receptive to what Jeremiah has to say to them. A direct confrontation with Hananiah at this point would have only turned the crowd against Jeremiah. In this contest of words, the people need to be the arbiters, and they should determine for themselves who is truthfully speaking for Yahweh. For that to happen, they need to know the fundamental distinction between true and false prophecy.

The phrase ***but listen*** introduces a contrary perspective (Lundbom 2004a, 334), against the one presented by Hananiah. It is significant that the priests are not included in Jeremiah's audience. They are perhaps intentionally excluded because Jeremiah knows that they are coconspirators with false prophets in promoting a false sense of peace and well-being in the land, and he is well aware of their opposition to his preaching (5:31; 6:13-14; 8:10-11; 20:6). ***This word*** (*dābār*) is not a word of revelation from Yahweh but simply a contrary perspective that Jeremiah wants to present to the people.

■ **8** Jeremiah sums up an essential component of the preaching of Israel's prophets who preceded him and Hananiah (v 8). **From *ancient* times** refers to the ancient past, and it could thus mean from the beginning days of prophecy in Israel. Though Hananiah is his antagonist, Jeremiah gives him equal status as a prophet (**the prophets who preceded you and me**), which is again a clever strategy on the part of Jeremiah to show that they both have something in common—their vocation as prophets. Jeremiah does not identify the prophets who preceded them. Perhaps he may have in mind their immediate predecessors, such as Amos, Hosea, Isaiah, and Micah, who have spoken severe words of judgment to Israel. Jeremiah reminds Hananiah and the people that the prophecies the prophets who preceded them included words about **war, disaster and plague against many countries and great kingdoms**. Here again, no particular country or kingdom is mentioned; obviously this reference includes Israel and the foreign nations.

In v 8, Jeremiah is not attempting to define prophecy in the past exclusively in terms of doom and destruction, but he simply attempts to show that speaking words of disaster is very much a part of the tradition that they both have inherited from the past. The question of what constitutes prophecy seems to be the issue that Jeremiah is trying to establish here. Do words of doom and disaster have a place in prophecy or is prophecy exclusively words of peace and well-being? Citing the content of the preaching of previous prophets, Jeremiah argues that oracles of doom are an essential component of Israel's prophecy.

■ **9** Having established the element of doom oracles as part of Israel's prophetic tradition, and by inference, having established himself as the one who stands in the tradition of Israel's previous prophets, Jeremiah now raises question about the authenticity of Hananiah as a true prophet (v 9). How can one know the legitimacy and authenticity of those who speak only words of peace? How can one know whether a person who speaks words of peace is a prophet sent by Yahweh? **The prophet who prophesies peace** in this context is clearly Hananiah, who has just spoken about Yahweh breaking the yoke of the king of Babylon and promised an immediate return of the temple vessels and the exiles in Babylon. Jeremiah applies here the Deuteronomic criteria of fulfillment or nonfulfillment of the prophetic word to test the authenticity of those who give peace and well-being oracles (Lundbom 2004a, 335-36). He seems to be saying to Hananiah and the people that they must wait to see fulfillment of Hananiah's words to determine whether he is a prophet **truly sent by Yahweh.** Jeremiah has elsewhere stated emphatically that the prophets who speak peace and well-being were not sent by Yahweh (23:21; 27:15). Jeremiah himself has made the strong defense during his trial that he is a prophet sent by Yahweh (26:12-15). At this point in this prophet vs. prophet encounter, Jeremiah does not say that Hananiah is not sent by Yahweh but simply raises the issue that Hananiah has not yet proven himself as Yahweh's true prophet. However, the subsequent action of Hananiah and Yahweh's word to Jeremiah would reveal the true identity of Hananiah as a lying prophet, a prophet not sent by Yahweh (28:10-15).

3. The Prophet vs. the Prophet—Round Three (28:10-11)

■ **10** Hananiah's response to Jeremiah was quick. He **took the *bars of* yoke off the neck** of Jeremiah **and broke it.** He would have understood the implications of Jeremiah's speech and the implied challenge to prove his legitimacy as a prophet sent by Yahweh. The burden is now on Hananiah to establish his prophetic authority. Since Jeremiah seemed to have been successful in the prophetic word against the prophetic word in the previous two rounds of this confrontation, Hananiah's strategy now is to respond to Jeremiah with action. Jeremiah's symbolic action conveyed a powerful message; now it is his turn to show the efficacy of his words and the inefficacy of Jeremiah's words and action. By taking the yoke off Jeremiah's neck and breaking it, Hananiah conveys the message to his audience that the fulfillment of his words of peace is set in motion by Yahweh, and that he has the authority to nullify Jeremiah's action and words.

■ **11** Hananiah's symbolic action is accompanied by a message allegedly from Yahweh (v 11). He follows the usual practice of Israel's prophets delivering a message following a symbolic action (13:1-11; 19:1-13). He repeats his message of Yahweh breaking **the yoke of Nebuchadnezzar king of Babylon** (see vv 2, 4). In v 3, **two years** is given as the time set for the restoration of the temple vessels and the exiles from Babylon. Here, **two years** is the time set for the end of the Babylonian hegemony over the vassal nations in the Syria-Palestine region. If we assume that this incident took place around 594-593 B.C., then the expected date for the fulfillment of this event would have been 592-591 B.C. Later, the community in exile would have concluded that Hananiah was a false prophet because of the continued domination of Babylon for another fifty plus years. But at the present time, Jeremiah's audience does not have enough evidence to determine who is speaking truthfully for Yahweh. They have heard two prophetic voices; Hananiah presents hope as an imminent reality and even performs a symbolic action to show that Yahweh's power is already unleashed to fulfill his prophecy. Jeremiah, on the other hand, simply raises questions about the legitimacy of those who prophesy peace, and he leaves the matter of the truthfulness of Hananiah's words for the people to decide. The narrator does not give us any indication of how the crowd responded but concludes this round with a report of Jeremiah's course of action.

At the end of this round of the prophet vs. the prophet confrontation, Jeremiah walks away without giving a rebuttal (v 11). Was it appropriate for Jeremiah to leave the scene without a rebuttal and further confrontation with Hananiah and without taking one final stand for truth and integrity? We cannot say that Jeremiah is admitting defeat or allowing Hananiah to have the last word. He has already spoken the truth about the Babylonian rule and called Judah and the nations to surrender to the yoke of the king of Babylon. He has presented his case, and there is nothing more to add to what he has already said. He leaves the issue for the people to reflect on and determine for themselves who is speaking to them the truth in Yahweh's name.

4. The Prophet vs. the Prophet—Round Four (28:12-17)

■ **12** In the final section of the narrative (vv 12-17), we find who indeed has the last word in this confrontation between the prophet and the prophet. Jeremiah is clearly established as *the* prophet and Hananiah is proved as *a* prophet who makes up lies in Yahweh's name. This final word is indeed Yahweh's verdict, and it is given to Hananiah by Yahweh's true messenger. The people or the priests are not mentioned here as the audience; so it is likely that here we have a personal and private confrontation of Jeremiah with Hananiah. If this is so, the people would not have heard the word Jeremiah spoke about Hananiah's death (v 16).

Verse 12 reports that Yahweh's word came to Jeremiah **after** Hananiah's symbolic action of breaking the bars of yoke off Jeremiah's neck. How much time has lapsed between these two incidents is not given.

■ **13** Yahweh commands Jeremiah to go and speak to Hananiah. Yahweh's speech that follows is his response to Hananiah's defiant action of breaking the bars of yoke off Jeremiah's neck. Jeremiah wore the bars of yoke upon his neck at the command of Yahweh; therefore, Yahweh is the One who is offended by Hananiah's action. It is Yahweh's word that Hananiah has challenged; therefore, Yahweh is the One who confronts him through his true prophet. Yahweh announces to Hananiah that what he has broken is bars of yoke made of wood, but through his action he has **made (*you have made*** in the MT) **bars of yoke of iron.** Hananiah's symbolic action has not rendered Jeremiah's symbolic action ineffective; instead, through this action, he has replaced the wooden yoke with yoke bars made of iron. The NIV reading **you will get a yoke of iron** lessens the impact of Hananiah's action and the role he has played in shaping Yahweh's judgment. His action was meant to convey an immediate end to the Babylonian domination. Yahweh now says that Hananiah's action aided only in prolonging the Babylonian domination and thus making it severe and difficult to bear. Lundbom says, "False preaching . . . aids in bringing about precisely what one wants not to happen" (2004a, 338).

■ **14** Yahweh reiterates his plan to place the nations under the Babylonian domination (v 14). Yahweh's word, **I will put an iron yoke on the necks . . . ,** echoes the Deuteronomic curse ("He will put an iron yoke on your neck until he has destroyed you" [Deut 28:48]). **All these nations** include Judah and the surrounding nations, particularly the nations that have sent envoys to meet Zedekiah in Jerusalem to plan a rebellion against Babylon. It is Yahweh's verdict that they **serve Nebuchadnezzar king of Babylon.** The LXX lacks **and they will serve him. I will even give him control over the wild animals.** The reference to control over the wild animals is hyperbole; it conveys the idea of Babylonians exercising total control over the lands of these nations. Nothing in these lands will be free.

■ **15** Jeremiah is the speaker in v 15. This verse introduces the defining moment in this narrative and settles the question of true and false prophecy. In his last speech to the people, Jeremiah has raised the issue of peace prophecy and the criteria for determining if a prophet is truly sent by Yahweh (see v 9). Though the narrative continues to speak of **the prophet Jeremiah** and **the prophet Hananiah,** only one has been truly sent by Yahweh. Jeremiah speaks directly and forcefully to Hananiah and declares to him that he is not **sent** by Yahweh. The judgment, **the LORD has not sent you,** means that Hananiah is a false prophet, an unauthorized individual speaking falsely in Yahweh's name. The question of true and false prophecy is thus resolved here. Yahweh's sending is the most important criterion that determines the legitimacy of true prophets. Yahweh's own verdict about the false prophets is that "I have not sent them" (27:15; also 23:21).

Jeremiah also tells Hananiah that he had "made this people trust in a lie" (v 15 NRSV). This is precisely Yahweh's assessment of the message of the false prophets ("They are prophesying lies in my name" [27:15]). "This people" refers to the people of Judah and perhaps the envoys from the neighboring nations assembled in Jerusalem (27:3). The function of true prophets is to lead the people to have trust in Yahweh by truthfully conveying the words they hear from Yahweh. By pretending to be a prophet sent by Yahweh Hananiah caused the people to trust in words that did not originate with Yahweh. His lying words have in turn influenced the people to turn their hearts away from Yahweh's true words spoken by Jeremiah, his true prophet.

■ **16** Yahweh is the speaker in v 16. The fate of the one that Yahweh did not send (*šlḥ* in v 15) is stated here. Hananiah pretended to be the truly sent prophet. Now it is Yahweh's decision to **send** (*šlḥ*) him **away from the face of the earth.** The one who is not sent, but claimed to have been sent, will be sent away! Expulsion from the land and destruction are among the fate of the people who listen to false prophecy and the prophets who prophesy falsehood (see 27:15). The second part of v 16 clarifies what this means. Hananiah the pretender who has swindled the people by preaching rebellion against Yahweh receives the verdict of death. **This year you will die** is a time-specific predictive prophecy and the final judgment on Hananiah. Hananiah gave a time-specific prophecy about the return of the temple vessels and the exiles in Babylon (vv 3 and 11). Now it is Jeremiah's turn to be specific about the time of Hananiah's death. Death is the penalty prescribed in Deut 18:20 for speaking presumptively in Yahweh's name. Hananiah not only promoted lies through false prophecy but also instigated **rebellion** against Yahweh. The LXX lacks the final part of this verse: **because you have spoken rebellion against Yahweh.** This sentence also echoes the penalty for false prophets and dreamers who promote rebellion against Yahweh in Deut 13:1-5 (see *sārâ* for "rebellion" in v 16 and in Deut 13:5).

■ **17** The narrative ends with a report about the fulfillment of Jeremiah's word about Hananiah's death. **In the seventh month of that same year,** two months after the initial confrontation between Jeremiah and Hananiah, Hananiah died. In the Jewish calendar, the seventh month is Tishri (September/October). The year would be 594-593, the same year of the events narrated in chs 27—28. Verse 17 in the LXX is brief: "and he died in the seventh month." Lundbom sees in this verse "the power and efficacy of the prophetic word" (2004a, 340). The issue of true and false prophecy has already been settled by Jeremiah's indictment of Hananiah as a prophet not sent by Yahweh (v 15). The fulfillment of Jeremiah's prophecy vindicates him as the authentic prophet; he has met the Deuteronomic criteria of true prophets (Deut 18:17-22).

FROM THE TEXT

Verse 3 indicates that a key point of controversy between Jeremiah and the official prophets was over the length of the Babylonian supremacy over Judah and the root cause of the current political crisis. Hananiah and his colleagues are convinced that the current crisis is short-term and that it is caused by Babylon, an aggressive and brute political power that invaded Yahweh's house and his land. Yahweh who is offended by this military power cannot and will not stand by the side and simply watch the continued power play of Babylon over Judah. He will promptly act and soon reclaim his property and his people, and demonstrate his power over Babylon. The authority and the boldness with which Hananiah spoke this message in Yahweh's name would have convinced the priests and the people of its authenticity as Yahweh's trustworthy promise.

However, this optimistic message of Hananiah does not deal with the issue of the moral and spiritual crisis that brought about the current political crisis. It simply anticipates an immediate end. With boldness and certitude he sets a time limit for God's action. This claim is a theological judgment firmly rooted in the view of Yahweh as the God who comes to the rescue of his people. Brueggemann labels Hananiah's claim an "ideological distortion" because his prophetic statement is not based on the discernment of new things that God is doing in the present situation (1998, 251). Though Jeremiah also anticipates the end, he sees it as part of the future plans and purposes of Yahweh; his immediate focus is on what Yahweh is doing now in the present moment to exercise his sovereignty over the world and particularly over his people who have broken their covenant with him. As far as Jeremiah is concerned, hope lies in the future. It is Yahweh who has placed Judah and the neighboring nations under the yoke of the king of Babylon (ch 27). It is Yahweh's will that Judah and the nations remain under the yoke of Babylon until the day of Babylon's judgment. Breaking the yoke of the king of Babylon is indeed yet another activity of Yahweh, the precise time of which has not yet been fully disclosed.

Contemporary interest in prophecy and prediction in some circles in the Christian church reveals a different approach to understanding current historical events. Some Christians view prophecy as a static word that God announced in the past about his future involvement in history. In such thinking, every event that happens in the world or every event that will happen in the future might be a fulfillment of a past word spoken by God. This way of perceiving history fails to take seriously into account God's creative power that he now manifests in the world through current historical realities. The biblical faith affirms that the God who shaped history in the past is the God who is shaping history in the present, and the God who will shape history in the future. Though the past is undeniably important, it does not hold the key to the unlocking of the present and the future. Rather, our understanding of the past helps us to properly discern what God is doing in the present. Such discernment of God's actions in the present can come only through a proper assessment of present realities, the first and foremost of which is an objective evaluation of the fidelity of God's people to their mission in the world and the condition of the world in general. That discernment may lead us to conclude that God's actions in the present are radically different from the ways in which he acted in the past. It is this kind of discernment of God and his work in the world that guided Jeremiah to insist on Judah's submission to Babylon in the sixth century B.C. as the will of the same God who delivered Israel from the power of Pharaoh in the thirteenth century B.C.

We should also ask the question, "What was wrong with Hananiah's message of grace and salvation to Judah?" His own name conveys the idea that Yahweh is a gracious God. His message conveys the idea of God extending his grace to Judah through his judgment of Babylon. This kind of grace comes cheap, without any judgment on sin and sinners. However, Jeremiah sees God's grace working in a different way and through a different avenue. As Fretheim points out, Jeremiah's preaching of judgment is an integral part of his understanding of God's grace at work on behalf of Judah (2002, 396). Judgment is the avenue through which Judah will experience God's grace. It is important for Wesleyan theology to emphasize this aspect of God's grace. Judgment of sin and sinners is part of God's gracious activity to bring hope and a future for sinners through salvation, which lies on the other side of judgment. This seems to be the message that Paul conveys in Ephesians when he states: "You were dead through the trespasses and sins . . . we were by nature children of wrath, like everyone else. But God, who is rich in mercy, out of the great love with which he loved us, even when we were dead through our trespasses, made us alive together with Christ—by grace you have been saved" (Eph 2:1, 3-5 NRSV).

C. An Unwelcome Letter (29:1-32)

BEHIND THE TEXT

A key source of the content of this chapter is a letter that Jeremiah sent to the exiles in Babylon (vv 5-23). This chapter indicates that an individual by the name of Shemaiah of Nehelam also sent letters to Jerusalem from Babylon; but the content of only one letter is specifically mentioned (vv 25-28; see *this* letter in v 29). The chapter as a whole is a narrative that includes summaries of both letters and other oracles of Jeremiah. In the LXX, this narrative is found in 36:1-32.

This narrative is commonly attributed to Baruch. The narrative frequently uses the introductory and concluding formulas of messenger style speeches (vv 4, 8, 9, 10, 11, 14, 16, 17, 19, 20, 21, 23, 24, 31, 32). Verse 2 indicates that Jeremiah sent his letter shortly after the exile of Jehoiachin in 597 B.C. Jeremiah's letter prompted Shemaiah to send his letter(s) to the people in Jerusalem (vv 26-28). The other oracles in this narrative also may be placed within a short period after the exile of 597 B.C.

We assume that the letters in this narrative in their original form had a formal beginning and ending. However, the narrative does not preserve those details. The narrator simply summarizes the details one would find in the formal introduction of a letter. In the case of Jeremiah's letter, we are told who sent the letter, to whom it was sent, and when and how it was sent (vv 1-3). In the case of the letter of Shemaiah, we are given information about the sender and the recipients (vv 24-25).

The narrative as a whole lacks proper structure and organization after v 14. There is clear organization up to this point with an introductory statement (vv 1-3) and the development of the primary message of Jeremiah to the exiles (vv 4-14). Verses 4-14 have three parts. In part 1 (vv 4-7), Jeremiah counsels the exiles to settle down and live a normal life in Babylon. In part 2 (vv 8-9), he counsels the exiles not to pay attention to the prophets and diviners among them who are prophesying falsely in Yahweh's name. The content of their false prophecy is not stated; it is likely that these false prophets were predicting an imminent return of the exiles to their homeland. In part 3 (vv 10-14), the prophet announces to the exiles that their return to the homeland is not imminent, but it will happen at a specified time in the future. He assures them that Yahweh will visit them. The letter thus ends with this hopeful note about the future.

Verse 15 seems to introduce a new segment in the narrative, but it is abruptly disrupted. This part may very well have been part of the original letter. However, this section shows no continuity with the preceding section. Two unrelated issues receive attention in vv 15-23. Verse 15 seems to introduce Yahweh's word to the exiles in Babylon who have made the claim that Yahweh has raised up prophets for them in Babylon; but there is no oracle from Yahweh as his response to this claim. The oracle that follows (vv 16-19) is a judgment word on Zedekiah and those who remain in Jerusalem. The LXX lacks vv 16-20, which complicates the textual problem here. Bright thinks that vv 16-20 were inserted here secondarily from another context and that they do not belong here (1965, 209). Verse 20 picks up the narrative that ended abruptly in v 15. Verses 21-23 contain an oracle about Ahab son of Kolaiah and Zedekiah son of Maaseiah, two false prophets in Babylon, and their fate. Holladay agrees with those who think that vv 16-20 belong between v 14 and v 15. Thus in his reordering of this section, he inserts vv 16-20 after v 14 and then places v 15 before v 21 (1989, 135).

It is likely that the disjointed sections of vv 15-23 may have been added as appendices to the letter, the primary purpose of which was to give hope to the exiles in Babylon. It is unclear why the appendix about Zedekiah and those remaining in Jerusalem is added to the letter; the purpose of it may have been to contrast the hope given to the exiles in Babylon (vv 5-14) with the tragic fate awaiting those remaining in Jerusalem. Taken together, the message of vv 5-19 shows close affinity to the message conveyed in ch 24 and thus there is some thematic continuity between vv 1-14 and vv 16-19. Also unclear is the reason for the addition of the words about Ahab and Zedekiah, two of the false prophets, to the letter. There is only a general indictment against them; their lies may have been prophecies about an immediate return of the exiles to Judah. If so, this oracle is another warning to the people. It continues the theme of vv 8-9 and exposes them as false prophets who speak lying words in Yahweh's name to the exiles. This oracle also shows that Jeremiah's message has opposition, both at home in Judah and among the exiles in Babylon. Jeremiah predicts that these false prophets will be put to death by Nebuchadnezzar.

Verse 24 begins with a directive to someone (from Yahweh to Jeremiah or from Jeremiah to someone in Babylon) to speak to Shemaiah of Nehelam. Lundbom thinks that v 24 preserves a fragment of a second letter that Jeremiah sent to Babylon (2004a, 346). The problem is that this directive could easily be understood as a directive from Yahweh to Jeremiah (Bright 1965, 212). Holladay thinks that the letter of Jeremiah closes with v 23; he treats vv 24-32 as a separate section from vv 1-23 (1989, 137). The message to Shemaiah is not recorded. What follows in vv 25-28 simply contain a summary of the letters that Shemaiah sent to the people and the priests in Jerusalem, and particularly to Zephaniah the priest, charging them with dereliction of duty because he did not take action against Jeremiah. Thus we have here a narrative that was most likely added to Jeremiah's original letter to show the chain of events that followed Jeremiah's message to the exiles. Later in the narrative, we find Jeremiah's word about Shemaiah addressed to the exiles, but not directly given to Shemaiah (vv 31-32).

Verses 29-32 report Jeremiah's message to the exiles. Lundbom designates this as Jeremiah's third letter (2004a, 362-63). **Send to all the exiles** (v 31) could be considered as a directive to send a letter (**send this message to all the exiles** in the NIV). It is possible that vv 31*b*-32 contain the contents of this letter (Holladay 1989, 146). This could also be understood as Yahweh's directive to give an oracle to the exiles and thus the final appendix to the letter. This oracle seems to show continuity with v 24. Instead of Jeremiah speaking a word to Shemaiah, he speaks now to the exiles about Shemaiah and reveals his identity as a false prophet. In this appendix, the narrator shows that Jeremiah's message to the exiles was met with a great deal of opposition, at least at the level of the Jewish leadership in Babylon. In this oracle, Jeremiah pronounces judgment on the false prophet and reiterates the hope given in his letter to the exiles.

It is difficult to determine the precise sequence of the various events in this narrative. It is likely that Jeremiah's letter (vv 4-14) sparked an angry response from the false prophets in Babylon, since it clearly contradicted the false hope they were feeding to the exiles. Shemaiah, perhaps the leader of this group, then sent letters to the priests in Jerusalem to rebuke and discipline Jeremiah (vv 24-28). Jeremiah, when he hears one of these letters read, sends a message directed to the people and announces to them that Shemaiah is not a prophet sent by Yahweh (vv 29-32). Thus the narrative in its original form may have had two parts: vv 1-14 and vv 24-32. The oracle about Zedekiah and the people remaining in Jerusalem (vv 15-19) and the oracle about the two false prophets (vv 20-23) may have been added to the narrative later to include Jeremiah's subsequent oracles given shortly after the letter was sent to Babylon.

IN THE TEXT

1. Unpack and Settle Down in Babylon (29:1-14)

■ 1 The narrative begins with an introduction that indicates that what follows (***these are the words***) is the content of **the letter** (*hassēper*); *sēper* is a general term for any kind of document such as a bill of divorce (3:8) or a scroll (25:13); in ch 29 this word refers to a letter (see also vv 25, 29) that Jeremiah sent from Jerusalem (v 1). Lundbom describes *hassēper* as a "letter written on papyrus, rolled into a scroll, and sealed" (2004a, 348).

Epistle of Jeremiah

The Deuterocanonical books (commonly known as the apocryphal books) include the Letter of Jeremiah, a letter that Jeremiah presumably wrote to those who were about to go into exile in Babylon (either in 597 or 587 B.C.). The letter begins as follows: "A copy of a letter that Jeremiah sent to those who were to be taken to Babylon as exiles by the king of the Babylonians, to give them the message that God had commanded him" (NRSV). In two major manuscripts of the Septuagint, this letter is located between Lamentations and Ezekiel; however, in a number of other manuscripts it is attached as chapter 6 of the book of Baruch. Most scholars think that this letter was inspired by Jeremiah's letter recorded in Jer 29. The letter is clearly a warning and exhortation against idol worship. It has numerous parallels to Jeremiah's sermon against idols in Jer 10 (see vv 1-16). This letter also reflects the language of Isa 40:18-20; 41:6-7; and 46:1-7. Scholars differ in their view of the date of this letter and the original language in which it was written. The commonly assigned dates range from the third century to the second century. The content of this letter indicates that the author was certainly concerned about the influence of idolatry and polytheism on the Jewish people at the time of the writing of this letter.

Verse 1 also identifies the recipients. They include the **elders** who survived the Babylonian invasion of 597 B.C. and the long journey from Jerusalem to their captivity in Babylon. The elders occupied a prominent place in the ancient Israelite society. They represented the people and had influential voice on important decisions (see 26:17). Ezekiel mentions "the elders of Israel" coming to him and seeking a word from Yahweh, during their captivity in

Babylon (20:1; see also 8:1; 14:1). The letter was also addressed to the **priests, the prophets,** and to **all the . . . people** who were taken **into exile** in Babylon by **Nebuchadnezzar.** The LXX omits *whom* **Nebuchadnezzar** *exiled* **from Jerusalem to Babylon** but inserts the phrase "an epistle to Babylon for the exiles." Second Kings 24:10-17 mentions princes, warriors, craftsmen, and smiths among those who were taken as prisoners by Nebuchadnezzar, but no mention is made there of the exile of priests and prophets. We know from Ezek 1:3 that Ezekiel the priest was among those who were taken into captivity in 597 B.C. The events of 597 are not mentioned in Jeremiah, except in v 2 and in 37:1 where mention is made of the appointment of Zedekiah by Nebuchadnezzar as king over Judah. In the LXX, **prophets** are designated as "false prophets" here and in v 8. Ezekiel's call to be a prophet came around 593 B.C., and we do not know of any other true prophet in Babylon during the early part of the exile; i.e., between 597 and 593 B.C.

■ **2** Verse 2 introduces additional historical data and it is a summary of 2 Kgs 24:12-16. The phrase **after . . . gone** *out* **from Jerusalem** indicates the exile of the people mentioned in this verse. It is likely that Jeremiah sent this letter shortly after the events of 597 B.C. **Jehoiachin** was Jehoiakim's son, and he was eighteen years old when he assumed the throne after the death of his father. He ruled only for three months (2 Kgs 24:8). **The queen mother,** Jehoiachin's mother Nehushta, the daughter of Elnathan, was among the members of the royal family that Jehoiachin surrendered to Nebuchadnezzar (2 Kgs 24:8, 12, 15). Jeremiah made a prediction about the exile of Jehoiachin and his mother in 22:26. Also among the exiles were the **court officials** (*sārîsîm*, plural of *sārîs*; translated in the RSV as "eunuchs"; *eunouchon* in the LXX), which is the most likely meaning of the Hebrew word here. Though some eunuchs may have functioned as servants in the palace during this period, the fact that they were among the exiles indicates that they were people of status and authority and thus "high-ranking officials" (Lundbom 2004a, 349). The NIV translation **court officials** is appropriate here (see also the NRSV). ***The princes*** (*śārîm*, plural of *śār*) **of Judah and Jerusalem** are members of the royal family, and thus part of Jerusalem's power structure. The exiles also included **the craftsmen and the artisans,** people skilled in the construction of buildings.

■ **3** Verse 3 identifies the individuals who took Jeremiah's letter to the exiles. They were part of a delegation that Zedekiah sent to Nebuchadnezzar, king of Babylon. The purpose of this mission is not stated. Zedekiah may have sent these people with his tribute payment or with some message to his master. One member of this delegation was **Elasah son of Shaphan.** Ahikam, one of the brothers of Elasah, saved the life of Jeremiah from the people who wanted to put him to death, following his trial for preaching the temple sermon (26:24). We do not know anything about **Gemariah son of Hilkiah.** The fact that he was a member of the group that represented Zedekiah indicates that he was a high-ranking member of the administration. His father, Hilkiah, may have been the high priest who found the book of the law in the temple and played a significant role in the reformation carried out by Josiah (2 Kgs 22:3, 8, 14; 23:4). Later in the fourth year of Zedekiah (594/593 B.C.), when the king himself went to Babylon, probably to present himself before his master, Jeremiah sent a scroll that contained words of judgment on Babylon. The messenger at this time was Seraiah the son of Neriah. The prophet asked Seraiah to read the words of the scroll and then to bind a stone to it and throw it into the Euphrates River (51:59-63).

■ 4 The letter is introduced here as the word of **Yahweh Sebaoth to all the exiles whom Yahweh exiled from Jerusalem to Babylon.** The first person verb *I exiled* clearly conveys the idea that this was Yahweh's judgment. The exile is not the display of Nebuchadnezzar's power and the consequence of geopolitical changes. Rather, it is Yahweh who is in power and it is his wrath that the people are experiencing in Babylon. Yahweh's word to the exiles also means that he is committed to his relationship with the exiled people. The judgment of the exile did not sever his relationship with them; neither is the judgment Yahweh's last word to them.

The letter itself has three parts. In the first part (vv 5-7), the prophet speaks to the exiles about establishing a normal life in Babylon. In the second part (vv 8-9), he repudiates the false prophets and their message. In the third part (vv 10-14), he announces Yahweh's visitation of the exiles after seventy years of captivity in Babylon.

■ 5 Jeremiah begins his letter abruptly. There is no introductory word of greeting or other formal elements. It begins with four imperatives (**build, settle down, plant, eat**) as Yahweh's command to the exiles. The command to build and settle down conveys the call to establish normal life in Babylon. Building and settling down are activities that bring some sort of permanency in the midst of disruption brought about by their uprooting from their own land. Planting and eating show activities that bring enjoyment to the life of the exiles. These commands negate any hope that the exiles may have maintained about an immediate release from their captivity and their return home. Also, these commands imply that the exiles had freedom to engage in these activities in Babylon. Ezekiel indicates that the Jewish exiles settled down as a colony at Tel Abib by the river Kebar in Babylon (Ezek 3:15).

Yahweh uprooted his people from the land of promise, the land of their ancestors. The exile is the action he has undertaken to build them and plant them in a foreign land. **Build** and **plant** are part of the vocabulary of Yahweh's call and commission of Jeremiah (1:10). These are also the actions that Yahweh has promised to undertake on behalf of the exiles of 597 B.C. (see 24:6). Building and planting here are activities that the people must undertake in Babylon as a necessary prerequisite to the fulfillment of Yahweh's promise of building and planting them in their own land. Though this command seems to be demanding from the people actions of disloyalty to their homeland, obedience to this command is necessary to the enjoyment of true freedom that Yahweh has for them in the days to come.

■ **6** Verse 6 contain five more imperatives—commands from Yahweh (***take, bring forth, take,*** **give,** ***multiply***) to the exiles in Babylon. This verse lists further actions the exiles need to take to establish a normal life in Babylon. These actions also affirm the message that the exile will last longer than a few years. ***Take wives*** is perhaps a command given to those who went to Babylon as unmarried individuals. Lundbom suggests that some of the exiles may have refused to marry and have children because of the uncertain times in which they lived (2004a, 351). To the people who are already married and have children, Yahweh's command is to find wives for their sons and husbands for their daughters, **so that they too may have sons and daughters.** The command, **increase in number there; do not decrease,** indicates that Yahweh's will for the exiles is that they fulfill the creation mandate (Gen 1:22, 28) even though they are in a foreign land. The exiles must increase in population in Babylon and become strong just as their ancestors multiplied in number in the land of Egypt, where they sojourned for over four hundred years (Exod 1:7, 20). Growth in number is necessary for the future of the exiles in Babylon. Not only is this a command from Yahweh, but also included here is the hidden promise that he will multiply them in number if they obey this command. Jeremiah anticipated that Yahweh will multiply the population when he restores them to the land of promise (3:16; 23:3; 30:19).

■ **7** In v 7 the focus shifts to the exiles' relation to the city where they live. Normal life in Babylon for the exiles requires peaceful relation to the people who took them into captivity. The exiles must not resent and hate their captors for uprooting them from their homeland and planting them in a foreign city, but instead, they must wish for **peace** (šālôm) to come to the city of their captivity. The command **seek** (drš) implies seeking with care and diligence, and thus an intentional act. This command together with the next command **pray** (pll) conveys the idea of diligent prayer to Yahweh on behalf of the city. The city is not specifically identified. It may refer to the city of Babylon or any other city where the exiles were located, or perhaps even to the land of Babylon (the LXX reads here "the land"). Fretheim notes that Yahweh's concern for the pagan city includes its inhabitants. The exiles' total involvement in the life of the city through their work and prayer would have a positive effect on their own lives; it would also have far-reaching effect on all who live in the city (2002, 403).

Treatment of the Enemy in the OT

Jeremiah's instruction to pray for the city of Babylon in which the Judeans are exiled by King Nebuchadnezzar is a radical idea in the OT. In Deut 20:10, Yahweh gives the command to Israel to offer terms of peace to the towns against which they will carry out the conquest campaign; Yahweh permits Israel to treat those who accept the terms of peace and surrender as forced laborers. However, Deut 23:6 forbids Israel from seeking peace with and prosperity for the Ammonites or the Moabites forever. Proverbs 25:21 instructs Israel to give food and water to enemies who are hungry and thirsty. The command to pray for the welfare of Babylon in Jeremiah echoes Jesus' command to his disciples to love their enemies and pray for those who persecute them (Matt 5:44).

■ **8-9** These verses deal with the issue of false prophets. The prophet now focuses on those who have been preaching a message of an imminent return of the exiles to their homeland. Again, it is the message of **Yahweh Sebaoth** that he is conveying to the exiles about false prophets. Verses 8-9 reiterate the message concerning the false prophets that Jeremiah gave to the envoys from the neighboring nations and to Zedekiah, the priests, and the people of Judah (27:9-10, 14-15, 16-18). These verses show that there were **prophets and diviners** among the exiles in Babylon. Prophets in these verses are certainly false prophets. Divination was a practice strictly forbidden in ancient Israel (Deut 18:10). It is likely that in Babylon where divination was a common practice, the diviners among the exiles would have found freedom to practice the art of divination (Lundbom 2004a, 352).

The final part of v 8 warns the exiles not to listen to the dreams of **dreamers** (the MT reads, "do not listen to your dreams"). The MT here and in 27:9 has *hălōmōtêkem* ("your dreams"). Lundbom and Holladay suggest the reading here as "your dreamers" by a slight vowel change in the text (*hālōmōtêkem*) or an emendation of the text (*hōlĕmêkem*) (Holladay 1989, 132; Lundbom 2004a, 352). This makes better sense. **You cause to dream** is also not clear. This perhaps conveys the idea of dreamers giving their dream messages because the people coerced them to have dream revelation. If that is the case, then the exiles were being influenced by the message of their imminent return by the false prophets in Jerusalem, and they may have demanded the false prophets among them in Babylon to give them the same message.

In v 9 Yahweh again denounces the false prophets, diviners, and dreamers. Their message is *falsehood.* They are spreading lies in Yahweh's name. There is no truth in the message they convey to the people. Their message itself is not specified; it is likely that it is about an imminent return of the exiles to Judah from Babylon. Yahweh makes it clear that these individuals are false prophets. The truth about them is that they are **not sent** by Yahweh. If they were prophets called and commissioned by Yahweh, they would have been speaking the truth about the exile, and they would have been in agreement with the message being preached by Jeremiah.

■ **10** Verses 10-14 contain Yahweh's actions that he plans to undertake on behalf of the exiles. Verse 10 confirms Yahweh's plan to bring the exiles back to their homeland. However, this is not an imminent event. Yahweh has allotted for Babylon **seventy years** to exercise its domination of Judah and other nations in the world. **When seventy years are completed for Babylon** conveys the idea that Babylon is simply serving Yahweh and his purpose in human history. **Seventy years** is not to be understood literally, but only as a set period of time for Babylon's service of Yahweh. "Seven" and "seventy" indicate totality or completeness. Moreover, seventy years do not mean the period of the exile in Babylon. In 25:12 "seventy years" is the period for Judah and the surrounding nations to serve Nebuchadnezzar, king of Babylon. Here in 29:10, Nebuchadnezzar is serving Yahweh for seventy years.

Seventy Years

In 25:11 ("these nations will serve the king of Babylon seventy years") and in 29:10 ("When seventy years are completed for Babylon") Jeremiah makes reference to "seventy years." Later traditions of Judaism interpreted the "seventy years" of Jeremiah as the period that God had allotted for the desolation of Jerusalem and the temple (see Dan 9:2; Zech 1:12; 7:5; 2 Chr 36:21). It is difficult to precisely date the "seventy years" of Babylon. This seems to correspond to the seventy-year period that spans from the end of the Assyrian power in 609 B.C. and the defeat of Babylon by Persia in 539 B.C. However, there was only sixty-six years from the rise of Nebuchadnezzar to power (605 B.C.) to the defeat of Babylon in 539 B.C. "Seventy years" in the Hebrew thinking indicates the full length of a set period of time (see "seventy years" as the full life-span in Ps 90:10). This number in Jeremiah thus may simply mean that Babylon will exercise its control over the nations the full length of time that God had set for it to do so, rather than a literal seventy years.

Yahweh promises that he will **visit** (*pqd*) the exiles and that he will **confirm** his **good word** (*dĕbārî haṭṭôb*, "my good word") (v 10). The good word is the trustworthy word of Yahweh. The purpose of Yahweh's visitation is to **bring** the exiles **back to this place. This place** is Jerusalem/Judah, the place of the origin of the letter. In contrast to the optimistic words of the false prophets concerning an imminent return of the exiles, the words of Jeremiah are not only optimistic but also realistic. He, too, is confident about the return of the exiles from Babylon to Judah; however, he is also aware that it will happen only at the end of a rather long period set by Yahweh for Babylon's service of Yahweh.

■ 11 In v 11, Yahweh makes clear to the exiles that their future is very much a part of his plans and purposes. **I know the plans I** *am planning* **for you** conveys the idea of Yahweh's wisdom and his intimate knowledge of his plans. The LXX lacks "I know the plans." These plans are for **peace** (*šālôm*) and **not for evil**. The goal of Yahweh's plans for the exiles is to give them *a future and a hope*. Lundbom describes this as "the hoped-for future" (2004a, 354). The LXX reads here, "to give you these." Wisdom instructions claim that those who find wisdom have a "future" and a "hope" (Prov 24:14 NRSV). The future of the exiles is very much a part of Yahweh's concern for them. He intends to bring them their *shalom* and promises to them that though at the present moment they are faced with conditions that may seem evil to them, his plan for them is not evil but good.

■ **12** Verse 12 anticipates that the exiles will seek Yahweh through prayer (*and you will call me and come and pray to me*). The LXX reads: "and you will pray to me and I will listen to you" (lacks the phrase "you will call upon me and come"). The NIV reading, **Then you will call upon me** (see the NRSV "Then when you call upon me") implies that the exiles will call on Yahweh when seventy years are completed for Babylon. The conjunction in Hebrew should be understood in its normal sense ("and"), rather than "then" as in the NIV and the NRSV. Deuteronomy 4:29 anticipates that the people whom Yahweh will send into exile among different nations because of their evil deeds will seek Yahweh "from there"; i.e., from the land of their exile. Yahweh's will for the people exiled to Babylon is that they maintain a living relationship with him throughout their life in exile by obeying his instructions (see vv 5-9) and keeping a prayer life (see Fretheim 2002, 404). Though Yahweh is planning future conditions of peace for the exiles, they must respond to Yahweh's promise through their restored relationship with them. Calling upon God is an act the faithful people perform particularly in times of need and distress (Ps 4:1; 17:6; 18:6). Though the exiles are away from the temple and though they are living in a foreign land, Yahweh promises to hear their prayer (see 1 Kgs 8:46-52).

■ **13** Verse 13 essentially reiterates the promise of v 12. The language of this verse is very similar to that of Deut 4:29. Yahweh promises to reveal himself to those who seek him. Seeking here means the act of prayer. The idea here is not that Yahweh remains hidden from the exiles and that only their prayer will bring him out of his hiding place. This verse emphasizes the possibility of experiencing Yahweh's presence through prayer. **When you seek me with all your heart** urges the exiles to involve their whole being in the act of prayer. The exiles' seeking Yahweh with all their heart could be understood as a condition for the experience of Yahweh's presence. Though the offer of peace and future and hope are all in the plans of Yahweh for the exiles, their wholehearted involvement in restoring relationship with Yahweh is essential for the realization of these promises.

■ **14** Yahweh promises in this verse that he will be **found** by the exiles who seek him with their whole heart. Verse 14 in the LXX is very brief; it simply states, "I will appear to you." Restoration is the key promise of this verse. This whole verse echoes Deut 30:3. Yahweh's plan of restoration includes the restoration of the fortunes of Judah (*I will restore your fortunes;* see NRSV). Lundbom notes that restoration of the fortunes is a theme found eleven times in Jeremiah—the fortunes not only of Judah (29:14; 30:3, 18; 31:23; 32:44; 33:7, 11, 26) but also of Moab (48:47), Ammon (49:6), and Elam (49:39). He also thinks that the fortunes refer not only to the temple vessels but also to the houses and properties that the exiles left behind in Judah (2004a, 355). The next phrase, **I will gather you from all the nations and places where I have banished you,** implies Judah's exile to nations and places other than Babylon (see 23:3). Since the letter is specifically addressed to the exiles who were taken to Babylon in 597 B.C., the reference to the restoration of the dispersed people in other nations and places seems out of place.

2. Another Word to the Bad Figs (29:15-19)

This section focuses on the fate that awaits Zedekiah and all who remain in the city. Verses 17-18 repeat the theme of 24:9-10. The phrase "who did not go with you into exile" (v 16) indicates that this section may have been part of the letter.

■ **15** It is very likely that this verse originally was an introduction to vv 20-23. However, there is no good way to explain its present position in the letter. This verse addresses those in exile who were claiming that **Yahweh has raised up prophets for** them **in Babylon.** Jeremiah would have heard reports coming from Babylon about this matter. We do not know if this claim coming from the exiles was a strong reaction to Jeremiah's preaching in Jerusalem concerning an extended stay of the exiles in Babylon. If this is so, the exiles consider the false prophets in Babylon who are preaching an imminent return to Judah as legitimate prophets called and commissioned by Yahweh to speak his message to them. They seem to claim that they do not need to listen to Jeremiah's preaching; they are a community with its own prophets of Yahweh.

■ **16** At this point we expect to hear what Yahweh's word is to the people who claim to have their own prophets in Babylon, but the letter shifts its focus to **the king who sits on David's throne and all the people who remain in this city** (see vv 16-19). The king who sits on the Davidic throne is Zedekiah. It is unlikely that Zedekiah's envoys who are carrying this letter would have reported the content of the letter to the king. It is also unlikely that the king would have screened the letter to see if there were any antiroyal sentiments in it. The following message is also about the inhabitants of the city who did not go into exile in 597 B.C.

■ **17** Verses 17-18 reiterate the message addressed to this same group of people in 24:9-10. In ch 24, Zedekiah and the people who remain in Jerusalem are described as bad figs. Though they now live in the land of promise, and perhaps think that they have escaped the judgment of Yahweh, Yahweh promises to **send the sword, famine and plague against them** (v 17; see 24:10). **Sword, famine and plague** are a familiar series of words in Jeremiah. **Sword** implies military invasion. **Famine** is usually caused by drought and is thus a natural calamity. The siege of a city by the enemy also results in famine. **Plague** also implies some natural calamity. Verse 17 announces that all of these will come as his judgment on Zedekiah and the inhabitants of Jerusalem. Yahweh also announces that he will make this people like "horrid" (šōʿārîm; Lundbom 2004a, 356) **figs that are so bad they cannot be eaten.** They will become a disgusting and offensive group of people, and their destiny will be like that of rotten figs that people discard because they have become useless to anyone.

■ **18** Verse 18 (compare with 24:10) also mentions **sword, famine and plague** as the instruments of Yahweh's judgment. Yahweh intends to make Zedekiah and the inhabitants of Jerusalem a ***horror* to all the kingdoms of the earth.** A series of curse words are used in this verse (***curse, desolation, hissing, reproach***) to convey the tragic and shameful fate of Zedekiah and his people. They will be dispersed as exiles among the nations who will regard them as people under the curse of Yahweh. ***I have banished them*** conveys the idea of Yahweh's action as having already taken place (prophetic perfect), though it is a future event. Yahweh has already unleashed the power of his judgment, which is already at work in the lives of Zedekiah and his people.

■ **19** The reason for this severe judgment on Zedekiah and the inhabitants of Jerusalem is stated in v 19. The main reason is that **they have not listened** to Yahweh's words (**my words**) that he **sent to them again and again by** his **servants the prophets** (see 7:25). Though Yahweh has persistently sent his prophets (see 7:13) to his people, they have not paid any attention to them or his words. However, they have been paying attention to the false prophets. This verse begins with a third person address (**they**) and then shifts to a second person address (***you did not listen;*** see also the RSV). The NRSV "they would not listen" assumes here a scribal error. The NIV attempts to clear up this problem by identifying the addressees as the **exiles (you exiles)** and sees it as a word now to the exiles in Babylon. Since the message as a whole is about Zedekiah and the people in Jerusalem, the possibility of a scribal error remains.

3. Because They Have Committed Folly (29:20-23)

■ **20** Verse 20 seems to provide a logical connection to the claim made by the exiles in v 15. The exiles are addressed directly (***you . . . all the exiles***). They are specifically identified as those whom Yahweh has **sent away from Jerusalem to Babylon.** The recipients of Jeremiah's letter are the exiles of 597 B.C. The command to them is that they now hear Yahweh's word to them. This verse thus introduces a transition in the letter.

■ **21** Yahweh's word to the exiles is not directly about them but about two individuals among the exiles. Verse 21 states the fate of **Ahab son of Kolaiah and Zedekiah son of Maaseiah,** two false prophets who speak falsehood in Yahweh's name. Ahab and Zedekiah are common names in the OT; we do not know anything more about these individuals, other than that they were popular false prophets among the exiles of 597 B.C. Yahweh intends to deliver these individuals into the hand of Nebuchadnezzar. The king of Babylon will strike them down before the eyes of the exiles (**before your very eyes**). The claim of the exiles that Yahweh has raised up for them prophets in Babylon (v 15) is thus effectively dealt with in v 21. Yahweh acts to silence the false prophets whom the people claimed to be Yahweh's prophets. The people made them prophets of Yahweh, but Yahweh does not permit them to live.

■ 22 The manner in which Nebuchadnezzar will carry out the execution of Ahab and Zedekiah is stated in v 22. In v 21, it is said that Nebuchadnezzar will **strike them down,** which suggests the use of sword as the weapon of execution. Verse 22 indicates that Nebuchadnezzar **roasted** (*qlh* means "to roast") these prophets **in the fire.** The usual word for burning is *śrp; qlh* is unusual and is perhaps used here to show the intensity of suffering at the time of their death. Burning a criminal was not an unusual method in the ancient world. The story of Dan 3 attests that this was a Babylonian practice. The manner of the death of these prophets will be the basis for a curse word among the exiles in Babylon. The curse, **Yahweh treat you like Zedekiah and Ahab, whom the king of Babylon *roasted* in the fire,** is a pronouncement of the fate of these false prophets.

■ 23 Verse 23 identifies the crimes that were committed by Ahab and Zedekiah. This verse begins with a general characterization of their conduct as foolish or **outrageous** (*nĕbālâ*), actions that are immoral and unethical. The specific crime they have committed is **adultery with their neighbors' wives.** They have broken the seventh commandment. Through this sin, they have brought disgrace and dishonor to the covenant community. They have committed this sin while they were claiming to be Yahweh's prophets. They have claimed to be leaders but failed to provide leadership through proper moral and ethical behavior. In addition to their covenant breaking, they have also **spoken lies** in Yahweh's name. Yahweh denounces them and characterizes their words as lies, words that he did not give them to speak. Yahweh is thus offended on account of two criminal actions of these prophets. Verse 23 (and the letter) ends with an announcement of Yahweh's full knowledge of the actions of these prophets. He is the witness of their actions. The community in exile may consider them as their prophets and their sins may be hidden from the people. As far as Yahweh is concerned, they deserve the death penalty for their gross violation of his moral and ethical demands and their claim as prophets who speak in his name.

4. Aren't You in Charge? (29:24-28)

■ 24 Verses 24-28 begin with a directive, most likely from Yahweh to Jeremiah, to speak Yahweh's word concerning Shemaiah, the Nehelamite (v 24). This section may very well be an appendix added to the narrative to show the chain of events that followed the letter of Jeremiah. We do not know anything about **Shemaiah the Nehelamite,** except that he was a false prophet (v 31). Also, the location Nehelam is unknown to us.

■ 25 The words spoken about Shemaiah are Yahweh's words, and they are addressed directly to Shemaiah. Evidently, in response to Jeremiah's letter, Shemaiah sent more than one letter to Jerusalem in his name. Yahweh's words sum up the content of letters that Shemaiah sent to the people and the priests in Jerusalem (vv 26-28). One recipient, **Zephaniah son of Maaseiah the priest,** may have been the chief officer in the temple and successor to Pashhur who put Jeremiah in the stocks (see 21:1-2) (Lundbom 2004a, 364). We do not know if Zedekiah son of Maaseiah (29:21) and Zephaniah son of Maaseiah were brothers. He is described as "the second priest" in the temple in 52:24 (NRSV). Zephaniah the priest was one of the two messengers that King Zedekiah sent to Jeremiah on two occasions with the appeal to pray for the nation (21:1-2; 37:3). He was among the key temple officials and other prominent officials of Judah who were arrested and put to death in 587 B.C. by the Babylonians (52:24-27; 2 Kgs 25:18-21).

■ **26** In the letter Shemaiah reminds Zephaniah his responsibility to maintain order in the temple. Yahweh has appointed him as priest to be ***overseers*** (*pĕqidīm*) in the temple. The NIV phrase **in place of Jehoiada** could also be translated as "under Jehoiada." The NIV reading (see also "instead of" in the NRSV) suggests Yahweh's replacement of Jehoiada with Zephaniah as overseer in the temple, and thus Jehoiada as the immediate predecessor of Zephaniah. The reason for use of the plural (***overseers***) is not clear. Zephaniah may have been the head of a group of priests who functioned as overseers in the temple.

According to Shemaiah, the responsibilities of Zephaniah as overseer of the temple include controlling every **madman** (*ʾîš mĕšuggāʿ*) ***who prophesies*** (v 26). Shemaiah makes this disparaging portrayal of Jeremiah because of the message he was preaching in Jerusalem. In his thinking only a madman would preach a message as unwelcome as the message that Yahweh has given Babylon supremacy over Judah and the nations for seventy years. Only a madman would prophesy that the exile would last for a while. Hosea's listeners also thought of Hosea as a "fool" and a "mad" person (*mĕšuggāʿ*; Hos 9:7 NRSV). Shemaiah reminds Zephaniah that his responsibility includes disciplining individuals like Jeremiah by putting them in **the stocks and neck-irons.** These are instruments of punishment that restrained individuals and kept their body in a stiff position with no movement possible. This is precisely what Pashhur did to Jeremiah when he spoke about the impending destruction of Jerusalem (20:2).

■ **27** Verse 27 is a charge against Zephaniah that he has not faithfully carried out his duty as overseer of the temple. Shemaiah is upset with Zephaniah because he thinks that the priest is being lenient to Jeremiah. His complaint is that Zephaniah has not taken steps to impose punishment on Jeremiah for prophesying to him and the people of Jerusalem. He seems to have extended kindness and courtesy to Jeremiah, and he may have been a sympathetic listener of Jeremiah.

■ **28** Verse 28 gives the reason why Jeremiah should have been disciplined by Zephaniah. He informs the priest that the exiles have received a letter from

Jeremiah and gives the summary of a brief portion of the letter. The focus is only on the length of the exile in Babylon and Jeremiah's counsel to the exiles to **build houses and settle down** and to **plant gardens and eat what they produce.** Verse 28 thus makes clear the real point of contention between Jeremiah and the false prophets. The false prophets expect an immediate return of the exiles to the homeland; Jeremiah preaches a long stay in Babylon. Shemaiah does not mention Jeremiah's words about the return of the exiles after seventy years of Babylonian supremacy. His focus is only on the exile as lasting a long time. He leaves the rest of Jeremiah's message out, and thus distorts the essence of Jeremiah's letter, by taking his words out of context. The goal here is to portray Jeremiah as a prophet of doom, a pro-Babylonian prophet who has no nationalistic sentiments.

5. He Will Not See the Good (29:29-32)

The final part of the narrative contains an oracle addressed to the exiles concerning Shemaiah. Yahweh's judgment on Shemaiah is given here.

■ **29** Shemaiah was upset and outraged that Zephaniah the priest reneged on his duty to discipline Jeremiah. However, in v 29 the priest shows further kindness and courtesy to the prophet by letting him hear the letter that Shemaiah sent to him and to the people and the priests.

■ **30-32** Verses 30-32 contain the oracle concerning Shemaiah. Verse 30 introduces this oracle as Yahweh's word that came to Jeremiah in response to Shemaiah's letter to Zephaniah. In v 31 Yahweh commands Jeremiah to **send a message to all the exiles.** The subject of this oracle is **Shemaiah the Nehelamite.** Lundbom says that Yahweh is now asking Jeremiah "to write another letter to the exiles" with his words of judgment against Shemaiah (2004a, 366). He considers this as Jeremiah's third letter in this chapter (2004a, 362). But it lacks any reference to the messengers who carried it to Babylon. This oracle may simply have been a word spoken to the exiles and not necessarily a letter sent by the prophet. Verse 31 also gives the reason for this judgment word against Shemaiah. He assumed the role of a prophet though he was not a prophet that Yahweh has sent to the exiles in Babylon. Moreover, through lying words he has caused the people to *trust in* a lie.

Because of his lying words and unauthorized activity as a prophet of Yahweh, Yahweh will *visit* (*pqd*) **Shemaiah . . . and his descendants** (v 32). The last part of v 32 (**declares the LORD, because he has preached rebellion against me**) is lacking in the LXX. The goal of Yahweh's visit is to bring his punishment on Shemaiah and his family. This false prophet and his family are not given any hope for the future. The prophet who rebelled against the future that Yahweh has planned for the exiles will end up without a future. None of his descendants will be **left among this people** (the exiles) to see the realization of Yahweh's promises to the exiles. The threat here is that Yahweh will remove them from among the exiles (threat of total extinction). Yahweh's plan is to do **good**

things for his people, but Shemaiah (and his descendants) will not have any part in it. This is the punishment for preaching **rebellion** against Yahweh.

FROM THE TEXT

Jeremiah's letter to the exiles begins with his instruction that they should engage in the normal daily tasks of building life in the land of their captivity. What is amazing about this directive is that it is given to those who are sent away by God in judgment. This directive in that sense seeks to lessen the harshness of punishment. They are told that the world outside of the land of promise is a world in which they will be able to experience the creative power and the presence of God the Creator who relates to his creation through his promise of blessing and prosperity and fruitfulness and growth (Gen 1:22, 28). God's command, **increase in number there; do not decrease,** is not only an invitation to participate in the creational mandate but it also conveys the promise of God's creational activity in the life of the exiles in Babylon. Moreover, even in exile in a foreign land, they will experience the blessings that God promised to Abraham, their ancestor (Gen 17:6). They will experience the same blessing their ancestors experienced in Egypt (Exod 1:7). Fretheim comments: "God's creational activity among the exiles is a crucial ingredient for what happens in redemption. Only in and through the growth of this people will God have anyone to redeem!" (2002, 409). This text thus reminds us that true life is possible for those who know God as Creator even in the most adverse conditions of life. In Hebrew thinking, God's creative work involves bringing into existence things that do not exist. Difficult circumstances of life may lead the faithful to think that God is no longer with them because they do not see his work in any dramatic way. This text reminds us of the faithful presence and life-giving activity of God even in the darkest days of life. Paul expresses his confidence in God's faithful presence when he states: "For I am convinced that neither death, nor life, nor angels, nor rulers, nor things present, nor things to come, nor powers, nor height, nor depth, nor anything else in all creation, will be able to separate us from the love of God in Christ Jesus our Lord" (Rom 8:38-39 NRSV). In such circumstances of life, God calls us to live life to the fullest and not yield to the temptation to give up hope.

Jeremiah asks in his letter to the exiles to seek *shalom* and prosperity to the city of their exile and to pray for it, and he promises that they, too, will benefit from its prosperity. Praying for the enemy is an idea virtually lacking in all the OT texts that deal with the treatment of the enemy. In light of this, we might consider Jeremiah's instruction as a radical idea, nonetheless an idea that introduces a new perspective on God's work in the world, then and now. This instruction is twofold: First, the exiled Judeans are to work toward promoting *shalom* in the city in which they live, and thus to engage in the welfare of the larger community. They must carry out this task while living in submission to foreign domination. This *shalom* does not come through violence and antigovernment activities, but through building homes, establishing family life, and engaging in normal activities of life. This *shalom* also comes not through isolation from the larger community, but through the fulfillment of civic responsibility in a city that is hostile to their existence. Seeking and finding and promoting peace in an enemy territory is not so much the order of the day for most people in the world today. The gospel reminds us that the purpose of Jesus' coming into our sinful world was to be our peace and to make peace in the world that was divided by hostility (Eph 2:14-17; Luke 2:14). Now it is the task of the disciples of Jesus to be peacemakers in the world (Matt 5:9). To them Jesus offers his peace that is quite unlike the peace that the world gives (John 14:27).

Second, the exiled Judeans are to pray for the city and its prosperity. This means praying for those who deported them and destroyed their land. Verse 7 also gives the rationale for Yahweh's radical command to the exiles. The future of the exiles by and large depends on the future of the city of their exile. If the city enjoys peace and prosperity, then the exiles will also have peace and prosperity. If the city suffers calamity, then the exiles also will suffer calamity. This way of thinking is different from the alternative, that is, to live in total hatred of the enemy, which is the basic human instinct, and what we commonly observe among communities that live in exile in the world today. Jeremiah's instruction here displays his deep theological conviction that God answers the prayer of the exiled people for the welfare of their enemies. The portrait of God here is that of the God who is active not only in the lives of his covenant people but also in the lives of the pagan Babylonians. God plans to do good things for the Babylonians, and this can be accomplished only through the prayer of his people. Thus even in the land of exile, the mission to the descendants of Abraham is to be a blessing to "all the families of the earth" (Gen 12:3 NRSV). This text reminds us of the responsibility of intercessory prayer for our communities, nations, and political authorities in our world, including those who persecute us (see Rom 13; 1 Tim 2:1-2). Jesus reminded his disciples to love their enemies and to pray for those who persecute them, for such a way of life and thinking is a characteristic of those that belong to the kingdom of God (Matt 5:44; see also Rom 12:14; 1 Cor 4:12).

Jeremiah's instruction to the exiles in 29:7 is extremely relevant to the contemporary readers of the book. We live in a world of multiple racial groups, diverse political, economic, social, and religious perspectives. How we live in such a world is a critical concern to Christians today. Some have opted for a life of isolation and sectarian existence because of fear of undue influence from others, particularly in the areas of education and politics. For them, any idea or perspective from others who are not like them is to be rejected because of a fundamental distrust of others and their perspectives. Some simply accept and tolerate others because of necessity, but not always with a willing spirit. They see diversity as a reality of life and find no way out of it and must tolerate it. Bracke sees in Jer 29:5-7 an alternative to isolation from and tolerance of others; that is, "to see those who are different from us as a gift from God" to enrich our lives. He finds here a challenge to the readers "to embrace and welcome diversity and relationships with others" not only for our own welfare but also for "the welfare of God's creation" (2000a, 223). This alternative will lead us, on the one hand, to a better understanding of others, and on the other hand, to clarify and give clear articulation to our own perspectives. It is very likely that Israel's creation faith in Gen 1:1—2:4*a* is a product of Israel's theological thinking during the Babylonian exile. If this is true, then it is also likely that it is Israel's interaction with the Babylonian culture and religion that led Israel to formulate a well-articulated creation doctrine and a worldview that is quite distinct from that of the Babylonians.

Jeremiah 29:11 is one of the often quoted verses in the OT. Many Christians have taken this verse to be a promise from God to each individual believer concerning God's special plans for his or her future. God's concern for the welfare of his people and their future is an undeniable truth in the Bible. However, v 11 needs to be understood in the larger context of Jeremiah's letter to the exiles and particularly in the more immediate context of vv 10-14.

Several things need to be noted as we hear vv 10-14 today. *First*, the present and future historical realities are planned and purposed by God, and they are part of his work of salvation that he intends to carry out among his people. God's plans for the people include both judgment and salvation; the destruction of the land, the exile of Judah, and the return of Judah to its land after seventy years are all planned and willed by God.

Second, shalom is the ultimate will or plan that God has for his people (***plans of peace;*** **plans to prosper you** in the NIV; v 11). This period of judgment, though it is an evil time, will not last forever. The future that God is shaping is a future of hope and peace. They do not need to fear evil or any harm. Though their evil actions resulted in their present predicament, the future that awaits them is not shaped by their past evil deeds but by the gracious activity of God on their behalf.

Third, the exile provides the opportunity for the people of God to pray and seek God with their whole heart, with a fully devoted and faithful heart. The God who promises to hear their prayer on behalf of the city of Babylon, the city of their captors, also promises to hear their prayer for their own needs. The call to prayer and seeking God comes at the end of a series of hopeful words that begin with an announcement of God's gracious words to a people under judgment. God announces to them his already planned gracious work on their behalf (vv 10-11) and then invites them to enter into a relationship characterized by spiritual renewal and total devotion to God. The promise of restoration in this text comes without any conditions. The exiled people are invited to enter into a relationship with God with a faithful heart at the present moment in history, while they are still in exile, while they are still passing through the days of judgment. Thus the possibility of finding God in exile in Babylon is asserted in vv 13-14. Thus on the one hand, God promises in vv 10-11 the return of the exiles (the end of judgment) when seventy years are completed. On the other hand, the people are asked to seek God with all their heart and pray so that God would hear their prayer and bring his promise to its fulfillment. This does not mean that if the people did not seek God and pray to him, he would be unable to do his will and purposes for them. Salvation is what God promises to his people. The text speaks loudly about God's commitment to fulfill that promise to those under judgment. Paul speaks of salvation as the work of God's grace, originating in the richness of God's mercy and love to those who are dead through their sins and trespasses (Eph 2:4-5).

"BUILD AND PLANT"

THE PROMISE OF RESTORATION (30:1—33:26)

Overview

Jeremiah 30—33 focuses on the theme of future hope and salvation. This section is often called Jeremiah's "Book of Hope," "Book of Consolation," "Book of Restoration," or "Book of Comfort." We find these chapters located between the oracles of judgment in the preceding sections of the book, and the narrative sections that deal with the destruction of Jerusalem and the beginning of the Babylonian exile of Judah (chs 39—40). In the present shape of the book, these chapters strongly convey the idea that Israel's salvation is already at work, even before the judgment words actually became a reality. Hope precedes judgment; in a real sense these chapters proclaim *grace that goes before* judgment (italics for emphasis).

Chapter 30 begins with Yahweh's command to Jeremiah to write down Yahweh's words in a book (30:2). Scholars think that the oracles in chs 30—31 make up the book of consolation proper. Poetic oracles dominate chs 30—31, except in 30:1-3, 8-9; 31:1, 23-29*a*, 30-34, 38-40. Scholars have given considerable attention to the so-called core materials (authentic preaching of Jeremiah) in chs 30—31. Some scholars limit the core materials to a few oracles, but most scholars consider most or all of the oracles in chs 30—31 as part of Jeremiah's preaching (see Keown, Scalise, and Smothers 1995, 84, for a summary of this issue).

Commentators in general think that materials in chs 30—31 were expanded to include the content of chs 32—33. Chapters 32—33 narrate the events that happened while Jeremiah was confined in the court of the guard in the royal palace shortly before the destruction of Jerusalem by the Babylonian army in 587 B.C. (32:1-3; 33:1). These chapters chronologically belong with ch 38, which places Jeremiah in the court of the guard (38:13, 28; see also 37:21). It is likely that chs 32—33 were added to chs 30—31 because of the emphasis on hope and restoration in these chapters. In the present arrangement the promise of the restoration of the "fortunes" of Israel and Judah in 30:3 and 33:26 serve as an inclusio or envelop around the materials in chs 30—33. These chapters thus begin and end with an emphasis on the theme of Judah/Israel's restoration (Lundbom, 2004a, 369; Miller 2001, 797).

A. Yahweh Promises to Restore Judah and Israel (30:1—31:40)

Overview

In the present form, the people of Israel and Judah are the primary subject of the oracles in ch 30 (see vv 3-4, 10, 18). In the LXX, the content of this chapter is found in 37:1-24. The LXX omits vv 10-11 and 22. Oracles in ch 30 contain both restoration (vv 1-3, 8-9, 10-11, 16-17, 18-22) and judgment themes (vv 4-7, 12-15, 22-23). The opening message of hope in vv 1-3 (in prose) is followed by a series of poetic oracles that continue through 31:22 (with the exception of 30:8-9, which is in prose). Lundbom thinks that 30:5—31:22 constitutes "the poetic core" of the Book of Comfort (he sees 30:8-9 as a prose addition; 2004a, 379). He also sees in this poetic core a careful chiastic arrangement of oracles that deal with the theme of judgment (30:5-7, 12-15, 23-24), hope (30:10-11, 16-17, 18-22), lament (31:15, 18-19), and promise (31:16-17, 20-22). At the center of this arrangement are two covenant formulas (30:22; 31:1) with a judgment oracle in the middle (30:23-24) (2004a, 379). The first judgment oracle contains a report (in the form of a lament by the prophet and the people) of the terror and anguish being expressed by the people (vv 4-7). Yahweh's word of hope (vv 1-3) is for the future, but the present reality is that of unbearable pain and agony for the people (vv 4-7). What good is hope for the people who do not see any escape from their present suffering? Yahweh responds to this lament with his solemn assurance that he will liberate his people from those who oppress them and that he will deliver them from their captivity (vv 8-9, 10-11). Though Yahweh promises restoration, he is, nonetheless, not detached from the present reality of the suffering of his people. In the next passage (vv 12-15) Yahweh laments about the incurable wound of his people and traces it to his punishment because of their sin. Yahweh, who laments the brokenness of his people, promises the judgment of the enemy of his people and the restoration of the health of his people (vv 16-17, 18-22). The chapter ends with the stark reminder, however, that what the people experience at the present moment is the devastating effect of the fierce tempest of Yahweh's judgment (vv 23-24).

Chapter 31 (ch 38 in the LXX) begins with the announcement of an eschatological covenant relationship between Yahweh and Israel (v 1). This is followed by an oracle that announces Yahweh's everlasting love and faithfulness to Israel and Israel's restoration and rebuilding (vv 2-6). This oracle also anticipates the people of the northern kingdom of Israel making pilgrimage to Zion/Jerusalem. Yahweh's gathering of his people from the various places he has scattered them and their joyous homecoming is the theme of vv 7-14. This oracle has many linguistic and thematic parallels to Isa 35:5-10; 40:11; 41:1, 5; 48:20; 58:11). Rachel's lament for her children and Yahweh's promise of the restoration of her children is the theme of Jer 31:15-17. Verses 18-19 convey the lament of Ephraim (northern kingdom of Israel). Yahweh responds to the lament with an announcement of his mercy to his dear son (v 20). Verses 21-22 contain a call to Israel to return from its wayward path. Judah's restoration is promised in vv 23-26. This is followed by another oracle that deals with the theme of the rebuilding of both Judah and Israel (vv 27-30). The restored nation receives the offer of a new covenant in vv 31-34. Verses 35-37 affirm Yahweh's enduring relationship with Israel. The oracles of consolation end with an eschatological promise of the rebuilding of Jerusalem as Yahweh's sacred city that will never again be uprooted (vv 38-40).

There is no consensus on the date of the oracles in chs 30—31. There seems to be an agreement among some scholars that the oracles that address Israel and anticipate the return of the exiles of northern Israel to their homeland originated in the early years of Jeremiah's ministry, during the period of the Josianic reformation (622-609 B.C.). However, the reference to the restoration of Judah suggests a date either immediately preceding the exile of 587 or soon after that event for the present shape of chs 30—31. It is possible, as some scholars suggest, that the earlier materials addressed to northern Israel in the context of Josiah's reformation were reshaped for Judah at the end of the prophet's career. Holladay prefers 588-587 B.C. for the final shaping of chs 30—31 (1989, 171). Lundbom favors a slightly later date, between 586 and 582 B.C., during the days when Jeremiah lived in Mizpah, among the people who were left in the land after the events of 587 B.C. (2004a, 378).

Some scholars have speculated on a later date for chs 30—31 because of their emphasis on hope and salvation, themes that are also found in Isa 40—55. There are also a number of parallels in language and thought between Jer 30—31 and Hosea. After an analysis of the verbal parallels between Jer 30—31 and Isa 40—55, and Jer 30—31 and Hosea, Lundbom concludes that influence of Hosea is clearly evident in these chapters, which is also evident in the early chapters of Jeremiah. He concludes that it is more likely that the writer of Isa 40—55 drew inspiration from Jeremiah, and not the reverse (2004a, 371-75; see also Holladay 1989, 156). Lundbom also notes that expressions in chs 30—31 are also found in other parts of Jeremiah, which in turn points us in the direction of Jeremianic authorship of the oracles in these chapters (2004a, 375; see Keown, Scalise, and Smothers for a list of verbal links between chs 30—31 and the rest of the book arranged under four categories [1995, 80]).

1. Write in a Book (30:1-3)

BEHIND THE TEXT

The Book of Consolation begins with prose introduction that announces Yahweh's future activity of restoring Israel and Judah to their homeland (30:1-3). Verse 1 introduces the content of chs 30—31 as Yahweh's word that came to Jeremiah. Chapters 32 and 33 each has its own introductory statements (see 32:1; 33:1). Verse 2 contains Yahweh's command to Jeremiah to write down Yahweh's words in a book. Verse 3 sums up the message of the book that Jeremiah was commanded to write (chs 30—31). This verse announces an eschatological event—Yahweh's activity to restore Israel and Judah to the land of their ancestors. Taken together, vv 1-3 function as the thematic introduction to what is presently the Book of Consolation (chs 30—33).

IN THE TEXT

■ **1-2** Following a customary introduction (v 1), the text opens with Yahweh's command to Jeremiah to **write in a book all the words** that Yahweh has spoken to him (v 2). The content of the book is not specified. **All the words** may be taken here to mean the prophecies we find in chs 30—31. The words are from **Yahweh the God of Israel.** The covenant God of Israel is the speaker; the words are directed to the covenant people Israel.

There is no clear purpose given for the writing of Yahweh's words in 30:2. It is obvious from the next verse (v 3) that the words are not judgment words but rather words of hope and restoration. Thus, the implied purpose of this book is to offer hope for Israel in exile—hope in their future return to their homeland.

■ **3** Yahweh's promise is stated in v 3. The phrase ***behold,*** **days are coming** is a frequently found phrase in the book (7:32; 9:25; 16:14; 19:6; 23:5, 7; 30:3; 31:27, 31, 38; 33:14; 48:12; 49:2; 51:47, 52). This phrase points to the future when Yahweh's promise will be realized in the history of his people. No specific time is given. Yahweh's promise is that in the days to come he will ***restore the fortunes*** of his people. ***And I will restore the fortunes*** (*wĕšabtî ʾetšĕbût*) conveys the central theme of chs 30—33 (see similar expressions in 29:14; 30:18; 31:23; 32:44; 33:7, 11, 26). Most recent translations translate this phrase as "I will restore the fortunes," though *šĕbût* (from *šbh*, meaning "to take captive") could also mean "captives." See Lundbom, who prefers the reading "I will restore the fortunes," for a detailed discussion of this expression (2004a, 355, 377). The NIV reading (**I will bring my people Israel and Judah back from captivity**) paraphrases the MT. Most commentators see here a reference to the national treasures that were taken out of the land as war spoils by the enemy nations. However, *šĕbût* in 30:3 and in 33:7 seems to have a broader meaning than simply material properties taken out of the land by the enemy. In these texts, where the theme of the repossession of the land and rebuilding of the people in the land immediately follows, the ***fortunes*** include the captives or the exiled people of Israel and Judah. The exiled people are considered in these texts as part of the national treasure of Israel and Judah. Yahweh still regards Israel and Judah as **my people,** his covenant nation. The phrase **Yahweh said** is yet another reminder that the promise comes from the covenant God of the people.

The second part of v 3 contains Yahweh's promise that he will bring the exiled people of Israel and Judah back to the land of their ancestors. *I will restore them to the land I gave their forefathers and they will take possession of it* further indicates that the exiled people are part of the "fortunes" that Yahweh plans to restore to the land. This restoration means Yahweh's faithful keeping of the promise of the land to the ancestors (see references to the gift of the land to the ancestors in 3:18; 7:7, 14; 11:5; 16:15; 24:10; 25:5; 32:22; 35:15; see also Gen 15:18-20). The exiled people who have temporarily lost their homeland will once again take possession of it. Yahweh's restoration will make it possible for the nation to reclaim their lost inheritance. The text is reminiscent of the taking possession of the land by those who were saved by Yahweh from their exile in Egypt in a previous era. "The restoration to the land," according to Brueggemann, "is the central, quintessential hope of the Jeremiah tradition, and much of the Bible." He goes on to say that "this tradition of hope knows that in the real world, no people or community will have dignity, security, respect, or well-being unless it has guaranteed land" (1998, 272). The text also anticipates the coming together of the nation as a whole, just as their **forefathers** took possession of the land under the leadership of Joshua.

FROM THE TEXT

God's words written in the book of Jeremiah (the written word—Scripture) are not only for the Judeans in exile but also for all who encounter these words in the days to come. What is written in a book/scroll is expected to have long life and be available for future generations. The inscribed words provide further testimony to the reliability of God's promises. The original recipients of the book of Jeremiah would have found in these words God's unwavering resolve to bring his exiled people to their home, the land of promise, and an invitation to live their life in exile in hopeful expectation of the fulfillment of God's promises.

This text also clearly conveys the truth that salvation is clearly the work of God. He promises salvation and guarantees its fulfillment. It is God's resolve to mend what was broken through human sin; it is his will to restore those who are alienated from him. Exile is not what God wills for his people or for the world. The good news in this text is that God authorizes and makes possible new life for those who live in exile and deathly circumstances of life. Contemporary readers of this text find here hope for their salvation in the continued resolve of God to *"gather up* all things" in Christ, "things in heaven and things on earth" (Eph 1:10 NRSV, emphasis added).

The homecoming of the exiled people of God is a key issue in this text and in chs 30—33 in general. The reference to the land in v 3 indicates that God is intensely concerned about the need for all human beings to be connected to a home and a land that they can call as their home and land. The land promised to the ancestors of Israel has a special focus in the OT. However, that does not mean that God is not concerned about the material well-being of others in the world or of their need for a home and a land. A home or a land is God's gift to a people. Every human being has a God-given place in this world. The promise of this text about God's plan to bring the exiles to their homeland needs to be heard in the context of the experience of millions of people in the world who are homeless, who have been forced out of their homes or lands by other human beings. When we rejoice with the Jewish people of our day who have returned and have reunited with their land after centuries of life away from that land, we also need to be intensely concerned about the Palestinians who have lived in that same land and have lost their home, when the Jews returned. God's intention is to fulfill the yearning of all people for a home. Therefore, it is critical that the church become a mediating force in the dialogue between Jews and Palestinians concerning the rights of each group to exist in the land, which they both call their home.

2. Comfort to Those Who Mourn (30:4-7, 8-11)

BEHIND THE TEXT

The hope conveyed in the prose introduction to the Book of Consolation is followed by a poetic unit (vv 4-7), the main theme of which is the distress and agony of Israel, which is the outcome of Yahweh's judgment. Verse 4 seems to function as an introduction to the oracles in chs 30—31. This poetic oracle is further introduced by a messenger formula (**For thus said Yahweh,** v 5*a*). This seems to suggest that the first person speaker in this poem (**I see;** v 6) is Yahweh (so Holladay 1989, 167). However, the first person plural form in v 5 (***we have heard***) implies more than one person as speakers here. Fretheim suggests that the voice here is that of the divine council, and he finds here God taking the lament and distress of his people and making them his own (2002, 416). Lundbom thinks that the prophet is expressing here the anguish of the nation that is being defeated by the enemy (2004a, 382). It is likely that the speaker here is the prophet who is conveying Yahweh's grief because of what he sees and hears in the land. In the book of Jeremiah, the lament of Yahweh and the lament of the prophet are seldom distinguishable. ***We have heard*** could thus refer to both Yahweh and the prophet. What they see and hear move them to enter into the midst of the suffering of the people. Yahweh not only enters into the very life of the people under distress but also offers them a word of hope and deliverance from their present trouble (v 7; **but he will be saved**).

Verses 8-11 continue the deliverance theme introduced in the last line of v 7. Verses 10-11 are a near duplication of 46:27-28. The LXX omits vv 10-11. Verses 8-9 are in prose [see NRSV] and the poetic section resumes in v 10. Verses 8, 10, and 11 all have the "oracle of Yahweh" introduction. There are two oracles of salvation in this unit; vv 8-9 with the theme of the liberated Israel serving Yahweh and the Davidic king, and vv 10-11 with its promise of Yahweh's salvation to Israel and Israel's return to their land. Verse 11 also includes a word about the judgment of the nations and Israel's judgment as Yahweh's just punishment of his people. Lundbom argues that vv 8-9 are a subsequent addition to the poetic section of chs 30—31 and that they break the continuity between vv 5-7 and vv 10-11. He views the salvation oracles in vv 10-11 as the response to the lament in vv 5-7, following the pattern found in the psalms, and thus serving a liturgical function (2004a, 387). Though this is possible, there is no need to view vv 8-9 as a later insertion. Verses 8-9 serve an appropriate function in the present literary setting. This salvation oracle introduces the theme of hope by announcing another **that day,** the day of salvation, in contrast to "that day," the Day of Judgment in vv 5-7.

These oracles (vv 4-7, 8-11) belong to the period immediately before the events of 587 B.C. In the present form, the oracles address both northern Israel that is already in exile and Judah that is about to go into captivity.

IN THE TEXT

■ **4** This introduction to chs 30—31 shows that the words of hope in these chapters are given to both Israel and Judah. The northern kingdom people lost their land and their statehood in 722 B.C. through the Assyrian invasion. The survivors of that nation have been scattered into various parts of the former Assyrian Empire. The southern kingdom people are now being faced with a similar destiny through the invasion of the Babylonians. In the present form of these chapters, the people of both kingdoms hear Yahweh's words, though originally at least some of the oracles may have been addressed to the people of Judah. The opening phrase, **These are the words,** is similar to the introduction to Jeremiah's letter (29:1; see also Deut 1:1).

■ **5** Yahweh's words are introduced with the typical messenger formula (***thus said Yahweh***). The messenger formula is followed by a lament of Yahweh and ***the prophet (we have heard) over the distress, anguish, and fear that they see*** in the land. What they hear in the land is ***a sound of trembling,*** cry of panic and fear, coming from the people who are being invaded by a ruthless enemy. What the people are experiencing is **terror** (*paḥad*) within their hearts, which comes as the consequence of their covenant disobedience (see "the terror [*paḥad*] that will fill your hearts" [Deut 28:67]). The prophet (and Yahweh) do not see any evidence of **peace** (*šālôm*) in the land. There is no experience of well-being and wholeness for the nation. **Peace** is Yahweh's gift and blessing to his people for their covenant obedience and faithful life (Num 6:26). The absence of peace in the land is not caused by the enemy invasion but is the direct result of the covenant breaking way of life (Deut 28:15-68). Yahweh has withdrawn his peace from his recalcitrant people. The people acknowledge elsewhere that they look for peace and a time of healing, but what they find instead is terror (Jer 8:15; 14:19).

■ **6** Verse 6 begins with a directive to someone; the identity of the individual to whom the directive is given is not needed because what follows is a rhetorical question. **Ask . . . see** imply that everyone knows the answer to the question that follows (**Can a man bear *a child*?**). It is utterly impossible for a man to give birth to a child. But what the prophet sees in the land is **every strong man** (*geber*) in the land with **his hands on his *loins*** (*ḥălāṣayim*; see the NIV "waists" in Isa 32:11). Lundbom thinks that *geber* refers to the soldiers who are fighting to defend Jerusalem (2004a, 384). It could also be a general reference to all the strong individuals in the land who have lost their courage and strength. The metaphor of every strong man in agony **like a woman in labor** conveys the intensity of the pain and distress of the nation (see this imagery in Isa 13:8; 21:3). There is hope for a woman in labor, because she will soon give birth and her agony will be over. But what is the hope for a man in labor? Since a man cannot give birth, his agony will continue. There will be no end to his pain; there will be no birthing and no new life. Fretheim sees in this unlikely metaphor of "men in labor" a deeper meaning. The people cannot make their future happen; "only God is able to bring a new generation of people to birth" (2002, 417). **Every face turned deathly pale** further describes the weak and feeble condition of the population. The look of death is on the face of all the people because of the terror and pain caused by the enemy invasion.

■ **7** Verse 7 begins with a ***woe*** statement (***Woel For great is that day***) and ends with an announcement of salvation to Israel. Prophets usually utilize the ***woe*** (*hôy*) utterance to convey the threat of an impending disaster and utter ruin. Verse 7 seems to mix the language of utter destruction with that of lament. The destruction that the enemy will cause will be terrible and it will be unlike any other destruction Israel suffered in the past. **That day** implies the Day of Yahweh (though "that day" in v 8 refers to a future day of salvation for Israel). Israel's prophets, beginning with Amos, spoke of the Day of Yahweh as the day of his judgment of Israel (Amos 5:18-20). It is unlikely that the northern kingdom people would have been among the original recipients of this oracle since the day of Yahweh's judgment had already come for that nation in 722 B.C. The reference here is most likely to the impending destruction of Jerusalem and the exile of the nation. That day will **be a time of trouble** (‛*et ṣārâ*) **for Jacob.** Wartime will bring distressing conditions, pain and agony, the absence of well-being, and exile into a foreign land. **Jacob,** though this name usually refers to the entire covenant nation, perhaps means here the people of Judah, since it is this part of the covenant nation that is now being faced with distressing conditions because of the Babylonian invasion. The **time of trouble** also includes the coming days of Judah's exile in Babylon.

Verse 7 ends with a word of salvation to Judah. Most commentators see this as a word of promise to Judah that Yahweh will save Judah from its present time of trouble. There is no need to read into this text the promise of an immediate deliverance, since it is not part of Jeremiah's message elsewhere in the book, and since no deliverance took place in 587 B.C. Lundbom agrees with Holladay's suggestion that originally this was a question ("and from it shall he be saved?") to which the answer was no. Jacob/Judah will not be delivered from the impending days of destruction (Lundbom 2004a, 385; see Holladay 1989, 150, 172). However, it is not unusual for laments in the Psalms or judgment words in the Prophets to end with a note of hope. **He shall be saved from it** most likely refers to the future restoration of Israel from the Babylonian domination and the exile of the nation, and therefore, it should not be treated as parallel to the promise of Jerusalem's deliverance in Isa 37:33-37. This promise is consistent with the overarching restoration theme in the Book of Consolation.

■ **8** Though "that day" (v 7) will bring a terrible time of distress for Israel, Yahweh announces to his people that there is yet another **that day** that he plans for them (v 8). The promise of this day, which expands on the promise in v 7 ("He shall be rescued from it" [NRSV]), comes from **Yahweh Sebaoth,** the sovereign Lord of the whole universe and all the powers in it. He has all the resources available to him to make this promise a reality. Events of **that day** (v 8) will indicate the reversal of the judgment of "that day" in vv 5-7. No other specific information or time table is given concerning that day, except that it will be a day of Yahweh's activity to bring salvation to Israel. On that future day, Yahweh will bring an end to Israel's servitude to other nations. **I will break** and (I) **will tear off** indicate Yahweh's direct involvement in the liberation of his people. Israel's **yoke** and **bonds**—the symbols of political servitude and bondage to other nations—will be broken. It is Yahweh who placed

Judah under the yoke of Babylon (27:2-15); now, it is again Yahweh who promises to break the yoke of Babylon from the neck of Judah (**his yoke from upon your neck and your bonds;** the NIV, **I will break the yoke off their necks and will tear off their bonds,** follows the LXX). Over a century earlier, Isaiah prophesied that Yahweh would break the yoke of Assyria from the neck of Judah (Isa 10:27). Nahum made a similar prophecy that Yahweh would break off the yoke and bonds of Assyria, which happened when the Assyrian Empire collapsed in 612 B.C. with the destruction of its capital city Nineveh. Yahweh's breaking of the Babylonian yoke also means that **strangers** (*zārîm*) or foreign nations will no longer be able to make Israel a servant nation.

■ **9** The end of Israel's political bondage (and bondage to foreign gods) means they will be free to **serve** (*ʿbd*) **Yahweh their God.** Yahweh will liberate them from the bondage to their political suzerains; their loyalty to foreigners will end. However, this does not mean that they will become an autonomous people. The nation's status as a slave remains, except that it will have a new master. In reality, it is a return to the old master with whom the nation had made a covenant long ago. Restoration of the Sinai covenant is implied here. Their servitude to Yahweh will be different from that of foreign political powers. There will no longer be oppression and suffering, but praise and worship and faithful and obedient life under the terms of the covenant.

In the days of restoration, Israel will also serve **David their king.** Serving the king conveys the idea of submission to the authority of the king and allegiance to his rule. **David their king** also conveys the prophet's hope that in the future an individual from the Davidic house will assume the throne of David, a king who in all essential attributes and qualities will be David to his people. The final phrase, **whom I will raise up for them,** clearly indicates that the restoration of the Davidic line and the restoration of Yahweh's covenant with David are clearly Yahweh's work. The nation that is now faced with the reality of the end of monarchy and the end of the royal line hears a gracious word of hope that the curse pronounced on Jehoiachin will be reversed (see 22:30).

■ **10** Verses 10 and 11 are oracles addressed directly to Jacob/Israel (see the repetition of these verses in 46:27-28). In the present context, both northern Israel and southern Judah hear this message. **Do not fear** is often found in the Bible as a word of salvation and reassurance. In some theophany accounts, God or an angel speaks this word to reassure those who are bewildered by their supernatural encounter with God (see Gen 15:1; 21:17; Matt 28:5; Luke 1:30). This is also found as a word of salvation to those who cry out to God in their deep distress (Lam 3:57). Isaiah often uses this word to announce salvation and to reassure those in exile that God is with them (41:10, 13, 14; 43:1, 5; 44:2).

In v 10, Yahweh addresses Jacob/Israel, whom Yahweh has promised to deliver from his foreign oppressors so that he may serve Yahweh (see v 9), as **my servant** (*ʿabdî*). Israel as Yahweh's servant is a metaphor developed out of Yahweh's covenant with Israel at Mount Sinai. It is important to note that even in the midst of judgment the servant status of Israel has not changed. Yahweh calls Israel his servant in spite of its long history of failure to live and carry out the task as servant of Yahweh (Fretheim 2002, 419). **Do not be dismayed** is another reassuring word. **Jacob** and **Israel** are interchangeable names for the whole nation, though Judah may have been the original audience of this speech. Yahweh promises to **save** Jacob/Israel from a **distant place,** which is **the land of their exile.** For the people of Judah, this means the land of Babylon. The focus of the promise here is the salvation of the **descendants** of Jacob/Israel. There is no hope given for an immediate return from the exile. The promise here is for a future generation. Verse 10 ends with the promise that ***Jacob shall return*** (šāb from šûb, meaning "to return") home from the land of exile. The goal of Yahweh's action is not only the salvation of his people and the end of their exile but also their life in their homeland in peaceful conditions. The exiled nation shall be ***at rest*** (ša'ănan from š'n, meaning "rest," "be quiet," "be at ease") in its homeland. Life in the land will be peaceful and secure. In the past, Israel existed in fear and dread of the nations, but in the days of restoration, **no one will *cause terror*** to the people that Yahweh liberated from their captivity.

■ 11 Verse 11 begins as a salvation oracle addressed to Jacob/Israel (**I am with you *to deliver you***) but its focus shifts to the judgment of the nations. The nation that is given the word about days of distress now hears a gracious word about Yahweh's presence. Judgment does not mean the withdrawal of Yahweh's presence. "I am with you" is the solemn promise that Yahweh gave to Jeremiah at the time of his call (1:8). This word of assurance comes not only to the prophet who was given the words of judgment to speak to Israel but also to Israel that hears the word of judgment. Just as Yahweh will deliver his prophet from his enemies, he will deliver his people who experience his judgment from their enemies.

Yahweh's salvation of Jacob/Israel also means the judgment of the nations. The language of making a ***full end of* all the nations** is hyperbole. Certainly, it is not the total annihilation of the population that is meant here. Perhaps this refers to the end of the nations' domination over Israel and the end of their political existence and power in the world. The doublet of 30:10-11 in 46:27-28 is preceded by a judgment word against Egypt (46:25-26). However, Egypt is also promised a future with a repopulation of the land "as in the days of old" (v 26 NRSV). See also 48:47 and 49:6, 39 for words about the fortunes of Moab, Ammon, and Elam. The nations that are destined to suffer Yahweh's judgment are not identified specifically, but only as the nations among which Israel has been scattered by Yahweh's judgment. The events of 587 B.C. resulted not only in the exile of Judah to Babylon but also in the scattering of the population to Egypt and other neighboring nations. ***But I will not make a full end of you*** introduces Yahweh's favorable attitude to Israel. Though Israel will suffer judgment, this will not lead to its complete destruction (see also 4:27; 5:10,

18). There will be a remnant left for Israel. Should Israel be completely destroyed, then there would be no future for Israel. That means the end of every relationship and every covenant that Yahweh established—with Abraham, with Israel at Sinai, and with David. Verse 11 ends with a modified view of Yahweh's judgment on Israel. The goal of Yahweh's judgment is not total annihilation of his people, but **discipline . . . with justice.** Judgment thus has an instructional purpose (*yāsar* means "to reprove," "discipline," etc.). Yahweh will carry out his judgment with restraint and compassion, and not with an outburst of anger. Yahweh's demand for justice requires him to punish Israel for its sins; there is no escape for Israel from punishment. **I will not let you go entirely unpunished** conveys Yahweh's resolve to punish his disobedient people.

FROM THE TEXT

God and the prophet who voice grief in vv 5-7 are not detached from the distress and agony of the community under God's judgment. Through this lament, both God and the prophet identify with the people who are afraid and live in terror, who have no peace, and who have lost all strength. Judgment and salvation are not arbitrary arrangements that God makes without any emotional involvement. Divine judgment brings grief to God, and he takes upon himself the agony and pain of those who suffer under his judgment. This divine participation with human suffering is at the center of God's promise of help and deliverance we find in v 7b (**he shall be saved from it**). This text reveals the God who enters into the thick of life, into terrifying situations human beings face in their everyday life, and offers hope in the midst of a dismal future.

Verses 8-9 convey a historical-political reality as well as the religious and spiritual outcome of God's salvation work he plans to carry out on behalf of the people of Judah/Israel. God promises to break the yoke from their neck and save them from their bondage to Babylon. This promised salvation is parallel to the salvation Israel's ancestors experienced long ago when they were slaves to the pharaoh of Egypt. God announces freedom to his people and calls them to have no fear, though they are living under terrifying conditions. The nation that is in panic and despair hears the good news of God's presence and resolve to save them. Deliverance from bondage, whatever type of bondage it may be, is God's will for humanity. Jesus' proclamation of the gospel includes "release to the captives" and freedom to the "oppressed" (Luke 4:18-19).

An important reminder of the text is that both judgment and salvation are the work of God. The One who chastises his people is the One who also offers them his presence and his salvation (v 11). The text thus interprets the present realities of Judah's pain and suffering and its coming exile to Babylon (and the suffering of the northern Israel during the Assyrian invasion in 722 B.C.) as Yahweh's just and fair punishment for their sins against him. The text makes clear that sin will not go unpunished. However, punishment of sin is not the end of the story. Those who hear the word of punishment also hear the word of God's gracious presence and the promise of salvation. The good news of salvation comes to those who are deeply aware of their predicament. The word they need to hear is not more condemnation of sin, but rather word of grace and hope. That is precisely the task of preaching the gospel today.

Verse 11 refers to a peculiar way of God's dealing with nations, Babylon in particular here in the present context, in contrast to God's dealing with Israel. God will visit both Israel and the nations to bring his judgment upon them. God announces the end of the nations. But Israel is told that he will not bring it to an end. The nations that acted violently and ruthlessly in the world and particularly against Israel will come to an end. However, Israel, the people oppressed and enslaved by other nations, will continue to exist. In the sixth-century situation, no one would have imagined the end of the mighty Babylonian empire, and no one would have thought that Judah will survive its days of calamity and destruction brought upon it by Babylon. God reverses that situation and announces the end of the powerful Babylon and the survival of the vulnerable Judah. God who speaks in this text is the God who turns "topsy-turvy" the "normal run of the world affairs" (Fretheim 2002, 419). He brings down "the powerful from their thrones" and lifts up "the lowly," and fills "the hungry with good things" and sends "the rich away empty" (Luke 1:52-53 NRSV).

3. I Will Heal You (30:12-17)

BEHIND THE TEXT

There are two short poems in this unit. The first poem describes the brokenness and pain of Judah (vv 12-15). In the second poem, Yahweh promises healing to Judah (vv 16-17). Some commentators treat these two as separate units. There is thematic continuity between the two poems. The overall theme of these verses is Yahweh's offer of healing to the nation that suffers incurable pain. This condition is caused by Yahweh who has struck the nation with a severe blow because of its numerous sins. Holladay views vv 12-15 as originally spoken to northern Israel that was destroyed by the Assyrians in 722 B.C. (1989, 156). The language of the poem fits with the broken condition of northern Israel. However, this may have been a freshly composed poem to convey the realities that southern Judah faced around 587 B.C. The language of vv 12-15 is similar to that of 8:21; 10:19; 14:17. Jeremiah 30:17 specifically refers to Zion. What is being said about Judah is also applicable to northern Israel and vice versa.

IN THE TEXT

■ 12 The poem begins with a messenger formula. Yahweh is the speaker. The addressees are not identified. The second person address implies Judah as the recipient of this word. **Incurable** (*'ānûš*, meaning "desperate," "incurable," "desperately wicked," "very sick," etc.) and **beyond healing** (*naḥlâ*, meaning "sick," "diseased," etc.) describe the desperately sick condition of Judah. These two words are paired together here to show the intensely hopeless condition of Judah. Judah's sickness is **beyond healing** by any human agency, but later in v 17, it is presented as healable by Yahweh. The words **your wound** (*šeber*, meaning "brokenness," "shattering," etc.) and **your injury** (*makkâ*, meaning "blow," "strike") are also paired together to show the intensity of pain and hurt inflicted on the nation (see the use of these words in 10:19 to describe Jeremiah's brokenness, and in 14:17 to describe the brokenness of Judah). The imagery in this verse portrays someone who has "sustained a vicious—perhaps mortal—blow and lies in a helpless state" (Lundbom 2004a, 395).

■ **13** Verse 13 continues the portrait of the hopeless condition of Judah. **There is no one to plead your cause** (lit., "there is none to judge your judgment") suggests the absence of anyone who would come forward and argue for an impartial judicial hearing of the case of this severely wounded and dying nation. Taking the vocabulary of brokenness and blow as conditions that necessitate proper medical judgment, Lundbom translates this as "there is none to diagnose your case of a sore" (2004a, 395). Whether we have here reference to the lack of a medical professional or of legal help, the issue here is that of the abandoned state of Judah. The nation lies without help, with **no remedy** for its **sore**, and without any hope of **healing** for its incurable wound. Healing from this deathly condition could only come from Yahweh, who is the healer of his people (30:17; 33:6; Exod 15:26; Ps 103:3). On the one hand, Yahweh is the One who inflicts this severe wound on Judah. That means no offer of healing is immediately available to Judah. On the other hand, healing will come to this dying nation. We find Yahweh's promise of healing in v 17.

■ **14** The first half of v 14 deals with Judah's abandonment by all of its *lovers* (*mě'ăhăbayik*). In Hos 2:5, 7, 10, 12, and 13, "lovers" refer to Baals, other gods that Israel worshipped. Most likely the reference here in Jeremiah is to Judah's political allies (see 22:20, 22; also Ezek 16:33, 36, 37). **All your *lovers* have forgotten you** because you (Judah) have forgotten Yahweh. In this dire situation, when Jerusalem is on the verge of being destroyed by Babylon, there is no help for Judah from any of her allies. No particular nation is mentioned. The nations that sent envoys to Jerusalem in 594 B.C. (27:3) have forgotten Judah. Egypt seems to be the only nation that extended help to Judah. In 588 B.C. during the initial stage of the Babylonian siege of Jerusalem, the Egyptian army came to help and the Babylonians withdrew for a short period (37:5). However, the Babylonians returned shortly to Jerusalem and there was no more help from Egypt. **They care nothing for you** because they are concerned about their own survival in the face of the rising power of Babylon.

The second part of v 14 gives the reason for the incurable wound of Judah and its abandoned state. The One who inflicts the vicious blow on Judah is Yahweh, the real **enemy** of the nation. The force of Yahweh's striking of Judah is like that of an enemy's attack. The goal of the enemy is to kill and not to spare. Judah is mortally wounded by the powerful strike of Yahweh. This is **punishment** (*mûsār* also means "correction," "discipline," etc.; see v 11 above for the verb form *yāsar*) from Yahweh. And it is severe in that it comes from a **cruel** enemy (***punishment of a* cruel** one). Though Nebuchadnezzar is the political enemy of Judah, he and Babylon remain in the background. What is taking place in Judah's history is the intense experience of Yahweh's judgment, which he mediates through the agency of Babylon. The reason for this cruel treatment of his people by Yahweh is clear. The ***iniquity*** of Judah is great and its **sins** are numerous. Yahweh's punishment, though it is portrayed using the language of an enemy's actions and cruelty, is not whimsical and arbitrary. Punishment is Yahweh's just response to those who have broken the covenant.

■ **15** This verse is lacking in the LXX. The first part of the verse is a rhetorical question addressed to the nation that is lamenting over its ***brokenness*** and ***incurable*** pain. Yahweh's question **why** does not seek an answer from the addressees; the answer is obvious, and the nation should know the reason for its present predicament. Judah's **cry** over its **wound** and **pain** indicates the lament of the nation in 587 B.C. The question implies that a guilty nation that receives equitable punishment for its sins has no reason to cry out in complaint to Yahweh or to anyone else. However, in the second part of the verse, Yahweh answers his own question and gives the reason for the brokenness and incurable pain of Judah. This condition is caused by Yahweh (**I have done these things to you**). What prompted Yahweh to bring pain and suffering to Judah is the multitude of Judah's ***iniquity*** and **sins**. Judah is suffering the consequence of its own actions. The intensity of its pain is matched only by the immensity of its sins. It is punishment well deserved, and no one else is to be blamed. ***Because your iniquity is great and your sins are numerous*** are words also found in v 14.

■ **16** There is sudden shift in v 16. The focus here is on the destiny of the enemies of Judah, who devour and plunder Judah. ***Therefore*** (*lākēn*) at the beginning of v 17 is difficult because in the Prophets this phrase usually introduces a judgment word preceded by an indictment. Here this phrase seems to follow what is stated in v 15. However, it is unlikely that Yahweh's judgment on Judah is the reason for his judgment on Judah's enemies. The NIV **but** is an attempt to remedy the ambiguity in the Hebrew text. All the nations that are being deployed by Yahweh to devour, plunder, and send Judah into captivity will face the same destiny. The consolation to Judah is that Yahweh is a fair and just God. In the end, the tables will be turned and the enemies of Judah also will be punished. The judgment on Babylon is most likely intended here.

■ **17** Verse 17 makes explicit Yahweh's consolation to Judah. Yahweh who inflicted wound and pain on Judah promises to bring ***healing*** to the nation in this verse. This promise of healing conveys compassion and comfort as Yahweh's gracious overture to his people under his judgment. **I will *heal* you** is the promise of Israel's healer. The nation refused to come to its healer (8:22), but here Yahweh the healer of his people offers to come to them with his healing. The reason clause (***because they have called you . . .***) suggests that the taunt of the enemies is what motivates Yahweh to heal and restore the health of his people. The enemies of Judah taunt and ridicule Zion by calling it an **outcast** and a forsaken city (**Zion for whom no one cares**). The verdict of the enemies is that even Yahweh has abandoned Zion, his chosen city and the place of his dwelling. The words of the enemies intensify the utterly helpless and lonely condition of Judah. But it is not the only motivation for Yahweh to act on behalf his helpless people. Healing the wounded, caring for the helpless, rescuing the abandoned are essential aspects of Yahweh's response to those who cannot help themselves. The promise of Zion's healing is also Yahweh's response to those who mock at her ruined state.

FROM THE TEXT

This text is filled with images of a seriously wounded and hurt, unhealed and uncared for individual who suffered a near mortal blow from a vicious attacker and is abandoned and left alone to die. Moreover, passersby do not offer any help but simply pronounce the verdict that the victim is an outcast who cannot expect help from anyone. The text makes it amply clear that the victim is not an innocent being who is under attack for no good reason. There is no one to blame for this incurable and helpless situation; the victim is told who caused this suffering and the reason for this suffering. Through vivid imagery, Israel is told that its present suffering is punishment for its numerous sins against God. The text then shifts to the judgment of the enemies whom God used as the agency of his punishment of his people. They will be judged with the very same judgment that came upon Israel. Their words of taunt of the people of God motivate God to restore the health and heal the wound of his people.

Brueggemann suggests that the verdict of the nations is what evokes God's "caring solidarity" with his condemned people. He goes on to say that "in the bottom of Israel's terrible humiliation before the nations, Yahweh found depths of love for Israel about which Yahweh did not heretofore know." Brueggemann calls it "Yahweh's transformed attitude and inclination" toward the hurt people of Judah (1998, 277-78). One cannot say that God suddenly found within himself the capacity to love or a reservoir of love he had that he did not know about previous to this verdict of the enemies of Judah. In Jeremiah's theology, both judgment and salvation, wounding and healing, come from the God who loves his people "with an everlasting love" (31:3). The promise of Israel's building and planting, which is rooted in God's love for his people, is at the center of Jeremiah's perspective of the future that lies beyond the days of Israel's uprooting and destruction (cf 1:10; see Fretheim 2002,

421). This text reiterates Israel's understanding of God as the healer of his people; he promises to heal not only the wound others have caused but also the wounds he himself inflicted on Israel (vv 15, 17; see also 3:22; 17:14; 33:6; Exod 15:26; Isa 30:26; 53:5; 57:17-19; Hos 6:1; 11:3; 14:4; Pss 30:2; 103:2-3; 147:2-3; Job 5:18). Jeremiah 30:17 affirms God's deep resolve to heal the wounded, help the helpless, rescue the abandoned, deliver the oppressed, and uplift the lowly and mocked. The promise, **I will *heal* you,** originates in God's love for the uncared for and the unattended. In the Christian gospel, the cross is the revelation of that love of God through Jesus Christ, who himself was rejected, wounded, ridiculed, and left to die a lonely death. The resurrection of Jesus Christ is the triumph of God's love and the hope for the healing of the broken and sinful world.

The healing God offers in this text and elsewhere in Jeremiah is the physical, material, and spiritual restoration of his people. It is also individual and communal in scope. We need to recognize in this promise of healing, the need for healing from the damaging effect of sin, God's willingness to forgive sins, and also the promise of God's deliverance from the power of sin. Healing that is being offered here is thus holistic. God's concern is for the total well-being of his people, both individuals and the community. This healing from God is essential for the enjoyment of true shalom.

4. A City Shall Be Built on Its Mound (30:18-22)

BEHIND THE TEXT

The promise of the total restoration of all things in this text follows the promise of healing in the preceding oracle. The oracle begins with a messenger formula (**For thus said Yahweh**). Most likely v 21 ended the oracle in its original form (see **the oracle of Yahweh** formula at the end of v 21). Commentators take v 22 as an editorial addition by the compiler of the Book of Consolation (Lundbom 2004a, 403). The shift from third person address in vv 18-21 to second person plural address in v 22 suggests that v 22 may not have been part of the original oracle. Verse 22 is lacking in the LXX, but the LXX omission does not justify the deletion of this verse, which in the present context completes the message of total restoration. Restoration of the fortunes of Israel and rebuilding of a city and a citadel suggests a period immediately following the destruction of Jerusalem in 587 B.C. as the possible date of this oracle of salvation. Verse 21 speaks of a ruler who will enjoy a special relationship with Yahweh. Some commentators place this text in the postexilic period. Many others attribute this oracle to Jeremiah. Holladay thinks it was originally addressed to northern Israel during the days of Josianic reformation (Holladay 1989, 156, 176). Most likely this oracle belongs to a period immediately after the events of 587 B.C. The people of Judah in exile hear in this oracle what life will be like in the days of restoration. Everything that has been lost will be restored, including their broken covenant with Yahweh.

IN THE TEXT

■ **18** The oracle begins with the promise from Yahweh that he will **restore the fortunes of Jacob's tents** (see 30:3). Yahweh promises in vv 18-21 his direct involvement in the total restoration of his people and the rebuilding of their life (**I will restore . . . have compassion,** etc.). As in 30:3, the reference here most likely includes both physical properties as well as human lives that were taken to Babylon as war spoils. **Jacob** in this context probably refers to Judah, though it has the broader meaning that includes northern Israel. **Jacob's tents** and **his dwellings** are the same. The promise here is that all that belongs to Jacob that the enemy has taken will be restored. Moreover, Yahweh also promises to have **compassion** on the ruined dwelling places of the people of Judah. The promise of restoration includes the rebuilding of the houses destroyed by the enemy.

The restoration promise also includes the building of *a* **city** and *a* ***citadel.*** Commentators view these indefinite nouns as collective nouns, thus referring to cities and citadels in general. The NIV treats them as definite nouns (**the city . . . the palace**) and assumes that the reference is to Jerusalem and to the royal palace. The text here speaks of building *a* **city** *on its mound* (*tēl*). A **mound** or "tell" is an artificial hill formed by the heap of rubble left when cities were destroyed by invading forces or by natural calamities. New occupants built their cities on the ruins left from a previous occupation. It is not unusual to find several layers of occupation in a "tell" in the ancient Near East, which gives evidence of various groups that occupied that location over a long period of time. The promise here concerns the building of the city of Jerusalem on its ruins. That means the city will be built on its very same location before it was destroyed and made a ruin by the Babylonians. Verse 18 ends with the promise that *a* **citadel** (*'armôn* also means "palace," "fortress," etc.) **will stand in its proper place.** The LXX reads here *naos* ("temple"; *templum* in the Vulgate; temple, according to the medieval Jewish commentator Rashi). The reference here may be to all the great buildings, including the palace and the temple, in Jerusalem that suffered destruction in 587 B.C. (52:13). The promise here is that they will be built again in their rightful places where they stood before they were destroyed by the Babylonians. Yahweh's intent is to restore the nation to its former state of glory.

■ **19** Verse 19 anticipates the return of normal life in Judah. When dwellings, cities, and citadels are rebuilt, **songs of thanksgiving and the sound of rejoicing** will be heard in them. The people who return from their exile will express their gratitude to Yahweh with songs of thanksgiving, the most appropriate response to Yahweh's deliverance of his people. Dwellings and cities where the sound of cry and pain was once heard will become places of joy and celebration. Yahweh also promises to multiply their number. The nation that has lost most of its population as victims of war and famine now hears echoes of the creation promise and of the promise to their great ancestor (***I will multiply them;*** see Gen 1:28; 17:2; also Hos 1:10; Jer 23:3; Ezek 36:10-11; Isa 54:1-3). Yahweh's plan is to make them a great nation, a nation with **honor** and significance in the world.

■ **20** The first line of v 20 speaks of the sons of Jacob (***his sons***) assuming their former state, like they were **in days of old** or in the ancient times. This line seems to continue the idea of their honor and significance mentioned in v 19. Perhaps the idea here is that Judah/Israel will return to the days of glory and honor in the world, which it enjoyed during the reign of David and Solomon. The second line seems to imply the restoration of Israel as a worshipping community (***His assembly* will be established before me**). The destruction of the temple and the exile brought an end to Israel's privilege to stand before Yahweh as a worshipping congregation. This promise implies the rebuilding of the temple and the restoration of worship in Jerusalem. Verse 20 ends with Yahweh's promise to **punish *all his oppressors;*** i.e., those who oppress Judah/Israel.

■ **21** The focus of v 21 is on a future ruler of Israel. The text probably originated in the context of the end of monarchy in 587 B.C. The people who are faced with an uncertain future because of the Babylonian domination hear in this verse the word of hope that **one of their own** will rise up as **their ruler** in the days to come. Two terms are used here to describe this ruler. The first word (*'adîr*) means a ***majestic one*** and the second word (*mōšēl*) means a **ruler.** Lundbom thinks that Jeremiah intentionally omits the term "king" (*melek*) here because the term has been tarnished by Jehoiakim and Zedekiah, the last kings to rule Judah (2004a, 408). He also suggests that the prophet's thinking may have been dominated by the idea that Yahweh is the only real King of Israel (8:19; 10:7, 10; 46:18; 48:15; 51:57) (2004a, 408). However, the text here seems to imply an anointed one, a messianic individual from the line of David (von Rad 1965, 218-19).

The second part of v 21 emphasizes the special relationship between Yahweh and the future ruler of Israel. **I will bring him near and he will *draw near* to me** conveys this ruler's privileged access to Yahweh. Yahweh promises to take the action to bring this ruler to his presence, and the ruler likewise will take the initiative to draw near to Yahweh. Yahweh's statement here echoes Moses' response to Korah and the Levites who challenged the priestly privilege of Moses and Aaron and claimed that everyone in Israel is holy. According to Num 16:5, it is Yahweh who chooses the one "who will be allowed to approach" Yahweh to carry out the priestly task (NRSV). The phrase **I will bring him near and he will *draw near* to me** suggests that the coming ruler will also have a priestly role. Commentators see in this statement an allusion to the priest-king idea, which received further development in the postexilic period (see the crowning of Joshua the high priest as ruler in Zech 6:11-13). Though the picture of a priest-king idea may be drawn from this text, it is more likely that the text deals with the special relationship between Yahweh and this coming ruler. Von Rad suggests that the text here conveys "a specific privilege at court," his "right of free access" to Yahweh (1965, 219). Verse 21 ends with the question, **for who is he who will *pledge his heart to approach* me?** The exact meaning of this question is not clear. The language of pledging one's heart as surety reflects the practice of "the deposit of a pledge or the giving of security" in the legal setting (ibid.). This rhetorical question suggests that though Yahweh will bring the ruler to his presence, the initiative of the ruler to approach Yahweh means to risk his life. According to von Rad, the question implies that "access on the part of the anointed one to Jahweh is only possible on the condition that he yields up his life" (ibid.). Von Rad, who also considers this text as a messianic prediction, says that in Jeremiah's view "the most important thing is that the anointed one risks his life, and in this way holds open access to God in the most personal terms possible" (ibid.). Jeremiah may be thinking here of the traditional belief that no one shall see God face-to-face and live (Exod 33:20; see the warning given to the people in Exod 19:21-25; also Judg 6:22-23).

■ **22** This verse sums up the goal of Yahweh's restoration activities outlined in vv 18-21. The covenant that has been broken by the people will be restored by Yahweh. **My people . . . your God** emphasizes Israel as Yahweh's special possession and Yahweh as Israel's only God (Lev 26:12; cf. Exod 19:5-6; Deut 7:6; see Jer 11:4; 24:7; 30:22; 31:1, 33; 32:38). The covenant promise comes without any conditions. Yahweh simply promises the restoration of the covenant relationship. All other promises concerning the future (vv 18-21) revolve around this promise of a restored relationship between Yahweh and his people. This gracious offer from Yahweh serves as a guarantee to the exiled Israel that it will have a future with rebuilt cities and citadels in its homeland, worship and joyous national and community life, and a ruler who will have open access to Yahweh.

FROM THE TEXT

The exilic readers of this text would have found in this text God's promise of new world that is clearly the opposite of their present world of chaos and disorder, despair and hopelessness, alienation from the homeland and from God, and exile and death sentence. Further, they would have found the God who speaks in this text as the source of their hope for life in a new and better world being promised here. The world that awaits them is a world that offers them new possibilities of relationship with God and true enjoyment of individual and communal life and well-being (shalom).

Contemporary readers of this text encounter in this hope-filled word from God a call to trust in God who is able to make all things new. The gospel of Jesus Christ, God's Anointed One, who yielded his life on the cross so that humanity, too, can have open access to God, proclaims newness with its promise of "release to the captives and recovery of sight to the blind," freedom to "the oppressed," and the freedom of the Jubilee Year (Luke 4:18-19 NRSV; see Isa 61:1-4). Entrance into the kingdom of God, according to the Gospels, is in reality the beginning of new life in the new and better world of God that exists through God's new covenant established through Jesus Christ. Moreover, this new world of God with all its possibilities and promises is open to all who wish to move beyond their present existence in despair and hopelessness and experience newness of life.

5. The Tempest of Yahweh (30:23-24)

BEHIND THE TEXT

Except for some minor variations, this poem is a near duplicate of 23:19-20. This judgment word, along with other judgment words (30:5-7, 11*b*, 12-15), disrupts the theme of hope in ch 30. This poem originally was spoken as a word of judgment on the people who subscribed to the message of false prophets (23:19-20). In ch 23, the poem announces what the prophet has seen and heard in the divine council as Yahweh's judgment words on the wicked. Its placement here following a powerful word of hope and the promise of restoration does create some confusion and difficulty of interpretation. Some commentators see here the reuse and fresh interpretation of an oracle originally pronounced in the context of false prophecy now in the context of the destruction of Judah and the exile of the nation to Babylon, and in the new theological context of the promise of hope and restoration of Judah. Thus they view these verses in ch 30 exilic in origin and as Yahweh's judgment word aimed to the enemy nations, particularly the Babylonians (Brueggemann 1998, 279; Fretheim 2002, 424). Another possibility is that this poem may have been reused by the prophet himself or by an editor in the context of the Babylonian invasion of Judah in 587 B.C. The Judean people who refused to pay attention to the prophetic words of Jeremiah are being reminded in these verses that the storm they are in is the direct outcome of their trust in the words of their false prophets. This is the storm of Yahweh on the wicked. The current events indicate that his prophecy is being fulfilled; the storm of Yahweh is indeed sweeping through the land to bring destruction of the wicked.

IN THE TEXT

■ **23** The poem reminds the people of Judah that the **storm of Yahweh,** a tornado-like whirling wind (*sa'ar*) that brings the destruction of the wicked is *sweeping* (*mitgôrēr; mithôlēl* in 23:19) through the land and it **whirls upon the head** of the wicked. In 25:32 Jeremiah describes the Babylonian army as "a mighty storm" (*sa'ar*) that is "rising from the ends of the earth." The storm imagery conveys intensity of the **wrath** of Yahweh against the wicked. The **wicked** (*rĕšā'îm*) are not specifically identified here. In 23:19-20, most likely the people of Judah are the wicked who will experience the storm of Yahweh's wrath (although some commentators think the wicked there are the false prophets, since 23:18-22 as a whole is about the false prophet; see 25:31 where the "wicked" [*rĕšā'îm*] are the nations). Here in 30:23 the reference is most likely to the wicked people of Judah upon whom the tempest of Yahweh's wrath is swirling.

■ **24** What the nation experiences is the **fierce anger of Yahweh** (*ḥărôn* [meaning "fierce," "burning"] is lacking in 23:20) that is bursting out like a destructive storm. It will **not turn back** until it has accomplished its purpose. It is already being unleashed against the wicked, and it will bring about their destruction. **Until *it* fully accomplishes the purposes of his heart** indicates the certainty of Yahweh's plans and his intention to carry out his words of judgment (see a similar statement about the power and efficacy of Yahweh's word in Isa 55:10-11). When Jeremiah originally spoke these words immediately before or during the Babylonian invasion of Judah in 587 B.C. the people would not have fully grasped the purposes of Yahweh's heart or his will. Instead, they would have raised questions as to why Yahweh has abandoned his people and his city during this dangerous time in their history. The prophet announces that **in days to come,** after Yahweh has fully executed his wrath, the people will **understand** the plans of his heart (**you will understand it**). Verse 24 lacks the word "understanding" (*bînâ*), which is in 23:20 (23:20 literally reads: "you will understand in it understanding," which in the NIV is "you will understand it clearly"). The post-587 B.C. community that hears this word is living through the days of judgment. They hear in this word a challenge to understand their present condition as the outcome of their wickedness. Thus in the midst of words of comfort, the prophet does not gloss over the present conditions of the wickedness of the people and the reality of Yahweh's judgment of the wicked. However, they are also told that their future is secure in the plans and purposes of Yahweh, though now they do not fully comprehend the meaning of the historical realities of their day.

FROM THE TEXT

Interpretation of this text that deals with the judgment of Judah hinges on our understanding of its relation to the oracles of comfort in chs 30—33. Soothing words alone cannot bring comfort and hope to those who experience pain and agony in their life. The first question people ask when they suffer is not how or from where or when or from whom they would receive comfort but why suffering has come to them. They want to know the reason for their suffering, especially when conditions or the context of their suffering do not make much sense. The prophet, though his primary goal is to convey hope and comfort in ch 30 to those who are faced with the impending destruction of their land and their exile into a foreign land, mingles his words of comfort with the reality of God's judgment (see also vv 3-7, 11*b*, and 12-15 for the words in judgment in ch 30). He fully recognizes the fact that the people are incapable of fully understanding the truth about God's plans and purposes because of the fearful and desperate conditions in which they live. They presently live in a world of God's judgment, the effect of which would have been the real life experience of the exilic readers of this text. Jeremiah's objective in this text is to persuade the Judean community to believe in the truth that God's plan is not to destroy them as he executes his anger because of their wickedness, but to fully restore them. But until that day of restoration comes, the people who are faced with God's judgment will have to wait patiently and live through the days of their suffering with trust in the good purposes of God for them. When the day of restoration comes, then they will be able to understand the full scope of God's actions—both his judgment and his salvific plans. In the meantime, they must walk by faith though they do not clearly see the intent of God's actions. Modern readers of this text should use caution when interpreting the words, **in the days to come, you will understand this.** The text here speaks clearly about understanding the salvific purpose of God's judgment. It does not mean that we will be able to fully comprehend at some later time the purpose of all the difficult and tragic situations that we may encounter in life. However, the text challenges us to live in confident trust "that all things work together for good for those who love God, who are called according to his purpose" (Rom 8:28 NRSV).

6. The Promise of Grace in the Wilderness (31:1-6)

BEHIND THE TEXT

In v 1, Yahweh offers his covenant relationship to the entire nation of Israel. Verses 2-6 are introduced with a messenger formula, but it seems that Jeremiah is the speaker in vv 2-3*a* (*From a distant place Yahweh appeared to me*). It is possible that vv 2-6 were originally addressed to northern Israel to announce the salvation of its exiled people (see v 4). Verse 5 implies the ruined condition of Samaria. The oracle ends with the anticipation of the people of northern Israel making pilgrimage to Zion. Most commentators place vv 2-6 in the early part of Jeremiah's ministry, and some connect it with Josianic reform and the centralization of worship in Jerusalem, perhaps around 622 B.C. (Bright 1965, 284). Lundbom suggests that v 1 was attached later, perhaps after 586 B.C., to give the hope to both Israel and Judah that all the tribes of Israel would once again be Yahweh's people and that Yahweh would be their covenant God (2004a, 419).

IN THE TEXT

■ **I** Verse 1 begins with reference to an unspecified time in the future (**at that time**) as the time when Yahweh will be God to all the ***tribes*** (*mišpĕḥôt*) of Israel and they will be a **people** (*'am*) who belong to Yahweh (**my people**). **I will be the God of all the clans of Israel, and they will be my people** is the promise of a covenant, and this promise is for the future. The covenant formula here and elsewhere in Jeremiah (7:23; 11:4; 24:7; 30:22) painfully reveals the truth that Israel exists without this relationship in its contemporary history. The promise is given to both the northern tribes and the people of Judah in the south. Brueggemann sees in this language Yahweh's loyalty to Israel and the process of gathering and unifying "separated and scattered small social units of Israelites to form them into one viable community" (1998, 282). Once before in Israel's past history Yahweh formed them as a people through his election and covenant with them when they existed without a national, political, or religious identity. The promise here is that Yahweh will again do what he did for Israel in Egypt when he "formed a new people out of disparate and hopeless social units" (ibid.). The phrase **at that time** clearly points out that the relationship that Yahweh promises to establish between himself and Israel is an eschatological event. At some point in the history of Israel, Yahweh will reestablish his covenant, which was broken by Israel. This action by Yahweh will usher in a new epoch in Israel's history in which the nation will enjoy a new beginning in its relationship with Yahweh. Verses 31-34 outline how Yahweh intends to fulfill this promise.

■ **2** This verse begins with the announcement that ***a people found grace*** (*ḥēn*) ***in the wilderness.*** Though this verse is introduced by a messenger formula (***Thus said Yahweh***), it is not clear here that Yahweh is the speaker. Lundbom thinks Jeremiah is the speaker in v 2 (2004a, 412). In the original setting of this oracle, the ***survivors of*** the sword probably meant the northern kingdom people who have been exiled into various parts of the Assyrian Empire. The Judean exiles in Babylon who have heard this oracle would have included themselves among the ***survivors of*** the sword. ***Grace*** (*ḥēn*) is Yahweh's gift; it is free and unmerited. The reference to the ***survivors of*** the sword emphasizes the truth that the people are indeed unworthy. They are in the ***wilderness*** and not in the Promised Land. Though Israel's devotion to Yahweh in the wilderness is mentioned in 2:2, references to wilderness as they related to Judah/Israel, for the most part, are found in the context of the sin of the nation or Yahweh's judgment of the nation (2:6, 24; 3:2; 4:11; 12:12; 13:24; 22:6; 23:10). Besides 2:2, 31:2 is the only other place in Jeremiah where the wilderness imagery conveys a constructive relationship between Yahweh and

Israel. "Wilderness" in 31:2 (NRSV) most likely is an image of the exile of the nation in Babylon, though it echoes the wilderness journey of the ancestors of Israel. In its past history, Israel escaped the sword of the army of the Pharaoh of Egypt and Yahweh brought them into the wilderness where he cared for them and sustained them with his gracious provisions (Exod 14—18). The sword in this text is the sword of the enemy, which in reality is the sword of Yahweh's judgment. Thus it is Yahweh's judgment that drove the nation into their wilderness existence. However, he promises to the nation his **grace;** they will share in the experience of their ancestors who also found Yahweh's grace in the wilderness. This verse thus anticipates the end of their exile and the beginning of their journey back in to their homeland.

The last line of v 2 is ambiguous. The Hebrew literally is ***walking/going to his rest*** (*rāgaʿ*) ***[is] Israel***. The subject seems to be Israel, and it appears at the end of the sentence. In the context of the preceding line, it would then mean that the people (Israel) who found Yahweh's grace in the wilderness are now on their way to their place of rest, which is their homeland. The NIV reads God as the subject here (**I will come to give rest to Israel**) and sees here the promise that God will give rest to Israel. The language of this verse has some parallel to Exod 33:13-14 where Moses asks Yahweh to show him Yahweh's ways so that he may know for sure that he has found "grace" (*ḥēn*) in the sight of Yahweh. Yahweh responds by saying that his presence will go with Moses and that he will give Moses "rest" (*nûaḥ*). In Deut 12:8-10, Israel's "rest" (*nûaḥ*) is its safety and protection from enemies that Yahweh offers to them in the Promised Land. The land is thus the land of rest in the ancient Israelite tradition. Israel's walk to its **rest** in v 2 is its journey to its homeland from the land of its exile, and it is being made possible by the favor/grace of Yahweh that it finds in the wilderness.

■ **3** Verse 3 begins with Jeremiah's announcement of Yahweh's appearance to him (**to me;** the NIV translates the MT singular as plural [**to us**], and assumes Israel as the speaker here). Though *mērāḥôq* can be translated as either "far off" or "long ago," the context here favors **far off**, thus implying a distant location and not a distant past as the NIV reading **in the past** suggests. The prophet seems to be referring to a revelation he received that announces Yahweh's love for Israel. The prophet speaks of Yahweh as a God "far off" (*mērāḥôq*) in 23:23. **Far off** here probably refers to Yahweh's dwelling place in heaven. The word that the prophet receives through revelation is that Yahweh has **loved** (*ʾahăbâ*) Israel with an **everlasting love** (*ʾahăbat ʿôlām*). This verse seems to be in tension with Jeremiah's message of Israel's sin and covenant breaking, and Yahweh's judgment of the nation and the termination of his covenant relation with Israel (Brueggemann 1998, 283). Though this tension is real and cannot be resolved, this verse implies that even in the midst of Israel's sin, and even when the covenant relationship between Yahweh and Israel was severed, and even in the midst of his judgment of Israel, Yahweh loved and continues to love Israel with his everlasting love. Yahweh's heart was broken by Israel's sin and covenant breaking, but his undying love for Israel is the source of hope for Israel's future. **I have drawn you with *covenant faithfulness*** (*ḥesed* also can be translated as "loving-kindness," "steadfast love," "covenant loyalty," etc.) reiterates the ongoing commitment of Yahweh to Israel. In addition to loving Israel with an everlasting love, Yahweh also draws Israel toward him with his *ḥesed*, his covenant loyalty and faithfulness to his people. Yahweh's love and faithfulness to Israel continue "by virtue of its drawing power" (Lundbom 2004a, 416). Brueggemann sees in this text Jeremiah who "lives very close to the heart of God's own heart." He goes on to say, "It is God's heart made visible here which gives Israel a new chance in the future" (1998, 283).

■ **4** Twice in v 4 and once in v 5 the prophet utilizes the word **again** (*ʿôd*) to indicate Yahweh's rebuilding and restoration of Israel following a total disruption of all the various aspects of community life, including agricultural activities, music, dancing, and merrymaking by the people. Yahweh begins his speech in v 4; **Virgin Israel** (*bĕtûlat yiśrāʾēl*) is the addressee. **Virgin** is a personification of the nation Israel. It implies that the nation has not yet reached its full potential; the future of Israel is not yet fully realized. It is still a young nation. Commentators think that the reference here is to northern Israel but later applied to the whole nation after the Babylonian exile. The nation suffered a tragic destruction while it was very young, and there was no hope for its future (see Amos 5:2 where the prophet offers a funeral song for the fallen virgin Israel with no one to raise her up). Yahweh promises to **build** the virgin Israel that is fallen and left without hope. She will be married and she will become a mother. The rebuilding of the nation Israel and its ruined cities and its increase in population is probably what is meant here (see Ezek 36:36). The rest of v 4 indicates the restoration of community life in the land. The imagery of a woman ***playing*** her **tambourine** and going out ***in the dance of those who laugh*** suggests the return of singing and dancing in the land, which ended when enemies invaded and destroyed the land and took the people into captivity (see Lam 5:15).

■ **5** Verse 5 indicates that this oracle was originally addressed to northern Israel. **Samaria,** the capital city of northern Israel, was located on a mountain and surrounded by mountains. These mountains, which were once inhabited but made desolate by the Assyrians, will be populated again. Farmers will plant vineyards in terraces on the slopes of the mountains of Samaria and the ruined places will become productive again. Planting vineyards and enjoying their fruit is a sign of restful life in peaceful time. Farmers will pursue their activities without fear of the enemy invading and consuming the fruit of their labor. This is a reversal of the covenant curses mentioned in Deut 28:30.

■ **6** Verse 6 anticipates the arrival of a future time (**there will be a day**) when pilgrims from northern Israel will make their way to Zion to worship Yahweh in the temple in Jerusalem. **The hills of Ephraim** stand for northern Israel.

Ephraim is often a substitute name for northern Israel in Hosea. **Watchmen** (*nōṣĕrîm*) will stand on elevated places in the land and call the people to begin their pilgrimage to Zion (see Ps 122:1). This verse suggests the end of worship in the local shrines in northern Israel and the recognition of Zion/Jerusalem as the only legitimate place of worship in Israel. Commentators see here Jeremiah's support for Josiah's effort to centralize worship in Jerusalem by destroying the altar at Bethel and the places of worship in Samaria (see 2 Kgs 23:15-20). The object of worship is **Yahweh our God.** Northern Israel will abandon its idolatry and Baal worship and confess Yahweh as their God. Jeremiah lays here the foundation of Israel's hope for its future—one undivided nation under one God with one place of worship.

FROM THE TEXT

This text speaks about God's grace, love, and covenant faithfulness that he extends to those who have walked away from their relationship with him. God's judgment of Israel and the loss of their land and life in exile in foreign lands did not mean an end to God's grace, love, and faithfulness to his people. They hear in this text the gospel—the good news of the possibility of experiencing God's grace, love, and faithfulness in their desperate and hopeless existence. The three times repeated **again** in this text is certainly good news for those who do not see any hope for their salvation, then and now. It is easy for us to accept grace, love, and faithfulness as God's way of relating to those who remain faithful to him. What about those who have broken their relationship with him and live in alienation from him? What about those who have refused to recognize and accept God's grace in their lives? Do they deserve God's continued gracious overtures toward them? The good news in this text is that God comes into the wilderness of our human existence with the announcement of his ***grace,*** **everlasting love,** and ***covenant faithfulness.*** The text reminds us that these are God's enduring attributes and thus the source of hope for all—sinners and saints alike. This text is a classic expression of the dynamic optimism of grace and the possibility of sinners to experience the joy of salvation and to sing the song of the redeemed. The text also reminds us that God in his grace, love, and faithfulness is the real builder of the lives of those who live a shattered and broken life.

7. With Weeping and Rejoicing They Shall Return (31:7-14)

BEHIND THE TEXT

This unit begins with a messenger formula, and with an imperative asking an unnamed group of people to proclaim and praise Yahweh and to make an urgent appeal to him to save his people (v 7). Yahweh responds to the appeal of the people and describes what he plans to do to restore Israel back to its homeland (vv 8-9). Verse 9 clearly indicates Ephraim/northern Israel as the object of Yahweh's restoration activity. The following verses (vv 10-14) contain Yahweh's word to the nations concerning his plan to restore Israel and their return to Zion. These verses begin with a call to hear Yahweh's word and ends with messenger formula (***oracle of Yahweh***). Yahweh's gathering of Israel is the theme of this oracle. In vv 10-11, the nations are charged to report to the people in distant coastlands Yahweh's gathering and redemption of Israel. Verses 12-13*a* describe in third person the joyous return of Israel to Zion and its satisfaction and joy over the abundance of grain, wine, oil, and livestock. Yahweh speaks in first person in vv 13*b*-14 promising joy, comfort, and satisfaction to both the priests and the people.

Some commentators keep vv 7-9 and vv 10-14 as separate units; however, they are treated here together because of their thematic continuity. The language of vv 7-14 has several parallels in Isa 40—55. This has led some commentators to assign vv 7-14 to the mid-late exilic or postexilic period. Lundbom suggests that these verses belong to Jeremiah and that any similarity to Isa 40—55 should be viewed as an adaptation of Jeremiah's language by the exilic writer of Isa 40—55 (2004a, 420). It is likely that Jeremiah's restoration oracle originally addressed to northern Israel in the days of Josiah in vv 7-9 would have been supplemented with words about the restoration of Judah (vv 10-14) either before or soon after the events of 587 B.C. It is not clear whether these verses have been later modified by the exilic community in Babylon to address their particular situation by incorporating into the words of Jeremiah the language of Isa 40—55. Though that possibility cannot be ruled out, it is highly unlikely that the exilic community would have distorted the original message of Jeremiah (Bright 1965, 285).

IN THE TEXT

■ **7** Five imperatives (***shout with joy, scream for joy, proclaim, praise, say,*** all in masculine plural) follow the messenger formula in v 7. It is not clear to whom these imperatives are addressed. Holladay thinks these imperatives are summons to heralds (1989, 170). Lundbom thinks Jeremiah is speaking to a "Judahite audience" (2004a, 426; see also, Brueggemann 1998, 284). Fretheim assumes these are addressed to all creation or more likely to those in Babylonian exile (2002, 430). It is equally possible to see here, as some commentators do, the nations as the addressees of these imperatives. If so, the nations are being asked here by the prophet to ***shout with joy*** for Jacob and to ***scream over the first of the*** nations (see vv 10-14, which begin with an announcement to the nations and a call to the nations to declare Yahweh's gathering of Israel to people on the distant coastlands). These parallel expressions convey the same meaning. The nations are to rejoice over Jacob in anticipation of what

Yahweh is about to do for his people. **Shout with joy** (*rānan*) is an expression often found in the psalms in the context of worship (see Pss 5:11; 33:1; 98:4; 132:9; 149:5). The verb *ṣāhal* means "scream" or "make a shrilling cry." Jeremiah also uses this verb to describe the "neighing" of horses (see 5:8; 8:16; 13:27). In v 7, *ṣāhal* is parallel to *rānan* and thus conveys the idea of screaming with joy (see also Isa 24:14). **Jacob** here more specifically refers to northern Israel (see the parallel "Ephraim" in v 9). The title ***first of the nations*** (*bĕrōʾš hag gôyim*) indicates the honorable place of Israel in the world. Amos sarcastically refers to the boastful claim of the aristocratic and wealthy citizens of Zion and Samaria as "the notables of the first of the nations" (*nĕqubê rēʾšît haggôyim*, 6:1 NRSV). Yahweh's salvation of Israel will restore its honorable place in the world as the first among the nations in the world. The nations are also being asked to ***proclaim*** and ***praise*** Yahweh to whom they are making the following urgent petition. The petition they are to make to Yahweh is this: **save your people, the remnant of Israel.** Some modern versions and commentators emend the text here to read "The LORD has saved his people" (RSV) based on the LXX reading (changing the MT imperative *hôšaʿ* ["save"] to a perfect form *hôšiaʿ* ["he has saved"] and the MT *ʿamměkā* ["your people"] to *ʿammô* ["his people"]). If we assume that the nations are making this petition, then it is best to retain the MT reading. The MT should be retained even if the petitioners are another group of people—perhaps Israel itself or the people of Judah. The appeal to Yahweh is to save his people, **the remnant of Israel** (*šĕʾērît yiśrāʾēl*).

The Remnant in Jeremiah

The remnant of Israel in 31:7 refers to the people of the northern tribes who have survived the military invasion and destruction of their land by the Assyrians in 722 B.C., those who are either left in the land or are living in exile in various parts of the Assyrian Empire. In 6:9 the "remnant of Israel" refers to the Judean population that was left as the survivors of the nation Israel after the Assyrians destroyed northern Israel in 722 B.C. In 40:11, 15, those who were left in the land under the leadership of Gedaliah, after the events of 587 B.C., are called the "remnant of Judah." Jeremiah also addresses the Judeans who escaped to Egypt after the murder of Gedaliah as the "remnant of Judah" (42:15, 19; 43:5; 44:12), though he did not give any hope for the future of this people. The future belonged to those who were exiled to Babylon (see 24:4-7; 29:10-14). In the oracles of consolation, the term is applied to all who have survived the deportations of 722 and 587 B.C.

■ **8** Yahweh responds favorably to the petition in v 8. He promises to **bring them**, the "remnant of Israel," **from the land of the north and gather them from the ends of the earth.** The land of the north refers in this context to Assyria, though after the Babylonian exile in 587 B.C. this would have also included Babylon. The reference to **the ends of the earth** does not mean a worldwide exile of Israel; it refers to the vast regions of the Assyrian Empire. No one will be left out in the lands of their exile from this saving activity of Yahweh. In his judgment Yahweh scattered his people (9:16; 13:24; 18:17), but in his salvation he promises that he will gather them (16:15; 23:3; 29:14; 32:37; see also Isa 43:5-6). The remnant that Yahweh gathers includes **the blind and the lame, expectant mothers and women in labor** (see Isa 40:11, 29-31). This group represents the most helpless and the most physically ill-fit to make the long walk from various parts of Assyria to the land of Israel. But they will be among those whom Yahweh gathers. No one will be left out. There is a hidden promise that Yahweh will give strength, care, and support to the weak and the ill-fit to travel with the rest on their homebound journey. Fretheim notes the lack of reference to the strong and the powerful and the elite in this list here. Though they will obviously be among the returning exiles, Fretheim sees in v 8 "a kind of democratization in the experience of deliverance" (2002, 431). The people that Yahweh gathers will be a **great** *assembly*. The picture here is that of a large crowd of people of all ages and physical conditions walking together on the road to their freedom. Yahweh's plan is to help them to **return** *here;* i.e., their homeland, where this oracle originates.

■ **9 Weeping** will be the response of the remnant of Israel as Yahweh gathers them to their homeland. It is likely that weeping refers to the repentance of the people, though it could also be a sign of their joy in the incredible experience of their salvation (Lundbom 2004a, 424). Fretheim introduces a plausible thought that weeping refers to the mourning of the people for those who were killed during the war (2002, 431). *I will lead them with supplications (favor)* seems to convey the idea that the people whom Yahweh gathers will make supplications to him to show their repentance, or that he will lead the people whom he gathers with his favor. The NIV **they will pray as I bring them back** is a paraphrase. The LXX reading "in comfort" or "in encouragement" (*en paraklēsi;* MT *bĕtaḥănûnîm* from *taḥănûn,* which means "supplication," "favor," "supplication for favor") conveys Yahweh's response of comfort or encouragement to the people who weep as they come home. Some commentators prefer the meaning conveyed by the LXX reading, which seems to make better sense. If we follow this interpretation, then comfort along the way (which is Yahweh's favor) is the response of Yahweh to the people who make their journey with weeping (repentance).

Yahweh also promises to bring the exiles to **streams of water.** Lundbom takes this to mean the Promised Land, which is described as a place with streams of water in Deut 8:7 (2004a, 425). This may simply be a metaphor in this text to convey the idea of constant nourishment along the journey. Unlike their ancestors who found no water in the wilderness when they came out of Egypt, the new exodus travelers will find streams of water all along their way (see Isa 41:18; 43:19-20; 44:3; 48:21; 49:10). Moreover, Yahweh will lead them **on a level path where they will not stumble** (see Isa 40:3-4; 42:16; 49:11). The

level path will provide a safe ground for "the blind and the lame, expectant mothers and women in labor" (v 8) to walk without fear of stumbling and falling down. However, it has significance for all those who return; the text indicates that their return journey will be free from the trouble and difficulty and dangers they faced when they were taken into the land of their exile.

Verse 9 ends with the reason for Yahweh's caring and comforting actions outlined in vv 8-9. These are the kinds of actions a father performs for his children. Yahweh claims that he is **like a father to Israel** and that **Ephraim is his firstborn son.** Ephraim here refers to northern Israel, and Jeremiah seems to be borrowing the imagery from Hos 11:1. This relationship is emphasized again in Jer 31:20. Father-son imagery describes Yahweh-Israel relationship in Deut 32:6 and Isa 1:2 (also Isa 63:16). Yahweh treats Ephraim as his firstborn son. In the Exodus tradition, the whole nation of Israel is Yahweh's firstborn son (Exod 4:22). Ephraim (or northern Israel), though it now constitutes only a part of the nation Israel, has not lost its status in the world as Yahweh's firstborn, a people with a special relationship with Yahweh. This is a privilege that the northern tribes share with the people of Judah from whom they have separated in 922 B.C.

■ **10** The unit begins with an imperative (**hear Yahweh's word**) directed to the **nations** (*gôyim*). This is followed by two more imperatives (**make known . . . and say**). The nations are being asked to declare in the **distant coastlands** what Yahweh is doing for Israel. Lundbom identifies the Greek Islands, Crete, and Phoenician colonies in the western Mediterranean as the distant coastlands (2004a, 428). In Isa 41:1 Yahweh's dispute is with coastlands, but in 42:4, the coastlands wait for his teaching or torah. In Isa 42:10, the prophet invites the people of the coastlands to sing praises to Yahweh. Here, in our text (v 10), the nations are being asked to proclaim in the coastlands Yahweh's gathering of Israel. **Israel** in this verse is most likely the northern tribes, though after 587 B.C., it would have included the exiled Judeans also. The nations in the world and all the inhabitants of the faraway islands need to know that it is Yahweh who has **scattered** Israel and it is he who will **gather** Israel. They need to know that Israel's dispersion in the Assyrian Empire was not the outcome of some geopolitical events, but that it was brought about by Yahweh as his judgment on Israel. At the same time, they also need to know that Yahweh's judgment on Israel does not mean the end of his relationship with that nation. He is still Israel's God, and he will bring his people back to their homeland. The nations are also asked to announce Yahweh's shepherd-like, watchful care and guidance of his **flock**—Israel. Israel was destroyed and scattered by the earthly rulers who were unfit shepherds of Yahweh's flock (see 23:1-2). Both northern Israel and southern Judah suffered judgment because of the irresponsible conduct of those who ruled these nations. The promise here concerns the northern people. In 23:3-4 this promise is given to the people of Judah.

■ 11 The nations are called to declare Yahweh's gathering of his flock (v 10), because it has already been accomplished by Yahweh. Verse 11 begins with a reason clause (*kî*). Yahweh has **ransomed** and he **redeemed Jacob from a hand** that is **stronger than his** hand—the hand of Jacob. **Ransomed** (*pādāh* means "ransom," "deliver," "rescue," etc.) and **redeemed** (*gā'al* means "redeem," "avenge" "ransom," "do the work of a kinsman," etc.) are in the perfect tense. In Jeremiah's thinking, Yahweh has already accomplished these actions (prophetic perfect); what Yahweh says is the same as what he does.

Yahweh the Redeemer of Israel

In Hebrew *pādāh* and *gā'al* are sometimes used interchangeably in the OT, since the outcome of these actions is the same. Both involve the idea of saving someone from a dire situation. The first term (*pādāh*) deals more with the act of deliverance or rescue (see Ps 25:22: "Redeem Israel, O God, out of all its troubles" [NRSV]). But the verb *gā'al* conveys a legal obligation an individual has to other members of his family or clan, such as avenging the murder of a kinsman, marrying the widow of a kinsman to perpetuate his family line, redeeming a relative from slavery, redeeming a relative's property, etc. This verb has its origin in the Exodus tradition. Yahweh redeemed (*gā'al*) Israel his firstborn from slavery (Exod 6:5; 15:13) and this redemptive activity of Yahweh has become the historical and theological basis for Israel's faith in Yahweh as its *gō'ēl* ("redeemer"; Pss 19:14; 78:35; Isa 41:14; 43:14; 44:6, 24; 47:4; 48:17; 49:7, 26; 54:5, 8; 59:20; 60:16; 63:16; Jer 50:34). Jeremiah sees the restoration of Israel to its homeland as Yahweh's redemption of Israel from its bondage to foreign political powers. The frequent reference to Yahweh as Israel's Redeemer in Isa 40—55 indicates the dominant influence of this idea during the Babylonian exile.

The exiles of northern Israel hear in this verse the promise of its redemption from Assyria. This promise comes from Yahweh, who redeemed their ancestors from the hand of Pharaoh. **A hand that is stronger than his** (Israel's) is the hand of Assyria. The power of Assyria was already beginning to decline with the rise of Babylon as a major political power when Jeremiah gave this oracle around 622 B.C. It is possible that this shift in world powers and the expectation of the downfall of Assyria would have given hope to the Judeans that the exiles of northern Israel would be returning home from the land of Assyria (Lundbom 2004a, 430).

■ 12 Verse 12 indicates that **Zion** will be the destination of the exiles who return home from the Assyrian lands. **Heights of Zion** implies the location of the temple in Jerusalem. The goal of the exiles' coming to Zion is to **shout for joy** or worship Yahweh who is their Redeemer. The rest of v 12 describes the **goodness of Yahweh** (*tûb yhwh*) over which the exiles will **rejoice** or **be radiant** (*nāhar* means "light," "burn," "flow," "stream"). Yahweh's goodness is his blessing upon his people, which is most evident in the abundance of **grain** . . .

wine . . . oil and increased **flocks and herds.** This experience of Yahweh's goodness means that northern Israel is no longer under the covenant curse (see Deut 28:47-51). Everything the people need for their existence will be given to them by Yahweh in abundance. The comparison of ***their soul*** (*napšām* from *nepeš*; in Hebrew, *nepeš* refers to the whole human being as a needy being (Wolff 1974, 10-25) to **a well-watered garden** suggests the well-being and satisfaction that the people will enjoy in their life. The final phrase, ***they shall not languish again,*** conveys the promise that Yahweh will meet all their needs in abundance and that they will never again faint or be weak.

■ **13** Verse 13 deals with the restoration of normal community life, in which there will be rejoicing and dancing and an end to sorrow and grief. A ***virgin*** (*bĕtûlâ*) dancing and rejoicing with ***young men*** and ***old men*** portrays a time of peace and well-being as well as a community where joy and happiness are characteristics at all times. Yahweh speaks in v 13*b* and promises to **turn their mourning** *to joy* and **comfort** *them* and ***make them joyful from their*** sorrow. Here again, the promise is for a reversal of all the sorrow and grief the people suffered when their land was invaded and they were taken to exile by the Assyrians. Yahweh is the One who brought upon them afflictions and sorrow. He will also be the One who will bring comfort and joy to them. Giving comfort (*nāḥam*) to his people is an important aspect of the divine nature of Yahweh (Ps 86:17; Isa 40:1; 49:13; 51:3).

■ **14** The oracle ends with Yahweh's promise of satisfaction and goodness to **the soul of the priests** and the **people.** *The soul of* the priests (*nepeš hakkōhănîm*) probably means the whole person. The priests are most likely priests in northern Israel who were among the exiled people. They were officials of the idolatrous worship in northern Israel and thus responsible for its moral and spiritual decay and consequently for the judgment that came upon that nation. They, too, shall receive the blessing of Yahweh. This verse thus anticipates their return to Jerusalem and becoming a part of the temple priesthood. The food for the priests came from the offerings that the people brought to the temple. Yahweh promises to satisfy the priests with ***fatness*** (*dāšen*), which most likely means an abundance of food, when they return to Jerusalem. Verse 14 ends with a promise to the people: ***my people with my goodness will be satisfied****.* The people of Yahweh will be satisfied with Yahweh's ***goodness*** (*ṭûb*), a reiteration of the theme in v 12.

FROM THE TEXT

This poetic unit in the Book of Comfort begins with the implicit theological claim that the nations have a special interest in the salvation and restoration of the remnant of Israel. They are called to sing and shout, praise God, and make petitions to God to save Israel (v 7). The second part of the text (vv 10-14) begins with a command to the nations to announce to the farthest part of the world that Yahweh's gathering of Israel is already taking place as a historical reality. The text assumes that the fulfillment of God's promise to bless all the families of the earth through Abraham (Gen 12:3) rests on God's restoration and salvation of Israel from its exile and their continued existence in the world as participants in God's plan of salvation and blessings for the whole world. Israel's comfort that is anticipated here may be seen as the prelude to the comfort of all the nations in the world. The prophet, by bringing the nations into this text as petitioners to God for Israel's comfort, and hearers of God's word about Israel's comfort, also shows the far-reaching and worldwide scope of God's comfort, which includes not only Israel but also the nations. This is also evident in God's promise that he will bring Israel **from the ends of the earth** (v 8). God who brings Israel from the ends of the earth is also the hope of the nations for their restoration and redemption.

The text also indicates that God's concern is also to gather and comfort all, including the weak, the helpless, and the powerless among his people. This far-reaching compassion of God does not exclude anyone but it is extended to the brokenhearted and those who live without hope in the world. God's goal is not to create an exclusive community of the strong and the powerful who would be the special mediators of his blessings to the world. Blessings to all the families of the earth would come through all of God's restored people; among them would be the blind and the lame—the physically and emotionally disabled—and the weak and the helpless. The people of God he gathers as the recipients of his gracious work of salvation are seen here as an inclusive community, a community in which all are welcome, regardless of their social standing or physical, mental, or emotional makeup. All participate in being the source of blessing and joy to the world. Moreover, the text portrays this community as a joyous community, in which songs of joy and gladness and praise will be heard at all levels of the community. Miller finds in this text the most "powerful or extravagant depiction of the Lord's future provision of the good of the people" and "an invitation to a party" that "goes on forever," "a marvelous party, where all are gathered before the Lord to enjoy all the benefits of God's goodness and celebrate in joy and singing and dancing" (2001, 815).

The Gospel of Luke portrays the community that gathered around Jesus as a community made up of the marginalized people, a people who rejoice not only in God's grace that is at work in their lives but also in God's grace that is at work in the lives of others (10:17-20; 13:10-17; 15:3-7, 8-10, 11-32). In the lives of those exiles of Israel whom we encounter in this text of Jeremiah, in the lives of those whom we encounter in the Gospel stories, and in the lives of those who experience God's redemption through the hearing of the gospel today, God's comfort comes through his grace, and this grace is most triumphant in those who consider themselves as weak and powerless to do anything to save themselves from their broken and hopeless existence. Such recipients of grace respond with joy and praise, because they have done nothing to deserve grace, but they totally depend on the richness of God's mercy and favor for their redemption and restoration.

8. Yahweh Comforts Rachel and Ephraim (31:15-22)

BEHIND THE TEXT

Verses 15-22 seem to have three parts. Part one presents Rachel's lament (v 15) and Yahweh's response to Rachel (vv 16-17). Verses 15 and 16 begin with a messenger formula (***thus said Yahweh***); vv 16 and 17 contain the oracle of Yahweh formula. Lundbom finds in these verses two literary units (v 15; vv 16-17). Though these verses begin with a messenger formula (v 15), Yahweh is reporting the lament of Rachel that he hears in Ramah. Lundbom thinks it is Jeremiah who is hearing the lament of Rachel (2004a, 435; Bright 1965, 282). According to Fretheim, though Yahweh is describing what he is hearing in Ramah, the language of this lament comes from Yahweh, which in turn indicates his own deep involvement in the suffering of the people (2002, 434). The prophet is conveying this report to his audience in Judah. The context of Rachel's weeping would have been the Assyrian invasion and deportation of northern Israel in 722 B.C. However, the report of Yahweh indicates that this lament was still being heard at the time when the prophet conveyed it to his audience, about a hundred years later. Rachel's sons refer more directly to the tribes of Ephraim and Manasseh, sons of Joseph, and the tribe of Benjamin. Ironically, Ramah was a transit point for the Judeans who were being exiled to Babylon in 587 B.C. (Jer 40:1). A bitter lament also would have been heard among these exiles of Judah who were in fetters and waiting in Ramah to make their long journey to Babylon.

Part two presents Ephraim's lament and Yahweh's response (vv 18-20). Verse 18 begins with Yahweh's first person speech that he has heard the moaning of Ephraim; this is followed by a lengthy confession that comes from the mouth of Ephraim (vv 18-19). In v 20 Yahweh responds to Ephraim's lament. The language of v 20 echoes Hos 11:1, 8-9. Commentators attribute vv 18-20 to the early years of Jeremiah's preaching addressed to northern Israel.

Part three (vv 21-22) contains Yahweh's invitation to virgin Israel to return home. These verses could be treated as a separate unit from the preceding unit, which ends with Yahweh's speech concerning Ephraim. There is no messenger formula in vv 21-22; however, the prophet is conveying Yahweh's words to Israel, calling her to return and to put an end to her backsliding behavior. Virgin Israel here is most likely a reference to northern Israel and thus it is possible to see this oracle as Yahweh's word to northern Israel in exile, spoken by Jeremiah in the early years of his preaching (see 31:4; Holladay 1989, 158). Lundbom sees Judah as virgin Israel and places the oracle in the context of the exile of 597 or 587 B.C. This is also possible if we connect this unit to the following unit, which speaks about Judah's restoration (vv 23-26). However, most commentators see vv 21-22 as part of the oracle (vv 15-22) addressed to northern Israel.

IN THE TEXT

■ 15 Jeremiah, Yahweh's messenger, conveys the report of what Yahweh hears **in Ramah** (*bĕrāmâ*). Some scholars think that the MT *bĕrāma* should be translated as "on a height" (Holladay translates v 15*a* as "A voice on the height may be heard"; 1989, 153). They cite the absence of the definite article in the MT in support of this view. The place name Ramah occurs almost always in the MT, with the exception of 31:15 and Neh 11:32, with the definite article either as *hārāmâ* "(the) Ramah" (13 times) or as *bārāmâ* "in (the) Ramah" (12 times). The LXX reads it as a place name (*en Rama*), which is also the reading in Matt 2:18. Most recent commentators and translations read here the place name ("in Ramah"). The precise location of Ramah is not known; scholars identify it either with er-Ram (located about five miles north of Jerusalem) or Ramallah (located about eight miles north of Jerusalem) (Lundbom 2004a, 436).

The voice that is being heard in Ramah is a **voice** of **bitter weeping**, and this is the weeping of **Rachel** for **her sons.** Rachel, the favorite wife of Jacob, and the mother of Joseph and Benjamin, is one of the great mothers of Israel. According to Gen 35:16-21, Rachel experienced great pain and agony when she gave birth to her son, and as she was dying she named him Ben-oni, which means "Son of my sorrow" (Jacob called him *Binyamin* [Benjamin] which means "Son of the south" or "son of the right hand"). Jacob buried her at an unidentified location between Bethel and Ephrath (which is identified as Bethlehem). First Samuel 10:2 locates Rachel's tomb in the territory of Benjamin. However, the traditional site of Rachel's tomb is near Bethlehem about four miles south of Jerusalem in the territory of Judah (see Gen 35:16-20). Both 1 Sam 10:2 and Jer 31:15 connect Rachel's tomb with a location north of Jerusalem. **Her sons** most likely refer to the Joseph tribes (Ephraim and Manasseh, the two leading northern tribes). The portrayal of Rachel here is that of a mother who refuses **to be comforted** upon hearing the news of the death of all her children. Some commentators see here the spirit of Rachel haunting her tomb weeping for her children, the northern tribes who had been deported to Assyria in 722 B.C. (Bright 1965, 282). However, Rachel is here most likely a personification of all mothers in Israel, who are grieving over the tragic loss of their children (see Fretheim 2002, 434). **They are not** conveys the idea that there is none left among her sons who could offer her comfort; she is grieving also because the loss of her children means the end of her motherhood and the loss of any hope for the future of the nation. The exile of the northern tribes in 722 B.C. was most likely the original setting of this verse. The text suggests that the bitter weeping of Rachel is also being heard in

Ramah as the Judean exiles of 587 B.C. are waiting there for their long journey to Babylon (40:1). One can only imagine the intense grief of the Judean mothers as their children were either slaughtered or taken away to Babylon, and as they saw no hope for the future of Judah. In Matt 2:18, Rachel is presented as weeping again, this time over the slaughtered infants of Bethlehem. In this portrayal of Rachel by the Gospel writer, she represents all the bitterly weeping mothers of Bethlehem who have lost their infants to the cruel decree of massacre by Herod.

■ **16** Verses 16-17 contain Yahweh's response to Rachel. The one who refuses to be comforted is being told to **restrain** or hold back her **voice from weeping**. The verb here is in the imperative; this is not a command that comes without compassion. The goal of Yahweh's speech is to offer comfort to Rachel. The comfort comes in the form of a promise of a ***reward*** or wage for her ***labor***. Her ***labor*** probably is her endless weeping over her sons. **They will return** to their homeland **from the land of the enemy** (Babylon is intended here). This will be the ***reward*** for the intense labor of Rachel. Yahweh hears the cry of a heartbroken mother and offers comfort to her. She will see her sons whom she does not expect to see again. Fretheim suggests that the language of reward in v 16, when understood in terms of Isa 40:10; 62:11, and the imagery of the story of Jacob-Rachel in Gen 29—33, conveys the idea that "the children born to 'Rachel' in exile are her 'wages' for her time in Babylon; these children will come back from Babylon to Canaan" (2002, 435). The weeping Rachel in v 16 could also refer to the land that is grieving over the deported people. The comfort being offered to Rachel is comfort to the land that it shall be reunited with its lost children. This is Yahweh's gracious response to a weeping mother, and this offer is made without any preconditions, including the repentance of the people in exile.

■ **17** Yahweh continues his speech in v 17. Rachel is given **hope** in this verse for her **future**. Verse 15 implies an utterly hopeless condition—the complete removal of her sons from the land. Verse 17 reverses that condition. Yahweh promises that her sons who were removed from her will return and that they will be reunited with their land. Yahweh gives Rachel the future that she did not think existed.

■ **18** Yahweh reports that he has indeed **heard Ephraim's moaning.** This is parallel to Yahweh hearing the bitter weeping of Rachel in v 15. **Ephraim** represents northern Israel in general as it does in Hosea. The word **moaning** (an intensive form of the verb *nûd* here could mean "shaking of lips in intense lament"). Fretheim sees here the image of a "person shaking or rocking back and forth in grief over what happened" (2002, 435). Ephraim's confession follows in vv 18-19. It begins with Ephraim's acknowledgment that Yahweh's discipline was upon the nation (**you disciplined me;** intensive form the verb *yāsar*, meaning "discipline," "chasten," "instruct," etc.) and that the nation was indeed disciplined by Yahweh (**I have been disciplined**). Ephraim also admits the truth that the nation was like an **untrained young bull** (*ʿegel lōʾ lummād*), an animal not yet under the yoke. Hosea portrays Israel as "a stubborn heifer" (4:16 NRSV) as well as "a trained heifer" (10:11 NRSV). This confession admits the truth that it was the nation's rebellious and unruly behavior in the past that brought upon it the judgment and exile of the nation in 722 B.C. Israel acknowledges these events as Yahweh's disciplinary actions that resulted in their intended outcome of obedience and instruction.

Verse 18 ends with a plea for return—***bring me back*** (Hiphil imperative of *šûb*, meaning "turn," "return," "repent") ***so that I may return*** (Qal imperfect of *šûb*, cohortative in meaning) followed by a statement of the reason for Israel's desire to return. This phrase also may be translated as "restore me so I may be restored," "bring me back and I will repent," "restore me and I will return," etc. The first use of *šûb* seems to focus on Israel's restoration from exile; i.e., return to its homeland. The second use of the verb *šûb* (*wĕʾāšûbâ*) most likely does not convey the idea that Israel will "repent" when Yahweh brings the nation back to its homeland. Repentance is, however, clearly expressed in the first part of v 18. Verse 19 also indicates that Israel has already repented. The second use of the verb *šûb* conveys the repented nation's earnest longing to be reunited with the land. Lundbom sees here Ephraim's request to be restored to Yahweh's favor, which cannot be ruled out (2004a, 443). To be restored to the land means to be restored to Yahweh's favor. Verse 18 ends with the reason for Israel's desire to be restored. ***You are Yahweh my God*** clearly is a confession of Israel's covenant faith that Yahweh is the God of Israel. The once untrained but now disciplined nation confesses its covenant relationship with Yahweh. This relationship had been broken by Israel's sins, but this confession indicates its desire to live in a restored relationship with Yahweh.

■ **19** Verse 19 begins with Ephraim's recognition of its ***turning away*** (*šûbî, my turning away,* from *šûb*). ***My turning away*** means an intentional deviation from the covenant way of life, which further implies Ephraim's willingness to take responsibility for such action. **I repented** (*niḥamtî*, from *nāḥam*, means "be sorry," "repent," "be comforted," etc.) also indicates an intentional act. Ephraim's repentance is perhaps the idea here, more than its being sorry for turning away from Yahweh. The LXX reading here ("for after my captivity, I repented") conveys the idea that the exile is what led Ephraim to repentance. The next line (***after I came to know, I slapped on my thigh***) also conveys the idea of repentance and sorrow that comes after one's knowledge of sin. What brought about this knowledge or understanding to Ephraim? How did Ephraim get this knowledge? Is it the knowledge of the exile as punishment, or is it the knowledge of its turning away from Yahweh? The text assumes some sort of repentance on the part of Ephraim during its exile. If so, ***after I came to know*** means Ephraim's knowledge of the exile as the reason for its punishment. Also, it is the experience of the exile that brought this knowledge to Ephraim. ***I slapped on my thigh*** reflects an ancient custom of expressing emotional pain or sorrow (Ezek 21:12 NRSV; Lundbom 2004a, 443). Ephraim also admits here that it **was ashamed and humiliated** because of the **reproach** it carried from its early days as a young nation. Ephraim admits here the long history of its turning away from Yahweh. The judgment of the exile is the final consequence of its accumulated sin and guilt, the shame and disgrace of which it has been carrying for a long time.

■ **20** In v 20 Yahweh responds with compassion to the confession and lament of Ephraim. In v 18, Ephraim makes a direct appeal to Yahweh (see the second person address). Yahweh's response addresses Ephraim in the third person; the speech is thus directed to someone else, perhaps to the prophet or to a Judean audience. Yahweh's response begins with two rhetorical questions (***Is Ephraim my esteemed son? Is he the child of delight?***), and the implied answers could be yes and no. Yahweh expresses his deep emotional connection and intimacy of relation to Ephraim. These questions also reflect his agony—the brokenness of his heart caused by Ephraim's long history of rebellion against Yahweh. These questions echo Hos 11:1-4. Ephraim is Yahweh's precious (*yaqqîr*) son who has gone astray. Ephraim is Yahweh's **child of delight** or the object of delight that has turned away from him. In spite of the long history of Ephraim's turning away, and in spite of Yahweh's frequent **speaking** words of judgment **against him,** Yahweh promises to remember his beloved child who has become a prodigal son (***I will indeed remember him still***). Yahweh's remembrance of his love for Ephraim is the hope for Ephraim's future. What Yahweh remembers is his child Ephraim whom he brought up with tender care and love, not the grown-up Ephraim who turned away from him. This father-child relationship that Yahweh remembers causes a raging of emotion within the divine being. The Hebrew phrase (ʿalkēn hāmu mēʿay lô) literally means, ***therefore, my bowels moan for him.*** The Hebrew word *mēʿîm* means "bowels" or "innards," but it can also mean "the womb of a woman." The verb **moan** (*hāmu*, from *hāmâ*, meaning "cry aloud," "mourn," "rage," "roar," "disquieted," "troubled," "growl," etc.) here conveys the idea of roaring or intense turmoil within Yahweh's being. This whole phrase taken together indicates the powerful emotion that Yahweh has within his being for his son (see similar inner turmoil in Hos 11:8-9). Yahweh declares that he will have **mercy** (*rāham*) on Ephraim, his rebellious but contrite son. This unit makes clear that ultimately Yahweh's mercy is the hope for the restoration of Ephraim/Israel.

■ **21** Yahweh's speech to virgin Israel utilizes five imperatives (**set up, *place*, *set*, return, return**). The first two lines convey the same idea. Yahweh asks virgin Israel to follow the **road markers** and **signposts** and to **set** her **heart** on the **highway** by which she traveled when she was taken to captivity by the Assyrians. Now, the call here is to retrace that same path and follow the same road signs as she returns home. **Road markers** (*ṣiyyunîm*) are stone pillars or monuments along ancient highways. Commentators recognize **signposts** (*tamrûrîm*, found only here in the OT, the meaning of which is not certain) as parallel in meaning to **road markers. Set your heart on the** highway is a call to focus on the highway of her travel without turning back or turning aside. The idea of a **highway,** a built-up road, as a path for the exiles to return home is also found in Isa 35:8; 40:3; 49:11; 62:10. Verse 21 ends with Yahweh's call to **return** given twice to virgin Israel. Return (*šûb*) here is a call to return to the land, though in Hebrew the word also means "to repent." This is made clear in the call to return to **these your cities.** The cities of northern Israel are meant here. Though in the context the call is given to northern Israel, the Judeans in exile after 587 B.C. would have heard in this text a call to return to their cities—the cities of Judah.

■ **22** The first part of v 22 presents a question from Yahweh to virgin Israel. The opening phrase **how long** (*ʿadmātay*) conveys a sense of hopelessness and frustration on the part of the one who raises the question (see 4:21; 23:26; Isa 6:11). Yahweh laments here about Israel's continued turning here and there—its "dillydallying" (Bright 1965, 276) and wavering conduct. They are not focusing their hearts on their homeward journey. The question is addressed to Yahweh's **backsliding daughter** (*habbat haššôbēbâ*). This epithet connects virgin Israel with the **backslider** (*mĕšûbâ*) Israel in 3:6, 8, 12, who committed adultery "on every high hill and under every green tree" (3:6 NRSV). It is ironic that here the address is to virgin Israel, but she is called a daughter who turns away or who "turns here and turns there" (Lundbom 2004a, 451). Yahweh's invitation to come home is thus extended to a people who are still in the habit of turning away from him. Though the call to return home has gone out to the people in exile, they have not paid attention to Yahweh's call. They remain in their backsliding and unfaithful way of life. The question then can be understood as an urgent call to the exiles of northern Israel to put an end to their vacillating conduct and to begin their return home.

The second part of v 22 gives the reason for Yahweh's urgent call to Israel. Yahweh calls his daughter who turns away from him to return to her home because he has **created a new thing in the land.** The verb *bārāʾ* ("create"), which is a key verb in the account of creation in Gen 1, is found only here in Jeremiah. God is exclusively the subject of this verb in the OT. This verb conveys the idea of God bringing into existence things that do not exist. **A new thing** (*hădāšâ*) conveys this idea. Most translations translate *bāʾāreṣ* as **on earth** as in the NIV, perhaps because of its parallel to Gen 1:1. But it is equally possible, and perhaps more likely, that *bāʾāreṣ* here means **in the land**—the land of Israel. This action is something that Yahweh has already performed and this condition is now in existence in the land. The last line states what that new thing is, but its interpretation is very difficult. We do not know the meaning of the line ***a female will surround/protect a man*** (*nĕqēbâ tĕsôbēb gāber*). The noun *nĕqēbâ* (**female**) is also found in the Genesis account of creation (1:27). The verb *tĕsôbēb* (from *sābab*, meaning "turn," "encircle," "surround") conveys the idea of protection (Lundbom 2004a, 451). The noun *geber* usually means a strong man or warrior. The whole phrase thus means that a female will surround/protect a strong man/warrior. Most commentators agree that this is a proverbial saying. The imagery of this proverb does not require literal meaning. Taken as a proverb, it expands on the idea of Yahweh doing a **new thing** (*hădāšâ*) **in the land**, something new and "surprising and difficult to believe" (Bright 1965, 282). This proverb echoes the words, "I am about to do a new thing [*hădāšâ*]" (Isa 43:19 NRSV). This new and unbelievable thing that Yahweh is creating for virgin Israel in the context of this verse is her restoration. Such a thing is difficult for Israel in exile to comprehend. Virgin Israel only needs to make her journey to her homeland by heeding to Yahweh's call to see his creative work of restoration that he has already performed for her in the land.

FROM THE TEXT

God hears the bitter weeping of a mother; he is moved with compassion and speaks tenderly to her and comforts her. No human being can adequately understand the depth of her pain and suffering. No human words would bring comfort to the mother who has lost all her children. God, who hears and responds to the cry of the mothers of Israel who are personified in this text by the image of weeping mother Rachel, is the same God who heard the bitter weeping of the mothers who lost their infant sons to the waters of the Nile, and the groaning and the cry of the enslaved Hebrews in Egypt (Exod 1:22; 2:23-25). Matthew's narrative of the slaughter of the Jewish infants by Herod's decree and the weeping of Rachel (all the Jewish mothers in Bethlehem) are wrapped up more intimately in the story of God himself. Jesus, God's Son, makes his entry into a world that is ruthless and where political powers act quickly to silence any threat to their power, even if it means killing innocent children (Matt 2:16-18). The incarnation of the Son of God, though it remains a profound mystery, in simple terms is God's coming into the world of sin and suffering and becoming a part of the suffering humanity. In the text of Jeremiah, in the Exodus narrative, and in the infancy narrative of Matthew, God does not enter into the scene of human pain and suffering, simply because that is what he is supposed to do as a just and righteous God. But as Fretheim suggests, the God of Jeremiah is a God who enters into the world of human pain and suffering and allows the suffering of the world to enter into his own divine life (2002, 434). The word of comfort that mother Rachel hears in Jeremiah is shaped by God's intimate involvement with those who suffer, those who have lost their land, lost their children, lost their identity and heritage, and are in exile in a foreign land. The word of comfort that comes from God who enters into the thick of human life and suffering has the capacity to bring comfort to those who refuse to be comforted by human words of consolation. God's comfort here is that Rachel's lost sons will return, their exile will end, her sorrow will turn to joy, and she will have a hope-full future.

This text, originally spoken to northern Israel, later heard by the Judeans who were being deported, and by the subsequent generation of exiles in Babylon, conveys comfort and hope to all who live in exile—its more immediate audience as well as the exiles in our own world today. The God of this text does not leave out anyone to never-ending weeping and sorrow. The God of this text does not leave out anyone to remain in exile as his or her permanent fate. The Gospel of John seems to be conveying this truth about God in his portrayal of Jesus in the story of Jesus, Mary, Martha, and Lazarus. In the Gospel story, Jesus the incarnate God enters into the sorrowful world of Martha and Mary and weeps with them. His words, "Your brother will rise again," are shaped by the pain and agony he experiences as he moves around in the world of the grieving sisters and their fellow Jews (John 11:23 NRSV). In the Gospel story also, comfort comes to those who refuse to be comforted, through the presence of Jesus and his compassionate, yet powerful words of hope. Today we hear the good news of God's comfort in the Gospels more profoundly and more meaningfully because it comes from God who actually suffered and died on the cross. The word of comfort we hear today is the same that the disciples heard from the Risen Christ: "I am with you always" (Matt 28:20*b*).

In the lament of Ephraim we find indications of deep sorrow and agony. Unlike the weeping of Rachel, Ephraim's (Israel) sorrow originates in the shame over the rebellious actions of his youthful days. Those who once stubbornly resisted God acknowledge their intentional turning away from God and God's judgment on them as his disciplinary action. The repentant Ephraim pleads with God to bring him home. God is deeply moved by the quivering voice of Ephraim, his beloved child. He cannot reject Ephraim, though his own inclination is to continue to speak words of judgment against his rebellion (v 20). Divine mercy wins and wrath is quickly overshadowed by compassion. Phyllis Trible, who sees in vv 15-22 a clear illustration of the maternal metaphor for God, also sees these verses moving from divine "grief" to "grace," from "desolate lamentation" to "redemptive compassion" (1978, 45). God's deep resolve to love his prodigal son in spite of God's actions of judgment and discipline in v 20 is a genuine reflection of the divine wrath and love in Hos 11. In Hosea and in Jeremiah, what ultimately saves the rebellious child is divine mercy rooted in divine memory (***I will indeed remember him still. . . . I will indeed have mercy on him***, v 20*b*; see Hos 11:1-9). The psalmist also speaks of the mercy, grace, steadfast love, and compassion that God shows toward human beings because he knows and remembers them as "dust" (Ps 103:8-14). Brueggemann states, "The God who *utterly remembers* is the God who *utterly has mercy*" (1998, 288). We hear in the words of the prodigal son in the Gospel of Luke an echo of the words of Ephraim in Jer 31:18-19. Likewise, the father who loves, welcomes, and rejoices in the homecoming of his wayward son in the Gospel story is a reflection of the loving, remembering, and merciful God of Jeremiah (Luke 15:11-32).

9. A Pleasant Dream (31:23-26)

BEHIND THE TEXT

In vv 23-26 the attention shifts to the restoration of Judah. The unit begins with a messenger formula in v 23. The first part of v 23 is in prose and the second part is in poetry. The second part of v 23 contains a blessing that will be heard among the restored people of Judah. Verse 24 is in prose, and it describes a unified Judah with farmers and shepherds dwelling together. Poetry is resumed in v 25. Yahweh is the speaker. The unit ends with a puzzling response by Jeremiah (v 26). References to the temple and Jerusalem as *righteous pasture* and *holy mountain* in v 23 have led some commentators to treat these verses as a later addition to the book, perhaps in the postexilic period. However, this oracle conveys the message of restoration, which envisions a reinstatement of Jerusalem and the temple to their place of glory and honor. There is nothing in the text that compels us to assign it a postexilic date. The ruined condition of Jerusalem and the temple in the aftermath of the events of 586 B.C. may have been the likely setting of this oracle.

IN THE TEXT

■ 23 Yahweh's speech is introduced with a ***thus said Yahweh*** messenger formula. **Yahweh Sebaoth, God of Israel** is the one who speaks here. Yahweh announces a blessing that will be heard **in the land of Judah and in its towns** when he restores their ***captives.*** The text contains the promise of restoration. A specific time for this activity is not given; it lies in the future. What follows is a word of blessing that those who return to their home will bestow upon the temple and the mountain where the temple is located. The blessing will be given in Yahweh's name. **May Yahweh bless you, righteous dwelling, holy mountain** may have been a blessing commonly heard in Judah before the temple was destroyed in 587 B.C. (Lundbom 2004a, 456). The epithet **righteous dwelling** (*nĕwēh ṣedek*) most likely refers to the temple. The Hebrew word *nāweh* usually means "pasture," and Jeremiah occasionally uses this term as a metaphor for the land of Israel (10:25; 23:3; 50:19). In Exod 15:13, the tabernacle is called "your holy dwelling" (*nĕwēh qodšekā*). In Jer 50:7 Yahweh is called *nĕwēh-ṣedek*; "righteous pasture" seems to be the best rendering in that context since it is used there as an epithet of Yahweh. **Holy mountain** (*har haqqōdeš*) refers to Mount Zion or Jerusalem where the temple is located (see also Isa 11:9; 27:13; 56:7; Pss 2:6; 15:1; 48:1). This mountain is holy because of Yahweh's dwelling there.

■ **24** Verse 24 anticipates the return of the Judean captives to the land of Judah and taking up residence in the cities of Judah. The first part of v 24 reads as follows: *Judah and all its cities will dwell in it together.* The NIV clarifies it by adding the word **people.** *In it* refers to "the land of Judah" mentioned in v 23. The second part of v 24 speaks of *ploughmen and they that will set out with the flock* living together in harmony in the land. In the ancient times these two groups lived in conflict and tension because of the scarcity of land suitable for farming and grazing activities. These two groups living in harmony portrays an ideal future of peace and tranquillity in the land.

■ **25** Yahweh states in v 25 that he has already taken the action to bring about the condition of peace and harmony in the land among farmers and shepherds. The perfect tense form of the verb (lit., *for I have saturated* . . .) conveys the idea that Yahweh's promise is already fulfilled, though it is a reality yet to be experienced by the nation in the days of restoration. Violence and conflict will end because Yahweh will satisfy all the physical needs of the people. The vocational groups that fight for survival, for food and water, will live in harmony because their *weary* and *languished soul* will be *saturated* with Yahweh's good and gracious provisions for them. **Soul** (*nepeš*) refers to the whole human being as a needy being (Wolff 1974, 10-25).

■ **26** This verse presents the prophet as the speaker. Most commentators view this verse as a later addition or a marginal comment by later editors. The meaning of this verse is not clear. It seems to convey the idea that the prophet had been asleep and that he had been dreaming. Yahweh's promise of bringing the exiles back to their land, the people repopulating the cities of Judah, the farmers and shepherds living together in harmony, and Yahweh satisfying the weary and the faint (vv 24-25) were thus probably part of a dream. This dream made his sleep a very pleasant experience. But when he woke up and looked around there was no change in the conditions of the land. Death, destruction, and the threat of exile are still all around. However, there is no indication that the future the prophet imagines is his wishful thinking. Perhaps what enables the prophet to sleep well at night in the midst of hopeless conditions is his pleasant dream of a future that is hidden in the promises of Yahweh.

FROM THE TEXT

It is difficult to imagine good days when life is lived in hardship and the future seems gloomy and without much hope. This text imagines for its readers good days that are coming, days when God will put all things back together for good. In the place where weeping is heard now, there will be songs of praise and worship. In the place where people live in conflict and violence, there will be peace, unity, and cooperation. In the place where there is weariness and fainting, there will be satisfaction and rejuvenation. Those who live in exile will come home. Those who have lost everything will find all their fortunes restored. This text imagines for Israel what it is difficult for it to imagine. This text dreams for Israel what it considers as an impossible and unbelievable dream. The goal of this text is to invite and urge its readers who are in difficult and unbearable circumstances to join with its author and fully utilize their capacity to imagine for themselves a future that is presently unimaginable. The text does not present such a future as an unrealistic and fanciful thought that only exists in the imagination of the author or its readers. This imagined future, which indeed is a vision of reality, is rooted and grounded in God's promise of restoration. The intent of this text is thus to give hope, and the prophet presents hope, in the words of Brueggemann, "as a dreamlike alternative imagination which accepts God's intent as more powerful than the present, seemingly intransigent circumstance" (1998, 289).

Hope-filled promises of God and his faithful working in history have provided God's people to continue to have dreams such as the one we encounter in this text. This dream has its parallel in the vision of the reality of God's kingdom as Jesus saw it and presented it to his audience in the first century A.D.—Palestine that existed in the hopeless conditions of the Roman rule. The author of this text also has his modern-day counterparts in people such as Dietrich Bonhoeffer and Martin Luther King Jr., who dared to imagine good days to come in the midst of hopeless conditions. On November 18, 1943, while waiting for his trial, Bonhoeffer refers to Jer 31:26 in his letter to Eberhard and writes: "the most difficult thing is getting up in the morning," perhaps knowing that conditions haven't changed at all. He is dreaming of freedom but he also is fully aware that in a few months he will be condemned. In the meantime he hopes to be reunited with his friends and family, and to be married to Maria (1971, 131-32). At a time when one could not imagine racial harmony in Black-White relations, Martin Luther King Jr. dreamed of a day when "on the red hills of Georgia, the sons of former slaves and the sons of former slave owners will be able to sit together at the table of brotherhood." Dreams and dreamers like Jeremiah, Dietrich Bonhoeffer, and Martin Luther King Jr. are still alive and at work in the history of nations all over the world today. The text also reminds us that it is a biblical imperative that the church engage herself in dreaming for those who cannot dream for themselves and keep alive the spirit of Jeremiah in our day.

10. All Shall Die for Their Own Sins (31:27-30)

BEHIND THE TEXT

This literary unit begins with an announcement of **the days** that **are coming** (v 27); Yahweh's words in vv 27-30 are thus directed to an unspecified future time in the history of Israel and Judah (see also **In those days** in v 29). The focus of vv 27-28 is on Yahweh's rebuilding of the nation Israel. Verses

29-30 present a proverbial saying and Yahweh's response. The proverbial saying, **The fathers have eaten sour grapes, and the children's teeth are set on edge,** is also found in Ezek 18:2. Yahweh's response in Jer 31:30 is also echoed in Ezek 18:4. Because of this parallel in Ezekiel, some commentators treat Jer 31:29-30 as a later addition. The proverbial saying was most likely a commonly heard complaint in Judah and in Babylon following the events of 597 and 587 B.C. Jeremiah is responding to this complaint; Ezekiel also addresses this complaint in Ezek 18.

IN THE TEXT

■ **27** Yahweh's speech is introduced with the phrase *Look,* **days are coming,** a customary announcement of future as the time of his activity. It is eschatological in the sense that it pertains to the future of the nation Israel. Yahweh's plan is to *sow* **the house of Israel and the house of Judah with the** *seed of human and the seed of beast.* The metaphor of sowing the seed, taken from agricultural activity (see Hos 2:23), portrays Yahweh as a farmer who generously scatters the seed of life throughout the land. This promise assumes the condition of a ruined and depopulated land and both human and animal life suffering the judgment of Yahweh. The promise is that Yahweh will repopulate the land with people and animal life, and thus the effect of judgment will be reversed. The promise is given to both Israel and Judah. Israel's national restoration is intended here. Also implied here is the idea of Israel and Judah as a united nation—one house of Israel as the recipient of this promise.

■ **28** In v 28 Yahweh promises to carry out his promise of restoration just as he fulfilled his words of judgment. He promised to "watch over" (šāqad) or fulfill his words of judgment in 1:12. Here he states that he **watched over** (šāqad) or fulfilled his words **to uproot and tear down, and to overthrow, destroy and bring disaster.** Now he promises that in the same way he will **watch over** (šāqad) or fulfill his promise **to build and to plant** Judah and Israel, the people and their land that were destroyed by his judgment. Building and planting reiterate the theme of sowing in 31:27. The theme of uprooting and overthrowing, and building and planting, first stated in 1:10, is a recurring theme in Jeremiah. Here in the Book of Comfort the prophet fulfills the commission "to build and to plant," given to him at the time of his call (1:10).

■ **29** Verses 29-30 do not have any continuity with vv 27-28 except that what is stated in these verses is a reality that will come into existence **in those days;** i.e., the eschatological days of Israel's restoration. The text seems to indicate that the statement, **The fathers have eaten sour grapes, and the children's teeth are set on edge,** was a popular saying among Jeremiah's audience. During Ezekiel's time, this continued to be a popular proverbial expression among the exiles in Babylon. Lamentations perhaps provides the best explanation of this proverb: "Our ancestors sinned; they are no more, and we bear their iniquities" (5:7 NRSV). The idea of children suffering punishment for the sins of their ancestors is conveyed by this saying. In v 29, Yahweh states that this saying will not be heard in the restored land (**in those days**), whereas in Ezek 18:3 Yahweh seems to refute this proverbial saying and demands an immediate end to it among the exiles. The proverbial saying attacks the system of divine retribution, which implemented penalty for one's sins not only on the perpetrator but also on his family and subsequent generations. The basis of this proverb is Israel's legal traditions on guilt and punishment, which is invoked at times by the Deuteronomic historians (see Exod 20:5; 34:7; Josh 7:24-27; 1 Sam 22:16-19; 2 Kgs 24:3-4; see also Jer 15:4).

■ **30** In v 30 there is no attempt to justify or defend the system of divine retribution. Neither is there an attempt to nullify it. Verse 30 simply interprets divine retribution using the standard of Deut 24:16: "Parents shall not be put to death for their children, nor shall children be put to death for their parents; only for their own crimes may persons be put to death." According to 2 Kgs 14:5-6, King Amaziah, when he executed his servants who murdered his father King Joash, followed the Deuteronomic law and accordingly spared the children of the murderers. The promise of restoration is indeed a reversal of the rigid idea of retribution in Exod 20:5 and 34:7. The promise means that there would be a corrective to the idea of inherited guilt and corporate punishment. It is very likely that both Jeremiah and Ezekiel were influenced by the Deuteronomic modification of the principle of divine retribution and by Yahweh's repeated promises of Israel's restoration. **Each individual in his iniquity shall die** emphasizes individual responsibility and accountability to one's actions.

FROM THE TEXT

This restoration oracle promises the reversal of the effect of judgment. The land that has become a desolate place without human and animal life due to war and exile will be repopulated with human and animal life. Restoration promised here is the restoration of all God's creatures. The entire created order stands to receive the benefit of God's work of salvation (Fretheim 2002, 439). The hope expressed in this text may be linked to the hope Paul anticipates in the freedom of the creation from "its bondage to decay" and its participation in the salvific work of God that leads to "the freedom of the glory of the children of God" (Rom 8:21 NRSV).

The text also announces the beginning of God's building and planting of his people. The days of uprooting, breaking down, overthrowing, and destruction are over. Now what the people can expect and hope for are days of their building and planting. Salvation that God offers here comes with the promise that the days of judgment are over. Those who enter into the experience of God's saving work find here an invitation to live not in fear of judgment, but in the joy of salvation and freedom from judgment. Sin brings judgment and death, but salvation offers life and hope for the future. The promise here is also that God will watch over to fulfill his promise of building and planting just as he watched over to bring judgment and death on Israel. That means the promise here is not empty words; its fulfillment is a certainty. We hear in this text an echo of the promise of freedom from "condemnation" and "the law of sin and death" that one finds in the gospel of Jesus Christ (Rom 8:1-2).

Verses 29-30 indicate that the events of 598 and 587 B.C. have brought to prominence the question of fairness and equity in the way God distributes the effect of the sins of the previous generations on a future generation. The proverbial statement in v 29 reflects the fatalistic thinking of the community that saw itself as totally helpless to do anything to change its destiny that was already determined for them by God's system of justice. Earlier generations that sinned against God escaped judgment, but the present generation is paying the price for the sins of their ancestors. The fundamental questions that are being raised by the people through this proverb are: will the future be always shaped by the sins and failures of the past? Will one generation be required to pay for the sins of the previous generation? If so, how can people ever have hope for a good future? How can they truly trust in the words of God building and planting them that they hear through Jeremiah? Is the newness that the prophet proclaims really a possibility for them? The text gives a firm and positive response to these questions. The future that God is shaping for his people will not be a replay of the past. The newness that God offers will be new in every aspect of their life and their relationship with God. God's people will not have to fear judgment for the sins of past generations. In the days that are coming, in the days of God's gracious activities of building and planting his people, each generation will be able to shape its destiny and relationship with God by their own actions. The new covenant text in the next section clearly affirms God's offer of forgiveness and forgetting of sins as part of the newness that is being promised here. Those who hear this text today find in it the gospel of God's grace and forgiveness through which he makes all things new. The old has gone, the new has come. As Paul affirms, this newness is the work of God (2 Cor 5:17-18).

Verses 29-30, though they are communal in orientation in its context, also speak to individuals in the contemporary hearing of this text. Those who live in hopelessness and despair, who see themselves as the victims of and in bondage to the failures and destructive ways of life led by their parents, find in this text God's offer of freedom and the promise of a new day. This text, like the gospel of Jesus Christ, also invites its listeners to trust in the gracious activity of God in their lives, which makes it possible for them to live in freedom from their bondage to the sins and failures of their own life and also of their parents and previous generations.

11. The New Covenant (31:31-34)

BEHIND THE TEXT

In the words of Bright, Jer 31:31-34 represents the "high point" of Jeremiah's theology, and "it is certainly one of the profoundest and most moving passages in the entire Bible" (1965, 287). This text has been the subject of intense theological reflection in Judaism and the Christian church (see Lundbom 2004a, 472-82, for a review of the new covenant in Judaism including Qumran, and the NT and the early patristic literature).

Though the new covenant oracle is popularly attributed to Jeremiah, some scholars have seriously questioned its authenticity. In 1901, Duhm (*Das Buch Jeremia*) described this text as "the effusion of a scribe who holds as the highest ideal that everyone among the Jewish peoples shall know by heart and understand the Law, that all Jews shall be scribes" (quoted in Potter 1983, 348). A most recent critic of the Jeremianic authorship of this text is Carroll, who sees here an expression of a post-Deuteronomistic hope in a "utopian future" and argues that "the utopian society" envisioned by the metaphor of this text "does not and cannot exist" (1986, 614). Scholars who argue for the Deuteronomistic editing of the book of Jeremiah attribute this text to the Deuteronomists (Nicholson 1970, 82). Nicholson, though he sees here "an expectation for the future," argues that this text "conforms to the pattern of a series of covenant renewal ceremonies in the Deuteronomistic presentation of Israel's history" (1970, 83). Others (Cornill, Moulton, Hyatt, Bright, Anderson, von Rad, Zimmerli, Wolff), however, see the text as authentic to Jeremiah (Lundbom 2004a, 465-66). Robinson, who argues for the Jeremianic authorship, finds in the themes and phrases of this text significant influence of the Hosea tradition (2001, 184). Holladay finds in the text expressions that are characteristic to the prophet and argues that the Deuteronomic diction in the text is "deliberate." He places the setting of the text in "the recitation of the Deuteronomic law during the feast of booths (tabernacles) in the autumn of 587, after the destruction of Jerusalem" (1989, 197). Lundbom says that since Jeremiah considered himself as "the prophet like Moses," and since the covenant at Sinai was established through Moses, it is only natural that "Jeremiah be the one to give Israel a new covenant" (2004a, 465).

The date of this text cannot be established with any certainty. The collapse of the covenant due to Israel's unfaithfulness to Yahweh is the general context of the new covenant promise. The Assyrian destruction of northern Israel in 722 B.C. signaled the beginning of the collapse of the covenant between Yahweh and Israel. The prophet would have seen in the deteriorating political conditions following the events of 597 B.C. and in the impending destruction of Judah by Babylon the end of the Sinai covenant. It is thus possible to place this central message of hope in the Book of Consolation in the period immediately before or following the events of 587 B.C.

Commentators and most translations consider this text as prose, though the NIV treats it as poetry. This unit shares with the preceding unit the same opening announcement, **Look, days are coming** (v 31; see v 27). The message that follows thus concerns Yahweh's activity in the days to come. In the setting of the Book of Consolation, the message of this text, the promise of a new covenant, follows the promise of Yahweh's new act of salvation or restoration of his people from their exile to their homeland (see vv 23-26, 27-30). The message is given to both Israel and Judah, the entire nation of Israel that exists without a covenant relationship with Yahweh. Each verse in this unit contains an *oracle of Yahweh* formula. Verses 31 and 32 announce Yahweh's plan to make a new covenant that will be unlike the covenant he made with Israel's ancestors. Verse 33 describes the new covenant and v 34 explains the outcome of the new covenant. Verse 34 begins with a lōʾ . . . ʿôd (**not . . . again**) statement and concludes with a lōʾ . . . ʿôd statement, the first referring to the deeds of the people and the second referring to Yahweh's actions, and both emphasizing a discontinuity with the past (Bozak 1991, 118).

The Essenes at Qumran regarded themselves as members of the new covenant community. Most Christians relate this oracle to the NT faith in Jesus as the Mediator of the new covenant (see Luke 22:20; 1 Cor 11:25; 2 Cor 3:4-14; Heb 8:8-12; 10:16-17).

IN THE TEXT

■ **31** The opening phrase **Look, days are coming** conveys the idea that Yahweh's action outlined in this oracle belongs to some unspecified time in the future. This phrase, found frequently in Jeremiah, conveys a future period of judgment or salvation (see 7:32; 9:25; 19:6; 23:5, 7; 30:3; 31:27, 38; 33:14). Eschatological oracles that contain a word of salvation, such as that we find in this unit, aim to give hope to those who live in hopeless conditions. The repeated occurrence of the *oracle of Yahweh* formula in every verse in this unit gives the audience the assurance that the hope-filled words concerning their future originate with Yahweh and that they can depend on the fulfillment of this word of hope. The message from Yahweh begins with the promise that he **will make** (lit., "cut") **a new covenant with the house of Israel and with the house of Judah**. The entire nation of Israel is the recipient of this promise. Thus there is clear continuity between those who stood at Mount Sinai as participants of the Sinai covenant and the community that receives this promise from Yahweh. Time and location may be different, but the recipients of the promise remain the same. The term **new covenant** (bĕrît ḥădāšâ) is found only here in the OT (see 31:22 where we find the phrase "new thing"; see also "new heart" and "new spirit" in Ezek 36:26).

The **new covenant** promise in v 31 implies that the old (Sinai) covenant is broken and that it no longer exists (see v 32). Also the term **new** does not mean the renewal or the reestablishment of the old covenant, but a relationship between Yahweh and Israel that is entirely *new* (italics for emphasis). However, as von Rad has pointed out, the new covenant introduces no change in the content of Yahweh's self-revelation at Mount Sinai (1965, 213). As we shall see later, the substance of the new covenant remains the same as that of the Sinai covenant.

Verse 32 also implies that this new covenant will not be associated with the past traditions of Israel's deliverance from Egypt. The text in its literary context (see vv 23-25, 27-28) makes it clear that the new covenant promise is linked to a new salvific event; i.e., Yahweh's deliverance and restoration of Israel from the lands of its exile. Just as the Sinai covenant was the culmination of the exodus event of salvation, the new covenant will be the culmination of Yahweh's new work of salvation on behalf of Israel. **I will make a new covenant** is Yahweh's gracious offer to give the house of Israel and the house of Judah another opportunity to enter into a brand-new relation with Yahweh. The establishment of the new covenant is also anticipated elsewhere in Jeremiah (see 24:7; 32:37-40; 50:5). This expectation is an important part of Ezekiel's view of Israel's restoration (Ezek 16:60; 34:25; 36:24-28; 37:26). Isaiah 59:12; 61:8; and Mal 3:1 also echo this hope.

■ **32** Verse 32 states that the new covenant will **not be like the covenant** that Yahweh made with the ***ancestors*** of Israel and Judah when he brought them out of the land of Egypt. (Verse 33 explains in what ways this new covenant will be dissimilar to the Sinai covenant.) Israel's exodus from Egypt is here portrayed as Yahweh's leading and guiding of his infant nation like a parent leading and guiding a child by holding firm the hand of the child to keep him or her safe from falling. The temporal clause, **When I took them by the hand to lead them out of Egypt,** echoes the theme of Hos 11:1, 3, 4 (see Robinson 2001, 191). Yahweh made his covenant with Israel's ancestors when the nation was in its state of infancy. Yahweh calls this covenant **my covenant,** the covenant that he initiated with Israel, the covenant to which he has ownership rights, and the conditions of which were willingly acknowledged by Israel's ancestors. **They broke** implies a defiant act, an encroachment of what truly belongs to Yahweh. Verse 32 thus makes clear the status of the Sinai covenant; it is broken by Israel and not by Yahweh. No particular act is mentioned here; it is likely that the prophet may be thinking of the long history of covenant violations, beginning with the making of a golden calf by those who were at Sinai (Exod 32) and the transgressions of the covenant by the later generations. The final phrase (***Though I was their husband***) implies another evidence of the broken relationship. Here Yahweh's role changes from that of a loving, caring parent (Jer 31:32*a*) to an ex-husband (v 32*b*). Israel was at one time Yahweh's covenant partner (wife) and Yahweh was Israel's **husband** (*baʿal* means "owner," "lord," "husband," "ruler," etc.; here it means the covenant partner with higher authority). That marriage relationship does not exist because Israel has broken the covenant and left her covenant partner. Hosea 2—3 and Jer 2—3 also convey the theme of the broken covenant by the use of the image of Yahweh as a husband rejected by his wife (see Bozak 1991, 120)

■ 33 Verse 33 explains in what sense this covenant will be a new covenant. The opening phrase, **This is the covenant,** refers to the new covenant in v 31. Here **the house of Israel** is the whole nation, and not just northern Israel (see v 31). The phrase *after those days* implies that it is an eschatological reality to be experienced at some time in the future history of Israel (see v 31). Yahweh's words, **I will put my law in their** *inner part and upon their heart I will write it,* show the new covenant's continuity and discontinuity with the Sinai covenant.

Yahweh's **law** (*tôrâ*) will be central to this new covenant just as it was to the Sinai covenant. Thus the new covenant will have continuity with the Sinai covenant. However, what the law entails is not clear. The text does not suggest a new *tôrâ*; only the covenant is called new. The Ten Commandments written on two stone tablets (Exod 24:12; 31:18) constituted the essence of the Sinai covenant. However, the legal tradition in the OT shows a complex system of ordinances and commandments. Some commentators take the view that the content of Yahweh's *tôrâ* in the new covenant will be the same fixed laws of the Sinai covenant "revealed as commandment, statute, and ordinance" (see Keown, Scalise, Smothers 1995, 134). Fretheim, however, sees *tôrâ* as dynamic and argues that "the law refers to the will of God for life in more general terms" (2002, 443). The focus of the text seems not to be on the specific content of Yahweh's *tôrâ*, but on the essence of it; i.e., Yahweh's will for his people that they wholeheartedly love and obey him and acknowledge him as their covenant partner.

Yahweh also promises that he will put his *tôrâ* in **their inner part** (*běqirbām*). The LXX translation conveys the idea of writing in the "mind" of the people (so does the NIV). **Upon their heart I will write** is parallel in meaning to Yahweh putting his law in the inner part. Holladay suggests the possibility, based on Jeremiah's use of inner part and heart elsewhere in the book, that these words could be understood to mean the city and the temple and that the text anticipates a "renewal of worship in the temple" (1989, 198). However, he goes on to include the commonly understood meaning of the text and sees here the idea of "Yahweh's law written in the interior intentionality of the people." Holladay also suggests that the singular use of the nouns (heart and inner part) conveys the idea of "the corporate will and intention of the people" (ibid.).

In the OT, **heart** (*lēb*) is the seat of emotions, human will, thinking, and planning. In Proverbs, parents admonish their children to write or bind their *tôrâ* (parental instructions) on their heart. Based on this parental teaching, Robinson suggests that "the new covenant is thought of in terms of parental affection," though he admits that the focus of the new covenant is on Yahweh's writing of his law on human hearts (2001, 195; see Prov 3:1-3; 6:20-

21). In the tradition of Deuteronomy, emphasis is placed on keeping the *torâ* in one's heart or remembering it (see Deut 6:6; 11:18). But what does Jeremiah mean here by introducing the thought of Yahweh writing his *torâ* on the heart? How will Yahweh write his *torâ* on the heart? Swetnam proposed the most unlikely explanation, that the text conveys the idea of "a direct contact between Torah and Israelite" (i.e., "God's Word acts immediately upon the faithful") as knowledge about the Law was imparted during synagogue worship (1974, 111-15; he comes to this conclusion by dating the origin of the synagogue worship in Israel and this text roughly at the same time). The text makes clear Yahweh's personal involvement of writing his law; it thus anticipates a grace event, similar to the promise that Yahweh will circumcise the heart in Deut 30:6. Von Rad explains this as the promise of a "change in the way in which the divine will is to be conveyed" to Israel (1965, 213). He suggests that there will be an end to the Sinai arrangement of Yahweh speaking and Israel listening and obeying; in the new covenant Yahweh will put his will straight into Israel's heart, so that humans will have "the will of God in their heart," and they will desire to do only that which is God's will. The picture here is that of a "new" individual, a person who is able to "obey perfectly" because of a "miraculous change of his [or her] nature" (1965, 213-14). McKane observes that this inner human disposition and motivation to obey the demands of the law is what makes righteousness possible in the new covenant. He goes on to say that the new covenant is "entirely the outcome of 'grace' and is a deep symbiosis of Divine Law (*torâ*) and human understanding of it, acquiescence in it and obedience to it." McKane also sees the new covenant resulting in "a harmony of divine and human wills" that "disposes of the tensions between obedience and disobedience to God's demands," and in one's "love of God with all the heart and soul" that originates in a "transformation at the core of being" (1996, 820).

Yahweh's writing of his law upon the human heart thus means that in the new covenant, heart will become the repository of Yahweh's *torâ* and that obedience will be the natural response of the human heart. Underlying this promise is the idea of Yahweh's gift of a new heart and a new spirit (see Ezek 36:26; also "one heart and one way" in Jer 32:39 NRSV). The new heart engraved with Yahweh's *torâ* will be the sign of a new relationship (new covenant) between Yahweh and Israel. This new heart stands in sharp contrast to the current condition of Israel—a people with the laws of the covenant written on two tablets of stone (Exod 34:1-5, 27-28; Deut 5:22), a people without heart or "foolish" (Jer 5:21), a people with "stubborn and rebellious hearts" (5:23), a people who do not acknowledge Yahweh "in their hearts" (5:24 NRSV), and a people with sin "engraved on . . . their hearts" (17:1 NRSV). Potter sums up Jeremiah's thought in this way: "As long as the Law is written merely on the tablets of stone, so long will sin be written on the tablets of the heart, and so long will forgiveness be impossible . . . In order for

God to forgive he must erase the sin written on the heart and replace it with the Law" (1983, 352).

The goal of the Sinai covenant law was to elicit love for God and obedience to him; however, the Sinai covenant law remained external to the individual, and as Israel's history has shown, it often failed to produce its intended outcome. Yahweh's writing of the law internally within the individual thus suggests not only a radical intervention on the part of Yahweh to forgive sin and transform the corrupt inner being but also a new kind of obedience from the people. The goal of the new covenant is the same as that of the Sinai covenant; i.e., Israel's acknowledgment of Yahweh as **their God,** and Yahweh's acknowledgment of Israel as his **people.** We may conclude that this relationship established by the new covenant will be sustained by Yahweh's faithfulness to his covenant and by the inner disposition and harmony of the people to the demands of Yahweh's *tôrâ* that is placed in their heart.

Deuteronomy and Jeremiah on the Heart

Deuteronomy 6:6 admonishes the people of Israel to "keep" Yahweh's instructions in their "heart" (see similar admonition in Deut 11:18 ("put these words of mine in your heart," NRSV). This instruction aims to elicit love for God with one's whole heart (Deut 6:5). Deuteronomy also calls Israel to "circumcise ... the foreskin of [their] heart" and not to be "stubborn any longer" (10:16 NRSV). To this we may also add the promise to Israel that Yahweh will circumcise their heart and the heart of their descendants (Deut 30:6). Deuteronomy recognizes in these passages three key issues: (1) the heart is the center of one's devotion to Yahweh; (2) the uncircumcised heart is unresponsive to the call to covenant obedience; (3) the future of Israel depends on the circumcised heart or the people's internal commitment to love and obey Yahweh. Jeremiah's own assessment of the heart of his contemporaries is rather bleak. He describes Israel's heart as stubborn, evil, and deceitful (5:23; 17:9) and thoroughly under the influence of sin (17:1). The new covenant promises the divine remedy for Israel's hopeless condition. The nation has broken the covenant and has no resources or ability within itself to bring about an inner change and transformation and to reenter a covenant with Yahweh. Sin is what is now "engraved on the tablet" of the heart of Israel (17:1 NRSV). The new covenant promise is thematically and theologically linked to the promise in 24:7 that Yahweh will give his people "a heart to know" him, and the promise of "one heart and one way" in 32:39 (NRSV) (see also Ezek 11:19; 18:31; 36:25-27 for Yahweh's promise of cleansing of his people and the gift of a new heart and a new spirit).

31:33-34

■ **34** Verse 34 sums up the outcome of the new covenant relationship. The beginning and the end of this verse with its repeated *lōʾ* ... *ʿôd* (***not ... again***) statements indicate a future that will be radically different from the past. In this new relation with Yahweh, the motivation to **know Yahweh** will not come from outside influences and teaching but from within the individual. **They shall not teach again—each one his neighbor, and each one his brother**—does not mean that *tôrâ* teaching will come to an end. The emphasis is on all the people of Yahweh knowing him without being reminded or taught by others. In the new covenant, the heart upon which Yahweh's *tôrâ* is written will know Yahweh and his saving actions that constitute the story of redemption. This includes the acknowledgment of Yahweh as the only true source of life and all provisions needed for existence. Knowledge of Yahweh also means personal and covenantal relationship with him, which in turn requires faithful obedience to the demands of Yahweh's *tôrâ*. Knowing Yahweh thus means an internal predisposition to obeying Yahweh. This eschatological promise is linked to the promise that Yahweh will give his people "a heart to know" him (24:7). Moreover, the new covenant promise is given to all people. The privilege of relation with God is available to all **(they will all know me)**; there will be no rank and no special privilege or status to anyone. No one will be left out in the new covenant relationship from the privilege of knowing Yahweh. **From the least of them to the greatest** will have access to this new relationship with Yahweh and have the opportunity to become full participants in the story of redemption and to fully embrace the laws written on their hearts.

Verse 34 ends with a grand promise from Yahweh, which is another significant new element in the new covenant. Yahweh's promise, **For I will forgive their *iniquity*,** places the new covenant in sharp contrast to the Sinai covenant. Some commentators have argued that this is really the new element in the new covenant (see Lundbom 2004a, 470). The Sinai covenant stipulated stiff punishment of sin and sinners. Forgiveness under the Sinai covenant came through prescribed rituals and the sacrificial system of worship. The new covenant with its promise of the law written on human hearts anticipates a new way of Yahweh's dealing with sin. Indeed the new relation between Yahweh and Israel is possible only because of (*kî*; **For**) Yahweh's forgiving grace. The offer of forgiveness of sin is intensified by the additional promise, **and their sin I will not remember again.** This is a total reversal of 14:10 ("now he will remember their iniquity [NRSV], **and he will visit their sin**"). This forgiving and forgetting of sin refers not only to Israel's past sins that have brought upon it the judgment of death and destruction and the exile, but also sins the people may commit in their renewed relationship with God. Yahweh's promise that he will not remember the sins of his people is intended to liberate them from the power of guilt and the fear of punishment in the new covenant relationship. No longer will they live in fear, but in the assurance of Yahweh's forgiveness of sins.

Forgiveness in the Sinai Covenant and in the New Covenant

Exodus 32 narrates the story of the mass execution of those who were involved in the golden calf apostasy and Yahweh's firm words that he will blot out those who have sinned against him from his book and that he will punish them on the day of punishment (see vv 31-35). The proclamation of Yahweh's goodness and mercy and forgiveness of sin in Exod 34 comes after intense pleading and intercession on the part of Moses (see Exod 33). Even then Yahweh makes plain that he will by no means clear the guilty but he will punish sinners to the third and fourth generation (34:6-7). Exodus 34:6-7 thus makes clear that forgiveness does not exclude the necessity of punishment of sin. The Sinai narrative portrays Yahweh as both forgiving and judging; however, the narrative seems to give more emphasis to the punishment of sin, and includes punishment as an important stipulation of the covenant relationship. Israel continued to experience Yahweh's forgiveness of sin in the course of its history not because it is Yahweh's obligation under the Sinai covenant terms, but because of Yahweh's mercy, grace, compassion, and covenant loyalty (Exod 34:6-7; see also Ps 103:8-14). The theme of punishment for sin is further elaborated in the theology of blessings and curses in Deuteronomy (see particularly chs 27—29). Joshua warned Israel that Yahweh will not forgive their sin (Josh 24:19-20). In the new covenant offer of forgiveness of sin, forgiveness is offered unilaterally and without conditions. God promises to break the vicious cycle of sin and punishment and offers sinners the possibility for new beginnings and new relation with God, and new opportunities to experience God's grace. This promise of forgiveness is a significant new element in the new covenant.

New Covenant in the Ancient Christian Fathers

Augustine saw in the new covenant text an explicit reference to the NT. Irenaeus saw both the old covenant and the new covenant originating from the same God, and Chrysostom argued that one and the same lawgiver gave both covenants. Chrysostom also finds in this text Christ's "pardon of the transgressions of all people . . . , the calling of the Gentiles, the superiority of the new law over the old law, the ease of access, the grace possessed by those who have believed and the gift given in baptism" (Wenthe 2009, 212-19).

FROM THE TEXT

The expression "new covenant" has been historically and theologically understood by the Christian tradition as God's new covenant initiated through Jesus Christ. Various NT passages (Matt 26:28; Luke 22:20; Rom 11:27; 1 Cor 11:25; 2 Cor 3:5-14; Heb 8:8-12; 10:16-17) either allude to or quote Jer 31:31-34 and make the claim of the fulfillment of the new covenant promise in and through the life events of Jesus Christ. Historically and theologically, the Christian community has thus understood itself as the people of God brought together through the new covenant.

This Christian perspective and reading of Jer 31:31-34, however, raises an important question about the promise of this text to the people of Israel. This text, understood in its historical and literary setting, affirms that God-

Israel relationship continues to exist even though Israel has broken the Sinai covenant. This relationship has a prior history, and God's continued relationship with Israel rests on his faithfulness to his covenant promises to Abraham. The eternality of God's covenant with Abraham is the subject of 31:35-37. The people of Israel, as heirs to God's covenant with Abraham, continue to hear in this text God's promise of the possibility of a renewed relationship with them, the promise of a heart that knows God, and the experience of total forgiveness of sins. The new covenant text reminds us that in spite of its announcement of a radical discontinuity with the past, the end of the history of broken covenant, God-Israel relationship continues at a deeper level. God comes to Israel in this text as a God who commits himself to this unfaithful people and offers them new possibilities for experiencing his grace and forgiveness. God's gracious way with Israel thus continues in this text. Christians, along with Paul, can only hope and pray that Israel will someday enter into a full participation in the new covenant relationship with God that has been initiated through Jesus Christ—the fulfillment of the promise far beyond all the expectation of the prophet (Rom 11:25-27).

The offer of the new covenant to the house of Israel and the house of Judah also raises an important question about a proper Christian appropriation of the promise of this text. The writer of Hebrews claims that the old covenant (Sinai covenant) has been made "obsolete" by God by initiating the new covenant (see Heb 8:13). However, it is also important to note that the writer of Hebrews while describing the old covenant as "obsolete," places the Christian hope in Jesus Christ alongside his claim that Christians are heirs to the covenant promises God made to Abraham (Heb 6:13-20; 8:13). Thus Christians need to hear the promised newness in this text as those who have been "grafted" into the community of God that God brought into existence through his covenant promises to Abraham (Rom 11:17-24). It is appropriate for Christians to hear the promise of 31:31-34 as a promise that came to its Jewish audience first, to which Christians are drawn and made full participants through the Christ event. Christian faith is in reality an affirmation of the experience of grace that is promised in this new covenant text. Thus members of the Christian community hear this text in the context of their experience and participation in a new relationship that God established through Jesus Christ that makes it possible for them to be God's people. The Christian reading of this text in this manner invites us to be grateful and humble for the experience of forgiveness of sins and the possibility of newness of life that God promises to effect within us through his new covenant promises. We must also remember, as Fretheim reminds us, that the new covenant promise is not yet "fully fulfilled" (2002, 450). The church still utilizes its resources to teach and promote the knowledge of God **from the least** to **the greatest.** In that sense, the promise of the new covenant continues to be a promise for the future, for the **days** that **are coming.**

The repeated first person emphatic statements in this text (**I will make, I** will put, I will . . . write, I will be, I will forgive) come from God who was offended by the sins of his people. The emphasis of this new covenant promise is on what God intends to do to make newness a possibility. God does not walk away from those who have broken their relationship with him, but he comes to them with the promise of their restoration and a new covenant relationship. Bozak comments that in the Sinai covenant emphasis is placed on God's "deeds of might and power," but in the new covenant emphasis will be on God's "deeds of mercy" (1991, 123). God in his sovereign freedom and grace commits himself to a weak, stubborn, broken, and unfaithful people, and pledges to be their God. His grace and forgiveness makes it possible for them to have a new beginning. This text is a classic expression of divine grace, the ultimate display of which is found in the Gospels in the person of Jesus Christ who came to "seek out and to save the lost" (Luke 19:10 NRSV).

The present condition of the addressees—the house of Israel and the house of Judah—is implicit in the text. The location of the text in the literary and theological context of the Book of Consolation makes clear that exile, displacement, and disrupted relationship with God are the present realities in which the people exist. The new covenant offer is the promise of new realities for people who live in desperate and hopeless conditions. The community that hears this promise also hears the promise of their salvation. Their salvation and restoration will culminate in a new covenant that God will make with them. The historical particularity of the text, however, does not mean that it is a promise fixed in history and given exclusively to a particular people at a particular time. As scripture, we hear in this text God's promise of newness through his gracious work of salvation extended to all dispirited people who live in broken relationship with God. Time, location, and setting may be different, but God's promise of newness and new realities for life is still the same.

In the new covenant the human heart receives special attention as the center of divine activity. God promises to write his law on the heart. Wesley saw here the difference between the law and the gospel. The law "shows duty," according to Wesley, but the gospel "brings the grace of regeneration, by which the heart is changed and enabled for duty" (1975, 2209). The writing of the law on human hearts clearly implies the gift of a new heart and a new inner disposition, and thus the beginning of a new life of obedience and trust in God. What is clearly anticipated here is a thorough cleansing of the corrupt human heart and its deliverance from the power of sin, thus making it ready for the reception of God's instructions. It is important to read this text of Jeremiah in tandem with Ezekiel's elaboration of the cleansing activity of God and the gift of a new heart and a new spirit (Ezek 36:24-27). Peter, in his speech at the Jerusalem Conference, testifies to God's gift of the Holy Spirit to both the Jews ("us") and the Gentiles and speaks of God's cleansing of the hearts of both Jewish and Gentile disciples by faith (Acts 15:8-9 NRSV). In the Christian interpretation of v 33, it is thus possible to include the cleansing and purifying work of the Holy Spirit as the necessary prerequisite to the writing of God's law on human hearts.

The new covenant offer comes to us not only with the promise of a new heart and freedom from the power of sin but also with the gift of pardon and forgiveness of sin. This gift makes it possible for sinners to make a new start without the fear of punishment and guilt of past sins. Whereas in the Sinai covenant God dealt with sin with the threat of punishment, in the new covenant he promises to deal with sin with the offer of grace, mercy, and forgiveness. This does not, however, mean that God has a new attitude toward sin and that sin is not subject to God's judgment in the new covenant. The new covenant promise of God's forgiveness of sin is echoed elsewhere in the Prophets (see Mic 7:18-20; Jer 33:8; Ezek 36:22-32; Isa 43:25; 44:22; 55:7; Ps 103:12). This promise does not give freedom to continue in sin and to subscribe to a false theology of cheap grace; but rather, the text invites its listeners to live in freedom from the power of sin, and to live in the joy of sins forgiven by God who does not remain angry forever (Ps 103:9).

The writing of the law on the heart establishes a new way of God relating with his people, in a more direct and personal way. In the Sinai covenant, God spoke through visible symbols of the presence of the law—the temple and the ark of the covenant where the tablets of the law were deposited—and the law was taught by the priests. In the new covenant, there will be no need for external reminders or the written law to elicit obedience from God's people. The law within is God's gracious will revealed to his people, the essence of which is loving God with one's whole being and loving one's neighbor (Luke 10:27). The law within is thus essentially the law of love, which is the essential basis of all relationships. Clarke explains the intended purpose of the law written on human hearts in this way: "all *within* and all *without* shall be holiness to the Lord" (1823, 337). This element of the new covenant reveals to us a relational God, who by placing within us his law, calls us to enter into a relational knowledge of him; i.e., knowledge of God through intimate involvement and participation in God's life through our love for him. This relational knowledge of God is also essential to our fulfillment of the law of "love your neighbor as yourself" (Luke 10:27).

The new covenant text anticipates a radical restructuring and reordering of community life. In the new covenant community life, there are no kings and priests and scribes and specially privileged people. There is no one left at the bottom of community life. All come to the covenant maker with the same need of the knowledge of God and forgiveness of sin. Moreover, the promises of the new covenant are for all; no one is excluded. From the least among the people to the greatest will all have equal access to the covenant. All will share in the knowledge of God. Forgiveness will be experienced by all.

Though the text is in the form of a unilateral promise from God, the promissory nature of this text anticipates human response through faith and obedience in order to realize the promise. In this regard, this new covenant offer is more like God's covenant promises to Abraham than the Sinai covenant offer to Israel at Sinai. Hidden in this promise is an invitation to its audience to a trusting and faithful response and participation in the relationship it offers. Moreover, this offer of grace and the divine work of writing the law in human hearts make it possible for human beings to do (that is, to obey God's instructions) what they cannot do for themselves. It is possible then to conclude that obedience in the new covenant relationship is grace initiated and grace enabled human response to God's offer of newness to those who live in broken relationship with him.

12. Yahweh's Enduring Relationship with Israel (31:35-37)

BEHIND THE TEXT

This poetic unit contains two speeches of Yahweh, introduced by the messenger formula **thus said Yahweh** (vv 35, 37). Most commentators treat these verses as one unit, but some treat only v 35 as poetry. In the LXX these verses follow a different order (vv 35-36 in the MT are in 38:36-37 in the LXX; v 37 in the MT is 38:35 in the LXX). The LXX sequencing of verses does not show a logical arrangement of the idea conveyed by these verses. Verses 36-37 utilize an "if" (*'im*) . . . "then/also" (*gam*) sequence or "protasis-apodosis sequence in which an impossible (or inconceivable) circumstance negatively reinforces the assurance" (Holladay 1989, 171). Yahweh's enduring relationship with Israel is the assurance given in these verses. Thus it has thematic continuity with the preceding new covenant passage. Huffmon identifies three other biblical texts (Gen 13:16; Jer 33:20-21; 33:25-26) where similar protasis-apodosis argument is found. He concludes that in 31:35-37 this distinctive style is used to reinforce the theme of the new covenant (1999b, 172-82). Its thematic continuity with the new covenant supports the placement of this oracle in the setting of the new covenant, either shortly before the events of 587 B.C. or shortly thereafter.

IN THE TEXT

■ **35** Jeremiah introduces Yahweh as the One who speaks in vv 35-36 and affirms his name as Yahweh Sebaoth. The language of v 35 is similar to that of a hymn of praise or doxology. Yahweh is identified here as the One who **gives** (*nātan*) **the sun *for light* by day.** The first part of v 35 reflects the work of creation on the fourth day (Gen 1:14-18; the verb *nātan* is also used in Gen 1:17). The phrase, who gives **statutes *of the moon and the stars,*** conveys the idea of Yahweh regulating the order and existence of the universe by placing **the moon and stars** as dependable sources of light at night. In Jer 33:20 Yahweh speaks of his unbreakable covenant with the day and his covenant with the night that guarantees the appearance of day and night at "their appointed time" (see also 33:25). The psalmist sees in Yahweh's placement of the sun, the moon, and the stars in the sky a clear evidence of his covenant love (*hesed*), which is worthy of praise (136:9). The final line of v 35, **Who stirs up the sea so that its waves roar—Yahweh Sebaoth is his name,** is also found in Isa 51:15. This line conveys the idea that it is Yahweh who by his stirring up of the sea causes the sea to produce its mighty and roaring waves. Elsewhere in the OT, the sea is sometimes depicted as the symbol of disorder and chaos; however, these texts also convey God's authority and power over the sea and the forces of chaos (see Jer 5:22; Pss 74:13-14; 89:9-10). The psalmist, speaking for the community of faith, describes their confidence in God's presence with them that leads them to have no fear even when the sea roars and threatens to harm their existence (Ps 46:1-3). Jeremiah 31:35 implies that the sea is part of Yahweh's creation and is under the control of the power of **Yahweh Sebaoth,** the sovereign Lord of all the powers of this universe. This hymnic praise thus seems to say that "the sea has no power even to make its own waves" (Keown, Scalise, and Smothers 1995, 136). This verse as a whole indicates that God rules both order (reference to sun, moon, and stars) and disorder (reference to sea) that are part of his creation (Brueggemann 1998, 296).

■ **36** Verse 36 introduces the first protasis-apodosis argument ("if . . . then"). ***These statutes*** refer to the permanent functions assigned to the sun, the moon, and the stars mentioned in v 35. The condition *if* introduces the impossibility of the sun ceasing to give light by day and the moon and stars ceasing to give light by night. They are part of the fixed order of creation, **statutes** of Yahweh that provide regularity and stability to the existence of the universe. It is inconceivable that these statutes will ***depart*** from before Yahweh who established this order of creation. Yahweh says that in the same way, it is inconceivable that **the seed of Israel will cease from being a nation** before him. Since the first (departure of the statues) is impossible, the second is also impossible. **The seed of Israel** (*zeraʿ yiśrāʾēl*) recalls the promise that God made to Abraham in Gen 15:5; 22:17; 26:4. In these Genesis passages, Yahweh's promise is that Abraham's descendants shall be as numerous as the stars in the sky. It is thus very likely that v 36 is a reaffirmation of Yahweh's covenant with Abraham (Lundbom 2004a, 486). Though the Sinai covenant is broken, what makes it possible for Israel to continue to exist as a nation is Yahweh's everlasting covenant with Abraham (Gen 17:13). ***All the days*** reiterates the eternal nature of the covenant with Abraham. It is likely that though this verse is an affirmation of the new covenant, the hidden promise of this verse (the continued existence of Israel) is not contingent on Israel's acceptance of the new covenant offer.

■ **37** The protasis-apodosis argument is used again to affirm Yahweh's covenant promise to Abraham. The first part introduces the protasis ("if" condition), the impossibility of anyone being able to measure **the heavens above,** which is so vast and beyond our imagination. In the same way it is impossible to examine **the foundations of the earth,** which is so deep and unfathomable. If these are impossible tasks for anyone to accomplish, then it is equally impossible that Yahweh will *reject all the seed of Israel.* Yahweh's covenant with Abraham is again reaffirmed here. The phrase *all the seed of Israel* implies the survival of Israel as a people. The destruction of northern Israel and southern Judah did not bring a total end to the nation. These historical events do not mean that Yahweh has totally rejected the whole nation. The surviving people are a testimony to Yahweh's faithfulness to his covenant with Abraham. The last line, **because of all they have done,** indicates that Israel's long history of covenant breaking would have been enough reason to justify Yahweh's total rejection of Israel. Israel's covenant breaking does not, however, evoke hostility and persuade Yahweh to break his covenant with Abraham. The hope of Israel for its future lies certainly in Yahweh's covenant faithfulness.

FROM THE TEXT

As Brueggemann points out, the function of this text is not to emphasize a "fixed" place for Israel "in the cosmos like heaven and earth" but to affirm God's covenant fidelity to Israel even in the midst of the harsh reality of his judgment of the nation (1998, 298). In the end, the future of the nation as a restored community that has received the new covenant offer solely depends on God's faithfulness to the promise he made long ago to Abraham. It is important to remember that God's covenant promise to Abraham also contains the promise of God's blessing to all the families of the earth (Gen 12:3). God's covenant promise is deeply rooted in grace, and the recipients of God's promise therefore have no legal claim on the promise that conveys grace. The text thus reminds us that the well-being of Israel or any nation or any community or any individual rests on God's grace. This grace is given to the worst of sinners as well as to the saints. Paul's testimony, "but by the grace of God I am what I am," is a clear affirmation of the truth about God and his grace as the fundamental premise of his relationship with us (see 1 Cor 15:9-10).

13. The Rebuilding of Jerusalem (31:38-40)

BEHIND THE TEXT

Chapter 31 ends with another eschatological oracle. In the MT the text preserves only **Look, days** and the rest ("are coming") is missing. Commentators think that the MT omission is due to haplography (accidental scribal error of skipping a word during the copying process because the word *baʾim* ["are coming"] and the preceding word *yāmîm* ("days") both end in *îm*). The message of this text is introduced as an *oracle of Yahweh* (v 38). The rebuilding of the city is the central theme here. This has led some commentators to see this as a postexilic add-on to the Book of Consolation. The oracle promises the rebuilding of the city and its landscape that was destroyed and remains in ruins. Lundbom attributes its authorship to Jeremiah and places it after the fall of Jerusalem. He sees in this oracle "a radical word from Yahweh and more daring preaching on the part of Jeremiah" (2004a, 489). It has continuity with the new covenant promise in that this oracle shares with the new covenant promise its eschatological orientation. To the people in exile, the message of the new covenant would have remained an incomplete promise without an additional word about the restoration and the rebuilding of Jerusalem. The new covenant offers Yahweh's forgiveness to his people. The promise of Yahweh's covenant faithfulness to Abraham offers hope for Israel's continued existence (31:35-37). This final promise reflects Yahweh's ongoing commitment to the city, and it serves as a fitting conclusion to the original Book of Consolation (chs 30—31).

IN THE TEXT

■ **38-39** Jerusalem is *the city* in v 38. The announcement that the city shall be rebuilt implies a ruined condition of the city. This message may have originated in the aftermath of the events of 587 B.C. The city will be rebuilt **for Yahweh.** Though this is a promise given to the people who were displaced from the city, the primary purpose of the rebuilding of the city is not to make it a place for the return of the exiled people but for Yahweh to inhabit it. The rebuilding of the city is also necessary to restore Yahweh's honor (see Ezek 36:22). When the city is rebuilt as Yahweh's city, then it will be a fitting place for the people to live.

The phrase **from the Tower of Hananel to the Corner Gate** introduces the boundaries of the city, the listing of which is continued in v 39. The locations mentioned in these verses were most likely the boundaries of the city before its destruction. **The Tower of Hananel** (see Zech 14:10; Neh 3:1) was in the northeast corner of the city, and in the northwest corner of the temple court, between the Fish Gate and the Sheep Gate (see the map of Jerusalem during the days of Nehemiah in IDB 3:1962, 533). Some scholars connect its location with the Antonia Tower rebuilt by Herod the Great. **The Corner Gate** was located on the western side of the city, where the present-day Jaffa Gate is located (Lundbom 2004a, 490). According to 2 Chr 26:9, King Uzziah built a tower at the Corner Gate.

Verse 39 uses the image of someone using a **measuring line** to mark the boundary of the city. The image of a measuring line is frequently found in Ezek 40—48 (see also Zech 2:1-5). The measuring line will go from the Corner Gate **to the hill of Gareb** and from there **to Goah.** These locations are not known to us. Commentators think that the hill of Gareb refers to the hill in the southwest corner of the city. Some have identified with the hill above the Ben Hinnom Valley (see Lundbom 2004a, 491). Goah could also refer to a location in the southern boundary of the city. Verse 39 thus seems to show the measuring line turning south at the Corner Gate and following along the western boundary to the southwestern corner of the city that borders the Ben Hinnom Valley.

■ **40** Chapter 31 concludes with an announcement that even the most defiled areas of the city will become holy in the eschatological day of the rebuilding of the city. **The whole valley where dead bodies and ashes are thrown** refers to the Ben Hinnom Valley in the southwest corner of the city where the Israelites sacrificed children to Molech (2 Kgs 23:10). **All the terraces *up to* the Kidron Valley** also will be made holy because this area was also a defiled place. The Kidron Valley area was also a dumping ground and a place for burning (see 2 Kgs 23:4, 6, 12). **The corner of the Horse Gate** refers to the eastern boundary of the city. The Horse Gate was located at the southeastern corner of the temple complex, and this gate would have served both the temple and the palace quarter (Lundbom 2004a, 493). The Horse Gate was the site of Athaliah's murder (2 Kgs 11:16). When the city is rebuilt, no part of the city will be left for unclean purpose. The entire city will be made ***holy to Yahweh***. ***Holy to Yahweh*** is an engraving on the gold rosette fastened to the turban placed on the forehead of the high priest (Exod 28:36-38). The assertion of this text may have contributed to the designation of Jerusalem as "the holy city" (Isa 48:2; 52:1; see also Rev 21:2, 10).

Verse 40 ends with Yahweh's solemn word that ***it*** (the city) ***shall not be plucked up and destroyed, again for ever.*** The phrases "pluck up" and "destroy" echo Yahweh's commission to Jeremiah in 1:10. The city had been destroyed again in A.D. 70 by the Romans. The emphasis of this word seems to be on ***forever.*** Jerusalem continues to exist as a remarkable testimony of Yahweh's faithfulness to the city.

FROM THE TEXT

The rebuilding and well-being of Jerusalem as God's holy city is a key concern in this text. The city had been made unclean by its inhabitants and as a result God was left with no option but to uproot and destroy it. As Fretheim points out, the rebuilding of Jerusalem is not for the returning exiles but for God (2002, 446). The promise here is that the city will be rebuilt and will become once again the place where God will be present (see a similar idea in the renaming of Jerusalem as "THE LORD IS THERE" in Ezek 48:35). Just as the new covenant offer marks the beginning of a new relationship between God and Israel, the newly rebuilt city marks the new relationship between God and his holy city. The newly rebuilt city will be the visible symbol of God's presence among his redeemed people. The days of uprooting and destruction are over;

the days of building and planting have begun (cf. 1:10). The remarkable and continuous existence of the city, in spite of its occupation by various political powers, is a reminder of God's gracious concern for the well-being of the city. In our modern-day understanding and appropriation of this text, we must take into consideration the fact that God's concern for the well-being of the city extends not only to the city but also to all of its present-day inhabitants—Jews, Arabs, and Christians. No one is left out of God's gracious concern in the new covenant. That message applies here as well.

B. Jeremiah's Confident Hope in the Future of Judah (32:1-44)

BEHIND THE TEXT

Chapter 32, which appears to be a part of the Book of Consolation, could easily have existed as an independent literary unit. Jeremiah's purchase of the field took place while the prophet was confined to the court of the guard. Based on vv 1-2, the events of this chapter could be dated to 588/7 B.C. The circumstances of his arrest and imprisonment are narrated in 37:11-21. Chapter 38 also contains incidents that happened during Jeremiah's confinement in the court of the guard. Chapter 32 thus chronologically belongs with chs 37—38. This chapter is perhaps placed here because of its theological and thematic linkage to chs 30—31.

Chapter 32 for the most part is made up of a mixture of biographical materials (vv 1-5, 6-15), Jeremiah's prayer (vv 16-25), and Yahweh's response (vv 26-44). Jeremiah's purchase of a field from his cousin Hanamel is a key incident reported in this chapter (vv 6-15). He purchased the field to symbolically convey his hope in the return of normal life in the land. This incident serves as the setting of Jeremiah's prayer and Yahweh's response.

There are some similarities between Jeremiah's prayer in vv 16-25 and that of Daniel (9:4-19) and Ezra (9:6-15; Neh 9:6-37). However, there is insufficient evidence to support the view that the prayer in its present form is the work of exilic or postexilic editors. The rationale and the objective of this prayer are not clear. Usually prayers are made to seek or confirm God's will before an action is carried out, whereas in this case Jeremiah's prayer comes after he performs the divine command. If this prayer was meant to raise questions about the wisdom of his purchase of the land under the current circumstances, then Jeremiah would have prayed this prayer prior to purchasing the land. Its present location after the transfer of the deed suggests a doxological function. The prayer is an acknowledgment of the power; nothing is too difficult for Yahweh.

Yahweh's response to Jeremiah's prayer comes in the form of three separate oracles (vv 26-35, 36-41, 42-44). The first oracle (vv 26-35) asserts Yahweh's power to do anything, including handing over Judah into the hands of the Babylonians. The second oracle (vv 36-41) affirms Yahweh's power to restore the people from the lands of their exile. The third oracle (vv 42-44) focuses on Yahweh's plan to restore normal life in the land, which had been disrupted by the invading army of Babylon.

IN THE TEXT

1. Jeremiah's Arrest and Imprisonment (32:1-5)

■ **1-5** Verse 1 reports the coming of Yahweh's word to Jeremiah **in the tenth year of Zedekiah.** This year is further identified as **the eighteenth year of Nebuchadnezzar.** The attempt to synchronize Zedekiah's tenth year (588/7 B.C.) with the eighteenth year of Nebuchadnezzar has some difficulty. According to Bright, this is correct if we count Nebuchadnezzar's accession in the fall of 605 as the first year, instead of his first official regnal year, which was 604/3 (1965, 236). The chronology of Zedekiah's kingship is synchronized here with the chronology of the king of Babylon perhaps because of the political domination of Babylon over Judah (Lundbom 2004a, 502). What follows in vv 2-5 is a parenthetical report that explains the precise setting of the coming of Yahweh's word to Jeremiah. The actual word that came from Yahweh is stated in v 7. Verse 2 reports that Yahweh's word came to Jeremiah when Jerusalem was being besieged by **the army of the king of Babylon.** This was also the time when the prophet was **confined in the court of the guard in the palace of the king of Judah** (v 2). Lundbom suggests that the siege mentioned here is the second and final siege of Jerusalem in the summer of 587 B.C. (2004a, 502-3). During this siege of the city, Jeremiah was in prison in the court of the guard in the royal palace complex.

Verse 3a indicates that Zedekiah had imprisoned him in the court of the guard. Verses 3b-5 recount Jeremiah's word spoken against Zedekiah and the city as the reason for the imprisonment of Jeremiah. These verses seem to imply that it was Zedekiah who imprisoned the prophet for his unpatriotic statements. This is different from the narratives in chs 37—38 that report Jeremiah's imprisonment.

The narrator reports Zedekiah's words in vv 3b-5, which presumably is a quotation of an oracle that Jeremiah uttered against the city and the king. The content of vv 3b-5 is somewhat similar to Jeremiah's oracle that he gave to Zedekiah in 34:2-3. Zedekiah begins with a question, **why do you prophesy,** followed by the oracle that Jeremiah uttered against the city and the king. Zedekiah's question and the oracle of Jeremiah thus explain the reason for the imprisonment of the prophet. Zedekiah's primary charge against Jeremiah is his prophecy against Jerusalem. The oracle Zedekiah quotes as Yahweh's word spoken by Jeremiah speaks of Yahweh's plan to give **this city into the hands of** *the king of Babylon.* This fate of the city has been a consistent and often-repeated message of Jeremiah (see 21:10; 32:28; 34:2, 22; 37:8-10; 38:3, 18, 23). Verses 4-5 of ch 32 describe the impending fate of Zedekiah. Yahweh also plans to give Zedekiah *into the hands of the king of Babylon.* The king will not escape the army of Babylon. What follows is the description of a face-to-face encounter between the king of Babylon and Zedekiah. The king of Babylon will speak to Zedekiah (*his mouth shall speak with his mouth*) and the king of Babylon will look into the eyes of Zedekiah (*his eyes shall see his eyes*) who will stand before him as a prisoner of war (see also 34:3). When the Babylonians eventually captured Jerusalem in 587 B.C. Zedekiah attempted to escape the city, but he was apprehended by the Babylonian army and he stood before Nebuchadnezzar who was at Riblah in central Syria. The Babylonian king pronounced his sentence on Zedekiah, the rebel vassal. The helpless Judean king witnessed the execution of his sons and the nobles of Judah, before he was blinded by Nebuchadnezzar (39:5-7).

Verse 5 of ch 32 contains the prediction of Zedekiah's exile to Babylon (see also 34:3). According to 39:7, after he was blinded, the Babylonians bound Zedekiah in chains and he was taken to Babylon. Blinded and chained, the Judean king would have been forced to walk the long road to the land of his exile as a prisoner of war. Yahweh also states that Zedekiah will be in Babylon until he *visits* (*pqd* means "visit," "attend," "punish," etc.) him. Though *pqd* conveys the idea of Yahweh's visitation to bring deliverance or salvation, here the idea is most likely his visitation to carry out his punishment on Zedekiah. What is intended here is Zedekiah's death in the land of Babylon as Yahweh's punishment. Zedekiah's death in Babylon as a prisoner is mentioned in 52:11. The oracle ends with a strong warning that Judah's attempt to fight the Babylonians will not be successful. The LXX omits the words *until I punish him, oracle of Yahweh, for though you fight the Chaldeans, you shall not succeed.* The MT has **you** in the second person plural form, which indicates that this warning is given to the people of Jerusalem as well as to Zedekiah.

2. Jeremiah Purchases Hanamel's Field (32:6-15)

■ **6-8** These verses contain Yahweh's word to Jeremiah and the fulfillment of that word. The word that came to Yahweh in the tenth year of Zedekiah, while Jeremiah was confined in the court of the guard, is again introduced with a customary introduction in v 6. Yahweh's word to Jeremiah is very brief. Yahweh announces to Jeremiah the news about the upcoming visit of Hanamel, son of Jeremiah's uncle Shallum, with his request to Jeremiah to purchase for himself Hanamel's field in Anathoth (v 7). What prompted Hanamel to sell his field is not clear. What is clear is that he owned land in the tribal territory of Benjamin. Yahweh also discloses the reason why Hanamel would be coming to Jeremiah with this request. According to Hanamel, Jeremiah has the **right** (*mišpaṭ*) *of redemption* (*gĕʾullâ*) *to acquire* Hanamel's field (v 7). The NIV reading (**because** as nearest relative it is your right and duty to buy it) is an explanation of the Hebrew text, which is literally, *yours is the right of redemption to acquire* it. Hanamel will request Jeremiah to act as a redeemer (*gōʾēl*) so that his field will remain in the family of Hanamel and Jeremiah.

Verse 8 reports the fulfillment of Yahweh's word. As Yahweh has spoken to Jeremiah, Hanamel came to Jeremiah who was confined to the **court of the guard,** and presented his appeal to the prophet. Jeremiah's confinement was perhaps not total isolation from the public, but rather he was free to receive visitors. Hanamel's speech to Jeremiah is a slightly expanded version of what Yahweh announced to Jeremiah in v 7 as the words of Hanamel. Hanamel's request to Jeremiah to **buy** the field in Anathoth is expanded to include its location **in the land of Benjamin. Yours is the right of redemption to acquire** in v 7 is expanded in v 8: **yours is the right** (*mišpaṭ*) **of possession** (*yĕruššâ* also means "inheritance") **and yours is the redemption** (*gĕʾullâ*); **buy it for yourself.** This appeal indicates that Jeremiah is the next person in the family who has the legal obligation to fulfill the duty to buy this field from Hanamel. If there were other relatives closer to Hanamel with more legal obligation and duty to buy the field, they could have declined and refused his request citing their own financial difficulty. The request begins and ends with an appeal to Jeremiah to buy the field for himself.

■ **9-12** Verses 9-12 give a first person report of the legal steps Jeremiah undertook to purchase the field from Hanamel. The text does not say who determined the price or what criteria was used to assess the value of the field. Neither do we know the size of the field. It is possible that Hanamel's request included the asking price for his property. However, it is likely that the land was not worth much due to the political situation of that period. The text simply reports that Jeremiah **weighed out for him** (Hanamel) **the silver—seventeen shekels of silver.** Since the intent of this symbolic act was to convey the message that life will return to normal in the land and that there will be land transactions as usual, it is possible to assume that the price he paid was the fair market value of the field under normal circumstances.

What follows in vv 10-11 is a summary of the steps that Jeremiah took to legally transfer the ownership of the field from Hanamel to him. The MT (**I wrote in the deed and I sealed**) seems to suggest that Jeremiah himself wrote the deed. However, since Baruch the scribe was present among others in the court of the guard (vv 12-15) where this transaction took place, it is more likely that the deed was drawn up by him at the instruction of Jeremiah. The MT (**I wrote in**) most likely refers to the signing of the deed by the prophet (see the NIV, **I signed and sealed the deed**). The phrase **I sealed** seems to suggest that Jeremiah placed his own seal on the deed. He also had **witnesses** called to witness this transaction, who also placed their signatures on the deed (see v 12). The transaction was completed when Jeremiah **weighed out the silver on the scales.** Verse 10*b* repeats the report of the payment of silver to Hanamel (see v 9). After the payment was made, Jeremiah took possession of the **sealed deed of purchase** as well as the **open copy** of the deed (v 11). Verse 11 informs us of the practice of making duplicate copies of legal documents in the ancient world on the top and bottom halves of a single sheet of papyrus. The copy on the top half of the sheet would be rolled up and sealed, and the copy on the bottom half of would be left open or unsealed (see Lundbom 2004a, 508, for a detailed description of the making of sealed and unsealed documents). The deed of purchase contained **the contract and the conditions** (MT literally means "commandment and the statutes") of the transactions.

After Jeremiah took possession of the deed, he entrusted the deed to **Baruch son of Neriah, the son of Mahseiah** for safekeeping (v 12). The witnesses of this action included Hanamel, **the witnesses who** signed the deed of purchase (**who wrote in the deed of purchase**), and **all the Judahites who were sitting in the court of the guard.** Verse 12 indicates that what appeared to be a private family business transaction was attended by a crowd of Judahites who were present in the court of the guard.

Baruch the Scribe

Baruch belonged to a prominent family of scribes. The names of various members of this family (Mahseiah, Neriah, Baruch) have been found on the Arad ostraca and on various seals that come from this period (Lundbom 2004a, 509). Baruch's brother Seraiah was an officer in the administration of Zedekiah. Jeremiah sent with Seraiah a scroll that contained his words of judgment on Babylon to be read in Babylon and then to be thrown into the River Euphrates with a stone tied to the scroll (51:59-64). At an earlier time, in the fourth year of Jehoiakim (605 B.C.), Jeremiah had utilized the service of Baruch to write on a scroll the words he dictated to him (36:1-4). However, here in v 12 we find the first mention of Baruch in the book. In 36:26 and 32, Baruch is identified as a "scribe" (*sōpēr*). Some scholars label the materials in chs 36—45 as the "Baruch Narrative" or "Baruch Document." Based on 25:1-13 and ch 36, most commentators think that chs 1—25 contain the oracles that Jeremiah dictated to Baruch in 605 B.C. It is very likely that Baruch was the prophet's personal scribe as well as a trusted friend, and thus the most suitable individual to keep the legal documents of the prophet. Baruch was taken along with Jeremiah by force by Johanan and his associates who accused Jeremiah of being unduly influenced by his friend Baruch. Baruch and the prophet were among the Judean refugees who settled down in Tahpanhes in Egypt (43:1-7).

■ **13-15** Verse 13 is a first person report of Jeremiah giving a command to Baruch. The command that follows in v 14 is actually a word from Yahweh, introduced with the typical messenger introduction, **Thus said Yahweh Sebaoth God of Israel** (v 14a). Yahweh's word is found again in v 15; thus Yahweh is the actual speaker in both verses. In v 14, Jeremiah commands Baruch to place both the sealed and the unsealed copy of the deed in an earthenware jar. There is no specific command to seal the jar, but it is implied in the following phrase (***in order that they may stand many days***). Verse 14 gives us a glimpse into the ancient practice of storing documents in clay jars. The Dead Sea Scrolls indicate the widespread use of earthenware jars to store documents by the community at Qumran. The command to Baruch shows that Yahweh's plan is to preserve a record of this transaction for future generations of Judah. There are no further instructions given on how and where to store the earthenware jar. Burying jars that contained valuable materials or hiding them at some safe place such as a cave was a common practice in the ancient times. Yahweh's word in v 15 (**houses, fields and vineyards will again be bought in this land**) makes clear the message that underlies Jeremiah's symbolic action. This deed will be the evidence of the truthfulness and the reliability of Yahweh's promise to Judah that life will return to normal and that the people of Judah will again be involved in normal business transactions such as buying houses, fields, and vineyards. The phrase **in this land** also conveys a strong message to those who may have misunderstood Jeremiah's instruction to those who were exiled in 597 B.C. to build houses and plant gardens in Babylon (29:5). The future of Judah is not in Babylon, but in this land, the land of promise. The exile is short-term; the people exiled to Babylon will return to their homeland, which is now being given into the hands of the Babylonians.

Bonhoeffer on Jeremiah 32:15

"'Houses and fields and vineyards shall again be bought in this land' proclaims Jeremiah (32:15), in paradoxical contrast to his prophecies of woe, just before the destruction of the holy city. It is a sign from God and a pledge of a fresh start and a great future, just when all seems black. Thinking and acting for the sake of the coming generation, but being ready to go any day without fear or anxiety—that, in practice, is the spirit in which we are forced to live. It is not easy to be brave and keep that spirit alive, but it is imperative." (Bonhoeffer 1971, 15)

3. Jeremiah's Prayer (32:16-25)

■ **16-17** Verse 16 is an autobiographical report that the prophet's prayer came after he had given the deed of purchase to Baruch son of Neriah. The first part of the prayer is acknowledgment of the awesome power of Yahweh who made the heavens and the earth by his ***great strength*** and by his **outstretched arm.** The faith in Yahweh as the maker of heavens and earth that is being expressed here is consistent with the creation theology in 27:5. In both texts Yahweh is described as performing his mighty work of creation by his great strength and by his outstretched arm (see Deut 9:29 where the idiom "great power" and "outstretched arm" is found in connection with the Exodus deliverance). Jeremiah's claim that ***nothing is too difficult*** for Yahweh is reiterated in Yahweh's response to Jeremiah's prayer (see v 27; ***Is anything too difficult for me?***).

■ **18-19** In vv 18-19, the focus of Jeremiah's prayer is on the righteous judgment and wisdom of Yahweh. Verse 18a sums up Israel's retribution theology (see Exod 20:5-6; 34:7), which guarantees Yahweh's **covenant faithfulness** (*ḥesed*) **to thousands** or to several generations of those who live in covenant relationship with Yahweh. Negatively, this retribution theology also guarantees serious repercussions of covenant breaking that will last for several generations. Future generations thus stand to inherit the blessings of covenant fidelity and the curses of covenant breaking. This rigid system of divine retribution is modified in Jer 31:30. **The laps of their children** is not literally one's lap but a figurative expression of recompense. The Hebrew word used here (*ḥêq*) refers to the pocket-like fold in a robe above the midsection large enough to carry infants or lamps (Lundbom 2004a, 512). Verse 18 concludes with a doxological acclamation of Yahweh as **the great God**, **the mighty,** whose name is **Yahweh Sebaoth.** In v 19, Yahweh is further praised for his excellent **counsel** and mighty **deeds** and for his watchful eye over all the children of humanity in order to distribute appropriately his justice that they deserve on the basis of their good or bad deeds.

■ **20-25** In vv 20-23, the focus of the prayer shifts to Yahweh's redemption of Israel from Egypt and Israel's rebellion. Yahweh is directly addressed here. The prophet recalls here that Yahweh has shown **signs and wonders in Egypt** and that he continues to perform such signs and wonders **in Israel** and **among all humanity.** There is no reference to any specific action he performed in the recent history of Judah. The prophet simply acknowledges here that Yahweh who performed mighty acts in the past history of Israel is involved in the same way in the present historical events. Yahweh's name is known not only in Israel but throughout the world as the One who performs signs and wonders. The clearest evidence of the power of Yahweh is the deliverance of Israel from its bondage in Egypt. **Signs and wonders** in that historical context refer to the ten plagues and the miraculous deliverance at the Sea (Exod 7:3). **Mighty hand, outstretched arm,** and **great terror** (Jer 32:21) are all typical expressions associated with the Exodus story (Deut 4:34). Through signs and wonders Yahweh delivered Israel from Egypt and gave them the land he promised to the ancestors (Jer 32:22). Jeremiah recalls here the conquest and settlement tradition. Jeremiah mentions Yahweh's past saving actions only to emphasize the rebellious response of Israel to Yahweh (v 23). The goal of the prayer at this point is to show that Judah's present calamities are Yahweh's just and righteous judgment upon a recalcitrant people. The nation is suffering the consequence of its long history of rebellion against Yahweh.

Verse 24 sums up the present historical crisis. The picture being drawn here is that of a city under siege with the effects of a terrible war seen all around. Siege ramps are found outside Jerusalem, and Yahweh has given the city into the hands of the Babylonian army. What one sees around the city is the wielding of sword and the devastating effects of famine and pestilence.

These things are happening precisely as what Yahweh said would happen to the people who have rebelled against him. Yahweh is a witness of all these terrible things that are happening to the city.

The intent of v 25 is not clear. This verse indicates that the instruction to buy the field with witnesses to the transaction came from Yahweh, though it is not stated in Yahweh's initial speech to Jeremiah concerning Hanamel's visit in vv 6-7. Commentators see here an expression of doubt or misgiving on the part of Jeremiah about the land transaction in light of the present circumstances of Jerusalem and Judah. But the overall doxological nature of this prayer leads us to consider v 25 as the prophet's agreement with Yahweh's seemingly impossible word. He has done what Yahweh had asked him to do. Now he is a partner with Yahweh and an actual participant with him in the shaping of Judah's future. He has been preaching about restoration; now he has put his money where his mouth is. The rest is now up to Yahweh. The only thing he can do is to wait for Yahweh to fulfill his word concerning the return of normal life activities in Judah.

4. Yahweh's Response (32:26-44)

■ **26-35** The first oracle that we find here as Yahweh's response to the prophet is essentially a reiteration of his judgment word against the city with a catalog of the sins of Israel and Judah that provoked him to turn against the city. Yahweh begins his speech with a solemn declaration that he is **Yahweh, the God of all flesh,** which parallels Jeremiah's acknowledgment of Yahweh as the maker of the heavens and the earth at the beginning of his prayer (v 17). This is followed by a rhetorical question, **Is anything too difficult for me?** This again echoes Jeremiah's claim that nothing is too difficult for Yahweh (v 17). He has the power to destroy and the power to save. The present situation is the work of Yahweh; he is the One who has given the city into hands of the Babylonians (v 28). The city is destined to be burned by the Babylonians. This fiery judgment will destroy the city and all the houses in the city that have been centers of Baal worship (v 29). The list of sins that Judah committed include burning incense to Baal and pouring drink offering to other gods (v 29), doing only evil from their youth (v 30), idolatry or doing evil with the work of their hands (v 30), turning their backs to Yahweh (v 33), refusal to take correction (v 33), defiling the temple by placing detestable idols in it (v 34), and building high places for Baal in the Valley of Hinnom and sacrificing their children to Molech (v 35). Verse 31 seems to suggest that from the day the city was built up, it was destined to be removed from Yahweh's presence. Most likely v 31 refers to the building up of the city with evil in its later history, and not to its original founding by David as his city, after taking control of it from the Jebusites (2 Sam 5:6-10).

Yahweh's speech thus justifies his judgment against the city. The current political situation that Judah faces is not the work of a despotic deity; neither is it the work of a massive military power that is engaged in the conquest of the world. Judah has determined its own destiny by its recalcitrant behavior. The nation alone is responsible for its actions. The present calamity is the direct consequence of Judah's sinful conduct and covenant breaking.

■ **36-41** Yahweh's second oracle contains the promise of restoration and eternal covenant (vv 36-44). Verse 36 reflects the pessimistic attitude of the people. They are well aware of the fact that Yahweh has given the city into the hands of the king of Babylon. What awaits them is the **sword** of the Babylonian army, and the devastating effects of **famine** and ***pestilence.*** Yahweh's message is to those who see no hope beyond the tragic consequences of the Babylonian invasion. Yahweh's speech assures them that the current political situation does not determine forever the future of Judah. Yahweh's plan is to gather his exiled people from all the lands of their exile and to bring them back and to ***make them dwell in safety*** in their homeland (v 37). The judgment of dispersion is the work of Yahweh; the One who drives them away in his anger and wrath is the One who will gather them and bring them back to their homeland where they will live under peaceful conditions. The repeated first person pronouncements (***I am gathering . . . I will bring them . . . I will make them . . . I will give them,*** etc., in vv 37-41) indicate emphasis on Yahweh's personal involvement in the restoration of the exiled people of Israel. Israel in exile does nothing to deserve Yahweh's salvation. The promise of peace and security is what Yahweh guaranteed to Israel prior to its entrance into Canaan under the leadership of Joshua (Deut 12:10). There is a new world that awaits Israel beyond the days of its exile. This new world is the creation of Yahweh who is the maker of the heavens and the earth. The experience of the people in this new world will be the same as that of their ancestors when they came out of their bondage in Egypt.

Yahweh's intent is to make Israel once again his people (**they will be my people**) and for him to be known as their God (**I will be their God**) (v 38). Verse 38 discloses Yahweh's firm resolve to restore Israel that has broken its covenant with Yahweh. Here we find the reiteration of the new covenant promise (see 31:33). Judah, by its senseless acts of unfaithfulness, has broken the covenant with Yahweh. However, Yahweh remains gracious; he is determined not to make the judgment of the exile a permanent disruption of his relationship with Israel. His covenantal solidarity with Israel, though interrupted by the exile, will continue as in the days of the Sinai covenant.

Yahweh's promise to the exiled people also includes "one heart and one way" (32:39 NRSV). The goal of this is to make it possible for the people to ***fear*** Yahweh ***all their days for their good.*** The gift of "one heart and one way" is implied in the promise of the new covenant wherein the law is written on human hearts (31:31-34; see also Ezek 11:19-20; 36:26-27). The phrase "one heart and one way" expresses "singleness of mind and purpose" (Bright 1965, 295) or a "new disposition toward Yahweh which permits full trust in God"

(Brueggemann 1998, 308). In the new covenant promise it is anticipated that all will "know" Yahweh (31:34). Here in 32:39, the gift of "one heart and one way" (NRSV) will lead everyone to **fear** Yahweh. Fretheim suggests that knowing Yahweh and fearing Yahweh are essentially the same reality: "knowing stresses the closeness of the relationship . . . while fearing (in the sense of awe) makes clear that the relationship is asymmetrical (God remains God and humans remain human)" (2002, 466-67). Those who fear Yahweh are mindful of his place as the Creator; he alone is the object of their praise and worship. Verse 39 indicates that the outcome of the people's fear of Yahweh is not only their own **good** but also the good of their children who come after them (Deut 4:10; 6:2-3, 24). What Yahweh promises here is a structured and orderly life for the community, wherein the goodness of the Creator will be in abundant supply. This condition will be enjoyed by all the future generations of the restored community.

Jeremiah 32:40 introduces the promise of a radically new relationship between Yahweh and Israel. The relationship between Yahweh and Israel has been disrupted by Israel's long history of sinful behavior. The exile is the clearest sign of the disruption of relationship between Yahweh and Israel. What Yahweh offers to Israel is not a simple mending of the broken relationship, but a radically new relationship that cannot be broken. Yahweh's promise is that he will make for them an **eternal covenant** (*běrît ʿôlām*; see also 50:5). Commentators think that this covenant is the same as the new covenant promised in 31:31-34. This covenant, unlike the Sinai covenant that is broken by Israel, is called **eternal** because it is given without any conditions, but only with promises. It is eternal because it is a unilateral offer on the part of Yahweh. There are no conditions that the people are called to keep. Whereas the future of the Sinai covenant rested on the faithful obedience of the people to the conditions of the covenant, the future of this new covenant rests on the faithfulness of Yahweh. Yahweh's eternal promise is that he will ***not turn away*** from his people and will not refrain from doing good to them.

Yahweh also promises to put his ***fear*** in their hearts to motivate the people to remain faithful to him (v 40); compare with ***I will place my law in their inward parts and on their heart I will write it*** (31:33). The positive outcome of Yahweh's gift of "one heart" to his people is a new disposition of the heart that orients them to a new perspective of Yahweh; i.e., to regard him with utter amazement and reverence in their hearts. Yahweh's promise also includes an anticipation of fidelity on the part of the people. The gift of one heart will motivate the people not to ***turn away*** from Yahweh, as they have done in their previous relationship with him. In the new covenant relationship, both Yahweh and his people will mutually enjoy covenant fidelity.

The second oracle ends with an announcement that Yahweh will **rejoice in doing . . . good** to the exiled community and that he will **plant them in this land *in truth*** (v 41). Yahweh was angry with his covenant people because of their covenant breaking way of life, and he drove them out of the land in his wrath and fury (v 37). The promise of restoration and the offer of a new heart show that Yahweh does not remain angry forever. The people who were uprooted from their land will be planted again in their land. The idea of Yahweh planting Israel echoes the commission to Jeremiah in 1:10 (see also 24:6; 31:27-28). Restoration is Yahweh's good work on behalf of his people, which he will perform with great joy. Yahweh will also carry out his work in **truth** (*'emet*), **with all** of his **heart** (*lēb*) and all of his **soul** (*nepeš*). **In truth** is an expression "normally reserved for the people and their commitment to Yahweh" (Lundbom 2004a, 521). Yahweh makes it known that he will be faithful to fulfill his promise, that his promise can be trusted, and that he is a trustworthy promise maker. Moreover, Yahweh makes this promise with "all of the divine heart and soul" (Fretheim 2002, 468). **With all my heart and with all my soul** is an expression found only here in the OT in reference to Yahweh (Lundbom 2004a, 521). Yahweh's command to his people is that they love him with all their heart, soul, and strength (Deut 6:5). Here Yahweh reciprocates the same degree of wholehearted and energetic love and loyalty to his people. He will be passionate about planting his people in their homeland, and he fully intends to keep this promise.

■ **42-44** In the final oracle Yahweh says that he is bringing about **all the good** that he has promised to his people (v 42). This oracle also interprets the significance of Jeremiah's purchase of the land. In the past the people have experienced **great evil** that Yahweh sent against them. However, the destructive days of judgment are over. What is ahead is a future filled with the good things Yahweh is planning for them. This future is just as certain as the judgment the people have experienced. **All the good** that Yahweh promises are return of the people from the land of exile and the resumption of normal life activities in the land of promise (vv 43-44). Fields will be bought in the land that the people now regard as a desolate place with no human or animal life, a land that has been given into the hand of the Babylonians.

FROM THE TEXT

The story of Jeremiah's purchase of the field is among a long list of stories in the Bible that conveys to us the faith of those who have gone before us, those who have dared to bet on the future when there seemed to be no future at all. From our human perspective and analysis of political realities and economic and financial data, we might conclude that Jeremiah made a bad investment. If we assume that fifteen shekels was all the prophet had as his worldly possession, then it is also possible to say that this transaction is analogous to someone emptying out the savings account to invest in a company that is selling off its once valuable stock for pennies a share. The story of this chapter is one of faith in action that may not make much sense to modern readers. In this kind of investment, one ventures to put all the stock knowing that there is no immediate return but only hope that conditions will turn around and that better days are ahead. Jeremiah's hope is in a future promised by God. He has been relentless in proclaiming this hope, and now he invests in that promised future though that future is completely closed off to his contemporaries. Moreover, he made this investment not for any personal gain, but for the sake of future generations to give them the guarantee of God's promised future for them. The prophet's hope and his invitation to his readers to trust in God's promised future for them originate in God's words. The God who makes promises in this text is the God who keeps his promises. Jeremiah is certain of that truth, and his faith is rooted and grounded in that truth. This text is thus a powerful challenge to its readers today to put their trust in God when it is difficult to trust God because of present realities of misfortune and painful situations in life. It is trust in the promise-keeping fidelity of God that equips us to bet on the future that does not seem to exist. Trust also makes it possible for us to see the future as secure under the sovereign control of God who alone has the power to shape our future and give us hope (cf 29:11).

Jeremiah's prayer and God's responses affirm one significant truth about God: nothing is too difficult for God. This text conveys not only the courageous and hope-filled actions of Jeremiah but also the solemn words of God that he is able to overcome any difficulties and obstacles to bring about new realities for his people. There is nothing that is too difficult for God. This affirmation of the power of God to do the impossible runs through the stories of the Bible, most importantly in the story of a barren couple whom God has called to be a blessing to all the families of the earth through their promised descendants (Gen 18:14; see Gen 12:3), and in the words of the angel to Mary, a virgin who was chosen by God to be the mother of Jesus the Son of God, the Savior of humanity (Luke 1:37). It is this power that is displayed in Ezekiel's vision of the rebirth of a nation out of the broken and dispirited condition of the exile (see 37:1-14). It is this power of God that makes it possible for us to enter the kingdom of God (Mark 10:27). It is this power of God "who gives life to the dead and calls into existence things that do not exist" that summons us to believe and to hope "against hope" (Rom 4:17-18 NRSV). It is this power that we find displayed most vividly in the death and resurrection of Jesus Christ, through which we are enabled to pass on from death to life, not only in the present world, but also in the world to come on the day of resurrection. The power of God to bring newness—to give the people of a stubborn and rebellious heart a new heart and a new spirit, to make the offer of a new covenant when the people broke the new covenant, to give hope for the future when the future seems utterly nonexistent—is the power of grace, God's pure gift to those who least deserve it. The God of this text—the God of Jeremiah—is the God who breaks into the impossible situations of life and creates a future filled with hope and his blessings to those who see no hope and escape out of their present miserable existence. He is indeed the God of grace and the God of wonders, the sovereign Creator and the Lord of the universe.

C. The Full Restoration of Israel (33:1-26)

BEHIND THE TEXT

Chapter 33 has two major parts; the first part (vv 1-13) is found in 40:1-13 in the LXX. The second part (vv 14-26) is missing entirely in the LXX. Chapter 33 begins with an introduction that places the origin of the content of this chapter in the court of the guard where Jeremiah was confined as a prisoner (33:1). This introduction links this chapter to ch 32, the setting of which is also Jeremiah's imprisonment in the court of the guard (32:1-2). In the first part (33:1-13) there are four oracles. Jeremiah is the recipient of the first oracle (vv 1-3). In this oracle, Yahweh promises to reveal to the prophet deep and mysterious things. The citizens of Jerusalem and Judah are the recipients of the remaining oracles. Oracle 2 (vv 4-9) announces the destruction and death of Jerusalem, but it also promises the restoration of Jerusalem. The first two oracles reflect a setting prior to the destruction of Jerusalem. Oracles 3 (vv 10-11) and 4 (vv 12-13) contain the promise of the restoration of Judah's social, religious, and economic life. The second part (vv 14-26) also has four oracles. The restoration of Davidic kingship is the subject of oracle 1 (vv 14-16). Oracle 2 (vv 17-18) announces a future in which Israel's royal and priestly lines will continue forever. Yahweh's undying fidelity to his covenant with David and the Levitical priests is announced in oracle 3 (vv 19-22). In oracle 4 (vv 23-26), Yahweh again affirms his fidelity to the Davidic covenant. The content of vv 10-26 assumes a situation after the fall of Jerusalem in 587 B.C.

Some scholars reject the Jeremianic authorship of ch 33 and place the content of this chapter in the exilic or postexilic periods. Carroll thus labels ch 33 as a "post-Deuteronomistic postscript to the cycle of salvation expectations in chs 30-31" (1986, 634). Those who assign this chapter to a later date see in this chapter the portrait of Judah as a devastated land. Bright places vv 1-13 along with the content of ch 32; however, he thinks that vv 14-26 were added to the book at a later time (1965, 298). Holladay likewise attempts to reconstruct the core of Jeremianic text in vv 1-13, but he places vv 14-26 in the postexilic setting (1989, 222-24, 229). Lundbom locates vv 1-9 between the symbolic act of the purchase of the field and the destruction of Jerusalem, somewhere between 587 and 586 B.C. (2004a, 529, 533). He places the rest of the chapter in the days immediately after the fall of Jerusalem (2004a, 537, 541, 542, 546).

IN THE TEXT

1. The Promise of Healing, Prosperity, and Security (33:1-13)

a. Yahweh's Promise to Jeremiah (33:1-3)

■ **1** Verse 1 provides the narrator's introduction, which locates the court of the guard as the setting of the first oracle (vv 2-3). This is a **second** occurrence of revelation from Yahweh to Jeremiah during his imprisonment, the first being the command to buy the field from Hanamel (32:6-8).

■ **2-3** This oracle begins with Yahweh's self-identification, which includes an emphatic claim of Yahweh as the maker of the earth and Yahweh's proclamation of his name (v 2). The third person feminine pronoun suffix (*it*) of the verb forms **made, formed,** and **established** in the MT most likely refers to "the earth"; most English versions have added **the earth** (following the LXX *gēn*) after the first verb to clarify the direct object. The verb forms **made** (*'āsāh*) and **formed** (*yāṣar*) belong to the vocabulary of the creation account in Gen 2:4*b*, 7-8, 19). **Yahweh is his name** appears in a slightly different form in Jer 10:16 and 32:18 (**Yahweh Sebaoth is his name**). In this self-acclamation, Yahweh reveals himself as the maker of heaven and earth, the all-powerful God with whom all things are possible, and his character and reputation as a trustworthy God. Verse 3 begins with a command given to Jeremiah to **call** to Yahweh in prayer, followed by Yahweh's solemn promise that he will answer Jeremiah's prayer. What Yahweh promises to reveal to Jeremiah are things that are **great** and **hidden,** things that Jeremiah has not yet known or experienced in his life. Lundbom states: "All genuine prophecy is hidden or inaccessible until Yahweh reveals it to his prophet" (2004a, 529). The oracle of the destruction of the city and its subsequent restoration in vv 4-9 reveals the hidden things that Yahweh alludes to in v 3.

b. The Restoration of Jerusalem (33:4-9)

This oracle has two parts: the first part (vv 4-5) serves as the setting for the second part (vv 6-9). In the first part the text conveys the tragic end of those who attempt to defend the city against the Babylonian siege ramps and the army. This is followed by a restoration oracle that promises Judah and Israel well-being and security in their life and relationship with Yahweh. The oracle was most likely given in the final days of Judah, before the collapse of the city in 587 B.C.

■ **4-5** The focus of attention in v 4 is the **houses of this city** and the **houses of the kings of Judah.** The text indicates that the houses inside the wall surrounding Jerusalem are being torn down to defend the city against the **siege ramps** and the Babylonian army that is wielding its **sword** outside the city wall. The reference is most likely to the houses that are near or attached to the city wall. These houses are being torn down by the defenders of the city to fortify the inside of the city wall (Lundbom 2004a, 531). Holladay suggests an emendation of the MT *heḥāreb* (**the sword**) to *haḥārakîm* ("crenels") and argues that the text indicates the demolition of the houses of the city to create battlements (small mound like merlons and crenels) to fight against the Babylonians (1989, 225). Though it is an interesting explanation, the emendation of the MT here is unnecessary. In v 5, the focus shifts to **those coming to fight the Chaldeans** (*bāʾîm lĕhillāḥēm ʾet-hakkaśdîm*). The oracle warns that the defenders of the city will fall by the sword of the Babylonians. The sword of the enemy is the weapon of Yahweh's **anger** and his **wrath** against the defenders of Jerusalem. The city is destined to suffer this tragedy because of the evil committed inside the city by those who are now attempting to defend it. Yahweh's anger, wrath, and hiding of his face—all express his uncompromising attitude toward the citizens of Jerusalem who have brought upon themselves the judgment of Yahweh through their evil. His verdict against them is that the houses they have demolished to fortify the city wall will become their burial ground.

■ **6** The oracle of restoration in vv 6-9 has two parts. The first part (vv 6-8) lists a series of actions that Yahweh will perform on behalf of the city and the people of Judah and Israel. The second part (v 9) describes the place of glory and honor Jerusalem will have in the future days. The restoration oracle begins with the promise that Yahweh is bringing to the city (**to her/it**) **new flesh** (*ʾărūkâ* means "the new flesh that grows at the wounded spot"; BDB 74) and **healing** (*marppēʾ*) (v 6). This is followed by another promise of healing (**I will heal them;** the NIV adds **my people**). Healing that leads to the restoration of the health of the city and the people is thus Yahweh's initial activity in the days of restoration. Yahweh the healer offers to come to the people who have rejected his earlier call to come to him for healing and restoration of health (8:22). The purpose of Yahweh's judgment is not the death of Judah. It will inflict a serious wound; but the One who inflicts this wound is also the healer of his people. Yahweh also plans to **reveal** to his people an **abundance of peace and security** (*šālôm weʾĕmet* literally means "peace and truth"; here this phrase is a hendiadys meaning "true peace"; Lundbom 2004a, 532). The Hebrew word for abundance (*ʿăteret*) occurs only in the Hebrew Bible. In Ezek 8:11, the noun construct *ʿătar* is often translated as "fragrance" or "smell" (of incense). Based on this meaning, both Holladay and Lundbom see here the divine promise that he will fill the city with the fragrance of peace and security that was once covered with the reverse—the stench of dead bodies (Holladay 1989, 223; Lundbom 2004a, 532).

■ **7** The focus of the promise in v 7 is on the restoration of the **fortunes** (*šĕbût* here probably means more than physical properties such as home or fields, but the captives; see 29:14) of **Judah** and **Israel** and their rebuilding in the land so that they will enjoy their life as in the days before their captivity.

■ **8** The cleansing and forgiveness of the people is an important theme in the oracles of restoration. In vv 6-8, this divine activity is stated as part of the program of restoration, but not necessarily a precondition to his healing and rebuilding of the people. Jeremiah is not describing these divine activities in any logical order. One would expect that the divine forgiveness is the fundamental premise of all the activities of restoration. The people who have sinned against Yahweh and defiled themselves with their *iniquity* hear the promise of Yahweh's gracious offer of cleansing. The promise of cleansing is an important aspect of the program of restoration in Ezekiel (36:25). The people who have **rebelled** against him hear the offer of his forgiveness of their *iniquities*. The offer of forgiveness is integral to the new covenant (Jer 31:34). It is important to note here that this offer of cleansing and forgiveness comes from Yahweh without any stated condition of the repentance of the people. It can be assumed, however, that the undeserving nature of Yahweh's grace might move the people to repent and to seek Yahweh with their whole heart (see 29:12-14).

■ **9** The focus of v 9 is on Jerusalem. In the days of restoration, Yahweh promises that Jerusalem (***it shall be*** in the MT; **this city will** in the NIV) shall become for Yahweh a ***joyous name, a praise, and a beautiful adornment*** in the world. All the nations in the world will hear about all the **good** Yahweh is doing to **them** (i.e., the inhabitants of Jerusalem; the NIV **it** implies the city, but in the MT the direct object is in third person plural). Though the city is the focus at the beginning and at the end of v 9, here the attention seems to be on the people who live in the city (see Lundbom 2004a, 533). The oracle ends with an anticipation that the nations will **tremble** and **shake** when they see Jerusalem as the recipient of **goodness** and **peace** from Yahweh. Yahweh's involvement in the historical processes is not only for the purpose of bringing judgment and salvation to Judah and Israel but also to make the nations in the world know that he is the sovereign Creator and Lord of the universe. The magnitude of the reversal of Jerusalem's misfortune will be such that all the nations in the world will recognize that it is Yahweh who is transforming the city into a prosperous and peaceful place. The nations' worship of Yahweh is not explicit here, though one may conclude that it is implied.

c. *A Place of Joy and Thanksgiving (33:10-11)*

■ **10-11** This brief oracle announces the restoration of social and religious life in the cities of Judah and in the streets of Jerusalem. The oracle assumes a condition of total devastation of the land and Jerusalem. There is no human or animal life. Thus it appears to reflect a condition after 587 B.C. The oracle may very well have been given immediately before the events of 587 B.C. When we read it along with the preceding oracle (vv 4-9), this oracle seems to serve the purpose of giving the reader a preview of the condition of the land when the city falls into the hands of the Babylonians. Again the emphasis here is not on the desolation of the land and the absence of human and animal life, but on the future days when the streets of Jerusalem and the cities of Judah will be filled with life and laughter, worship of Yahweh, thanksgiving and celebration of his love (*ḥesed*) that is eternal. Variations of the refrain, **Give thanks to Yahweh of hosts, for Yahweh is good, and for his love is eternal,** are found in a number of psalms and in Chronicles (Pss 106:1; 107:1; 136:1; 1 Chr 16:34; 2 Chr 5:13). The silence brought about by death and destruction will be broken by the laughter of the people and the joyful sounds of brides and bridegrooms. The people will respond to Yahweh's goodness to them with thanksgiving and praise. Worship in the temple will be resumed with people bringing their thanks offering to Yahweh in his house. All these will become a reality because Yahweh will **restore the fortunes of the land.** Houses and fields and properties that were destroyed by the enemy will be restored, and life will return to normal as in the old days.

d. The Restoration of Pastoral Life (33:12-13)

■ **12-13** The brief oracle in vv 12-13 is similar to that of the preceding oracle. Here the promise is the restoration of the pastoral life in the uninhabited wasteland of Judah. The desolate places of Judah will become pastures for the flocks and herds of shepherds (v 12). The picture of shepherds and their flock resting in pasture reflects peaceful conditions. This picture is extended to the cities in the various regions around Judah and Jerusalem. These regions include the hill country, the Shephelah in the southwest, the Negev in the south, and the land of Benjamin (v 13). The phrase **the flock shall pass under the hand of one who counts it** refers to the counting of the flock by the shepherd as they pass under his rod (Lundbom 2004a, 536).

2. Yahweh's Faithfulness to His Covenants (33:14-26)
a. A Righteous Branch for David (33:14-16)

■ **14** At this point in ch 33, the theme shifts to a future that will witness the reemergence of the Davidic kingship (vv 14-16). This oracle also introduces a collection of oracles that deal with the political and religious future of Israel (the Davidic kingship and the priestly ministry) in the second part of ch 33. Verses 14-16 are very similar to 23:5-6. Lundbom thinks that vv 14-16 expand and modify 23:5-6. He also thinks that this oracle could have been given anytime after the destruction of Jerusalem but rejects the view that it is a late exilic or postexilic work (2004a, 537-39). The opening phrase, **The days are coming,** indicates the eschatological orientation of this oracle. The audience is told that they can anticipate a time in the future when Yahweh will **fulfill his good word** (*haddābār haṭṭôb*) **to the house of Israel and to the house of Judah** (v 14). The entire nation is the recipient of this good word. Yahweh's word is good in that it is trustworthy and dependable; it is a word spoken for the welfare of his people. Based on the content of v 15, we may assume that the good word implies Yahweh's covenant promise to David concerning a permanent royal house and the perpetuity of the Davidic kingship (2 Sam 7:12-16).

■ 15 The specific action of Yahweh that confirms the good word spoken to Judah and Israel is described in v 15a. The opening phrase, **In those days and at that time,** again conveys the eschatological nature of the fulfillment of Yahweh's word. Yahweh promises here to **make sprout** (*'aṣmîaḥ*) **for David a Righteous Branch** (*ṣemaḥ ṣĕdāqâ*). (In 23:5 the verb is "raise up," which conveys the same idea.) The term righteous Branch is generally considered as a messianic designation (see comments on 23:5 in Varughese 2008, 281-82). This messianic king will **perform justice** (*mišpāṭ*) **and righteousness** (*ṣĕdāqâ*) **in the land.** These are qualities that are lacking in the king who now sits on the throne of David. It is obvious that the oracle means to convey a negative evaluation of King Zedekiah, whose name means "Yahweh is righteousness."

■ 16 The people of Judah are currently living in fear and in dangerous conditions because of the Babylonian siege of the city. The current political regime is responsible for the wartime conditions in which the people now live. The oracle promises that in future days under the faithful rule of the righteous Branch, there will be salvation for Judah and safety for the citizens of Jerusalem (see 23:6, where it is Israel that will live in safety). The city will be known by a new name in those days: **Yahweh is Our Righteousness** (*yhwh ṣidqēnû*). In 23:6 this name is given to the future messianic king, the righteous Branch. Here it is the name by which the city will be known. This new name for the city is a play upon the name Zedekiah, who has failed to live up to the significance and meaning of his name. Ezekiel says that in future days Jerusalem will be called **Yahweh is there** (Ezek 48:35).

b. Davidic Kings and Levitical Priests (33:17-18)

■ 17 The main theme of this oracle is the political and religious future of Judah. This future depends on the continuation of the Davidic house and the priesthood that performs offering and sacrifices. The oracle reflects a condition that threatens the continuation of Judah's royal and priestly lines. The oracle may have been given by Jeremiah in anticipation of the Babylonian takeover of Judah and the impending destruction of the temple. It is also possible that this oracle was given immediately after the events of 587 B.C. In v 17 the oracle promises that the royal line of David will continue. There will always be someone who will be the legitimate heir to **the throne of the house of Israel** (see 1 Kgs 2:4; 8:25; 9:4-5 where this promise is stated with conditional clauses). The throne of the house of Israel is the throne of David. This promise is grounded in the Davidic covenant in 2 Sam 7:12-16. This promise reverses and modifies the judgment speech against Jehoiachin, which seems to give no hope for the continuation of the Davidic line through Jehoiachin (Jer 22:29-30).

■ 18 The focus shifts to the continuation of the priestly line in v 18. **Priests** from the Levitical family (*hakkōhănîm halĕwiyyîm* literally is **the priests, the Levites**) will always be available to perform the task of offering the **burnt offering** and burning the **cereal offering** and offering **sacrifice**. Numbers 25:13

speaks of a "covenant of perpetual priesthood" (NRSV) that Yahweh made with the priests of the house of Aaron. In the whole burnt offering the entire animal is consumed on the altar. The cereal offering is a gift offering of grain or flour. In some earlier texts, Jeremiah seems to maintain an antiritual view (see, for example, 6:20; 7:21-22; 14:12). Here in 33:18, offering and sacrifices are treated as an essential part of Yahweh worship in the temple. The phrase **before me** suggests the continuity of worship in the temple. If the oracle was given immediately after the events of 587 B.C., then it is possible to assume that this verse anticipates the rebuilding of the temple.

c. Yahweh's Eternal Covenants (33:19-22)

■ **19-21** The next oracle focuses on two issues: (1) Yahweh's unbreakable covenant with David and the Levitical priests (vv 20-21) and (2) Yahweh's promise of the multiplication of the descendants of David and the Levites to the extent that they cannot be numbered or measured (v 22). Verse 19 is the typical introductory formula of the oracle. Verses 20-21 utilize the **if . . . then** formula. The protasis (**if**) in v 20 states an utterly impossible matter. Yahweh's **covenant with the day** and his **covenant with the night** cannot be broken by the people (*if you could; you* is masculine plural, referring to the people). Day and night were established by God on the first day of creation (Gen 1:5) to appear **at their appointed time**. No matter what the people would do to offend God, he would remain committed to his fidelity to his creation. This covenant is between God and his creation, and it is unlike the Sinai covenant between Yahweh and the people, which the people were able to break. The Genesis account does not refer to a covenant that God made with day and night. However, God promises that "day and night shall not cease" in the context of his covenant with Noah (Gen 8:22 NRSV; see 9:8-17). Yahweh's fidelity to his **covenant with David** and the ***Levitical priests*** (*halĕwiyyîm hakkōhănîm* here is a reversal of the word order in Jer 33:18; the phrase means "the Levites, the priests") is just as firm and sure as his covenant with day and night. The phrase ***also*** (my covenant) ***with the Levitical priests my ministers*** comes at the end of the verse in the MT, which suggests that perhaps this may have been a later addition. Again the "covenant of perpetual priesthood" mentioned in Num 25:13 (NRSV) may be intended here. The people through their sins cannot break the covenant that Yahweh made with David and the Levitical priests. Neither would Yahweh break his covenant with David and the Levitical priests because of the sins of the people. Both of these are covenants to which Yahweh is bound with his unconditional promises. David, Yahweh's servant, will always have a descendant to **reign on his throne**. In the same way, there will always be Levitical priests serving as ministers in the temple.

■ **22** The oracle ends with the promise that reminds us of God's promise to Abraham, Isaac, and Jacob about the numerous descendants they would have that cannot be numbered or measured (Gen 15:5; 22:17; 32:12). The ***host of***

heaven (*sĕbā' haššāmayim;* **the stars of the sky** in the NIV) is a general term that would include the sun, moon, and stars (Lundbom 2004a, 544). The language here as in the patriarchal promises simply conveys the idea of the increase of descendants. Fruitfulness and multiplication is part of the creational mandate (Gen 1:28*a*). Jeremiah 33:22 implies that ***the seed of David*** and **the Levites** would fulfill that mandate through Yahweh's covenantal blessing to them.

d. God's Fidelity to Israel (33:23-26)

■ **23-24** The final oracle in ch 33 has two parts. In the first part (vv 23-24), Yahweh repeats to Jeremiah a disparaging statement that is being said about the two families that Yahweh has chosen. In the second part (vv 25-26), Yahweh affirms his covenant with the patriarchs and with David. Verse 23 is a customary introductory formula that announces a revelation from Yahweh. Yahweh's word to Jeremiah comes in the form of a question addressed to the prophet concerning what is being spoken by ***this people*** (v 24). The identity of this people is not given. It is possible that the nation Judah is intended here, though some commentators entertain the possibility of another nation making a reproachful statement about Judah. In the context of the events of 587 B.C. other nations would have made such disparaging statements about Israel. The quote implies two things: (1) Yahweh has ***chosen*** the ***two families;*** (2) he has ***rejected*** them both. The identity of the two families (*hammišpāḥôt,* meaning "tribes" or "families" or "clans") is not clear. Some commentators think Judah and Israel are meant here (**the two kingdoms** in the NIV is clearly an interpretation leaning in this direction). If the nations are making this disparaging comment, and if this statement is about Judah and Israel, then the nations seemed to have perceived Judah and Israel as Yahweh's two chosen families. If the statement is coming from the people of Judah, then it would be difficult to make sense of the reference to two families since both Judah and Israel are part of the one family—Israel—that Yahweh has chosen (see Amos 3:1). The final phrase, **they despise my people and no longer regard them as a nation,** comes from Yahweh (v 24). The nations (**they**) no longer consider Israel, Yahweh's people (**my people**), as a nation among the nations in the world.

■ **25-26** These final verses seem to be a restatement of vv 20-21. These verses also follow the **if . . . then** pattern. Yahweh's covenant with **day and night** is reaffirmed here. An added element here is the covenant with the **fixed laws of heaven and earth** (v 25). Verse 26 makes two things clear: (1) Yahweh is eternally committed to his covenant with **the descendants of Jacob and David;** (2) Yahweh is committed to his covenant promise to take from the descendants of David ***rulers*** for **the descendants of Abraham, Isaac and Jacob.** The unconditional covenants that Yahweh made to Abraham and David are reaffirmed in v 26. He remains committed to these covenants even though Israel has broken the Sinai covenant. The offer of the new covenant (31:31-34) is the hope that remains for Israel for a totally restored relationship with Yahweh. Yahweh thus promises an unbroken continuity with the past in the days of restoration, with the added element of the new covenant in the days to come. The oracle ends with an affirmation of Yahweh's promise to **restore the fortunes** of Israel. What is at the root of this gracious work of Yahweh is his **compassion** or mercy (*rhm*). Israel receives from Yahweh the offer of his grace, his unmerited favor to an undeserving people, which alone is the hope for its future.

FROM THE TEXT

God's invitation to Jeremiah to call to him (in prayer) and his promise to reveal hidden things to the prophet suggests some significant lessons about God-human relationship (v 3). It seems that God is saying to the prophet that it is his conversation with God that will lead him to have knowledge of God's future plans and actions on behalf of Israel. This text leads us to the following conclusions about this invitation from God that are instructive to us.

First, the text does not mean that our calling upon God will lead us to have knowledge of the mysterious things about God. In the context of this text, what is being promised is a fuller knowledge of God's work on behalf of Israel and its future that is hitherto not made known to Jeremiah. Further revelation to Jeremiah means things that are related specifically to the restoration of Israel. As we read this text, we need to remind ourselves that scriptures of the church as the full revelation of God disclose to us all that we need to know, and are capable of knowing, about God, not only through his words, but also through his actions in history—most importantly through the Word that became flesh—Jesus of Nazareth, the Son of God. This means that there are no great and hidden things about God outside of the Scriptures waiting to be revealed to us through some other form of revelation.

Second, the text does not mean that our calling upon God will lead us to have knowledge of future events that are not yet known to us. In this text, the future is made known to the prophet and the initiative of this offer comes from God. The text thus speaks against our modern tendency to predict the future through calculations and interpretations of symbols and imageries in the Bible. In this text what God reveals to Jeremiah is a future that involves both judgment and salvation in the history of Israel. In this future, there is brokenness but healing, displacement but restoration, break up of social, political, and religious life but the return of normal life in the land. It is a future that hinges to a great extent on the past and the present ways of the life of God's people. The admonition of the text to its modern readers is to be less concerned with knowing the future or predicting the future through some pedantic ways and be more concerned with living life in the present in a faithful manner that will certainly have an impact on our future. Again, scriptures give us instructions on how to live our lives, which by and large determines our future with God. In the Bible, this present life is more important than our claim of the knowledge of future events.

Third, the text suggests the possibility of a conversational life with God. Conversational life with God means a life of uninterrupted conversation with God. It is possible to say that the one with whom God is engaged the most is the one who is fully engaged with God in a conversational relationship. What is otherwise hidden from us because of our sinfulness (broken relationship with God), the text seems to say, will be revealed to us when we live in conversation with God. Jesus says to his disciples that what they are unable to understand about him, they will come to know through the ministry of the Holy Spirit (John 16:12-13). In Wesleyan theology, the Spirit-filled life and Spirit-guided life—our conversational life with God in and through the Holy Spirit—is not only the means of knowing the truth about God but also the genuine mark of an authentic Christian life.

Fourth, our conversational life with God leads us to have a holistic vision of the future that God desires for us. The future that God reveals to the prophet includes recovery of health and healing, prosperity, restoration of the lost fortunes, cleansing from the guilt of sin, forgiveness of sin and rebellion, renewed relationship with God, return of joy and gladness among the people, worship and thanksgiving to God, and return of normal life under the leadership of faithful political and religious leaders. This text combines all aspects of life—spiritual, social, material, political, religious—together in its vision of the future of God's people. Salvation—wholeness—is what God promises to sinful humanity. Our broken lives have hope because God remains gracious and faithful to the covenant he made with us through the sacrificial death of his beloved Son. The text reminds its readers that God's desire for the sinful human beings is their total restoration—healing, health, forgiveness, cleansing, joy and gladness, worship and thanksgiving, and life under the leadership of God's faithful leaders. The text also reminds the readers of the possibility of living a life of wholeness because of God's gracious mercy that comes as a gift to an undeserving people.

"BUILD AND PLANT"

DESTRUCTION BEFORE RESTORATION (34:1-22)

Overview

Chapter 34 is set apart from other chapters in the book that belong to the days of Zedekiah (see chs 24, 27—29, 37—39). Chronologically, this chapter belongs with ch 37. Perhaps it is placed here to contrast the covenant breaking done by the citizens of Jerusalem with the covenant faithfulness of the Recabites in ch 35 (Lundbom 2004a, 548). The siege of Jerusalem by the Babylonians, and their temporary withdrawal from Jerusalem because of the news of the Egyptian army advancing toward Jerusalem to render help to Judah serve as the general context of this chapter as well as ch 37.

This chapter begins with Yahweh's word, which announces the capture and the burning of Jerusalem by the Babylonians (v 2), and it ends with the same judgment word (v 22). These verses that envelop the content of ch 34 convey the focus of this chapter; the city of Jerusalem is destined to be destroyed by the Babylonians. The destruction of the city is thus established as a necessity before its rebuilding can happen in the days of restoration promised in chs 30—33.

BEHIND THE TEXT

Chapter 34 has two major literary units. In unit one (vv 1-7), we find Yahweh's word concerning the personal fate of Zedekiah. In unit two (vv 8-22), Jeremiah announces Yahweh's judgment on the people of Jerusalem and King Zedekiah for breaking a covenant they have made proclaiming freedom to their Hebrew slaves.

It is likely that the oracle in vv 1-7 was given when Jeremiah was freely moving around in the city. Verses 1 and 6 indicate that Jeremiah spoke to Zedekiah just prior to the siege of the city by the Babylonians in 588 B.C. Jeremiah's words to Zedekiah in vv 2-4 have some similarity to the words given to him in 32:3-5. Both speak about the personal fate of Zedekiah. The prophet offers the king a peaceful death though he would be captured by the Babylonians.

The second part of this chapter (vv 8-22) begins with a narrative introduction (vv 8-11) that sets up the setting of the long oracle from Yahweh (vv 12-22). The narrative introduction indicates that Zedekiah made a covenant with the people of Jerusalem and proclaimed freedom to their Hebrew slaves but afterward they turned around and reclaimed their slaves. There is no indication of when this covenant breaking occurred. It is possible that the covenant and the proclamation of freedom to the Hebrew slaves were made during the siege of the city by the Babylonian army that began in January 588 B.C. (Holladay 1989, 239). This covenant making would have been an attempt to appease Yahweh and to seek his favor to the city under siege. Some commentators think that this action was taken to draft the freed slaves into Zedekiah's beleaguered army that was engaged in defending the city. Others entertain the view that the freeing of the slaves was done to relieve the slave owners of the burden of feeding the slaves during the siege when there was a shortage of food in the city. It is not clear when the slave owners reclaimed their slaves. It is possible that this occurred when the Babylonians lifted the siege because of the news of the Egyptian advance toward Jerusalem sometime during late spring or early summer 588 B.C. (Bright 1965, 223). Holladay speculates that the covenant making and the proclamation of freedom to the slaves were announced in the feast of weeks in late spring 588; he assumes that the reclamation of the slaves took place in the summer of 588 (1989, 239).

The oracle section (vv 12-22) has two parts. The first part (vv 12-16) is a summary of how both the ancestors of Israel and the present generation broke the covenant law concerning the release of the Hebrew slaves every seventh year, which Yahweh established as part of the Sinai covenant. The second part (vv 17-22) announces Yahweh's judgment. The covenant breakers will face dire consequences. Both they and the city in which they live will be handed over to the Babylonians. Some commentators see in this section extensive work of Deuteronomic editors, while some others attribute this section to postexilic writers. There are also a number of scholars who find in this section an authentic report of an event that happened during the final years of Zedekiah. This commentary considers this section as an authentic report of an event during the final years before the fall of Jerusalem. This narrative may be placed along with other Baruch materials in the book.

IN THE TEXT

1. A Tragic but Hopeful Word to Zedekiah (34:1-7)

■ 1 Verse 1 provides the historical context for the oracle in vv 2-5. The unit concludes with another reference to the historical setting (vv 6-7). Yahweh's revelation came to Jeremiah when Nebuchadnezzar and his army and a coalition of vassal states of Babylon were waging war against Jerusalem and the neighboring cities. Reference to **the kingdoms of the earth under the dominion** of the king of Babylon indicates that the vassal states were demonstrating their loyalty to Nebuchadnezzar the overlord by providing him with the military assistance as required by his treaty with them (Lundbom 2004a, 549).

■ 2 Yahweh instructs Jeremiah to speak to King Zedekiah. It is possible that Zedekiah may have given the order to arrest and confine the prophet (see 32:2-5) because of his words to the king in 34:2-5. However, 37:11-17 gives us another account of Jeremiah's arrest and imprisonment. In 34:6 we are told that Jeremiah spoke to Zedekiah in Jerusalem. It seems that Jeremiah was free to move around in Jerusalem at this time and that he was not yet a prisoner in the court of the guard. Yahweh's word to Zedekiah is firm. He is **giving** Jerusalem into the hand of Nebuchadnezzar king of Babylon and "he shall burn it with fire" (NRSV). This prediction simply announces what one could have anticipated as the fate of any city that resisted a conquering nation in the ancient world at that time.

■ 3 The focus of Yahweh's word now shifts to the personal fate of the king in vv 3-5. Verse 3 is similar in wording to 32:4. The message of the final phrase of v 3 (**to Babylon you shall go**) is reiterated in 32:5. The siege of the city means that there is no escape for Zedekiah from the hand of Nebuchadnezzar. Yahweh announces that Zedekiah will be captured and he will be **given** into the hand of the king of Babylon. This will be Yahweh's work and judgment against his infidel king. Yahweh will treat Zedekiah in the same way he will treat his holy city. Zedekiah will stand before the king of Babylon and see his eyes and hear from his mouth Nebuchadnezzar's judgment pronounced to his rebellious vassal (see comments on 32:4-5). Verse 3 of ch 34 ends with the pronouncement of the exile of Zedekiah to Babylon as a prisoner (see Zedekiah's fate in 39:5-7; 52:9-11).

■ 4-5 The oracle to Zedekiah ends with unexpected good news to the king though the tone of the preceding statement is rather ominous. He will not be executed as a criminal by Nebuchadnezzar though he has rebelled against Babylon. He will ***die in peace*** (52:9-11 indicate that he died while in prison in Babylon). This simply means that his death will not be by violent means, ***by the sword*** of his captor. The oracle announces that he will be spared a grim and brutal end. Zedekiah, nonetheless, witnessed the execution of his sons, was blinded, chained, and made to walk the long journey to Babylon. The words of consolation to Zedekiah continue in 34:5. He will receive some of the funeral rites that other Judean kings received at the time of their death. Roland de Vaux cautions us not to confuse the phrase ***they shall burn for you*** with cremation. He adds that this refers to the practice of burning incense and perfumes near the dead body (1965, 57). Lundbom notices here an irony in this statement about burning for the king since it comes directly after the verdict about Nebuchadnezzar burning the city with fire (2004a, 552). Moreover, the people will lament for their dead king by saying ***alas Lord***. His death will be a loss to the people. Making lamentation was also a part of the ancient funeral customs. Yahweh's word of consolation thus mitigates the judgment word about his capture by the Babylonians. This word is given to Zedekiah as a guarantee from Yahweh (***I have spoken the word***).

■ **6-7** Verse 6 indicates that the prophet spoke these words to the king somewhere in Jerusalem. This means he had access to the king. We do not know if this happened in a private encounter between the prophet and the king or in a public setting. Verse 7 again reiterates the Babylonian siege of Jerusalem as the historical context of this oracle. All other cities of Judah except **Lachish** and **Azekah** and Jerusalem were already taken by the Babylonians. The Babylonians were on the move to take control of these three remaining fortified cities. Lachish and Azekah were fortified during the reign of Rehoboam, Solomon's son who became king of Judah in 922 B.C. (2 Chr 11:9). The well-known Lachish Letters indicate that Lachish was destroyed before the fall of Jerusalem.

2. The Consequence of Covenant Breaking (34:8-22)

■ **8-9** Verse 8 indicates that Zedekiah initiated the covenant with the people of Jerusalem to make a proclamation of freedom to all their male and female Hebrew slaves. Lundbom links the phrase ***proclaim to them freedom*** (*'liqrō' lāhem dĕrôr*; see Isa 61:1 for *liqrō' dĕrôr*, "to proclaim freedom," which implies the Jubilee Year release) to the Jubilee Year release (2004a, 560-61). The Hebrew term *dĕrôr* ("freedom") is also found in Lev 25:10 in connection with the law of the Jubilee Year release.

Sabbatical and Jubilee Year Freedom of the Slaves in Ancient Israel

The law permitted the Israelites to hold other Israelites as slaves (Exod 21:1-11; Lev 25:39-43; Deut 15:12-18). Debt and poverty were the conditions that forced someone to become a slave of another person or to sell children as slaves to others. The law also stipulated that each Hebrew slave shall go free in the seventh year after six years of service. This Sabbatical release is stated in Exod 21:2 and Deut 15:12. However, the law in Lev 25:39-43 stipulates a general release of all the Hebrew slaves in the year of Jubilee (fiftieth year). Some speculate that the Jubilee Year release was mandated because of the failure of the people to obey the Sabbatical release.

We do not know if Zedekiah's covenant and proclamation of freedom to the Hebrew slaves were carried out in observance of the Sabbatical Year law or Jubilee Year law. Lundbom makes a strong case for the latter (2004a, 560-61), though one could argue that in the present situation, this would simply have been an act of piety or demonstration of repentance during a national emergency to seek Yahweh's favor, and not necessarily part of the observance of either Sabbatical Year or Jubilee Year.

■ 10 The people agreed and they entered into the covenant that they would not keep their fellow Hebrews as slaves and they set them free according to the covenant they made (v 10). How they entered into this covenant is not stated here. One key aspect of the ritual that accompanied this covenant making is found in vv 18-20 (see discussion of vv 18-20). Again we do not know if the slave owners agreed to this covenant for political, economic, or religious reasons. Verse 15 indicates that this was an act of repentance (see notes on v 15).

■ 11 The text does not say what prompted these covenant keepers to change their mind and renege on their covenant making with Yahweh. The freedom they proclaimed to their slaves was short-lived. Whatever repentance they displayed was also short-lived. The Hebrew phrase here, **they turned around . . . they took back** (*yāšûbû . . . yāšībû*) is a play on *šûb* ("repent," "turn around"). The citizens of Jerusalem broke their covenant and brought their former Hebrew slaves under bondage again. It is likely that they would have interpreted the lifting of the siege by the Babylonians and the withdrawal of the Babylonian army from Jerusalem as a sign of Yahweh's favor and response to their repentance. As soon as freedom came to them, they decided to go back into their covenant breaking way of life and put their fellow Hebrews into slavery. Bright describes the whole episode a typical example of "foxhole religion" (1965, 224).

■ 12-14 Yahweh's word came to Jeremiah (v 12) after the citizens of Jerusalem violated the covenant they had recently made with Yahweh (v 11). The first part of Yahweh's word mentions the Sinai covenant making (v 13) and the establishment of the law of the Sabbatical release of the slaves in the seventh year (v 14). Verse 13 specifically refers to Yahweh's liberation of Israel from Egypt their **house of bondage.** This freedom that Yahweh brought to Israel is the theological basis for his commandment concerning the Sabbatical release of the Hebrew slaves in Exod 21:2 and Deut 15:12. In both passages, the Hebrew slaves work for six years and in the seventh year, their owners are required to let them go free. This law is restated in v 14. The second part of v 14 suggests that this law had been disregarded by the ancestors of the present generation. This was an intentional act of disobedience to Yahweh on the part of the previous generations.

■ **15-16** Verse 15 contrasts the obedience of the present generation with the disobedience of the previous generations. ***And you, you turned around one day*** (*wattāšūbû ʾattem hayyôm* could also be translated as "and you, you repented recently") indicates that the present generation, though it also had neglected the Sabbatical release law, recently repented of their covenant disobedience. They did what was **right** in the eyes of Yahweh and proclaimed **freedom** (*děrôr*) to their fellow Hebrew slaves and made a covenant before Yahweh **in the house** that is called by his **Name.** Verse 16 sums up their covenant breaking soon after the covenant was made in Yahweh's house. ***But*** the citizens of Jerusalem have ***turned around*** (*wattāšūbû*, "but you have turned around," from *šûb*) or nullified their repentance. Yahweh describes the act of taking back their slaves whom they have sent away free as profanation of his **name.** Holladay says that Jeremiah is using a priestly expression, "profaned" Yahweh's "name," found six times in Leviticus and five times in Ezekiel, to point out the "awesome wrong of the people's conduct. They have profaned, polluted Yahweh's very identity" (1989, 242). The covenant was made in the temple with Yahweh as the witness of their proclamation. Their covenant breaking was in reality a total disregard for Yahweh who witnessed a solemn act of obedience that was carried out in his presence in the temple that bears his name.

■ **17** The sentence of judgment (vv 17-22) begins with an announcement of freedom to Zedekiah and his people who have not proclaimed freedom to their fellow Hebrew slaves. The freedom that awaits them is the **freedom of the sword, *the pestilence,*** and ***the famine.*** Yahweh does not recognize the freedom they have proclaimed to their slaves when they made the covenant as an act of obedience because they reneged on their promise. Those who have taken their fellow Hebrews back into slavery themselves will be slaves to the power of their enemy and to the siege conditions of plague and famine. They will be a ***horror*** to **all the kingdoms of the earth,** an object of contempt and hatred in the world.

■ **18** The destiny of those who ***transgressed*** (ʿ*br*, "to pass over," "overstep," "transgress," etc.; BDB 717) the covenant they have made with Yahweh is stated in v 18. Yahweh will make them **the calf they cut in two and then walked** (ʿ*br*) **between its pieces.** When they **made** (*krt* literally means "to cut") the **covenant,** they **cut** (*krt*) a calf in two pieces, walked between the pieces, and invoked on themselves the same fate of the calf if they should break the covenant. This recalls the story of God's covenant making with Abraham narrated in Gen 15:9-11, 17-21). Though this ritual is not mentioned in the account of the Sinai covenant, the text there refers to the sprinkling of blood (Exod 24:6-8). In Jer 34:18, Yahweh unleashes upon those who have failed to keep the words of their covenant with him the power of the curse they have spoken against them.

■ **19-20** Verse 19 mentions all those who were involved in the covenant making ritual, those who have walked between the two halves of the calf and then turned around and violated the covenant. These include the **officials** of Judah and Jerusalem, the *eunuchs*, and **the priests and all the people of the land.** Zedekiah is not included here but is mentioned in v 21. Yahweh will hand them over to the Babylonian army, their **enemies who seek their lives** (v 20). They will receive no burial, but their dead bodies will become food for the **birds of the air and the beasts of the earth.**

■ **21** Verse 21 deals with the fate of King **Zedekiah** and **his officials.** Yahweh will hand them over into the hand of **the army of the king of Babylon.** Babylonians are the enemies who are seeking the life of Zedekiah and his officials. They have withdrawn from Jerusalem only temporarily. There is no mention of their dead bodies becoming food for the birds and the animals. Why Zedekiah was exempt from dishonorable death and nonburial is not clear (see vv 4-5). Was he not directly responsible for the covenant breaking? Was this primarily an act of infidelity on the part of the prominent citizens and other leaders of Jerusalem? Perhaps so.

■ **22** The oracle ends with Yahweh's word that he is giving the command and that he will **bring** the Babylonians **back** to Jerusalem (see 37:8 for another word about the return of the Babylonians to Jerusalem). Lundbom sees here another wordplay. The people who "took back" (*tāšibû*) their slaves are now faced with the threat of Yahweh "bringing back" (*hăšībōtîm*) the Babylonian army to Jerusalem (2004a, 567). The siege will be resumed and the Babylonian army will **take** the city and **burn it *with fire*** (see v 2). Verse 22 ends with a curse that the cities of Judah will become desolate places without inhabitants. Total desolation of the land is the outcome of Judah's breach of the covenant they have made not only with Yahweh but also with their fellow human beings.

FROM THE TEXT

A key issue emerges out of the narratives in ch 34. King Zedekiah and his people sealed their destiny of destruction and death when they reneged on their commitment to covenant fidelity. When they walked between the two parts of the calf they cut, they invoked on themselves death if they should fail to keep their word. They knew full well the consequences of their oath and the violation of that oath. However, with full knowledge of the price they will have to pay for their infidelity, they have decided to nullify the covenant they have made with God. In other words they have started on the path of the choice of life and then turned around to resume their journey on the path of death. They showed gestures of fidelity to God but ignored the enormous price of infidelity. They showed signs of good faith, perhaps a frantic attempt to save themselves from an immediate threat, but failed to make fidelity a way of life and relationships, with God and others in the community. When fidelity is lost in relationships—at the family, local, national, and global level—there is no future. It seems likely that the slave owners reneged on their covenant commitment to reclaim their wealth and power over others (see Brueggemann 1998, 326-27). The positive outcome of their fidelity to the covenant would have been national and social well-being, the blessings of the covenant. However, in deciding to reclaim power and wealth by reinforcing slavery, they welcomed back into the community the power of the covenantal curses—death and destruction and disruption of social, religious, and political life. The irony in the text is that it announces to those who have reclaimed wealth and power by exploiting the poor in the society their own death and destruction by a greater political power (Babylon) that is intent on expanding its power and wealth through conquest and exploitation. The text also makes clear that Babylon is simply an instrument that executes God's covenant curses on Judah for its total disregard for the covenant it has made with him.

It is also important to note that God's judgment on Zedekiah and the people of Jerusalem begins with a reminder of his gracious redemption of Israel from its slavery in Egypt (v 13). The people who have received grace from God are portrayed in this text as those who have lost the memory of God's gracious work in their own lives. The freedom they enjoy, the freedom that God brought to them, is freedom they refuse to share with others. Their reinforcement of slavery, after they have made a covenant with God to release their slaves, shows that their lives and actions are not shaped by the memory of God's act of saving and freeing them from their slavery. Though they are free, they live in bondage to their self-centered ways of life. They refuse to give grace to others, though they themselves are recipients of God's grace. In the end, they live without remembrance of their history; so, God denies them a future, at least until he fulfills his promise to enter into their history once again to lead them out of the land of Babylon, in a new exodus experience.

"BUILD AND PLANT"

FIDELITY IN RELATIONSHIP (35:1-19)

Overview

Chronologically, this chapter has no continuity with the preceding chapters. Chapter 26 is the last chapter that recounts events that happened during the reign of Jehoiakim. However, ch 35 has some thematic connection to ch 34. This chapter focuses on the uncompromising faithfulness of the Recabites to the commandment given to them by their ancestor; here we find Jeremiah conveying a lesson on covenant fidelity to the citizens of Jerusalem who have broken their covenant with Yahweh (ch 34). Chapter 36 narrates an incident that happened in the fourth year of Jehoiakim, which has thus chronological linkage with the narrative in ch 35. The exiled nation would have heard in this narrative a call for stubborn loyalty and devotion to Yahweh as the appropriate response to his promises of restoration and rebuilding of Israel.

BEHIND THE TEXT

This chapter has three major segments. In the first section, the narrator recounts a symbolic act (Holladay 1989, 246) that Jeremiah performed (vv 1-11). Two oracles follow this narrative. The first oracle is addressed to the people of Judah (vv 12-17). The second oracle is addressed to the Recabites (vv 18-19). The chapter belongs to the period of the reign of Jehoiakim. Most commentators generally acknowledge the historicity of the event reported in this chapter. The narrative preserves great details, including the precise location where the incident took place. In the LXX this narrative and the subsequent oracles are found in ch 42.

Commentators are not certain about the date of Jeremiah's encounter with the Recabites in the temple. According to 36:5, Jeremiah was barred from entering the temple in 605 B.C. We do not know for how long this debarment continued and when Jeremiah was finally permitted to enter the temple again. The reference to Jeremiah entering into one of the chambers in the temple with the Recabites has prompted some to conclude that this incident took place before 605 B.C., the fourth year of Jehoiakim, when he had access to the temple, or after the death of Jehoiakim in 597 B.C. (Lundbom 2004a, 571-72) when Jeremiah would have felt it safe to move around in Jerusalem. Verse 11 indicates the presence of the Recabites in Jerusalem during the days when Nebuchadnezzar was conducting a military campaign against Judah with the assistance of the army of the Syrians (Arameans). According to Bright, Nebuchadnezzar dispatched the Babylonian army to Judah along with bands of soldiers from the neighboring vassal states to punish Jehoiakim for his rebellion against Babylon in 601 B.C. (see 2 Kgs 24:2). Nebuchadnezzar himself did not arrive in Judah until the end of 598 B.C. The military campaign against Judah by Babylon and its allies took place in 599/598. Bright places the incident reported in ch 35 in 599 or 598 (1965, 190; Holladay 1989, 246). Verse 11 supports a later date, possibly late 598 or early 597, just prior to the death of Jehoiakim. It is also possible that the intent of v 11 is not to be specific but to give a general reference to the time when the Recabites were living in Jerusalem. We assume that Jeremiah would have been free to enter the temple during this politically unstable period in Judah. The Recabites, who were tent dwellers, were obviously living in Jerusalem during this wartime in Judah because of the unsafe conditions elsewhere in the land.

The Recabites

The Recabites, like the Nazirites (see Num 6:1-21), were a religious community in ancient Israel. The members of this community have chosen for themselves peculiar ways of life following the instructions and commands established by their ancestor and founder Jonadab son of Recab during the reign of Jehu (842-815 B.C.). Second Kings 10:15-27 reports that Jonadab son of Recab was a witness to Jehu's massacre of those who were left in the house of Ahab in Samaria and also of Baal worshippers in the temple of Baal. Apparently, its founder believed that living in tents, refraining from sowing seed and planting vineyards, and abstaining from wine were essential to preserving the purity of faith and the worship of God. It is likely that this community lived in the desert as tent dwellers and rejected the luxuries of settled life in villages and in the urban areas.

IN THE TEXT

1. A Symbolic Act (35:1-11)

■ 1 The narrative of the symbolic act has four parts. Part 1 (v 1) gives a third person narrative introduction that indicates **the days of Jehoiakim** as the general time period when Jeremiah received this revelation from Yahweh. The more precise setting is found in v 11. Part 2 (v 2) contains Yahweh's command to Jeremiah. Part 3 (vv 3-5) reports the obedience of the prophet to Yahweh's command. In part 4 (vv 6-11) the Recabites speak to Jeremiah about their obedience to the command of their ancestor concerning wine and other aspects of their lifestyle.

■ 2 Yahweh's command to Jeremiah comes without any explanation or rationale. Yahweh asked the prophet to **go to the house of the Rechabites**, bring them to **one of the chambers** in the temple, and give them wine to drink (v 2). **House** here most likely means family or clan (Lundbom 2004a, 572; Fretheim interprets this as a house where they lived in Jerusalem; 2002, 494). The chambers were the rooms in the three-level outer structure that surrounded the holy place and the holy of holies (1 Kgs 6:5-6). These rooms were for priests, singers, stewards, doorkeepers, officials, and for storage of temple vessels and offerings that came into the temple (see v 4; also, Ezek 40:45-46; 2 Kgs 23:11; 1 Chr 9:33; 2 Chr 31:11-12). The objective of the command to give the Recabites wine to drink is not given here, but it is made clear in the oracle in 35:12-17. The whole symbolic act becomes a lesson for the people of Judah and the citizens of Jerusalem.

■ 3-4 Verses 3-4 give a first person report of Jeremiah's obedience to Yahweh's command. Jeremiah brought the family of Jaazaniah and the rest of the Recabites to the temple, into the chamber of the **sons of Hanan . . . the man of God**. Jaazaniah may have been the ehad of the Recabite group that Jeremiah brought in to the temple (Holladay 1989, 247). The title **the man of God** given to Hanan is a customary title for prophets in the early days of Israel's history (see 1 Sam 9:6-10). The **sons of Hanan** may have been part of the temple prophets. It is likely that the entire group of Recabites were brought into this chamber. Lundbom thinks that the chamber could not have accommodated a large number of people, and so there could not have been many of them (2004a, 574). Verse 4 ends with the specific location of the chamber of the sons of Hanan—near the chamber of the officials, and above the chamber of **Maaseiah, *the doorkeeper,*** the priest who perhaps controlled the entrance to the temple area (2 Kgs 22:4). Maaseiah may have been the father of Zephaniah the priest (see Jer 21:1).

■ **5** The first person narrative continues in v 5. Jeremiah placed before the Recabites pitchers full of wine and cups and he asked them to drink some wine. Where did he get the wine? Did he bring it with him? Or did he get it from the storage area in the temple where wine was kept? The text does not answer these questions.

■ **6** The immediate response of the Recabites was a refusal to grant Jeremiah's request (v 6). Their reason for not drinking wine is stated in v 6. They are following the command of their ancestor **Jonadab, son of Rechab,** who commanded them and their children not to drink wine.

■ **7** In v 7, the Recabites relate further instructions they have received from Jonadab. This includes a rejection of settled life as an agrarian community. They were not to build houses or sow seed or plant vineyards, but they were to live in tents all their life in the land where they resided. Lundbom says that the Recabite vow has all the marks of desert life (2004a, 575). Jonadab instructed this way of life as necessary for their long life in the land. In Deuteronomic theology, obeying the Sinai covenant is the condition for long life in the land (Deut 4:40; 5:16). The final phrase, **in the land where you *sojourn*** (NIV **where you are nomads**), indicates that the Recabites, though they were part of the Israelite population, considered themselves sojourners, as were the patriarchs, in the land.

■ **8-10** The Recabites state how they have faithfully obeyed the command of Jonadab their ancestor (vv 8-10). None of their family members drink wine. They do not build houses for their habitation. They have no fields or vineyards. They live in tents and have obeyed all the commandments of their ancestor.

■ **11** In v 11, the Recabites explain the reason for their presence in Jerusalem. They have moved out of the countryside or the desert area where they lived and sought safety in Jerusalem because of the danger they faced when the Babylonian army and the army of the Syrians came up against Judah. It is likely that they were living in tents within the walls of Jerusalem when Jeremiah's encounter with them took place (Lundbom 2004a, 576).

2. The Message to Judah (35:12-17)

This section has two oracles from Yahweh. Yahweh speaks first to the people of Judah and the citizens of Jerusalem. The oracle contrasts the long history of their covenant disobedience with the faithful obedience of the Recabites to the command of their ancestor. It ends with a word of judgment against Judah for its lack of response to Yahweh (vv 12-17). In the second oracle, Yahweh extends a special promise to the Recabites as a reward for their obedience to the command of their ancestor (vv 18-19).

■ **12-13** Jeremiah has faithfully carried out the command to test the Recabites, and they have proven their fidelity to the command of their ancestor. Now Yahweh sends Jeremiah to speak to the people of Judah and the inhabitants of Jerusalem. The oracle begins with a question from Yahweh: *"Will you not take discipline to listen to my words?"* Discipline (*mûsār*) is chastening or correction that comes from an authority figure, which the recipients are required to follow. In the past Yahweh brought his punishment upon Israel as a disciplinary action, but Israel rejected it as discipline from Yahweh (see 2:30; 32:33). Holladay sees here a challenge to hear the announcement of their doom (1989, 248). It is more likely that to **take** or accept **discipline** (*mûsār*) from Yahweh means to be prepared **to listen** to his words (Brueggemann 1998, 333). The word that Judah is invited to listen to is both a lesson on obedience and a word of judgment (35:14-17).

■ **14** The Recabites' obedience to the command of their human ancestor is contrasted in v 14 with Judah's disobedience to Yahweh's words that he has spoken to them persistently in the past. The issue of not drinking wine is singled out as an illustration of the obedience of the Recabites. The command was given at one time long ago, but the people obey it even **to this day**. However, Yahweh has spoken continuously to Judah, but it has failed to listen to him.

■ **15-16** Verse 15 sums up Yahweh's failed attempts to call the covenant nation to reform. Yahweh has persistently sent **all** his **servants the prophets** to the covenant nation (see 25:4; 26:5). Yahweh's message to Judah through his prophets sums up Jeremiah's message of reform (35:15*b*; see 7:3-7). There are three basic demands in this speech: (1) The people of Judah must **return** (*šûb*) from their evil ways. This is a call to repentance. (2) They must be involved in doing good (**make good your doings;** NIV: **reform your actions**). The call here is thus to put an end to evil, and instead to do that which is good and pleasing to Yahweh, that which leads to the welfare of the covenant people. (3) The covenant people must not **walk after** other gods and **serve them.** They must show fidelity to the first commandment. Meeting these conditions is essential to Judah's continued existence in the land (see 7:7 and 25:5 for the same emphasis). In Deuteronomic theology, obedience to the Sinai covenant is the condition for the people's continued life in the land (Deut 5:32-33). Here, the repentance of the people is the condition, which implies that the land will be lost if they fail to repent of their evil. Jeremiah 35:15 ends with Yahweh's disappointment and frustration that the people did not turn their attention to him and listen to his voice. Verse 16 again contrasts the loyalty and obedience of the Recabites to their ancestor with Judah's disobedience to Yahweh with whom the people of Judah have made a covenant (see v 14).

■ **17** The oracle ends with Yahweh's pronouncement of judgment on the people of Judah and the inhabitants of Jerusalem. He is to bring on them **all the evil** he has spoken against them. The reason for this judgment is that they have not listened to Yahweh, though he has spoken to them, and they have not answered though he has called them. Evil is what Judah can expect from Yahweh for its blatant disregard for Yahweh.

3. The Message to the Recabites (35:18-19)

■ **18-19** These verses contain a brief oracle to the Recabites. Yahweh will reward them for their faithfulness and obedience to the command of their ancestor. They receive a promise similar to what Yahweh made to the house of David and the Levitical family (**Jonadab son of Recab will never fail to have a man to stand before me all the days;** see 33:17-18). The phrase **stand before me** conveys the idea of standing before God in worship, for intercession, to receive a word from Yahweh, or in the service of Yahweh (Lundbom 2004a, 579). Baruch (45:4-6) and Ebed-Melech (39:16-18) also received a word of promise from Yahweh for their faithfulness. Those who are obedient will live, but the disobedient will perish. That seems to be the lesson of this symbolic action and the accompanying word from Yahweh.

FROM THE TEXT

The Recabites in this text present themselves as a countercultural community that is committed to an alternative way of life totally alien to the dominant culture of Israel. They are a minority in the land, and they live in a transient setting, without any of the comforts of those who live a settled life in the land. However, the focus of this narrative is not on the peculiar lifestyle of the Recabites; the narrative is neutral on this issue. There is no indication in the narrative that in order for a community to maintain its integrity it must separate itself from surrounding cultures and live in isolation from the rest of the world. What is significant in this narrative, however, is the issue of listening and faithfulness in action. The Recabites listen and remain faithful to the commands of their ancestor; they remember their past, and they maintain deep-rootedness to their own particular history within the history of Israel. The Recabites shape their identity by their faithfulness to the commands given to them by their ancestor a long time ago. It is important to note that the text does not speak about the Recabites' fidelity to God's commands. However, there is fidelity in their life—to a human ancestor. Their fidelity has its historical basis in their ancestor Jonadab's peculiar understanding of what it means to be a community that maintains its religious purity. The text credits the community with a quality—fidelity in relationship to someone who gave them a pattern for its future life. In contrast, Jeremiah's audience—the majority of Israel—does not listen to God; neither are they faithful to him. Israel's ancestors made a covenant with God at Mount Sinai to listen to God and obey his commands. Israel's history, however, has been a history of continual resistance to God and unwillingness to listen to his voice, even though God has spoken to Israel persistently through his prophets and continues to speak through Jeremiah. The point of this story is to show that Israel shapes its identity not by its listening and obedience to God's word, but by listening to its own self-directed ways. It does not honor the commitments it made; it does not show fidelity to the covenant its ancestors made at Sinai. Because of the covenant-breaking ways of Israel's life, it is faced with a serious crisis—the judgment of God that is unfolding through contemporary political events, which it will not be able to withstand.

This text speaks to us today about the urgent need for shaping our personal and community life by our commitment to be a listening and obedient people of God. Those who claim to be the people of God cannot have an authentic existence apart from God's eternal and trustworthy Word that gives guidance and direction to their life. The fact that God speaks—which in itself is God's gracious gift to us—requires the response of listening and faithfulness in action. It is this speaking-listening-obeying activity that binds us into a faithful relationship with God. Not listening to God means listening to our own voices, or being autonomous in our thinking and actions. This further means that life is lived not in trust and dependence on the One who gives life to us as a gift and permits it to continue, but by our own cleaver schemes and trust in our own resources. Jesus, in the Gospel of Matthew, at the end of his Sermon on the Mount, invites his audience to act wisely—to hear and to act according to his teachings (Matt 7:24-27). The Gospel also indicates that the life that is derived from this listening-responding relationship with God has the potential of surviving the crises of life. On the other hand, autonomy means fragile existence on shaky foundations, waiting for its collapse at the slightest storm.

"BUILD AND PLANT"

A DEFIANT KING AND THE INDESTRUCTIBLE WORD (36:1-32)

Overview

This narrative, though it has some chronological connection to the preceding chapter, does not have direct linkage to chs 27—34 or chs 37—44. The story of ch 45 also is dated to the fourth year of Jehoiakim; Jeremiah's oracle to Baruch has literary and chronological continuity with ch 36. In contrast to the devotion, loyalty, and commitment of the Recabites to the commandment of their ancestor (which exists only as an oral command given by Jonadab; 35:6), King Jehoiakim shows utter disdain for Yahweh's message given to him in the written form, a permanent record of Yahweh's message to Israel. He destroys the scroll that contains Yahweh's words, because he recognizes in the scroll words that hold him accountable to Yahweh, and culpable of Judah's destruction by the Babylonians (v 29). He attempts to nullify the words of judgment by destroying the scroll. The remaking of the scroll shows the resurrection of the word of Yahweh and the survival of the prophet's message. The following chapters (chs 37—44) show the tragic outcome of the king's defiance. Jehoiakim's action became a model of behavior for Zedekiah, who also continued on the path of rejecting the prophetic message. The narrative scheme of chs 37—44 seems to show that Jehoiakim's burning of the scroll has set in motion the judgment of Yahweh on Judah. The outcome of the king's action was the ultimate destruction of the land, the exile of the nation, destruction of the city and the temple, and further deterioration of social and political life of even those who were left in the land by the Babylonians.

BEHIND THE TEXT

This chapter comes about as close as possible to a description of the technology of the collection and preservation of prophetic oracles (see Clements 1988, 210; Bright 1965, 181). That is to say, in the narrative of a production of the first scroll and its multiple readings before its destruction, only to be replaced with a second, expanded edition with "many similar words . . . added" (36:32), the reader gets some kind of view into the shift from a predominantly oral culture to a predominantly written one.

The specific command to *write* the prophecies in this chapter seems to represent a significant development not just for the history of culture but also for the book of Jeremiah itself. Jeremiah's call narrative in ch 1 doesn't have writing as a key component of his prophetic vocation. So here is another step toward the final preservation in writing of oracles that were originally spoken. First Samuel 9:9 indicates a change in the phenomenon of prophecy [**What used to be called a seer** (*rōʾeh*) **is now called a prophet** (*nābîʾ*)]. Here, we see the beginnings of a new development; can one say that "What once was called a prophet is now called a writer"? Perhaps!

Chapter 36 is also very interesting for discussions of direct speech, reported speech, and intermediaries. Yahweh's word is mediated by Jeremiah the prophet to whom the oracle is originally given. Jeremiah's words are further mediated by Baruch who **wrote them down in the scroll in ink** (36:18, "in ink" being a most interesting detail).

When Baruch reads the scroll, he is mediating the words of Jeremiah (the words of Yahweh), which now exist in written form (36:10). And then Micaiah mediates the words of Baruch, which are the words of the text that mediates the words of Jeremiah who mediates the words of God (36:13). And Baruch mediates the text again through his interaction with all the officials in the court (36:15). Finally, Jehudi the king's servant mediates the words of the text in which Baruch mediated the words of Jeremiah (36:21). Jehoiakim destroys this text and demands that Jeremiah be arrested (36:23-26). But then Yahweh comes back into the picture, giving Jeremiah a command to rewrite the scroll and mediate God's words again (36:27-32). Jeremiah does so with Baruch mediating his words into a text that mediates those words and includes with it many other similar things. Thus essentially we are dealing with multiple levels of proclamation and mediation even within the relatively straightforward story of the production and dissemination of a scroll, its destruction, and the subsequent production of a second edition. In the LXX, this narrative is found in 43:1-32.

The narrative has five parts. Part 1 narrates the production of the first scroll (vv 1-7). The second and third parts report Baruch's reading of the scroll, at first in the hearing of all the people (vv 8-13) and later to the officials (vv 14-19). The fourth part narrates another reading of the scroll, this time by Jehudi to King Jehoiakim, and its destruction by the king (vv 20-26). The narrative ends with the report of the making of the second scroll (vv 27-32). Verses 1 and 9 place the events described in this chapter in the fourth and fifth year of Jehoiakim (605-604 B.C.).

IN THE TEXT

1. Production of the First Scroll (36:1-7)

■ 1 The passage begins with the historical note that Yahweh's word came to Jeremiah in the fourth year of Jehoiakim. Earlier in the book, the reader was informed that this "was the first year of King Nebuchadrezzar of Babylon" (25:1 NRSV). Given the importance of Nebuchadnezzar as one who determined, as Yahweh's "servant" (25:9; 27:6), the fate of the nation of Judah, the significance of the year in which he became king should not fail to capture the attention. However, it is clear that the text here has to do with a message directed at Jehoiakim, his officials, and the Judean community.

■ 2 Yahweh commands Jeremiah to write down in a scroll the oracle that he is about to receive. This is a clear development upon what has been encountered previously. Perhaps it is because Jeremiah **cannot go to the LORD's temple** (v 5) that the oracle must be written and presented through two intermediaries: Baruch as the reader of the text and the text itself. Yet another possibility presents itself, however; namely, that the change from oral to written prophecy as evidenced by this chapter signals a profound cultural shift from an exclusively (or, at least, predominantly) oral culture to one in which the written word will play an increasingly greater role. The focus of this written prophecy is to be, according to the second part of this verse, a summary of all of Yahweh's words **concerning Israel, Judah and all the other nations** (v 2).

This verse also places the beginning of Jeremiah's prophetic career sometime in the beginning of the reign of King Josiah. Other references to the reign of Josiah (who died at the hands of the Egyptian Pharaoh Neco II in 609 B.C.) are found in 1:2; 3:6; and 25:3. The last of these references is particularly relevant for the passage under consideration, for there Jeremiah himself says that the word of Yahweh has been coming to him "from the thirteenth year of Josiah son of Amon king of Judah until this very day" (25:3). The thirteenth year of Josiah was 627 B.C. Considerable debate has occurred over the significance of this year. The majority position, represented by Clements (1988, 4) and by Varughese (2008, 21), is that Jeremiah's call came in this year to a young boy. This may be called a "high chronology" of Jeremiah's life. Against this view is a "low chronology," or later dating for Jeremiah's life, held by such scholars as William Holladay (1986, 1) and James Hyatt (1956, 779). What is clear is that Jeremiah's prophetic career was a long one, involved at a deep level with the waning days of Judean independence. Unfortunately for the nation, his word was not well received. If it had been, then perhaps the events narrated could have been avoided.

■ **3** In typical fashion, this verse expands upon the command to prophesy (in written form) by suggesting that the people, upon hearing the warning of impending disaster, might change their ways. This verse thus raises the possibility of repentance and thus for a possible reversal of judgment (see 4:1-8; 7:1-15). Repentance is what Yahweh wills for his people; however, destruction is the path the people have chosen for themselves.

■ **4-6** Jeremiah fulfills Yahweh's command to write the prophecy down by summoning his scribe Baruch.

Scribes in the Ancient Near East

Scribes filled a very important role in the ancient Near East. Jeremiah 36 bears many marks of being familiar with the work of scribes, a fact that causes Walter Duckat in his work on biblical trades to cite it four times. Scribes served many important functions in many different societies, including maintaining sacred literature archives, serving as royal secretaries, administering land, produce, and taxation records, transcribing letters between various nonroyal dignitaries, and cataloging lists of army conscripts and battle spoils (Duckat 1968, 213-17). The "scribe's knife" that King Jehoiakim uses to cut the scroll and throw it in the fire (36:23) was normally used by scribes for erasures and for cutting papyrus rolls to suitable size for use. In addition, especially in cases where literacy was not widespread, the scribe was an indispensable member of the royal counselors as well as a sought-after, and therefore very wealthy, member of society at large. The degree of literacy among Judean society in the seventh to sixth centuries B.C. is a matter of some debate; nevertheless, the importance of scribes is beyond question. This is clear from the involvement of many scribes in the events related in ch 36.

It is interesting to note that, while Jeremiah himself is not directly responsible for the writing, nevertheless by having it commissioned, he is obeying Yahweh. It is only in v 5 that the word **command** (*wayĕṣavveh*) appears, with Jeremiah commanding Baruch to **read to the people from the scroll the words of the LORD** that he had written at Jeremiah's dictation (v 6).

■ **7** Finally, Jeremiah essentially repeats the possibility of redemption voiced by Yahweh back in v 3, with the added suggestion that **the anger and wrath pronounced against this people by the LORD are great**. Jeremiah thus makes clear here that it is Yahweh's anger, and not his own, that is pronounced against the people. Jeremiah might well have been justified in being angry at the people in light of their ill-treatment of him. Yet he does not take personal affront at their rejection of his message; he merely suggests that rejection of his message is a rejection of the One who sent him (see Luke 10:16).

2. Baruch's First Reading (36:8-13)

■ **8** The scroll written at Jeremiah's dictation is presented for the first time in the hearing of all the people. The text says that Baruch carried out Jeremiah's instructions to the letter. In this way, Baruch demonstrated his fidelity to Jeremiah just as Jeremiah demonstrated his fidelity to Yahweh in having the scroll produced in the first place. Both Yahweh and Jeremiah are convinced in this passage, as noted, that if the words of Yahweh are given a proper hearing, then perhaps the nation will repent. To that end, Baruch faithfully did what was commanded of him.

■ **9** The second date reference (the fifth year of Jehoiakim; 604 B.C.) seems to indicate that producing the scroll took some time, as the project was begun in the fourth year of Jehoiakim. At the very least, the command came in the fourth year. The text is unclear whether Jeremiah and Baruch got to the project right away or whether the start of their work was sometime removed from the initial command received by Jeremiah. Either way, it was clearly important to the compilers of the book that the reading of the scroll be connected to a specific fast time in the temple. It is not certain if a fast **in the ninth month** was a usual practice. It could rather have been called in response to the advance of the Babylonian army against Ashkelon in November 604 (Clements 1988, 212; Keown, Scalise, and Smothers 1995, 205). This fast proclaimed by the people (or the religious authorities, so Carroll 1986, 659) therefore serves as the religious context for all the people as well as relevant officials to hear the words of the scroll that Baruch reads to them.

■ **10** This verse relates again that Baruch read from the scroll, adding specific information regarding where Baruch was when he read. Finally, as though this was not already known, the verse concludes with the declaration that the reading was in the hearing of all the people. That the reading took place in the chamber of Gemariah son of Shaphan is a significant point. The family of Shaphan played a significant role in the book of Jeremiah (see sidebar on page 56 on the Shaphan Family)

■ **11-13 Micaiah son of Gemariah, the son of Shaphan** was among those who heard Baruch's reading of Yahweh's word from the scroll. Perhaps recognizing the seriousness of what he heard, he rushed off to find the king's councilors in executive session (v 12). This council included **Elishama the secretary, Delaiah, Elnathan, Gemariah, Zedekiah,** and **all the other officials.** After all of this detail, v 13 sums up the discussion by relating that Micaiah reported to these assembled persons the contents of the scroll read by Baruch.

3. Baruch's Second Reading (36:14-19)

■ **14** Upon hearing the words of Micaiah, repeating the words of the scroll that Baruch read, the officials summon Baruch to appear before them. They send Jehudi to order Baruch to come to them with the scroll from which he has read Jeremiah's prophecies. Baruch, ever the compliant scribe, comes at Jehudi's bidding, with the scroll in his hand, to the royal councilors.

■ **15-17** Once Baruch arrives in the chamber before all the officials, an interesting exchange occurs. The officials first ask Baruch to read the scroll to them, as if they were not already familiar with its contents from Micaiah's reporting and, possibly, from other reports as well. On second glance, however, it appears they want merely to confirm what they have already heard. They are struck with fear because of what the scroll has to say (v 16) and suggest that the king must be informed at once. They then question Baruch as to the manner of the scroll's composition (v 17). They want to know, specifically, if Baruch wrote the scroll and if indeed Jeremiah dictated these words to Baruch. They want to make sure that, before they report these words to the king, the words they hear are indeed Yahweh's words mediated through the prophet.

■ **18-19** Baruch's answer to this question is one of the more startling revelations in this lengthy and complicated story. The officials have asked him if he wrote the scroll at Jeremiah's dictation. He says that Jeremiah dictated the words of the scroll and he wrote them down **in ink.** To modern ears, "in ink" connotes permanence, as opposed to "in pencil," or in some other erasable medium.

This point about permanence will become important in the final two scenes of the chapter. Before then, the officials, still afraid because of what they have heard, warn Baruch that his and Jeremiah's lives will be in danger. They are to hide themselves, and thus protect themselves from a potential judgment. This advice given to Baruch mimics the motivation for writing down the prophecies—if Baruch and Jeremiah heed this warning, they might come out alive, just as, if Judah heeds the warning of the scroll, it may yet survive and not suffer the punishment for its sin.

4. Third Reading and Destruction of the First Scroll (36:20-26)

■ **20** Just as, after the first reading, Micaiah rushed off to the officials' chamber and reported to them what he had heard, so now after the second reading, the officials rush off to the king to report to him what they have heard. The detail that they failed to bring the scroll with them lends a sort of comic element to the scene. Why the officials did not take with them the scroll they had in their possession when they went to the king is not known.

■ **21** The king sends Jehudi out again to fetch the scroll from the chamber where the officials had left it. That it is Jehudi who is so sent makes him, so to speak, a mirror image of Baruch. Like Baruch, Jehudi carries out his orders seemingly without complaint (though see 45:3 for a complaint of Baruch), going back to the place from which he had just come. Upon his arrival back at the king's winter palace, he reads the scroll to the king. The officials are there also, now hearing the scroll's contents for a second time. This is not to mention poor Micaiah, who by this time is sitting—or, rather, standing—through his third time hearing the disturbing words of Jeremiah and Baruch's scroll.

■ **22-26** The story now introduces a new element, however. There will be no further reporting of the contents of this particular scroll, and it will never be read again. The king, not nearly as impressed as his officials were with the scroll, rather casually slices it up, bit by bit, as Jehudi did the reading, and throws it into the fire until it is all destroyed. Though the king and his servants heard all the words of Yahweh, they were dispassionate and defiant (v 24). The unrepentant king destroyed Yahweh's word and thus closed the door to Yahweh's offer to retract his words of judgment. Verse 25 seems out of place somewhat, in that it reports that the king paid no attention to some of the officials' entreaties not to burn the scroll, even though v 24 informs the reader that all had already been destroyed. Perhaps v 25 is added here as a parenthetical note to show that Jeremiah's sympathetic supporters did attempt to persuade the king to pay attention to Yahweh's word mediated through the prophet. Finally, the king not only defies Yahweh but also sends his deputies to arrest the mediators of Yahweh's word, Baruch the scribe and Jeremiah the prophet (v 26). The posse includes the king's own son Jerahmeel and two other loyal soldiers. But Jeremiah and Baruch had apparently followed the advice given in v 19, for the text claims that Yahweh hid them, not allowing the king's soldiers to find them.

5. Production of the Second Scroll (36:27-32)

■ **27-29** Following the third reading of the text and its destruction by the king, Yahweh commands Jeremiah to create another scroll containing all the words contained in the scroll that King Jehoiakim destroyed (v 28).

A judgment upon Jehoiakim for having burned the first scroll comes next. It would certainly be enough to indict Jehoiakim simply for burning the scroll. Therefore, it is curious that the oracle contains words that the king presumably said while he destroyed the scroll. The previous narrative (v 23) portrays, instead, Jehoiakim as rather dispassionate while destroying the scroll, without saying anything against the prophet or against the troublesome words written on the scroll. In v 29, the king's purported speech is addressed directly to Jeremiah, who was not present when Jehoiakim burned the scroll. This oracle presents Jehoiakim as a ruthless king who dared to destroy the scroll because in it Jeremiah dared to write Yahweh's word concerning the destruction of the land and human and animal life by the king of Babylon. The oracle is addressed to a king who exercises his power not only to silence Yahweh's messenger but also to destroy his written word. The king's purported speech reveals his fear that the content of the scroll written "in ink," if it is preserved will reveal his culpability, should the words announced in it come true. It seems that this detail in v 29 has been added to further enforce the picture the text yields of Jehoiakim.

■ **30-31** In vv 30-31 Yahweh pronounces his verdict on the wicked king. This follows the typical pattern of an oracle of judgment: ***Therefore, thus says Yahweh concerning Jehoiakim, King of Judah.*** The judgment pronounced on the king has three related dimensions. First, **no more of his line shall sit upon the Throne of David.** The NIV's **he will have no one to sit on the throne of David** does not properly catch the sense of the end of the Davidic dynasty. This is a negative fulfillment of the promise given to David in 2 Sam 7:11b-16 and 1 Chr 17:10b-14.

The second part of the judgment against Jehoiakim has to do with the mistreatment of his body. Instead of being afforded a proper royal burial (or, in the idiom of 1 and 2 Kings, to ***sleep with the ancestors***), Jehoiakim's body will be cast out to the elements.

The third and final element in the judgment against Jehoiakim widens the focus a bit to include the entire nation. Yahweh declares that he will punish the king's sons, attendants, and everyone in the land for their wickedness. This is, essentially, a reaffirmation of the designs for punishment Yahweh has had in mind for the nation throughout the book of Jeremiah. The last statement of the oracle recalls the earlier stated motivation for producing the first scroll in v 3, but concludes negatively that the people and the king **have not listened** to the threat of judgment of which Yahweh through the prophet has consistently warned. Had they listened and changed their ways (see 7:5-7; 18:7-9), then the punishment could have been averted. However, they did not repent, and so Yahweh will not retract his words of punishment.

■ **32** The narrative ends with a summary statement that Jeremiah took another scroll and gave it to Baruch and Baruch wrote down on it all the words contained on the first scroll that Jehoiakim destroyed. This scroll contained many similar words added to the words on the first scroll. Scholars think that this expanded second scroll contained much of the materials that we find in chs 1—25 in the present form of the book.

FROM THE TEXT

Though the narrative gives us valuable information on the process of the making of the book of Jeremiah, its primary focus is on the rejection of the word of God by both Jehoiakim and the people of Judah. Two issues are important for us to consider when we reflect on the theme of the rejection of God's word in this narrative.

First, there is no point of no return. Though the text only describes the content of the two scrolls in summary fashion, the particular summary it gives is instructive. God's word is that hope yet remains for Judah. In a way, this point is similar to that announced by the story of Jeremiah's visit to the potter's house in ch 18. In that story, God declared that if he had decreed disaster on a nation whose people subsequently repent, then he will turn away the disaster he had previously planned for them. It seems that even at this late date within the history of Judah, with the army of Babylonia marching across the land, the possibility yet remains for God's punishment to be turned back.

The implications of this for present society are clear. A Wesleyan view of the world maintains that it is fallen and sinful, yet God is still able to redeem it if individuals and communities would but turn to receive in faith the grace God offers. Wesleyan theology is in harmony with the majority of Protestant thought that humans cannot earn their way into salvation through good works, although good works are required of those who receive salvation by grace through faith. Humans do not have the ability in themselves to choose good and turn away from evil; this is all the gift of God. Salvation is the offer of God through Jesus Christ to all who repent and turn away from their sinful way of life, including those who live a life full of sin and repent at the hour of death. God's desire for sinners is not their death but their salvation.

Second, God's word cannot be silenced or destroyed. In this story, Jeremiah and Baruch could certainly have given up hope once the word they had been given by God was rejected at the highest level. The witness of this text, along with the abiding witness of Scripture, is that even if God's word is rejected, it cannot be silenced or destroyed. It is possible also that Jehoiakim, by destroying the scroll, is trying to destroy the evidence of his own complicity in the events that lead up to the destruction of Jerusalem and Judah. God's command to Jeremiah to produce a second scroll with all the same words plus some clearly demonstrates that the divine word survives any and all human efforts to silence it.

Just like the possibility of salvation remaining even after all hope seems to be lost, so also the indestructibility of God's word is a very positive message. Though it may mean judgment on the leaders, their attempts to stamp it out will ultimately be unsuccessful. At the same time, however, there is a promise of salvation held even for the leaders who would scorn God's word in the way Jehoiakim did in this passage. If they would return to God, just as if the people would return to God, then even at this late date God would turn back the punishment he had promised to bring about on the land. However, the narrative also warns its readers to be cautious; continued rejection of God's word and actions like that of Jehoiakim may ultimately lead to a point of no return, though that may not need to be the case. The tragedy of 587 B.C. in the history of Judah is a stark reminder of this reality.

"BUILD AND PLANT"

THE DEATH OF A NATION (37:1—44:30)

Overview

Chapters 37—44 narrate the events immediately following and after the Babylonian invasion of Judah in 587 B.C. that resulted in the total collapse of the nation, the destruction of Jerusalem and the temple, and the deportation of the citizens of Judah to Babylon. These chapters also show the further deterioration of conditions in post-587 Judah that eventually prompted the remaining people of Judah to escape to Egypt in fear of Babylon. However, these chapters not only narrate the story of Judah but also portray the prophet's personal suffering. Some commentators have called these chapters the *via dolorosa* chapters of Jeremiah or the "passion narrative" of Jeremiah (Lundbom 2004b, 50). It is generally agreed that these chapters contain the work of Baruch, the scribe and biographer of Jeremiah. This section is followed by Baruch's own personal narrative (ch 45), which might be considered Baruch's signature chapter, which in turn concludes the so-called Baruch Narrative (chs 36—45).

These chapters portray judgment as a reality that is taking place in the history of Judah. The words of threat pronounced in chs 1—25 are being fulfilled. Judah is being dismantled, uprooted, and torn down. These chapters thus convey the veracity of Jeremiah's words of judgment. What now remains for Judah is the fulfillment of Jeremiah's words about Yahweh's building and planting of Israel. In that sense, the end of Judah narrated in these chapters is not the end, but only the beginning of a future for Judah, the days of its restoration and rebuilding and the enjoyment of life in a new covenant relationship with Yahweh.

A. Zedekiah-Jeremiah Encounters with Interludes (37:1—38:28a)

BEHIND THE TEXT

Chapters 37 (LXX 44) and 38 (LXX 45) narrate the interaction of Jeremiah with Zedekiah, the last king of Judah, and they also contain significant information on the personal suffering of the prophet. The king was apparently a rather ineffective ruler, partly because he only came to power at the behest of the occupying Babylonians. He is shown to be easily manipulated, with regard to both domestic and foreign policy. After a brief introduction of the king (37:1-2), the text plays out the tête-à-tête between the prophet and the king in three episodes (37:3-10, 17-21; 38:14-28a), separated by two interludes in which the prophet is accused of treason (37:11-16; 38:1-13). These meetings and Jeremiah's imprisonment took place in the days immediately preceding the collapse of Judah (588-587 B.C.). The events narrated in chs 37—38 are more or less in sequential order.

The interaction of Jeremiah and Zedekiah leads up to the first story of the fall of Jerusalem in ch 39. Another version may be found in ch 52, with the two together appearing like a theme and its reprise in a symphony. The first introduction of Zedekiah is separated a bit from the narrative of the fall of Jerusalem, whereas in ch 52 they are adjacent.

IN THE TEXT

1. Prelude: Introduction of King Zedekiah (37:1-2)

■ 1 The introduction of the king is reminiscent of the short introductions of the kings of Israel and Judah throughout the books of 1 and 2 Kings. This verse gives the lineage of the king, saying that he was the son of Josiah and that he succeeded Coniah, or Jehoiachin, the last popularly elected king of Judah. See 52:31-34 for a discussion of what happened to Jehoiachin after the exile. Verse 1 also indicates that Zedekiah was placed on the throne as a puppet ruler of the Babylonians by King Nebuchadnezzar.

This fact contributes to the generally negative impression Zedekiah seems to have made on the populace (see, among others, ch 28). Missing from this introduction in comparison to 2 Kgs 24:18 is a note of how old Zedekiah was when he began to reign and how long his reign lasted (see 52:1-3). These details about Zedekiah were probably more important in the historical report of 2 Kings than in the text here (37:1). However, the narrative introduction in v 1 situates itself more or less precisely in the history of Judah (see 1:1-3).

■ 2 One element typical of 1 and 2 Kings, however, does remain. This comes in the judgment that Zedekiah and his associates did not listen to Yahweh or to Jeremiah. Yet this statement is only a summary compared to 2 Kgs 24:18-

20. Again, however, the difference is to be explained according to the specific functions of Jeremiah and 2 Kings rather than a deficiency in Jeremiah or an unnecessary addition on the part of 2 Kings. The summary judgment on Zedekiah in v 2 portrays the king as a weak, sinful ruler, allowing himself to be blown along by the wind rather than take a positive stand for Yahweh.

2. Zedekiah Sends Officials to Jeremiah (37:3-10)

■ **3-5** The first encounter between Zedekiah and Jeremiah begins with the king dispatching two of his advisers to seek a prophetic oracle from Jeremiah. Another example of community leaders seeking such an oracle from Jeremiah may be found in ch 42. In addition, v 4 indicates something interesting about the treatment of the prophet by the leadership. On a surface reading, there is a conflict between 36:5 (in which the reader learns that Jeremiah **was prevented from going to the House of Yahweh**) and 37:4 that indicates he was still able to move about as he wished. This tension, however, can be resolved in two ways. It is likely that Jeremiah's disbarment from the temple and his hiding from Jehoiakim's deputies ended with the death of Jehoiakim and Zedekiah's accession to the throne in 597. Chapters 37—38 portray Zedekiah as a sympathetic but powerless ally of Jeremiah. It is also possible that Jeremiah's freedom **to come and go among the people** did not necessarily include the freedom to go to the temple. If this is the case, Jeremiah's disbarment from the temple does not mean he is in prison and not free to otherwise move about as he wished. Carroll resolves the tension a bit differently. He suggests that 37:11-16 (see below) is a distinct story of how Jeremiah was thrown into prison, set against 32:2-5 (Carroll 1986, 675). This explanation is also plausible, but definitive conclusions suffer from the lack of evidence.

A temporal note is given in v 5, suggesting the Babylonians **withdrew from Jerusalem** upon hearing of the Egyptian advance. This sets up the oracle in v 8. Therefore, there is an internal logic to the narrative of ch 37. Verse 5 refers to the Egyptian army under the leadership of Pharaoh Hophra advancing toward Jerusalem around 588 B.C. These events may have prompted Zedekiah and his people to put their misguided hope in Egypt as a political ally, interpreted as help sent by Yahweh (see 2 Kgs 18:21 for a similar saying about hasty reliance on Egypt).

■ **6-10** The remainder of the first episode is divided into two separate oracles that Jeremiah gives the officials for the king. The first one in vv 6-8 puts down any hope for deliverance from the Babylonians that might have been placed in the Egyptians. Rather than, as hoped, the Babylonians turning back and going home, it is the Egyptians who will turn back and go home. As it turns out, according to v 8, the Babylonians will in fact turn back, but they will come back to Jerusalem, besiege the city once again, overrun it, and burn it down. Even if the Babylonian army is reduced to the wounded, they would rise up and burn the city (v 10). This is, according to the oracle, the fate of all those who trust in Egypt for deliverance. One further point can be noted, in reference to the issue of mediation of words discussed in the commentary on ch 36. Zedekiah himself is not present in this episode, as he will be in the others in this chapter, and so the oracle is given in a kind of mediated fashion: first from Yahweh to Jeremiah, then from Jeremiah to the advisers, with instructions to deliver to the king what the prophet and Yahweh had told them.

This word would surely not have been well received either by the officials or by the king who sent them. Nevertheless, Jeremiah is compelled to say exactly this (see 1:7; 20:9). The reader can certainly empathize with the position in which Jeremiah has been placed. He does not want to call for the destruction of his nation, surely; but the events before him and the word of Yahweh that has come to him make such a conclusion inescapable. Brueggemann's comments on what Zedekiah receives and what he gets are instructive: "The king had asked for a word of prayer *addressed to Yahweh* in intercession. Instead, however, he receives from the prophet *a word from Yahweh*, more of the same word to which he would not listen. The king wants God's help, but gets only God's harsh guidance" (1998, 355-56). Seeing as the Babylonians have already successfully laid siege to Jerusalem before, there is nothing to suggest they will not be successful again. Even with the possibility of Egyptian aid coming, the ultimate defeat of Jerusalem and a second (and third!) exile seem inevitable.

3. Interlude: Jeremiah Accused of Treason (37:11-16)

■ **11-13** As mentioned above, both of the interludes in the extended conversation between Jeremiah and Zedekiah involve the former being accused of treason. The temporal note given in this verse recalls vv 5 and 8, which also indicate that the Babylonians had temporarily abandoned the siege of Jerusalem. Naturally, this should have been cause for celebration, or at least for relief, among Judeans. However, Jeremiah's oracle given to the king's officials declared in no uncertain terms that the temporary withdrawal of the Babylonians was indeed a temporary withdrawal. Jeremiah and Yahweh said that they would come back, with force! When they did come back, the city would not be able to stand against them, but would be destroyed by fire.

In the present text, however, the lifting of the siege gives Jeremiah an opportunity to leave the city in order to receive his inheritance in the land of Benjamin (v 12). This narrative unit, while it gives the reader a glimpse into the generally negative treatment the prophet is supposed to have experienced (Clements 1988, 219), also recalls the story of the land deal in ch 32, during Jeremiah's confinement in the king's prison house.

In this version of Jeremiah's arrest and eventual imprisonment, the charge is simple treason. Not knowing what business Jeremiah is about—and perhaps not caring—the guard Irijah accused him of **deserting to the Babylonians**. This accusation is understandable given the state of affairs around Jerusalem. Perhaps the guard made this accusation because he may have mistakenly taken the prophet's words about the return of the Babylonians to Jerusalem as unpatriotic and an indication of his pro-Babylonian political view. It is then not difficult to understand the guard's suspicion of Jeremiah as an ally of Babylon and his leaving the city as an attempt to desert to the Babylonians.

■ **14-16** Jeremiah very simply protested his innocence and denied the charge, though he oddly did not offer any further justification, such as the real purpose of his leaving the city, indicated in v 12. Although Jeremiah is not compelled to give his reason, this would seem to be a critical piece of information in his own defense. The focus of the text is on the charge and the prophet's denial of the charge against him. In any event, Irijah **would not listen to him,** so it is actually unclear whether Jeremiah tried to justify his action and this justification was rebuffed as well. Jeremiah is put into the house of Jonathan the ***scribe,*** which had been converted into a prison. This location of Jeremiah's confinement will come into play later on in episode two of the interaction between Jeremiah and Zedekiah.

The mistreatment that Jeremiah receives at the hand of **the officials,** which is probably some kind of catchall term for royal bureaucrats, is symptomatic of the negative reaction that the prophet's words have been receiving all along. Jeremiah often complains that "the word of the LORD has come to me and I have spoken to you again and again, but you have not listened" (25:3). At times, the resistance to Jeremiah's preaching flared up into persecution and imprisonment.

4. Jeremiah Meets Zedekiah in the Palace (37:17-21)

■ **17** In the second episode of their extended interaction, Jeremiah and Zedekiah meet together in the palace. Zedekiah exercised his royal prerogative and had Jeremiah taken out of the prison house to be brought to him. Yet in spite of the king being able, in theory, to do whatever he wished, there is still a hint of sneakiness to this conversation, for the king speaks to Jeremiah ***secretly in the palace.*** The NIV's **privately** seems not quite strong enough when seen in this light. Jeremiah was a persona non grata by this point, and even the king could have tainted his reputation by speaking with him openly. This may also further indicate Zedekiah's general ineffectiveness as a ruler, for he seems in this text to be somewhat afraid of how his interactions with Jeremiah will make him look in the eyes of the rest of the people, and his officials in particular. He also, apparently, was fearful before Yahweh, as indicated by the hesitating question he asks of the prophet, **"Is there any word from the LORD?"** What the king hoped to hear was reassurance from Yahweh that Judah would be saved from the Babylonians; instead, what he received as Yahweh's word was bad news about his own capture by the Babylonians. Yahweh will soon hand him over to his enemies. Obviously this is not what the king wanted to hear but, again, Jeremiah can say nothing else than what Yahweh has given him to say.

■ 18 Jeremiah continues the dialogue with a question of his own directed to the king. He wants to know what wrong he has committed against the king and his officials that they treat him like a criminal. He wants to know why his attempt to follow the commands of Yahweh was interpreted as a jailable offense. Jeremiah's claim of innocence here matched very closely his protest of innocence made to the arresting officer. There, as here, he did not give a lengthy justification for his actions, as the reader might have expected. So, even though he did fully state his case before Irijah, he does so before Zedekiah.

■ 19 Jeremiah lent further support to his claim by asking after the whereabouts of the prophets who prophesied that the Babylonians would not again come up against the city. This claim is reminiscent of the dueling oracles scene with Hananiah, the other (false) prophet of Yahweh (ch 28). Hananiah may well be included in the statement Jeremiah made to the king. Jeremiah himself was still around, but it seems that those who gave a word alternative to that which he gave were nowhere to be seen. According to the logic of the Deuteronomistic test for prophets (see Deut 18:15-22), Jeremiah is therefore in the right, and all the other prophets are in the wrong.

■ 20-21 Jeremiah continued his speech to the king with an urgent plea. In so doing, he seemingly left behind for the moment his protestations of innocence. If he must be confined, then he asked that he be imprisoned in the court of the guard rather than the house of Jonathan the scribe, converted as it was into a prison house. His request conveys his fear that his enemies will kill him if he is sent back where he came from. Zedekiah granted this request and also ordered that Jeremiah be given a daily allowance of bread **until all the bread in the city was gone** (see 52:6, 34). The narrative anticipates severe shortage of food in the city and the eventual end to the food supply when the Babylonians return and resume the siege of the city. Moreover, the text anticipates the fulfillment of the words spoken by Jeremiah to Zedekiah in 37:6-10.

5. Interlude: Jeremiah Accused of Treason Again (38:1-13)

In this chapter the reader again faces something of a confusion regarding Jeremiah's whereabouts. Specifically, it is unclear where Jeremiah was before the officials threw him into the cistern. Does 38:1-6 report another instance of the arrest of the prophet and his mistreatment by the officials? Or, did the officials take him from the court of the guard where he was confined under the order of Zedekiah (37:21)? In 38:13 and in v 28, he is confined again in the court of the guard. Since the text of ch 38 is unclear, there is reason to assume that Jeremiah was taken from the prison in the court of the guard and thrown into the cistern, which was also in the court of the guard (v 6). After Ebed-Melech's rescue of the prophet, he was returned to the court of the guard (v 13). So it is possible that the narrative deals with moving Jeremiah from one place of confinement to another (to a cistern) and then back to the previous place. Texts like the land transaction narrative in ch 32 clearly indicate that Jeremiah was able to give oracles while confined to the court of the guard. However, the officials' action indicates that their intent was to cut him off from any contact with the public and possibly to let him face death in the cistern.

■ **1-5** For all his demonstrated ineffectiveness and indecisiveness as a ruler, Zedekiah at the very least has not revealed the content of the *secret* conversation he had with the prophet in the palace (37:17). That this is so is revealed by the fact that the various officials named in v 1 now accuse Jeremiah of treason based not on what he has said to the king, but for what he had been **telling all the people**. Except for their names, we do not know anything about the individuals mentioned in v 1; neither do we know for sure their political views, though the text seems to imply that they were powerful and influential nationalists among the royal officials who advocated resistance against the Babylonian imperial power. Evidently Zedekiah was afraid of going against the demands of these officials (v 5). The phrase **all the people** perhaps means at least a representative sample of the Judean population. As used here and elsewhere in the book, it implies Jeremiah's purported reputation as a public figure. His words have gone out among **all the people** and have caused them to lose heart, as the officials will claim before the king, and so he must be silenced (v 4).

The content of the oracle itself (vv 2-3) is interesting. Jeremiah, speaking the words of Yahweh, is directly advocating desertion to the Babylonians. The oracle announces death and life issues; inside the city is not where one would find life because Yahweh's word to those who opt to stay in the city is their death by sword, famine, and pestilence—all the terrible and devastating affects of war. Life is to be found outside the city, more precisely, in the camp of the Babylonian army. Those who desert to the Babylonian side receive here Yahweh's offer of life. Statements like this can be found elsewhere in the book (see 21:4, 9; 22:25). Brueggemann suggests that in this oracle "Jeremiah preaches his characteristic word that God is now the active enemy of the Jerusalem enterprise" (1998, 362). He had earlier suggested that the "book of Jeremiah in its main parts has a decidedly 'pro-Babylonian' slant" (1998, 361). However, this need not necessarily be the case, as Huffmon persuasively argued: "Jeremiah [the prophet] is not to be characterized as pro-Babylonian, though many of his contemporaries so viewed him, but as pro-Israel. This stance did not demand political independence" (1999a, 267). In other words, to suppose that Jeremiah was "pro-Babylonian" because of statements like this is to accept at face value the charges of treason leveled against the prophet. Such a reading flatly ignores Jeremiah's theological contention, namely that the events about to happen are at the behest of and through the power of Yahweh, and not a display of might by the Babylonian imperial military machine. By speaking thus, he called into question the power of the empire and the inviolability of Jerusalem at one stroke.

Since the officials cannot do anything to stop the Babylonians from executing their plans, they are now engaged in doing what they are able to do; i.e., to stop the prophet from his continued call for surrender to the Babylonians and thus to resist the power of Babylon. They demand to the king that Jeremiah **should be put to death** because he is speaking words that destroy the morale of the nation and particularly that of the soldiers. They say to the king that the prophet **is discouraging the soldiers** (*hûʾmĕrappēʾ ʾetyĕdê ʾanšê hamilḥāmāh*), which literally means, **he is weakening the hands of the soldiers.** The soldiers are unable to grasp their weapons because of the preaching of Jeremiah, which has weakened their hands just as effectively as would a wound or a muscular disease.

The response the king gives is rather curious. In a phrase that sounds very much like the permission God gave to the Satan in the book of Job, the king tells them **"He is in your hands."** But then he goes even further than God does in Job and says, **"The king can do nothing to oppose you."** It is likely that this is yet another expression of the ineffectiveness of Zedekiah as a ruler. He was not even strong enough to oppose those who would put one of his citizens to death. It may well be that Zedekiah agreed with their suggestion of a death sentence for Jeremiah, but this is not what he said in v 5. The effect of this statement is that, even if Zedekiah had wished Jeremiah to remain alive, he would not, because the king by this time is devoid of all his authority.

■ **6-13** Jeremiah was not immediately put to death, however, in spite of the officials making that intention clear and the king having given them leave by default. It seems that if the officials were so upset at what Jeremiah was preaching, they should have just run him through rather than throwing him into a cistern to starve. For that matter, why lower Jeremiah with ropes? On the other hand, however, perhaps the officials want Jeremiah's suffering to be great on his way to death. On this reading, they are not satisfied merely to kill Jeremiah. It is an odd sentence to be sure, but one that would achieve the punitive purpose quite well.

In the later course of the story, this turned out to be a blunder on the officials' part, for even when Jeremiah himself appears powerless, he has powerful allies who work for his benefit. Ebed-Melech the **Ethiopian,** a eunuch in the service of King Zedekiah, appealed to the king that his officials **have acted wickedly** by putting Jeremiah into the cistern where he will die of starvation (v 9). It is significant that the conversation took place outside the palace (v 8). The **Benjamin Gate** is hardly a secret place; he was perhaps sitting there to hear cases that the people brought to him and to render judgment, which was part of his official function. It is possible that Ebed-Melech took advantage of this opportunity to present his case of injustice done to an innocent person by the royal officials (see Lundbom 2004b, 71).

In the course of his appeal to the king, Ebed-Melech's statement that **he will starve to death when there is no longer any bread in the city** (v 9) provides a nice contrast with the statement that Jeremiah was to be fed in the court of the guard "until all the bread in the city was gone" (37:21). Moreover, the narrators may perhaps be trying to say something about the roles of foreigners in the history of Judah. Jeremiah is a prophet without honor in his hometown (see Luke 4:24), but he seems to enjoy much support from foreigners. First, here, he is freed from the cistern and returned to prison by a foreigner, the Ethiopian Ebed-Melech. Later, he is freed from the prison by a foreigner, the Babylonian Nebuzaradan (39:13-14; 40:5).

The king's decisive response to Ebed-Melech (38:10) renders ambiguous the judgment that he is an ineffective ruler. It is difficult to determine the shifting portrayal of Zedekiah in these narratives. On the one hand, he acts decisively on certain issues (v 10; see also 37:21; 38:16); on the other hand, he admits he is powerless to do anything to save the life of the prophet and he acts in fear of his officials (38:5; see also 37:17; 38:24-25).

Ebed-Melech carried out Zedekiah's instructions faithfully (vv 11-13). At the end of the narrative unit in v 13, the prophet is back in the court of the guard again. Whereas it was unexpected that officials bent on mistreating or killing Jeremiah should lower him down into the cistern with ropes, here Ebed-Melech not only uses ropes but tosses down rags for Jeremiah to place under his arms—probably meaning in his armpits—so as to lessen discomfort as he is pulled out of the cistern. For his faithfulness and efficiency in seeing to Jeremiah's release, the Cushite earns an oracle of comfort in 39:15-18.

6. Jeremiah Meets Zedekiah at the Temple (38:14-28a)

■ **14** In the final episode of the interaction between Jeremiah and Zedekiah, the king **had him brought to the third entrance to the temple of the** LORD. This may have been the entrance to the temple from the court of the palace and thus a private place (Lundbom 2004b, 76). The intent of Zedekiah's private meeting with the prophet is to ask the prophet a question; it is not clear what the question is, but based on Jeremiah's response, we assume that the question was about the course of action he should take to save himself and the nation from the Babylonian army. Evidently he is aware that the prophet has the divine word, and he demands the prophet not to **hold anything back** from him. He wants to know in detail the fate that awaits him. This demand is a bit ironic in that Jeremiah has not in any way been demonstrated as one who is willing to hold things back (see 20:7-10).

■ **15** In response to the king's demand, the prophet suggests that he is not on the same level as the king's counselors; **you would not listen to me** (v 15). This statement cuts two directions. On the surface level, Jeremiah expressed his fear that honesty will earn him nothing but a death sentence. Below the surface, however, this is an attack upon the king's counselors who have consistently led him on the wrong path. Precisely because the king is weak and not able to make firm decisions for himself, the counselors have seized the opportunity for power and have conspired to eliminate Jeremiah as a potential rival for the ear of the king. Essentially, Jeremiah has told the king here that, had the king listened to him instead of the advisers, then the situation that was taking place would certainly have been averted. Though this has been a common theme of Jeremiah's preaching, he was ultimately unsuccessful in converting enough people and turning away Yahweh's wrath.

■ **16-18** The king swore on oath not to give Jeremiah over to death. Along the way, he finally did assert some kind of independence from his advisers, promising not to **hand** Jeremiah **over to those who are seeking** his **life** (v 16). Zedekiah wanted to hear the word of Yahweh from the mouth of the prophet, and promised to protect him for delivering it faithfully. Yet, he also wanted to protect his own life and his apparently shaky hold on the throne. Even though, assumedly, the power of the Babylonians was behind him, the imperial army was occupied elsewhere and thus Zedekiah could very well have been the target of a coup d'état organized by the most bold among his supposed counselors.

Thus assured at least of temporary protection, Jeremiah again suggested that Yahweh has given the city into the hand of the Babylonians. If Zedekiah and the other Judean survivors surrender to the Babylonians, then all will be well. **You and your house may live** (v 17) may also be a promise of the survival of the Davidic dynasty (the NIV's **you and your family will live** is too narrow). If not, **this city will be handed over to the Babylonians and they will burn it down; you yourself will not escape from their hands** (v 18). This is similar to the statements attributed to the prophet throughout the book regarding submission to the Babylonians. It is understandable, therefore, why Jeremiah should have been charged with treason.

■ **19-23** In typical fashion, Zedekiah responded to Jeremiah's repeated prediction with fear and uncertainty. Yet, it is worded slightly different here. Whereas the entire conversation was occurring in secret for fear of the royal officials who disagreed with Jeremiah's interpretation, now Zedekiah is said to be afraid of those who have already gone over to Babylon. It is surely a part of the presentation of Zedekiah as a pathetic figure that he is never able to make a firm decision on his own. He is always worrying about what people will say or do to him. So Jeremiah reassured the king that if he did what was commanded of him, **then it will go well with you, and your life will be spared** (v 20).

Verses 21-23 report, however, an entirely different sort of punishment that will come to Zedekiah for his disobedience. Now the penalty does not seem to fall on him or the city, as it did previously, but on his family. Like the rest of the Judean citizenry, the women and children in the palace of Zedekiah will suffer the ill-effects of Zedekiah's poor judgment. At the end the final judgment is repeated once more: Zedekiah **will be captured by the king of Babylon; and this city will be burned down** (v 23).

The poem in v 22 deserves special comment. The poem cited there is also quoted in Obad 7. Jeremiah creatively reuses a taunt originally delivered against the nation of Edom (see 49:7-22). Moreover, the fact that it is **those women,** the women who are brought out of the king's harem and given to the Babylonian officials, heightens the critique of Zedekiah. Not only do his advisers manipulate him, not only do the first exiles mistreat him, but now even the members of his own household malign him. The last couplet of the taunt echoes in an odd way the experience of the prophet in the cistern: **Your feet are sunk in the mud; / your friends have deserted you** (see 38:6). Whereas Jeremiah did find a friend in the perhaps unlikely source, Ebed-Melech the Ethiopian, now King Zedekiah is completely friendless. Even though he was given many chances to repent and follow Yahweh's leadership as communicated by the prophet, he failed to do so, and this is only one of the ways in which he failed miserably as king of Judah.

■ **24-28a** In the final exchange, Zedekiah warned Jeremiah not to reveal the contents of the conversation to anyone, on pain of death (v 24). He even gave Jeremiah a scripted line with which to respond to any questioning (vv 25-26). In this way, Zedekiah shows a little bit of shrewdness, even if it is ultimately based on a fear of what the officials will do to the king himself. As it turned about, giving Jeremiah a line to feed the officials was a smart move on Zedekiah's part and would have a chance at success, **for no one had heard his conversation with the king** (v 27). It seems all was not well for the prophet, for he did remain confined in the court of the guard **until the day Jerusalem was captured** (v 28). It is interesting that the prophet is under a double death threat. Zedekiah threatens him with death and demands that he keep their conversation a secret from the officials. On the other hand, Zedekiah is also aware that the officials might threaten the prophet with death and demand him to share the content of his conversation with the king. Caught in the middle of this danger to his life, the prophet decides to be truthful to the king. Clarke notes that the king was asking Jeremiah to tell "the truth, and nothing but the truth, but not the whole truth" and that Jeremiah was "most certainly not obliged to relate anything" other than "what was necessary" to the officials (1823, 358-59).

FROM THE TEXT

Several theological lessons can be gleaned from the behavior of the various characters in the story. The basic contrast is between acting with integrity with respect to God's word and acting only with regard to one's self-interest. On the one hand, we should perhaps not be so quick to criticize the officials. The decisions they make are in line with their desire to save their own lives and the life of their nation. On the other hand, we should also perhaps not be so quick to praise Ebed-Melech. Perhaps his only motivation is to redress what he sees as an injustice in the treatment of a political prisoner. Yet, the book is very clear in its judgment on these two courses of action. The elaborate plans explicitly attributed to the royal officials and implicitly to the king ultimately, in the book and in the history, come to naught. In the case of Ebed-Melech, his care for Jeremiah earns him a special commendation from God. Whatever his actual motivation might have been—for there is no information on this point—he is blessed by God for having taken care of God's prophet. In the end, those who are acting in their self-interest and in the political interest of the nation receive in the narrative a negative evaluation because they attempt to destroy God's prophet, which in reality means an attempt to silence God at that critical time in Judah's history. The narrative also shows that God's prophet survived through the intervention of a person, most likely not a member of the community of faith, but who was committed to doing that which is just and right. The preservation of the life of the prophet also means in the narrative the ongoing opportunity for the nation to continue to hear God's word—the word of life and death. This privilege is made possible to the community of faith by the actions of a "righteous Gentile."

A further contrast can be drawn between the behavior of Zedekiah and Jeremiah throughout this narrative. On the one hand, Zedekiah is presented in a somewhat conflicted way. At times, he is shown to be either incapable or unwilling to refuse his officials' plans to kill the prophet. However, he is also shown to be something of a shrewd operator, trying to shore up his own rather tottering reign in the midst of a difficult time for the nation. Jeremiah, by contrast, is presented as unflinchingly resolute. This is certainly an outgrowth of his sense of a call, which also makes him willing even to commit treason in the service of an even higher, theologically informed patriotism.

Paradoxically, Jeremiah in this text resists the power of the state (Babylon) by encouraging submission to the power of the state (Babylon). That this move can be made is due to the theological foundation that has been consistently built throughout the book. Even though the attempts made by Judeans to reassert their independence from Babylon—the appeals for aid from Egypt, returning to the worship of previously disregarded deities or attempting violent military rebellion—and even though each may have some advantages, according to Jeremiah these options are all demonstrably unfaithful to God. Again, it does not matter if such a judgment is fair to the alternative positions (and it is not); what is important is that the text mentions the alternative positions in the first place. The reader is then obligated to take seriously these alternatives, even going back behind what the text reports about them in order to discover something of the dramatic conversation taking place in sixth century B.C. Judah.

The counterintuitive nature of the perceptions ascribed to the prophet cannot be overstressed. As has already been seen, the charge that Jeremiah the prophet was a pro-Babylonian sympathizer at best and a Judean traitor at worst has a great deal of merit when one considers the totality of the statements attributed to him. The word of God in this passage, and in particular the promise to Zedekiah that he would not be handed over to the Babylonians by those who had already surrendered, seem to run against the grain. However, this is precisely the point: radical obedience to what God requires will often run contrary to what makes sense from a human point of view. While this does not mean that faith and intellect or reason are ultimately opposed to one another, it does mean that sometimes even the best and the brightest among humans have a rather limited view when it comes to the things of God.

B. The Fall of Jerusalem (38:28b—39:18)

The destruction of Jerusalem by the Babylonians is, without doubt, the most important axis on which the book of Jeremiah turns. In fact, the book has two parallel versions of this and related events—the first here at the end of ch 38 through ch 39 and the second, somewhat more lengthy, account in ch 52. These relate to one another like musical variations on the central theme of an opera. Therefore, in the present commentary, the latter story is called a reprise of the former in order to indicate the organic connection between them. In the first version the reader encounters a summary statement of Jerusalem's fall, along with accounts of what happened to three particular men—or, at least in one of the cases, what was promised to happen to him—after the fall of the city. These three men are King Zedekiah, the last king ever to sit on David's throne, the Prophet Jeremiah, and an otherwise unknown Ethiopian ("Cushite," 39:15) named Ebed-Melech, who ministered to Jeremiah when the latter was in prison for his preaching.

1. Summary Statement (38:28b—39:3)

BEHIND THE TEXT

In certain ways, the whole book of Jeremiah has been leading up to this point. For here the threats of Yahweh through the prophet to destroy Jerusalem and allow its citizenry to be deported are finally realized. The reader can appreciate the importance attached to the Babylonian siege and conquering of Jerusalem in the meticulous detail given to its description. Even though here the details are rather scarce, with the fuller description left to the "reprise" in ch 52, still there is enough here to warrant the suggestion that the final editors of the book of Jeremiah were quite concerned to locate the events of the exile within a specific set of historical circumstances. On the one hand, this lends a kind of historical credibility to the work, for once these details are included they can then be checked against the details of other documents (for example, the Babylonian chronicles). On the other hand, however, the editors of Jeremiah were not overly concerned with proving the validity of their arguments, but rather with testifying to Yahweh's leadership even over the terrifying and terrible events of the exile. Even though the Promised Land was violated at this time, another motif running through the book is that this does not represent a complete end for the people. Seen in this light, the exile is not only punitive but purgative. In other words, the point of exile is not punishment for its own sake, but to purify the remnant of the people for a renewed relationship with Yahweh after the exile is concluded.

IN THE TEXT

■ **38:28b** In the MT, v 28 ends with the phrase, *and it happened when Jerusalem was taken.* This text immediately presents the interpreter with a problem. The second half of 38:28 seems not to fit where it lies. This is because 39:1-3 go on to describe in a certain amount of detail circumstances leading up to the fall of Jerusalem, beginning with the siege of Nebuchadnezzar and the Babylonian army. The MT recognizes this problem by setting off 38:28b with marks indicating the limits of a passage.

Four major possibilities present themselves for dealing with this issue, any of which seem perfectly acceptable. Moreover, each has varying levels of support among principal English translations. The first is an idiosyncratic option offered by NKJV. It leaves 38:28 intact and translates, "Now Jeremiah remained in the court of the prison until the day that Jerusalem was taken. And he was there when Jerusalem was taken."

Second, the reader may attach 38:28b to 39:1, resulting in variations of **this is how Jerusalem was taken.** (Related to this is seeing the phrase as a title for ch 39, though this is not found in any principal English version.) This option is also adopted by NIV, NASB, TNIV, NCV, and ASV. Keown, Scalise, and Smothers agree (1995, 227). The ASV resolves the issue by making 39:1-2 a long parenthetical comment, which appears somewhat strained (this is adopted by Carroll 1986, 691).

The third option is to delete 38:28b as dittography (a scribal error doubling a line of the biblical text). This is preferred by NLT, CEV, The Message, KJV, ESV, and the 21st century KJV. These translations follow the Septuagint. Thompson's commentary favors this option (1980, 641).

The fourth option is to move 38:28b to a spot between 39:2 and 39:3. This is adopted by the present commentary. This translation recognizes in a footnote that "many authorities" believe that 38:28b was placed where it was because of an error. Among the commentaries, John Bright takes this option (Bright 1965, 241). The NRSV seems to follow this option by placing 38:28b at the beginning of 39:3 ("When Jerusalem was taken . . .")

■ **39:1-3** As indicated above, these verses describe in summary fashion the events leading up to the capture of Jerusalem. The reprise in 52:4-27 is, as will be seen, much more detailed. Preserved here are the essential details of what happened when the Babylonians invaded Jerusalem. The siege of Jerusalem began **in the ninth year of Zedekiah king of Judah, in the tenth month** (see the addition "tenth day" in 52:4; 2 Kgs 25:1). Though this text gives the date for the beginning of the siege (v 1) and the fall of Jerusalem (v 2), there is no consensus among scholars on the specific date of these events. There is a one year difference in the reckoning of these dates due to different ways of correlating biblical references of dates with the Babylonian and Jewish calendar systems. Some scholars place the beginning of the siege in January 587 and the fall of Jerusalem in July 586, whereas others place these events in January 588 and July 587 respectively. This commentary follows the latter. The note in v 2 that the breach of the wall occurred **on the ninth day of the fourth month of Zedekiah's eleventh year** reminds the reader of the historical note given in 1:1-3. In 1:3, one learns that the word of Yahweh came to Jeremiah all the way up to the eleventh year of Zedekiah, ***until Jerusalem went into exile in the fifth month.*** The narrator does not give any details of the events between the siege and the fall, except one key development that happened when the city was taken by the Babylonians. Four chief officers along with **all the officials of the king of Babylon came** and sat **in the Middle Gate.** King Nebuchadnezzar himself was not present; v 5 indicates that he was at Riblah. In ancient Israel, the city gates were the places where elders sat and settled disputes and pronounced judgments. The narrator implies by this brief statement that the fate of the city and its population is now in the hands of the officials of the king of Babylon. Verse 3 may be a veiled reference to the fulfillment of Jeremiah's words in 1:15-16. In spite of the brevity of vv 1-3, however, it is clear that this text was meant to give a clear sense of where the siege and fall of Jerusalem fit into the overarching historical picture (see From the Text in the next section).

2. Zedekiah After the Fall (39:4-10)

BEHIND THE TEXT

Jeremiah 39 is one place where the differences between the Septuagint and the MT are very significant. Verses 4-13 in the MT are missing in the LXX (ch 46 has vv 1-3 and then vv 14-18). One must stop short, however, either of saying this text is "missing" from the Septuagint or that it has been "added" to the MT. Using either one of these terms is to prejudice the discussion of which of the two versions may represent something closer to the original words of Jeremiah. A neutral explanation for this difference is to invoke the scribal error of haplography, wherein a copyist's eyes would skip from one phrase to a similar one and leave out the material in between (Parke-Taylor 2000, 210). Some scholars think that a shorter Hebrew text is the source that underlies the Septuagint. However the divergence is to be explained, the question remains as to how ancient readers, such as the early Christians, who considered this text as their scripture would have understood the meaning of this text. One may also ask how understanding of the text today would be different had the general tradition of biblical translation followed the Septuagint rather than the MT.

IN THE TEXT

■ **4** Though Zedekiah, as king of Judah, had the duty to protect the city from attack, he nevertheless fled from the city as soon as it was clear that the wall had been breached. The "reprise" version of Jerusalem's fall in ch 52 has a bit more detail about what happened to Zedekiah in his escape attempt, but the summary given here is rather enough. He escaped with **all the soldiers**, a phrase that may in fact be limited to his personal bodyguards, for it seems unusual that all of the soldiers defending the city would have been able to escape the detection of the Babylonians. However, making such fine distinctions is not the point of this narrative. Rather, this narrative has short descriptions and nearly breathless language, describing the events of the fall. At this point in the narrative the focus is simply on Zedekiah's attempt to escape the city.

■ **5-7** Again, the "reprise" narrative has a bit more detail, namely that the detachment of soldiers commissioned to protect the king fled from him when the Babylonian army caught up with them (52:7-8). Just as Zedekiah abandoned the city in its time of need, so the soldiers abandoned him in his time of need. The situation was indeed very dire in Judah at this time. Yet even though Zedekiah and his soldiers were able to escape the city and elude detection by the Babylonians, his absence was soon noted and the enemy soldiers (**the Babylonian army**) took off in pursuit (39:5). Again, it is probably not the case that the entire contingent of the army of the Babylonians in Jerusalem at that time pursued Zedekiah. This detail in v 4, however, is parallel to the account in 52:8. The Babylonian army captured Zedekiah in the plains of Jericho and brought him to Nebuchadnezzar, who had set up his command post at Riblah, an ancient city in central Syria, which the Babylonians used as their military and administrative center in that region (39:5). Where the NIV reads in v 5 **he pronounced sentence upon him**, the Hebrew may also be translated *he put him on trial*. But this trial was in no way a fair affair. The outcome is assured before the trial begins, so it captures the point nicely to say that Nebuchadnezzar pronounced sentence upon Zedekiah without the bother of a trial.

The narrative continues with the rest of the punitive actions that Nebuchadnezzar carried out to put an end to any further Judean resistance to his plans (vv 6-7). In accordance with the previous prophecies of Jeremiah, perhaps the Babylonians would not have been so brutal with Judah and Jerusalem had the king and his officials not revolted against them. The way in which Nebuchadnezzar carried out the removal of potential threat to his power is interesting, even if its violent nature is abhorrent. The killings take place in order of importance; that is, those closest to power (**the sons of Zedekiah**) are the primary targets of the Babylonians. After that the attention is turned to **the nobles of Judah,** those who stood in line next as potential leaders of Jerusalem in the absence of the royal family. In the next chapter of the book of Jeremiah, the reader will discover that the elimination of the royal line was not complete, and there would again be a revolt in Judah that attempted to reestablish Judean independence and the Davidic succession (40:13—41:18).

Moreover, Zedekiah is forced to watch these things before he himself is blinded (39:6). Jeremiah had given a prophecy to Zedekiah that the king "will not escape out of the hands of the Babylonians but will certainly be handed over to the king of Babylon, and will speak with him face to face and see him with his own eyes" (32:4). Yet the sentence passed on Zedekiah represented a violent reversal of this prophecy. The last thing that Zedekiah saw was the coming to naught of all the hope that had rested in the Davidic dynasty—as the kings chosen by God—for centuries. It is not an overstatement to say that these events, and their preservation in the book of Jeremiah, had a profound psychological impact on the remnant of Judah. Indeed, the reader will see further evidence of the fear of Babylonian might that is brought about in Judah by events like this, especially in the aftermath of the rebellion of Ishmael (chs 40—41). For now, blinded Zedekiah is taken off in **bronze shackles** to die in Babylon. His fate is much worse than that of his predecessor Jehoiachin, in whom some semblance of admittedly ambiguous hope survives even after the land is devastated and the temple destroyed (see 24:1-10; 52:31-34).

■ **8-10** After the slaughtering of the king's sons and the Judean officials, and the blinding of Zedekiah, the text rather simply reports that **the Babylonians set fire to the royal palace and *the house* of the people and broke down the walls of** the city. Again, it will be left for ch 52 to expand upon this, and the reader finds great detail there (see 52:13-14). Verse 9 of ch 39 similarly reports in a summary fashion that Nebuzaradan, the captain of the guard, deported to Babylon those who were left in the city and **those who had gone over to him** (most likely Nebuchadnezzar is intended here). See the commentary on 52:15 for a more extended treatment of this, but at first glance it seems odd that those who voluntarily surrendered are deported. Nevertheless, the Babylonians for whatever reason did not spare them; only the poorest of the land are left over, to tend fields and vineyards, presumably for the benefit of the empire.

FROM THE TEXT

When the Babylonian army came and laid siege to Jerusalem, all hopes for Judah's future came to an end. The people may have held hope in the jailed Jehoiachin (see 52:31-34), but the tragic events that followed the capture of the city by the Babylonians must have darkened any ray of hope for the nation's future. Their city was taken by the enemy, their king abandoned them, and those who were sworn to protect the king abandoned the king. The murder of the king's sons and all the royal officials, and the exile of the blinded king to Babylon would have only added intensity to the hopelessness that was spreading through the land.

The only ones who seem to benefit from this situation are the poorest of the land and, in a way, this rights a wrong previously complained of by the prophet. He announced God's judgment on the higher levels of society for mistreating their slaves, particularly for taking back their slaves whom they had set free (see 34:8-22; Stulman 2005, 317). Nebuzaradan's (the commander of the Babylonian army) decision to give the poorest people, who owned nothing, the land once owned by the wealthy perhaps should be rightly understood as making things right by God who cares for the poor and demands justice in the land. In reality, the land now belongs to the imperial power, which could have used the land and its resources to benefit itself and its program of expansion and maintenance of its army. But strangely enough the commander of the imperial army gives the land to the poorest in the occupied area. One might also see here the concern for justice by another "righteous Gentile" in the book of Jeremiah.

The point of this is perhaps that, even in a situation where all positive feeling seems lost, yet a bit of hope remains. Even though the Babylonians probably did not act in this way only to give a benefit to those previously oppressed, that they did so leaves a hint that not all is destroyed, that in fact new life can go on in the Promised Land after the exile is over. As will be shown later, another point driven home by the book of Jeremiah is that the experience of exile is not only punitive (intended to punish the nation for its sins) but also purgative (intended to purify the nation for better service to God). This note of the benevolence of the empire to the less fortunate in Judean society certainly contributes to this dual function of the exile; the empire lays the foundation for the restoration of proper social relations, which is essential for the restoration of proper relations with God.

3. Jeremiah After the Fall (39:11-14)

BEHIND THE TEXT

The fate of the Prophet Jeremiah is something of a concern in the book. This is so even in spite of his general absence from the narrated fall of Jerusalem, both here in ch 39 and in the "reprise" version in ch 52. As will be shown, the slight differences in detail between 39:11-14 and 40:1-6 is a matter of perspective and not a real divergence. Stulman's comments on this divergence are balanced and enlightening. He writes: "As is often the case in the book, linear categories of time are not of foremost importance, even in historicized accounts . . . The text's lack of coherence may present a ready opportunity to recognize its own focal concerns and theological interests" (2005, 318). Carroll, by contrast, states rather flatly: "These stories are the equivalent of the variations on the interview motif and indicate the variety of story-telling used to portray Jeremiah . . . The stories cannot be harmonized, but they share central themes" (1986, 693).

At the end of the day, the text as we have it is concerned to note what happened to the principal character. However, this is not the primary concern, as evidenced by the fact that Jeremiah immediately again drops out of the story for three chapters. Thus it is important to keep in mind, as Stulman suggests, "while tidying up the 'mess' may make the text more readable by modern standards, it may also distort its own inner logic" (2005, 318). Jeremiah only shows up again in the conversations following the assassination of Gedaliah. These four verses can be divided further into two pairs, the first dealing with the command of Nebuchadnezzar and the second with its execution.

IN THE TEXT

■ **11-12** It is unclear on the surface why the Babylonian king should take such interest in a Judean prophet. The text does not inquire after the motivation, so that an assessment from a somewhat wider viewpoint becomes necessary. It is certainly within the realm of possibility that Nebuchadnezzar had heard of Jeremiah's preaching, and specifically his repeated predictions that Babylonia would take control of Jerusalem and the land of Judah (see, among many others, 32:4, 36; 34:3; 37:17; 38:3, 18). Skinner suggests a role for Gedaliah in this, which becomes explicit in 39:14. He writes: "Gedaliah would have made enquiries about Jeremiah, and then applied for his release partly in the ground of personal and family friendship . . . Such a request, accompanied by information about the prophet which could not fail to commend him to the Babylonian government, could not reasonably be refused" (1922/1963, 274). Furthermore, Jeremiah had also encouraged his fellow citizens to voluntarily surrender to the Babylonians, for that, he said, was the key to survival (see 21:8-9; 38:17). Finally, Jeremiah had sent a long note of consolation to the exiles in Babylon, exhorting them essentially to work for the advancement of the city of Babylon, "because if it prospers, you too will prosper" (29:7).

All of these things may have contributed to the Babylonians' perception of Jeremiah as a willing supporter of their intentions for Judah. Indeed, this view was apparently current among Judeans as well (see 37:17). This has led commentators to a sometimes heated debate over the political alignment of Jeremiah. Huffmon's perspective that Jeremiah was "pro-Israel" seems to be an appropriate understanding of Jeremiah's political affiliation (1999a, 267). In other words, both the Babylonians and the Judeans were wrong regarding Jeremiah. He was neither anti-Judah nor pro-Babylon, though it is plain enough to see how his preaching could be taken in that way.

The text next reports Nebuchadnezzar's specific instructions regarding the fate of Jeremiah. He was to be given whatever he asked for (v 12). That the prophet received this special consideration from the empire surely contributed to whatever ill-will Judeans continued to have for him. Nevertheless, his supposed pro-Babylonian stance is rewarded by the empire and he is given a choice as to where he will go. This is made more explicit in the parallel story of his release by Nebuzaradan in 40:1-6.

■ **13-14** The text then names three persons, along with **all the other officers of the king of Babylon** who carried out the emperor's orders concerning Jeremiah (v 13). The indication that so many people were involved in this is typical of expanded readings in the MT. Comparison with the LXX, however, is impossible since, as has already been indicated, vv 4-13 are not found there. Functionally, it certainly would only have been necessary for Nebuzaradan to do this, perhaps assigning the task to an underling. The Babylonians entrusted Jeremiah to Gedaliah, a member of the Shaphan family, and the governor appointed by the king of Babylon over Judah (v 14; see 40:5). As noted above, though Jeremiah **remained among his own people** (39:14) he soon disappears from the narrative until after the flight to Egypt that follows the assassination of Gedaliah and the fear of Babylonian reprisal.

FROM THE TEXT

The OT witnesses in abundant and various—but still consistent—ways to a God who takes special concern for the welfare of those who have dedicated their lives to him. In the same way that Israel is God's ***special possession*** out of all the earth, even though all the nations belong to him (Exod 19:5), so also are those called to serve God. The consistent assurance that God "will be with" those whom he calls is a characteristic feature (Josh 1:9; Exod 3:12; Jer 1:8; and many others). Thus these four verses detail the concern for God's prophet and put Jeremiah in that stream of God's chosen agents for whom special deliverance is often accomplished.

However, the story of what happened to Jeremiah after the fall of Jerusalem should not generate a false sense of security. That is, one should not extract from this text the supposition that, should prophets/preachers but remain faithful to the word of God then they will never have to experience rejection or loss. Such a principle not only contradicts experience but also creates great difficulty for the doctrine of God. It seems undeniable that persecutions of various sorts and degrees always attend the life of a minister, and perhaps a greater degree or more severe sort of persecution more clearly indicates the correctness of the path one is on. This text, along with the stories of the intervention of members of the Shaphan family and Ebed-Melech to rescue of his life, relates a few "good days" in the life of the prophet, who otherwise lived a rather trouble-filled life. On the other hand, interpretations that say the life of faithfulness must necessarily be easy and prosperous make God into an employee in a work-for-hire contract. Nowhere in Scripture is it promised that the faithful life will be free from heartaches and difficulty, and perhaps even danger (in some cases life-threatening). Rather, it is the opposite, as the Epistle of James indicates that those who endure hardship will be blessed (Jas 1:12). Yet, even in the face of these persecutions, the promise of a text like Jer 39:11-14 is that God will provide a way of escape for those who are faithful to his call in the midst of trying circumstances.

4. Oracle of Comfort to Ebed-Melech (39:15-18)

BEHIND THE TEXT

The oracle of comfort to Ebed-Melech the Cushite (i.e., Ethiopian) looks back to what this man had done for Jeremiah (38:7-13). At the same time, it looks forward to a similar oracle of comfort for Jeremiah's scribe Baruch (45:1-5). This oracle has many of the elements typical of this genre but, as we shall see, there is no repetition of the words of the complainant (see 45:3). Even though this element is lacking, however, one can still feel confident in a designation of it as an oracle of comfort.

IN THE TEXT

■ **15** The text begins with the command of Yahweh to Jeremiah as well as the setting of the oracle. In view of the remainder of the text, it is safe to assume that this took place after Ebed-Melech's ministrations to Jeremiah, rescuing him from the pit and petitioning the king to have him placed in the court of the guard. Thus the oracle to follow is Yahweh's response to what Ebed-Melech has done in caring for the prophet. The implications of this will be drawn out more fully below (see From the Text).

The Release of Jeremiah

When was Jeremiah released? The promise to Ebed-Melech the Cushite (v 16) comes in between two narratives that deal with the release of Jeremiah (vv 11-14; 40:1-6). This has led some to wonder if the two stories of Jeremiah's release reflect two different occasions or only one. Stulman provides a helpful summary of how this issue has been treated in previous scholarship (2005, 318). However, the promise to Ebed-Melech need not be seen as an intrusion. An alternative is to see this promise as a note of hope that flies in the face of the terrible events being narrated. When it seems that everything is going wrong, God, through Jeremiah, promises that Ebed-Melech, who had helped Jeremiah before (see 38:7-13), will not lose his life in the capture of Jerusalem. Another example of a message of hope to an individual that seems not to belong where it has been placed is the promise to Baruch, Jeremiah's scribe, found in 45:1-5.

■ **16** Here one finds the direct command of Yahweh to speak, to whom the message is to be addressed, and the beginning of its content. Yet immediately the reader is faced with somewhat of a logistical problem: how, exactly, is Jeremiah to go anywhere, to say anything to anyone, when he is confined in the prison house? The text is not concerned with this detail; the assumption is implicit that the message that Yahweh orders Jeremiah to speak will get to the one for whom it is intended. To a degree, this episode is a working out of the promise Yahweh gave Jeremiah at his call, that he ***will go*** [NIV: must go] ***to all to whom I send you, and will say everything I have commanded you*** (1:7).

The specific content of the message is spelled out in the remainder of the oracle. A typical element of an oracle of comfort, which is lacking in this example, is a restatement of the complaint. We do not know if the complaint, if it ever existed, was simply left out by the narrator. It is more likely that Ebed-Melech never made a complaint or cried out to God, as Baruch did (see 45:3). Nevertheless, he had done something worthy of receiving the oracle. He had used what power he had to save Jeremiah from a certain death, v 18 calls it an act of ***trust in Yahweh.*** In his speech to Ebed-Melech, Yahweh reiterates his intentions for Jerusalem. The unique element in this instance having to do with Ebed-Melech is that the Cushite will see all of Yahweh's intentions for the city and the land come about—these things will happen ***in [his] presence.*** Perhaps this element serves as further indication that Yahweh's word is true (that is, Ebed-Melech should believe it because he himself will see it), but otherwise the reason for this detail is unclear.

■ **17-18** In these verses, the oracle goes right on to the promise of deliverance: ***I will save you on that day*** (v 17). This may be a reason why it was important in v 16 to indicate that Ebed-Melech would himself witness the carrying out of Yahweh's intentions for Jerusalem: even in the midst of all these calamitous events that he is to witness, he himself will not fall victim to those of whom he is in dread. Another unclear element is the precise identity of these people. It could either be the invading Babylonian army or, perhaps less likely, some in the Judean hierarchy who are angry on account of Ebed-Melech's care for Jeremiah related back in ch 38. The oracle concludes with another word of salvation (v 18). Yahweh promises to save him from the calamitous effect of war. What Yahweh offers him is his life as a ***prize of war*** (*šālāl*), the same promise that we also find in Yahweh's speech to Baruch (45:5). This is Yahweh's reward to Ebed-Melech for his trust in Yahweh. As indicated earlier, Yahweh acknowledges Ebed-Melech's action to save the prophet's life as an act of trust in Yahweh, trust perhaps not only in Yahweh's involvement in the events of that day but also in the prophet as Yahweh's spokesperson.

Clements offers an interesting suggestion for the function of this oracle: "the promised survival of Ebed-melech served to corroborate a major theological point. God took an interest in the destinies of individuals who showed loyalty to him. Such indications of a personal survival of disaster could be presented as tokens of a larger national hope" (1988, 228).

FROM THE TEXT

God cares for faithful people, whether or not they acknowledge him. The lack of complaint in the text, coming from Ebed-Melech, suggests that God's word of salvation is simply God's faithfulness to him for his courageous involvement in the life of another person. The story of his involvement in the life of the prophet in ch 38 does not indicate that he acted because of his trust in God. In that narrative, it is simply an act of mercy or deep concern to do the right thing—that is, to save the life of a person who is the victim of injustice committed by some powerful people. We do not know if Ebed-Melech, as a Cushite, even recognized the God of Israel, or that he acted on the basis of his faith in God. However, he does, though an outsider to the covenant community, what members of the covenant community are expected to do, but have failed. He is making things right—the injustice committed by members of the covenant community. Though an outsider, he participates with God, most likely not knowingly, in the advancing of God's plans and purposes. God's promise of salvation clearly suggests that God cares for those who care for others, whether or not they acknowledge him. Moreover, God recognizes this act as an act of trust in God. In the biblical tradition, trust like this is what God reckons as righteousness (Gen 15:6).

God's offer of salvation comes without respect to what we have done. As we will see when we consider the similar oracle of comfort to Baruch in 45:1-5, a persistent temptation is to read these and similar stories as if God is "paying back" faithfulness previously offered. In contrast, salvation is never something that is earned, but it is the free gift of God's grace extended to all humanity. While there is a response required to this free gift, the response cannot be seen as earning one's way into God's favor. Even the Ten Commandments recognize this: they do not begin with the First Commandment (**You shall not have any gods before me**) but with a restatement of what God has done for the children of Israel, [**I am the LORD your God, who brought you out of the land of Egypt, out of the house of slavery, (therefore) you shall not have any gods before me** (Exod 20:2-3)]. The response of faithful people who follow God's commands is always an offering of praise and thanksgiving for what God has already done for them and for all his people, even to those who have not yet acknowledged his existence and action on their behalf.

Whatever we have to fear, God promises deliverance. Whether Ebed-Melech feared the Babylonians or some other Judean hierarchy is unclear. However, no matter who Ebed-Melech was specifically afraid of, the promise of God delivered through Jeremiah is that he would have his life as a prize of war—that is, he would achieve victory and would be able to save his life throughout all of the terrible events that he was about to see, that were about to take place in his presence. By affirming that his words against the city were about to take place, God showed Ebed-Melech that his designs for him would also come to fruition. Because Ebed-Melech trusted in God and, by implication, should go on trusting in God, he would see the deliverance for which he longed, the promise of which comes to him as a surprise in the midst of his fear and anxiety, in the midst of uncertain and difficult days.

C. Judah Becomes a Province of Babylon (40:1—41:18)

BEHIND THE TEXT

Babylonian influence and control was operative in Judah at least as far back as the appointment of Zedekiah as king after the first siege of Jerusalem in 598-597 B.C. However, Judah continued as a more or less independent state during the reign of Zedekiah. The second text in this unit (40:7-12) narrates the final stage in the political takeover of Judah by the Babylonian empire as its province after the Davidic line had been finally cut off. This is preceded by another narrative on the courteous treatment of Jeremiah by Nebuzaradan, the captain of the guard of the Babylonian army (40:1-6). The third text in this unit describes an attempt by one of royal blood to reestablish the Davidic line and Judean independence by force (40:13—41:18), a move that would not have been necessary had the Babylonians allowed Judah to maintain the same kind of existence after 587-586 B.C. as it did after 598-597 B.C. In the LXX this narrative is located in 47:1—48:18.

IN THE TEXT

1. Jeremiah's Support of Gedaliah (40:1-6)

■ **1-3** This short text holds three surprises for the reader. The first comes in the words ascribed to a Babylonian general. The second comes in the interesting option given to the prophet by the Babylonians. Third, this text relates the appointment by the Babylonians of Gedaliah son of Ahikam to be the governor of Judah. Thus, even though this text is short, it contains much invaluable material that moves the story of the exilic period along in significant ways.

Although this text is not an oracle in the strict sense, v 1 nevertheless introduces it as a message from Yahweh delivered through the prophet. To clear up any resulting confusion, the first phrase in v 1 could perhaps be translated *the thing that Yahweh brought about for Jeremiah* or **what Yahweh caused to happen to Jeremiah.** This is a minor issue but still one that perhaps has some significance for interpretation. The NEB translates this verse, "The word which came from the LORD concerning Jeremiah." On the basis of this, Thompson suggests that the "next verses are evidently seen as a declaration of the mind of Yahweh about Jeremiah" (1980, 652 n. 10).

The text follows on the heels of a parallel description of Jeremiah's release from prison and the choice given to him. The Septuagint lacks the story of Jeremiah's release in ch 39, thus correcting the problem. Immediately after this text comes a narrative that deals with events that happened in Judah when Gedaliah ben Ahikam was elevated to the governorship of Judah (40:7-13). Thus there is a bit of confusion as to the narrative sequence. In 40:1, the details of the release of Jeremiah are somewhat different. Whereas in 39:11-14, Nebuzaradan, the captain of the guard, releases Jeremiah from the place of his imprisonment and entrusts him to Gedaliah. Here in 40:1, Jeremiah is bound in chains among the exiles in Ramah, the holding place before their journey to Babylon when Nebuzaradan speaks to him and releases him from chains (vv 1-4). What is somewhat a surprise here is Nebuzaradan's words to Jeremiah, which sums up the Deuteronomic theology (vv 2-3). These verses state two issues that are important to Deuteronomic theology: (1) Yahweh the God of Israel is the One who pronounced **this disaster** that came upon **this place** (Jerusalem); (2) Yahweh has done this because **you** (second person plural) **sinned against Yahweh and did not obey him.** It is obvious here that Nebuzaradan is not speaking to Jeremiah but rather it is a word to the exiles about their culpability for the tragedy that happened to them. In that sense, vv 2-3 have the function of an oracle from Yahweh.

There seems no particular reason that a Babylonian general would on his own adopt the dominant perspective articulated in the Book. Brueggemann suggests that here "Jeremiah is publicly recognized as a proponent of the Babylonian conquest" (2007, 106). Though this is plausible, it may be following the text a bit too closely. As we have stated earlier, there is no clear indication that he was pro-Babylonian in politics; on the contrary, evidence seems to suggest that his politics were grounded in his theology, which seeks to explain what Yahweh is doing in the history of his people.

■ **4-6** These verses describe the good treatment Jeremiah received from Nebuzaradan. The Babylonian offer to the prophet is extremely generous and appealing to anyone. It is ironic that the one who gives freedom to Yahweh's prophet, who is a prisoner falsely accused and mistreated by the community of faith, is an officer of the Babylonian army, the enemy of the state of Judah and a member of the pagan community. For once in his life, Jeremiah is free to go wherever he pleases to go—to Babylon or anyplace in Judah. Nebuzaradan assumes personal responsibility for the welfare of the prophet, if he chooses to go to Babylon with him (v 4). Apparently the suggestion that Jeremiah is a pro-Babylonian sympathizer, even though steadfastly denied by the prophet (see 37:11-16), has reached as far as the Babylonian court. This Babylonian generosity speaks in part to the possibility that some actual benefits could be found for the remnant in Judah. Nebuzaradan leaves the decision to Jeremiah and recommends that if he decides to stay in Judah, then he return to Gedaliah, the governor appointed by the king of Babylon. Perhaps he perceived that Jeremiah would be safe from his enemies under the protection of Gedaliah. **Go anywhere else you please** (v 5) is Nebuzaradan's final word to Jeremiah. The Babylonian goodwill toward the prophet also includes a food allowance and a present he received from Nebuzaradan before the prophet left to go to Gedaliah (v 5). Verse 6 indicates that Jeremiah went to Gedaliah at Mizpah and decided to remain among those who were left in the land. This verse sets the stage for the prophet's involvement in the aftermath of Gedaliah's assassination (see ch 42). Mizpah in the Benjaminite area (probably modern Tell en-Nasbeh), located about eight miles north of Jerusalem on the Nabulus Road, was an important town in the days of Samuel (1 Sam 7:15-16; 10:17-24; Lundbom 2004b, 103). The narrative here indicates that the Babylonians set up this town as the provincial center after the destruction of Jerusalem (Lundbom 2004b, 104).

2. Gedaliah as Governor (40:7-12)

■ **7-8** Verse 7 seems to indicate that the Judean army still had some forces left **in the open country** (*baśśādeh* literally means "in the field"). Lundbom thinks that the area being referred to here is the hill country north of Jerusalem (2004b, 110). It is not clear what these officers and their men were doing there. It is safe to assume that they were either part of a resistance movement within the army that rejected the idea of surrender to the Babylonians (somewhat similar to the Zealot movement during the Roman occupation of Judah), or those who managed to escape when the Babylonians invaded Jerusalem. The goal of Babylon was the destruction of the capital city and the death and/or deportation of anyone who was a potential threat to the empire. The Babylonians accomplished that goal and thus there was no further need for a continuation of the Babylonian military campaign in Judah. When the captains of the Judean forces left in the country areas heard about Gedaliah's appointment as governor over **the poorest in the land,** they came to him ostensibly to swear allegiance to him and, by extension, to the Babylonians. Verse 8 lists the identity of these officers; not much is known about any of these gentlemen, except what the immediate context of the book of Jeremiah reports of them. The narrative later reveals that one of these officers, Ishmael ben Nethaniah, a member of the royal family, had plans of his own to continue the resistance movement, which would include the murder of the governor (ch 41). In next section (40:13-16), Johanan ben Kareah, one of the officers, warns Gedaliah of the evil designs Ishmael has in mind, but the governor refuses to believe it.

■ **9-10** Gedaliah takes **an oath to reassure them** (v 9), most likely to guarantee their safety and welfare; if they were part of a resistance movement, then this means that he would not turn them over to the Babylonian army. Moreover, he instructs them to have no fear in serving the king of Babylon. His assignment is to stay in Mizpah and his mission is to represent the people who are left in the land before the Babylonians. This perhaps included the role of mediating between the Judean rebel forces and the Babylonian army. Obviously these forces had taken control of some villages (v 10); so he asks them to go back to their villages, live in peace, and resume normal life activities, which include gathering summer fruit, wine, and oil, and storing them. Lipschits finds here "a tendency toward reconciliation with Babylonian authority" and hope in "the possibility of national rehabilitation under Babylonian rule immediately after the destruction of Jerusalem" (2005, 349).

■ **11-12** The final two verses round out a nice literary structure for this unit. Whereas vv 7-8 told of army officers hearing of Gedaliah's appointment, here some other Judean exiles or, more properly, Judean refugees who escaped to Moab, Ammon, and Edom and in other lands, hear about it and return to Judah thinking that there may be a time of peace immediately forthcoming. There is a sense in which these refugees are also submitting to the power of the Babylonians, at least for the sake of expediency. These people ***came to Gedaliah, and they gathered lots of wine and figs*** (v 12). Apparently they believed that the situation had stabilized somewhat after the destruction of Jerusalem and the temple, and so they pledged themselves to live in the pax Babylonica, to paraphrase a term from the usage of a later imperial organization. That the situation in Judah is about to take a turn for the worse turns a text like this into a darkly ironic scene. This irony has already been built into the narrative by the presence of Ishmael among those generals and other leaders who pay homage to Gedaliah, and so the two of them together make the impending darkness seem rather thick indeed. For not only Gedaliah but also some innocents will come under the deadly gaze of Ishmael, perhaps even some of those who returned to Judah from their refugee camps in 40:11-12.

3. The Rebellion of Ishmael (40:13—41:18)

Israel-Ammonite Conflict

Ammonite involvement in the affairs of Judah had been an ancient and persistent problem throughout its history. In the oracle against Ammon (49:1-6), there is doubtless some reflection of the ignoble circumstances that brought about the origin of the Ammonites, at least in Israelite/Judean religious tradition (Gen 19:37-38). Interestingly, Deut 2:19 suggests that Ammonite territory is not to be taken, for it was given to the descendants of Lot, and thus the Judeans' distant relatives. This is placed against the stricture in Deut 23:3 that forbids Ammonites and Moabites from entering and thereby defiling the temple of Yahweh. The Israelite judge Jephthah also had extensive dealings with the Ammonites (Judg 11—12; see also 1 Sam 10:27—11:11; 2 Sam 10:1—11:1). It is not completely surprising that Ammonite involvement in Judean affairs should cause further problems in the exilic period.

■ **13-16** The narrative implies that some time has lapsed between the meeting of the leaders of the Judean army with Gedaliah (vv 7-8) and the meeting of Johanan and the army officers with Gedaliah (v 13). That the text presents Johanan as the leader of the delegation that delivers news of the coming attempt on Gedaliah's life presages in an important way the role that Johanan will take on after the assassination. In the same way as Jeremiah is presented as pro-Babylonian, or at least perceived to be such, so Johanan, in trying to save Gedaliah's life, is implicitly supporting Babylonian policies and interests in Judah. This stance will change under the stress of shifting events, but for now Johanan seems to be concerned with maintaining peaceful relations with the Babylonians. That is, through the perception of attempting to preserve Gedaliah's life, Johanan is, though perhaps unknowingly, advancing the claims of the empire on the life of the people remaining in the land.

This stance taken by Johanan directly contrasts that of Ishmael, who takes matters into his own hands, trying through force to reassert Judean independence and, so it seems, to restore the Davidic monarchy, presumably with himself on the throne (see below). Verse 14 reports the warning of Johanan and the officers of the army concerning the Baalis-Ishmael plot to assassinate Gedaliah. Verses 14*b*-16 describe Gedaliah's fatal naïveté, first, as his refusal to believe the warning that Johanan and his associates give him; and, second, by refusing to give permission to Johanan who spoke secretly with Gedaliah and volunteered to go and kill Ishmael. However, Gedaliah's response to Johanan may be understood as a serious attempt to separate himself from any activity that would lead to the collapse of an already fragile community. Any violence in the land would destabilize the newly formed provincial government. Even if he suspects Ishmael as a potential threat to his life, he recognizes that his role in this proposed preemptive strike would further damage his reputation and that of the whole Shaphan family that receives a rather favorable treatment in the biography of Jeremiah. It seems that in the absence of lack of clear evidence (which Johanan fails to produce), Gedaliah chooses to take a risk rather than jeopardize his relationship with Babylon and the future of the people that Babylon entrusted to his care. On the other hand, Johanan's main concern seems to be the welfare of the remaining population (**the remnant of Judah,** v 15). He views violence as a justifiable act to save this small and fragile community from dispersion and ruin. Though in this text, Johanan appears to be concerned more about the people, later the narrative portrays him as an insolent individual who has his own self-interest, who refuses to believe in the words of the prophet (43:1-3). It is not clear at this point in the narrative if Johanan had his own political aspirations. However, it is clear that he perceives Ishmael as a traitor who should be dealt with, and he needs the approval of the governor.

His concern for secrecy when speaking to the governor may be a hint of more revealing aspects of his character to come later in the narrative (v 15).

■ **41:1-3** These verses prove the authenticity of the report of Johanan to Gedaliah concerning Ishmael's plot to assassinate the governor. The narrative focuses on Ishmael's terrorism, which leads to the further deterioration of the fragile state of affairs in the post-587 Judah.

Ishmael's actions rather dramatically illustrate the perception that Babylonian rule should be resisted violently. The key to the passage and to the action of Ishmael is in the somewhat hurried exposition of v 1. The text reports almost as a side note that Ishmael **was of royal blood and had been one of the king's officers.** Thus, it seems likely that by assassinating Gedaliah, Ishmael is committed to continuing, or restarting, the Davidic line. Verse 2 indicates that Ishmael killed Gedaliah because he was an appointee of Babylon over Judah. Does this mean Ishmael was upset with the Babylonians for appointing over Judah a person who was not a member of the royal family? It is also possible he desired the throne for himself and was perhaps chafed at having been passed over by the Babylonians, or perhaps had aspirations for gaining independence for Judah from imperial rule. Yet this narrative may be read from the Jeremiah tradition's perspective of the culpability of the royal family for the disaster of 587 and subsequent tragedies. Ishmael's actions only serve to highlight the book's perspective that the royal family's ruthless actions and "self-serving ideology and total contempt for the concerns of justice and righteousness in the land" did not end with the end of the Davidic kingship in 587 (Varughese 2004, 319-28). The Ishmael-Gedaliah episode illustrates the role of the royal family in the final scattering of those that the Babylonians allowed to remain in the land. The narrator's specific identification of Ishmael as a member of the royal family (41:1) thus may be an intentional attempt to portray the dark side of the royal family. Especially important is the note that Ishmael and his men committed the murder of Gedaliah and **while they were eating *bread* together** (vv 1-2). The narrative suggests that the royal family is capable of any act of treachery including the killing of those who fellowship with its members at the table.

Verse 3 reports that **Ishmael also killed all the Jews who were with Gedaliah at Mizpah;** the narrative strikes the reader as a bit of sensationalizing, especially when it reports that the victims of Ishmael and his band of ten men also included the Babylonian soldiers. The atrocities that he committed may explain, however, the negative reaction that Ishmael receives among the populace. Ishmael's violent action is presented as something that the people do not appreciate, and indeed they are fearful of Ishmael when he takes them captive after killing Gedaliah.

■ **4-10** This text continues the preceding portrayal of Ishmael as a cold, ruthless, and calculating killer of even unsuspecting people, including pilgrims, and a hostage taker of those who had no one to protect and defend them. As noted, the narrative does not make clear the motives of Ishmael. Neither does the text report much of Ishmael's speech, indeed attributing only a short sentence to him (v 6b). This absence notwithstanding, this chapter is nevertheless a good example of perceptions of the propriety of resisting Babylonian rule.

The text does not say what prompted Ishmael to kill seventy of the eighty pilgrims from Shechem, Shiloh, and Samaria, who were on the way to Jerusalem. Verse 5 describes the ritual signs of their grief and mourning; the goal of the pilgrimage was to offer grain offering and incense offering at the site of the ruined temple. Why Ishmael was weeping as he came out to meet the pilgrims as they were passing through Mizpah is not clear. Is he pretending to be grieving along with the pilgrims to gain their trust? He welcomes the pilgrims in the name of Gedaliah into Mizpah, which a day before was the scene of a massacre. It seems that Ishmael is trying to earn the trust of the pilgrims and make everything look normal in the city. The unsuspecting and trusting pilgrims who enter the city expecting to enjoy the hospitality of Mizpah soon become victims of a savage attack; seventy of them are butchered and their dead bodies are thrown into a cistern that the Judean King Asa made when he fortified Mizpah during his war with King Baasha of northern Israel (v 9; 1 Kgs 15:22 alludes to the fortification of Mizpah, but not to the cistern). The NIV attempts to resolve a textual difficulty in the MT by translating the phrase *běyad gědalyāhû* (which literally means "by the hand of Gedaliah" or "because of Gedaliah") as **along with Gedaliah,** thus giving the impression that Gedaliah's dead body was also thrown into this cistern. The first part of v 9 probably means that Ishmael killed the pilgrims to cover up his murder of Gedaliah. Ten pilgrims are spared because of their offer to give the killers food supply that they have hidden in the fields. The killers continue their villainous acts by taking the people including the daughters of King Zedekiah as hostages and head toward the Ammonite territory (v 10).

■ **11-18** These verses indicate the further deterioration and destabilization of conditions in Judah in the post-587 period, following the murder of Gedaliah, the provincial governor appointed by the king of Babylon. It had seemed like the land would have some measure of peace under the Babylonian regime, for apparently any threats had been removed. When the governor was killed, the situation became dangerous again. Two individuals vying for power emerge; vv 11-15 indicate that though Ishmael and his group were initially successful in taking control through their acts of terror, they were forced to abandon their hostages and escape to the Ammonites because of the forces of Johanan who pursued them. Obviously Ishmael realized that he and his **eight men** (v 15; we do not know what happened to two of his men; see v 2) cannot succeed in a battle with Johanan and **all the army officers** (v 11). Ishmael's hostages are free and now they are under the protective custody of Johanan and his forces (v 16). However, this does not mean that conditions are back to normal and the people rescued by Johanan are free from trouble. Johanan, fearing Babylon's swift retaliatory actions for the murder of its governor, decides to take the group and proceeds in a southern direction, intending to take the people to Egypt (v 17). They come to a place called **Geruth Kimham,** a village near **Bethlehem.** Johanan is thus clearly the leader of the Judean remnant, at least the group of Judeans with which the book of Jeremiah is concerned.

This text highlights an interesting similarity between Johanan and Ishmael, although on the surface of the text they oppose one another. Both seek support from nations for help against the empire. Ishmael ostensibly has nationalistic—and perhaps dynastic—ambitions. His plan was ultimately Ammonite in origin, and one can presume, foundational for greater ambitions on the part of the Ammonite King Baalis (40:14). Further support for this Ammonite connection comes in the fact that Ishmael flees to Ammonite lands after being routed by Johanan (41:15). The perception of this text is that Johanan and those associated with him, regardless of their request for a directive oracle from the prophet (see 42:2-3), had already determined to go to Egypt in order to escape the Babylonian retaliation for the murder of Gedaliah. Thus the text introduces a significant difference between the perceptions of Jeremiah the prophet and those of the leadership of the community. The former sees the future of the nation in terms of submission to Babylon; the latter sees it in its dependence on foreign nations, other than the imperial power of Babylon.

FROM THE TEXT

It is difficult to make sense of Ishmael's actions in this narrative. It seems that the destroyer nation Babylon, though it disrupted community life in Judah, has also made some provisions for life to continue in the land. The narrative does not view this as an expression of the goodness of an evil empire, but as God's provisions for life to continue in the land. Though there was a glimmer of hope for the people of God for a brief moment, that was destroyed by the actions of Ishmael, a member of the royal family to which God has given the task of protecting and preserving life in the land. Ishmael in this story reminds us of the capacity of evil to create havoc in the midst of God's good plans and purposes for his people. Evil here is the manifestation of selfish plans and motivations of power where there is no regard for the dignity of human life and its worth. Ishmael in this narrative sees his victims as objects that can be easily disposed, eliminated, and discarded. It is painful and difficult to make sense when such evil comes from those who are entrusted with the responsibility to lead and guide, protect and preserve life, and make life possible for all who are under their care. Violence done against human dignity and worth by those who are in power is not always bloodshed as we see it in this narrative. In our world, it also shows up in more subtle ways that seek to promote the selfish interests of those who hold power over others in the community.

In present-day Jewish worship, the Fast of Gedaliah is observed on the third day of Tishri every year. Specifically designed to commemorate the incident related in Jer 40:13—41:18 (and the much shorter treatment in 2 Kgs 25:25-26), the fast occurs during the High Holy Days, between the Jewish New Year (*Rosh Hashana*) and the Day of Atonement (*Yom Kippur*). Although historically Gedaliah may have been assassinated on the first day of Tishri, the commemoration was moved to the third day because no fast can occur on a festival day like Rosh Hashana. In addition, if Rosh Hashana begins on a Thursday evening, then the Fast of Gedaliah is postponed until Sunday, or the fourth of Tishri, as no fast can be observed on the Sabbath.

That Jewish sages should have instituted a formal fast to commemorate these events speaks to their endurance as an occasion for mourning. As with rituals of remembrance tied to other, similar events in various cultures, this is not an occasion to celebrate. Instead, it is an opportunity to reflect on a good situation turned bad. The story at its core resonates with something deep in the human psyche. The remembrances of communal tragedies are times of sorrow, to be certain, but they are also times to explore new and fresh possibilities for moving into a life beyond tragedy into hope. For hope does not disappoint, even in the face of apparently inconsolable communal grief over unspeakable communal tragedy.

D. The "End" of Life in Judah (42:1—43:7)

BEHIND THE TEXT

The assassination of Gedaliah set in motion a calamitous series of events, as related in the texts comprising this unit (42:1—43:7). In the LXX, this section is located in 49:1—50:7. In these chapters a new leader for the community emerges who does not agree with the prophet's view of events. In addition, the remaining survivors—or at least those with whom the book of Jeremiah is concerned—abandon Judah and flee to Egypt, a decision taken even in the face of dire consequences foretold to follow.

The assassination of Gedaliah must have caused great confusion among the surviving Judean population. In a way, this was the culmination of a series of events that spelled the "end" of life in Judah. It can only be spoken of as an "end" in a limited sense. In contrast to the OT reporting, inhabitation of Judah basically continued uninterrupted throughout the entire Babylonian period. The books of Chronicles are the most extreme in suggesting that the land was completely emptied (see 2 Chr 36:20-21). The book of Jeremiah, by contrast, recognizes something of the continued settlement of the land in 39:10 and 40:7. That being the case does not exclude taking the text seriously as a perception of the exile, however. Jeremiah is, by and large, concerned with only the upper tiers of Judean society. The lower classes, given some kind of good treatment by the Babylonians, are thereafter forgotten as meaningful players in the story.

In view of these traumatic events, the reader must understand that it was a live question whether the Babylonians would come back, essentially, to engage in genocide against the Judeans after the assassination of the governor and the imperial troops. More will be said about this when the focus turns to the "reprise" version of the story of Jerusalem's fall in ch 52. The Judean leadership (Johanan and his commanders) is convinced that this will happen, although Jeremiah does not agree. In the first episode of the narrative (42:1-6), the Judean officials come to Jeremiah to ask him for Yahweh's advice while the group was temporarily located at Geruth Kimham. Jeremiah responds with a rather lengthy speech warning the officials about the consequence of going to Egypt (42:7-17, 18-22). As 43:1-7 indicates, they have already made the decision to go to Egypt, and they were merely seeking prophetic confirmation. When such does not come, they proceed anyway.

IN THE TEXT

1. Request for an Oracle (42:1-6)

■ 1-3 Verse 1 claims that, not only the key leaders, but also **all the people from the least to the greatest** approached the prophet with the request recounted in vv 2-3. The phrase **all the people** probably reflects the "empty land" ideology so pervasive throughout the book of Jeremiah, even in spite of the tempering of it in chs 39—40 (see 4:7; 44:22; and 46:19 with reference to Egypt). The order of procession, so to speak, is interesting as well, especially in light of the counterpart in v 8. First come all the army officers, then Johanan son of Kareah and Jezaniah (Septuagint: Azariah) son of Hoshaiah, and finally all the people from the least to the greatest. In v 8 the order of the first two parts of the procession is reversed, so that Johanan comes first, then the soldiers, and then the rest of the people. This is another example of the literary artistry of the authors/compilers of the book of Jeremiah, in which they make changes in their own language to create the desired effect. The desired outcome in v 8, most likely, is to elevate the role of Johanan as the leader who has the responsibility to pay attention to Yahweh's instructions given in response to the appeal made to him.

Another example of creative reuse of older traditions comes in v 2 with the introduction of the concept of the remnant. This important theological concept will be used in a variety of ways, mostly negative, in the next couple of chapters. Here, the people who have come to Jeremiah indicate that they were once many; now only a few remain. Under normal circumstances, this would be a cause for celebrating the goodness of Yahweh in not making a full end of the people (see 4:27; 5:10, 18; 30:11; 46:28). The people were trying to preserve what little of the once great nation remains. So they have come to the prophet to seek a word from **Yahweh your God** (vv 2-3; see change to **Yahweh our God** in v 6). Verse 3 sums up the specific request: **where we should go and what we should do.** The group wants Yahweh to show the direction for its conduct. It is difficult to determine the sincerity of this request, since it is likely that the group has already made its decision to go to Egypt (see 41:17). Lundbom agrees that the way in which the request is worded makes it clear the decision has already been made: "If it has, the question may simply be which route to take . . . The request now is for Yahweh's favor regarding the journey they have undertaken" (2004b, 137). However, it is also possible that 41:17 may be a conclusion that the narrator has drawn about the intent of the group based on its later actions. If this is so, the request here may be considered sincere.

■ **4-6** Jeremiah agrees to their request. It is interesting to note that the people request the prophet to pray to **Yahweh your God,** which implies a distance between them and Yahweh (vv 2-3); here the prophet tells them that he will pray to **Yahweh your God.** The prophet's response is perhaps intended to assure the people that *his* God is indeed *their* God and that they will be bound to the direction they seek from him. He says, further, that he will keep nothing back from those who have inquired of him. This phrase will be echoed later in the report of the oracle itself, which clearly conveys the consequence of their disobedience to Yahweh's word. The impression given by v 4 is that the prophet responded, as the American idiom goes, "in good faith," trusting that the people would receive his word. As the story proceeds on, however, it becomes clear that a decision has already been made. Jeremiah is put in a rather difficult situation by these events. On the one hand, if he had given Johanan and his associates the word they wanted to hear, he would perhaps have been treated as a kind of national hero, possibly even having a key advisory role in the new community of "voluntary exiles" in Egypt. On the other hand, he is compelled to say whatever Yahweh has told him (1:7; 20:9), and so he cannot hold back anything of what Yahweh gives him to say (42:4; 20:9; 38:14).

The people insist on their determination to do whatever Yahweh tells them to do through the prophet, even calling on Yahweh to testify against them should they fail (v 5). This statement will be turned against them, in the pattern already demonstrated, when the oracle is returned from Yahweh. For now, however, the people have insisted that they will do whatever Yahweh tells them. The final clause of v 6 essentially restates the Deuteronomistic theology of blessing and curse following, respectively, on obedience and disobedience. Things have gone bad for the people to this point, such that they are but ***few in number*** (v 2), so they are seeking some way to turn their fortunes around. Perhaps better stated, they are seeking after the fact divine confirmation of a fortune-turning decision they had already made in their hearts, even if they were not ready to admit it with their lips.

2. Oracle: Do Not Go to Egypt (42:7-22)

■ **7** **Ten days later,** or ***after ten days*** (the difference being possibly significant), Jeremiah returned to the community with a word from Yahweh. The request of the people and Yahweh's response, though they are two different episodes as indicated by the reference to **ten days,** are treated together in this chapter to demonstrate the literary unity of the whole narrative. Though the narrative does not indicate disconnection between the request for an oracle and its delivery, there will indeed be a disconnection, typified by the Judeans' unwillingness to follow what Jeremiah will reveal to them from Yahweh. It will be shown that this unwillingness is more than likely an indication that a decision has already been made.

■ **8-9** After having assembled all the people together, Jeremiah gave them the word he had received from Yahweh. Once again the text goes into great detail regarding the names of the people there, at least until it comes to **all the people from the least to the greatest.** It would certainly have been sufficient to say only this, for **Johanan son of Kareah and all the army officers who were with him** are surely included. Yet, as has been seen, at least the Hebrew text of Jeremiah characteristically gives as much detail as possible. This is demonstrated again in v 9, where Jeremiah reminds the people that they had sent him to Yahweh **to present your petition.** The much shorter Septuagint texts reads merely, "Thus says Yahweh."

■ **10-18** The heart of the passage is the delivery of Yahweh's message to the people. As is typical of the words of Yahweh in Jeremiah, both the positive and the negative are spelled out with their respective implications. The answer Yahweh gave is in line with previous oracles generally accepting Babylonian rule. The key difference between this passage and earlier texts advocating submission to the Babylonians is that, before Jerusalem's fall, it was not at all clear that submission would mean remaining in the land (see 38:2). Here, by contrast, remaining in the land is equated with submitting to the Babylonians. Moreover, remaining in the land is necessary for them to see the fulfillment of Yahweh's intent to build them and plant them (v 10; see 1:10).

Yahweh's conditional promise in 42:10 concludes with a statement that introduces a peculiar understanding of the events of 587 and the disruption of community life: **I am grieved over the disaster I have inflicted on you.** One way of reading this statement is that a change or a development has taken place in Yahweh's mind and his stance toward the people of Judah. The destruction of Jerusalem and the exile of Judah have been as much a heartache and source of deep sorrow for Yahweh as they have been for the people. Yahweh's promise of restoration is thus deeply linked to the experience of his grief at the devastation of judgment that the people experience in their life.

Yahweh's speech continues with a series of admonitions, promises, and warnings (vv 11-18). These statements need to be understood from the standpoint of the implied political awareness of the respective characters in the narrative. This awareness has a number of points. First, all of them were aware that Gedaliah's assassin was a Judean. This is so even though Jeremiah was absent from the narrative after his decision to stay with and support Gedaliah's administration in Mizpah (40:1-6). Second, seeing that not only Gedaliah but also the detachment of Babylonian soldiers were killed by Ishmael and his men surely would not have escaped imperial notice. The death of yet another Judean would hardly have caused concern, even if he was the appointed imperial governor. Martial law could be imposed as a simple response to such impunity. However, the slaughter of soldiers could be considered an act of rebellion.

Third, and most important, the imperial army probably was on the way to Judah. The central disagreement was within the Judean remnant concerning exactly what their response would be. On the one hand, Johanan—who had become the leader of the community after the death of Gedaliah—and his associates are of the opinion that the imperial response will be swift and deadly. Verses 11-18 indicate that Jeremiah and, by implication, Yahweh, however, hold a contrary opinion. Possibly lying behind this alternative is at least a degree of imperial goodwill for Johanan having routed Ishmael and chased him back to his Ammonite allies (41:13). Jeremiah, with authorization from Yahweh, tells the people, **Do not be afraid of the king of Babylon, whom you now fear** (v 11). While the belief suggested here is only implicit in the text, it seems a reasonable explanation. Moreover, it follows the suggestion in Skinner's classic study: "The mischief done by the ruthless act was irreparable, or seemed so to be to Johanan and his fellow soldiers . . . If they had kept their heads and stayed on in the country, trusting to an impartial investigation by Nebuchadnezzar's government, all might have been well" (1922/1963, 282).

42:10-18

The advice/divine command not to go to Egypt is couched in theological language. Yahweh's promise in vv 11-12 includes both Yahweh's actions as well as the actions of the king of Babylon. On the one hand, Yahweh promises to be with his people to save and rescue them from the hand of the king of Babylon. On the other hand, the promise is that the king of Babylon will show mercy to the people who are afraid of him. This promise perhaps reflects the prophet's belief that Nebuchadnezzar will relent in his punishment of Judah precisely because the Judean assassin of his governor has been chased away by Judeans. In any case, the prophet maintains the view that Nebuchadnezzar is a tool in Yahweh's hand, even after the events of 587, though this time for good—or, at least, neutral—rather than evil (**he will have compassion on you and restore you to your land;** v 12). The promise thus assures that good things are to come for those who show obedience to Yahweh. Again from Skinner: "It was a settled conviction of Jeremiah's later ministry that the Babylonian empire was the power ordained by Yahwe [sic] for the maintenance of civil order in the world . . . To seek safety beyond the pale of the great world-empire was to flee from the presence of Yahwe" (1922/1973, 338).

Verses 13-18 describe the negative side, disobedience to the word of

Yahweh and the implications that will follow. The first two verses essentially repeat one another, using different language to express the same intention, namely, going to Egypt instead of remaining in Judah. The important theological concept of the remnant is employed in a certainly sarcastic way in v 15. It should be noted that the phrase **remnant of Judah** is not found in the Septuagint. In the two oracles against the refugees in ch 44, the prophet announces that the remnant of Judah will be almost completely destroyed. Skinner once again puts it well: "To abide in the land, trusting to the promise of Yahwe and the clemency of the king of Babylon, was the course of safety and of duty; to go down to Egypt was an act of apostasy and rebellion, which would be punished by all the evils they sought to escape" (1922/1973, 338). The disobedience encapsulated by the impeding decision to go to Egypt will cause another change in Yahweh's mind regarding the surviving Judeans (see v 10): **As my anger and wrath have been poured out on those who lived in Jerusalem, so will my wrath be poured out on you when you go to Egypt** (v 18). This makes explicit the view that Yahweh took on the matter, even without having to speculate on what the Babylonian response to the events might have been.

■ **19-22** Jeremiah continues speaking in v 19, though now he is surely giving his own words supplementing Yahweh's oracle. The wording of this prophetic speech invites speculation that the decision may have already been made, even before the angry reaction in 43:1-7. Verse 20 of ch 42 is curious, suggesting that the sin of the people was not only deciding to go to Egypt—a decision that was already made, as the prophet seems to realize—but in sending the prophet to inquire of Yahweh in the first place: "The prophet reminds the listeners that they have promised allegiance to his teaching. Now they are reneging. The danger is double. It is wrong to go to Egypt. It is wrong to vow to listen to the prophet and then to disobey. On both counts, this remnant community has placed itself in profound jeopardy" (Brueggemann 1998, 394). Jeremiah perhaps understood here again a little more than his contemporaries gave him credit for. For, in v 21, he tells the rest of the people that **you still have not obeyed the LORD your God in all he sent me to tell you.** While too much should not be made of it, the fact that Jeremiah says, **Yahweh your God,** in v 21 surely contrasts to the original request for an oracle in v 3 of this chapter: "Pray that **Yahweh** your God will tell us where we should go and what we should do." By reminding the people that Yahweh is their God too, Jeremiah told them that their decision, which they had already taken even before seeking the advice of Yahweh, would result in nothing but punishment and devastation.

The promise of punishment is couched in the same terms as was the promised punishment for the sins of the people before the exile: **you will die by the sword, famine and plague in the place where you want to go to settle** (v 22). However, whereas at least some of the threats of punishment before the exile seem to suggest a possibility of punishment being turned back (for example, 7:5-7), here it is clear that since the decision has already been made to flout what Yahweh commands, Yahweh has himself made an irrevocable decision to blot out the remnant of Judah. Only a few will remain (see 44:14)! Here, then, is another inversion of the theological concept of the remnant: a remnant of Judah goes down to Egypt and is severely punished by Yahweh because of it; only a remnant of the remnant will return to the land of Judah to live there.

3. Response: Jeremiah Is Lying (43:1-7)

■ **1-3** The text begins with the assertion that what Jeremiah said to the people as he spoke in Yahweh's name was indeed the words of **Yahweh their God**, thus leaving no doubt in the minds of readers that the prophet was not giving his personal opinion as his response to their request (v 1). Two of the leaders of the group including Johanan, and **all the arrogant men** accuse the prophet of lying. Those who asked Jeremiah for a word from **Yahweh your God** (42:2-3, 5) react by claiming that **Yahweh our God did not send you** (43:2), when they hear a word they did not want to hear. Now they are certain of their relationship with Yahweh. At least the assumption of the people is that Yahweh will not stand in their way. Even though the leadership asked for an oracle, it becomes clear in the succeeding verses that the decision has already been made. The rejection that Jeremiah's word encounters is symptomatic of the reactions he has been getting throughout his prophetic career. Rejection added on to negative reaction added on to accusation of treason added on to suspicion of deceit yield the result, in the next chapter, of a disillusioned, bitter prophet delivering a scornful final public message (44:26-30). The leaders and all the rest of the people do not give any credibility to the word that Jeremiah delivers here, even in spite of the fact that, according to the narrative, all of his predictions to this point have been demonstrably accurate.

In 43:3, the leadership also accuses Jeremiah that he has been incited by his scribe Baruch. The supposed involvement of Baruch in this incident is interesting, and also introduces a bit of irony into the scene. The readers know more than most of the characters, for the narrator has already informed the readers that Jeremiah did in fact seek Yahweh's advice rather than that of Baruch. However, the charge is that there is a Baruch led conspiracy to hand Johanan and his group over to the Babylonians. The leadership sees the prophet and Baruch his scribe as agents of the Babylonian regime, and his prophecy as a ploy to keep them in the land until the Babylonians arrive to take them into exile. For Jeremiah, if it is a question of going to Babylon or going to Egypt or staying in the land, the answer is clear. The first and the third clearly mean submission to Yahweh's will. Babylon, though ruthless it may have been in its dealings with Judah, nonetheless is a tool in Yahweh's hand. Egypt, on the other hand, is the last place in the world where Yahweh would want his people to be—a place from where he saved them a long time ago. Jeremiah very clearly saw the return to Egypt as return to slavery (2:14-18).

■ **4-7** The immediate decision to go to Egypt, in the opinion of the narrator, is disobedience to the voice of Yahweh (vv 4, 7) and thus a great sin on the part of the Judean community. Jeremiah the prophet, Yahweh, and the narrator are all convinced that the people had made the wrong decision. Adding further to the judgment that they had therefore sinned against Yahweh is the designation that the leaders were "arrogant" people (v 2), an adjective not found in the Septuagint of 49:2. The rest of the paragraph details some of the people who went along, including Jeremiah and Baruch—who, it may be surmised, went under protest. The text ends with another condemnation of the people's decision, thus forming a nice frame to this short literary unit.

FROM THE TEXT

The text begins with the people and their leadership seeking a word of guidance from God. The prophet intercedes and gives God's response in a faithful manner, clearly indicating God's plan for the people, offering God's mercy, and explaining how his mercy will be worked out through the mercy shown to them by the king of Babylon. God's response through the prophet also warns of the dire consequences of their decision to go to Egypt. The leadership rejects the voice of the prophet—the voice of God they sought—as a lie and set out on the course of action they have already determined prior to their plea for God's guidance. Against the prophet's strong warning not to go to Egypt, the leadership takes the people, including the unwilling prophet, to their self-imposed exile in Egypt. The text makes clear that though the Babylonian exile of the Judean community was necessary for the future of God's people, those who remained in the land in submission to his will also had a future in the land. Life, whether lived in exile or in the land of freedom, should be a response to God's gracious work—in the case of the community in the text here, a life lived in anticipation of the fulfillment of God's promises. On the part of God, he promises to be faithful to his word; nonetheless, he allows the people to have their freedom—to stay in the land or to go on their own self-directed way. In this case, that self-directed way (i.e., Egypt) means erasing from the history of God's covenant people their salvation from Egypt through God's mighty and wonderful acts. Though God has his plans for the future of his people, the text makes clear that they, through their disobedient actions, shape their own future, in total disregard for the clear and repeated warnings of the consequences of such action. It is ironic that the people promised to obey God's voice whether it is good or bad (42:6). However, in the end, they chose for themselves a path that in their thinking was good, and rejected the good plans God had for them. The narrative clearly shows that what was good in their thinking was indeed bad and that they have chosen for themselves the word of judgment and rejected the word of salvation (Miller 2001, 867).

E. A Sign-Act and the First Two Oracles in Tahpanhes (43:8-13; 44:1-14)

BEHIND THE TEXT

The story of the voluntary exiles in Egypt is one that, according to the narrator of Jeremiah, is not successful. In fact, the Babylonian army of which they were so afraid is about to follow them to Egypt. Therefore, even though they had left the land in order to save their lives from the Babylonians, soon enough there will not be many of them left to save.

The city of Tahpanhes to which the voluntary exiles have come was in the lower Nile region, near the eastern extremity of Egypt. This frontier town (modern Tell Defineh), bordering on Sinai, was located on the caravan route leading to Palestine and Syria (Lundbom 2004b, 143-44). It is not clear when Johanan and the Jewish exiles arrived here; some scholars consider the murder of Gedaliah three months after the fall of Jerusalem (see 39:2; 40:1; Holladay 1989, 296). Others think that it took place three or four years later and relate it to the third Judean deportation to Babylon in 582 B.C. carried out by Nebuzaradan (see 52:30; Lundbom 2004b, 115). In either case, the Jewish exiles arrived in Egypt during the reign of Apries/Hophra (589-570 B.C.). Tahpanhes is mentioned earlier in 2:16, in the context there of leaning on Egypt for support against the Babylonians. In a way, that is what the Judean exiles have done again, leaned for support on Egypt. The first text in this unit contains an instruction from Yahweh to Jeremiah to perform a sign-act (symbolic act) and to speak a judgment word against Egypt (43:8-13; LXX 50:8-13). The Judean exiles in Tahpanhes are the implied audience of 43:8-13; thus it is a judgment word against them. This is, essentially, a restatement of the implications that will follow the negative choice made in the previous episode: spurning Yahweh by not remaining in the land. The second text (44:1-14; LXX 51:1-14) is a judgment oracle given directly to the Judean refugees who came to live in Tahpanhes.

IN THE TEXT

■ **8-13** Verse 8 is the narrator's introduction, which serves as a superscription for vv 9-13. Verse 9 is an instruction from Yahweh to the prophet to perform a sign-act. This is followed by the oracle that Yahweh gives him to deliver (vv 10-13). Like other sign-acts in the book (see, for example, chs 13, 27, and 51), the text here reports only the command of Yahweh for the prophet to do something; there is no report of the prophet carrying out the sign-act. The symbolic action here is commanded by Yahweh in order to set up the remainder of the oracle in vv 10-13. The command in v 9 is to take two large stones and bury them with **clay in the brick pavement** (or lay them with clay/mortar in the pavement; the clay/mortar thus serves as the binding agent; Lundbom 2004b, 145) at the entrance of the palace of Pharaoh in Tahpanhes in the sight of **the**

Jews. In contrast to the episode with the yoke, the two stones are the location for Yahweh's action, rather than what Yahweh uses to accomplish his purposes.

Though there is no narrative report of the prophet performing the sign-act and delivering the oracle, it is reasonable to assume that he did both. The message of v 10 is clear. At the very same place where the prophet laid the stones, the Babylonian king Nebuchadnezzar will set up his rule over Egypt. Verse 10, in addition, exhibits the theologically striking phrase that **Nebuchadnezzar is my servant,** a tool in Yahweh's hand. This time, the tool is to be used not, as in times previous, against Judah (25:9) or the other nations (27:6), but against Egypt. As mentioned above, the Judeans who have come to live in Egypt as voluntary exiles will themselves come under judgment; they will experience the pain that Nebuchadnezzar and Yahweh inflict upon Egypt.

It is unclear whether the presence of the Judeans in Egypt was what brought this oracle against Egypt, though that is a plausible explanation. Stulman writes: "The point of the narrative is direct: there is no skirting the will of God. Egypt will not provide sanctuary from Yahweh's judgment. The immense Egyptian empire is no less under the sovereign rule of Yahweh than is Judah" (2005, 338). It is reasonable to assume that this message is given to the Jews mainly because the symbolic action and its interpretation in the form of an oracle take place in the sight of **the Jews,** not the Egyptians. Moreover, Yahweh's punishment of a land to which his people had gone into exile is a recurring motif in the exilic and postexilic prophets (for a few examples, see Jer 25:12; 30:10; and Ezek 39:28).

Jeremiah 43:11-13 go on to describe in vivid detail what Nebuchadnezzar will do when he comes to Egypt. Ezekiel's last dated oracle (571 B.C.) also makes reference to Nebuchadnezzar's invasion of Babylon (29:17-20). Jeremiah's oracle here and in ch 46 clearly anticipate Nebuchadnezzar's invasion of Egypt. Extrabiblical records indicate a Babylonian invasion in 582 B.C. and another one in 568 B.C. (Lundbom 2004b, 147, 208). Lundbom cites Josephus's report that Nebuchadnezzar invaded Egypt in 582 B.C. and took Jews into exile in Babylon; he thinks that if an invasion did occur in 582, then the prophecy of Jeremiah would have been fulfilled not long after the Jewish exiles arrived in Tahpanhes in 582 B.C. (Lundbom 2004b, 147). Verse 11 echoes the language of 15:2. This verse announces the judgment of death and deportation to the Jewish exiles in Egypt. Verses 12-13 focus on the destruction of the temples of the gods of Egypt and obelisks of Heliopolis.

■ **44:1** The focus next shifts to the first *proper* oracle against the refugees, even though the oracle against Egypt in 43:8-13 is a veiled oracle against the refugees. It also has a bit of a wider focus, addressing the refugees not only in **Tahpanhes,** to which Jeremiah had been taken, apparently against his will, but also Judean communities in **Migdol, Memphis,** and **Upper Egypt** (that is, in the southern extremities of the country, perhaps the source of the south-to-north flowing Nile river). The wider audience of 44:1, as opposed to the more restricted addressees of 43:7-13 (i.e., those in Tahpanhes) raises the question of the extent of the Jewish migration/voluntary exile to Egypt at this time.

The first possibility is that the narrative in chs 42—43 is limited in its awareness of the extent of the Judean migration. This may indicate different source material. The second possibility is that the oracle against the refugees in 44:1-14 comes from a different time than the narrative framework in chs 42—43. More than likely it is later, on the basis that more expansive treatments are usually—though not always—later than more restricted ones. The third possibility argues from a strictly literary standpoint that Jeremiah delivered his symbolic action and oracle in Tahpanhes because that is where he had gone. This is not a satisfactory solution, however, for it tends in the direction of rendering the other groups of exiles irrelevant. The fourth possibility, and perhaps the most defensible, is that these two renditions represent different perceptions of the same event, namely the voluntary exile of the Jews to Egypt. The size and location(s) of the community was apparently variously estimated. One group of perceptions believed it to be quite small (see also 42:2). At least one other, as represented by 44:1-14, considered it rather large. Whichever of these possibilities is chosen, there are logical and logistical problems to be dealt with, but it seems like the fourth option does not read too many conclusions out of too little evidence, as the others might tend to do.

■ **2-6** This first oracle against the refugees actually contains three oracles preceded by the usual formula **Thus says Yahweh.** The first of these, contained in vv 2-6, is a kind of historical retrospective, recalling for the various Judean communities what has happened to Judah. The connection between the calamities that came upon Judah at Yahweh's bidding and the Jews' presence in Egypt is clear. For the most part, it is because of what happened to Judah that they have come to Egypt in the first place, and in this way Jeremiah links the present experience of the people to the past. The irony of the refugees' situation could certainly have been on people's minds, for this was not the only time that Israelites had migrated to Egypt because of difficult events in Israel. Rather, a migration from Canaan to Egypt in the book of Genesis sets up the severe oppression and miraculous liberation in the book of Exodus, the foundational event of the nation of Israel and its faith in Yahweh (but see Jer 16:14-15; 23:7-8).

Verse 3 repeats the same charges that have been levied at the people throughout the book of Jeremiah. The terrible things that happened to Judah took place, says Yahweh, because **they provoked me to anger by burning incense and by worshiping other gods that neither they nor you nor your ancestors ever knew.** This note of intergenerational sin is not found in the Septuagint. Verse 4 also repeats a characteristic phrase of Jeremiah, suggesting that **again and again I sent my servants the prophets,** who warned the people of the judgment that was going to come if they failed to turn away from their evil. Where the NIV translates **again and again,** the sense is roughly equivalent to the American idiom *early and often.* The phrase, sometimes worded slightly different, is also found in 7:13, 25; 11:7; 25:3-4; 26:5; 29:19; 32:33; and 35:14-15.

The point of the phrase is that Yahweh was, from the earliest days of Judah's bent toward sin, about the business of trying to bring about repentance and reconciliation. This is essentially also the driving force behind the conclusion of the retrospective oracle in vv 5-6. Even though the prophets were sent *early and often,* the people refused to listen, and this is the reason why all the disaster has come upon Judah.

■ **7-10** Whereas vv 2-6 formed an oracle looking back on what happened in the past, the next short oracle has as its focus the present situation. This oracle, in other words, accuses the people in Egypt of not having properly learned the lessons of the past. They are continuing to **provoke me to anger with what your hands have made, burning incense to other gods in Egypt.** Idolatry, so it seems, was a persistent problem, judging by the amount of time the prophets spend complaining about it. Yahweh was a God who insisted on exclusive, aniconic (that is, without images) worship. Any deviation from that would be severely punished, as was the case for all the people in Egypt. They had seen these things with their own eyes but still failed to amend their ways appropriately. The question raised by Yahweh in v 9 implies that the Jewish exiles in Egypt have forgotten the fact that they are in exile in Egypt because of the sinful ways of their ancestors, the kings and queens of Judah, and their own sins when they lived in Judah.

Verse 10, at the end of this segment, seems to shift the focus from second to third person. While the accusation of sinfulness in the present was directed toward the people in vv 7-9, v 10 is a kind of editorial comment or aside castigating the people for showing no contrition or fear of Yahweh and for their failure to live by his commandments. Stulman captured the thought well: "Thus, Judah's entire history is construed as one of obduracy and incognizance, leading to the present disaster . . . This word [of God] is faithfully declared by Jeremiah, God's spokesperson, but it is decisively rejected by king and people" (Stulman 1998, 90). While there is no "king" to accept or reject Yahweh's word—the last one to hold that title having been blinded and carried off in chains (39:7; 52:11)—nevertheless, the point of rejection of the prophetic word is driven home with finality.

■ **11-14** These verses look to the future, to punishment that Yahweh intends to bring on the remnant from Judah.

Negative Uses of Remnant in Jeremiah

Though remnant is a theological concept in the Prophets that receives a favorable treatment, in 44:14, the remnant of Judah in Egypt is given no hope at all. The theology of the remnant in Jeremiah finds expression in the phrase "I will not make a full end of you" (see 46:28, among others). The prophet addresses Johanan and his people who asked for Yahweh's guidance (42:1-6) as the remnant of Judah (meaning, as those who have received Yahweh's favor and those who constitute the nucleus of the future community of Israel) (42:15). However, Yahweh also warns them of the dire consequences of going to Egypt in 42:16-17. In 44:14, Yahweh announces the total end of the remnant of Judah in Egypt. Yahweh here has turned his face against the people because of their evil, in contrast to promises regarding the remnant throughout the prophetic literature. In a way, this announcement is an inversion of the oracle of Yahweh delivered in ch 42, for there it is said that Yahweh is "grieved over the disaster I have inflicted on you" (42:10). The relationship between Yahweh and the Judean remnant is, therefore, complex. The editors of the book of Jeremiah show great skill in using this concept for fresh and creative, though not entirely unanticipated, purposes.

A text such as this is relevant to perceptions of Babylon as an imperial power because the people have sought refuge in Egypt from Babylon. However, such refuge will not be found, for Babylon will come to destroy Egypt as well. Yahweh's intent is to **take away the remnant of Judah who were determined to go to Egypt to settle there** (v 12). This indicates very clearly that Yahweh and, possibly also Jeremiah, knew that the decision to flee to Egypt had already been made even though the people did come to the prophet seeking the advice of Yahweh. Finally, v 14 indicates the complete nature of the designs Yahweh has against all of the refugees in Egypt, whether those among whom Jeremiah was to be found in Tahpanhes or any of the other places. The remnant of Judah that came to settle down in Egypt has no future. They will not escape or survive Yahweh's judgment; neither will this remnant return to Judah, except some who will escape as fugitives when the Babylonians invade Egypt. This is a difficult word to hear in any case, but it seems that Yahweh has finally turned his back on his people.

43:8—
44:14

FROM THE TEXT

Jeremiah 43:8-13 is consistent with the prophet's view of God's sovereignty over history and the kingdoms of the world. As Miller notes, there is an interesting interplay in this text between what God intends to do and what Nebuchadnezzar will do. In a strange way, the text mixes the "politics of God" and the "politics of the nations." This text is a clear example of how God manifests his "divine sovereignty . . . through human sovereigns" (Miller 2001, 867). The Babylonian king is not portrayed as someone acting on his own behalf, displaying his power over other nations and people. He continues to play the role of God's servant, an instrument in the hands of God to accomplish God's sovereign plans and purposes. The message of 43:8-13 is rather dark. Those who received mercy from God (and those who were given the promise of the mercy of the king of Babylon) are now given over into the hands of the king of Babylon, to their death and destruction (see 42:22). The land to which they escaped from the will of God itself will be destroyed. The destruction of Egypt means the destruction of those who hoped to make a life there, according to their own plans and purposes. They rejected God's offer of life; instead, they have chosen for themselves a life of their own. In the end, they will have neither the promised life nor the life of their own making.

We find in 44:1-14 an invitation to learn from the past, and shape our present life in light of the lessons from the past—particularly mistakes of the past. The text offers no future to the Jewish community in exile in Egypt, to those who refuse to learn from the mistakes of the past. They do not recognize that mistakes of the previous generations and of their own are what brought them into their present situation. They are set on pursuing the same path, the end of which will be their total ruin. The text ends without any hope given to the recalcitrant people. The note of hope that seems to be taken completely away in this text is the same that has been articulated throughout the book. Those who would return to God would be saved. The text also reminds us of God's faithfulness in sending his servants to remind those who may suffer loss of memory of the past the need to listen and learn from the experiences of the past and to avoid the path others have taken that have led them to their destruction. It also speaks of contrition and fear of God and obedience to his instructions as key to finding life even when we stray from the path he has placed before us. That speaks volumes about God's mercy to sinners who spurn his love for them.

F. Debate with the Devotees of the Queen of Heaven (44:15-30)

BEHIND THE TEXT

This unit has the form of a debate between the Judean exiles in Egypt and the prophet on the critical issue of the cause of the calamities that came upon Judah. In response to the prophetic word that more calamities are in store for them for their continued disobedience in the land of their voluntary exile, the people present an alternative understanding of the events that happened and defiantly say that they will not listen to the prophetic voice (vv 15-19). The prophet gives his response in vv 20-23 and simply reiterates what he has been preaching all his life. This is followed by two oracles from Yahweh (vv 24-25, 26-30), the first dismissing the claim of the people, and the second asserting Yahweh's involvement in Judah's life and the history of the nations.

The debate here focuses on why these tragedies occurred. The text contrasts the perspective of the prophet with that of those who have considered the worship of cult images as critical to their daily existence, prosperity, and safety. The particular deity in question here is **the Queen of Heaven**. The people perceive their decision to discontinue the worship of this goddess as the cause of these disasters, whereas the prophet insists that the disasters came upon the people as punishment for their idolatry.

IN THE TEXT

■ **15-19** This is the second and more important text mentioning the Queen of Heaven and the cult associated with her. The other is 7:16-20, more of a polemic sideswipe than a debate. Here in ch 44 we encounter a somewhat broader picture of what was involved in the cult of the Queen of Heaven. Moreover, the devotees of the Queen of Heaven are represented in ch 44 as speaking for themselves, rather than, as in ch 7, merely described. While ch 7 is a bit more detailed in terms of describing the involvement of all the family members in the cult, ch 44 reports the women's direct speech in defending their actions, apparently with the full support of their husbands. Most importantly, ch 44 presents in a succinct way the conflict over the interpretation of the events of the exile between Jeremiah and those who participate in the cult of the Queen of Heaven. Thus this is entirely different from the conflict between Jeremiah and Hananiah in ch 28 over the interpretation of the exile of 597 and the role of Babylon in the affairs of Judah. There in ch 28, both prophets interpret historical realities affirming faith in Yahweh; whereas Hananiah projects the end of the power of Babylon over Judah within two years, Jeremiah sees it lasting for a while—for seventy years (see 29:10). The astounding feature of this text is the content of the speech by the devotees of the Queen of Heaven (44:15-19). They are united in their decision not to listen to the prophetic word spoken in Yahweh's name (see vv 1-14). Moreover, they are determined to fulfill their vows and make offerings to the Queen of Heaven, and thus continue what they and their ancestors and their kings and their officials used to do in Judah (v 17). They say that as long as they carried out their responsibilities with regard to the cult of the Queen of Heaven, they found blessedness. However, as soon as they began to neglect these responsibilities they found failure and, in addition, have seen many of their number die by the sword and famine (v 18). It is not clear when the people neglected this cult, which was most likely introduced during the days of Manasseh (2 Kgs 21:3). Josiah's reform brought an end to this cult (2 Kgs 23:4-5). The reference in Jer 44:18 may be to the suppression of this cult since the days of Josiah. If this is so, the people see the calamities that came upon Judah in 597 and 587 and afterward as the result of their neglect of the worship of the Queen of Heaven. Verse 18 is remarkable for two reasons. First, in spite of the obvious differences, the devotees of the Queen of Heaven seem to follow a similar line of thinking as do the Deuteronomists, particularly in the way judgment and redemption follow, respectively, on sinfulness and faithfulness. Second, the declaration that the people have suffered death by the sword and famine employs typical language of the judgment sections in the book of Jeremiah. Thus, it is significant that these two competing theologies use the same process of reasoning to arrive at their very different conclusions. The people's response ends with the renewed commitment of the women to make offerings to the Queen of Heaven; they claim that they have done so in the past with the full knowledge of their husbands (v 19).

The Queen of Heaven

Who was the Queen of Heaven? Scholars have suggested many different options, though none of them have reached the level of consensus. Some of the suggestions include Asherah, the consort of Baal from Canaanite religion; Ishtar, the warrior goddess from Babylonia, or her Sumerian counterpart Innana; Astarte from Canaanite religion; and a host of others. For interpretation of the book of Jeremiah, however, it is ultimately unimportant what particular goddess this epithet addressed. What is of much greater significance is the window this text, and its shorter, more polemical companion in ch 7, give the reader into the critically important debates in sixth-century Judah (and elsewhere) concerning the reasons for and the significance of the exile.

■ **20-23** Jeremiah's response to the devotees of the Queen of Heaven is what the reader has come to expect by this point in the book. He argues that Yahweh *could no longer stomach* (v 22) the great evil of the people in worshipping other gods, and in particular the Queen of Heaven; Yahweh acted in judgment and made the land a desolate place because of the abominable practices of the people of Judah. The calamities that happened are clearly the outcome of their sin and disobedience to the voice of Yahweh. In Jeremiah's speech there is no direct response to the claims of the devotees of the Queen of Heaven, but rather, a straightforward affirmation of the Deuteronomic theology of blessings and curses. What the people consider as an act of faithfulness to the Queen of Heaven is in the judgment of the prophet an abomination and the cause of desolation.

■ **24-25** Yahweh's first response (vv 24-25) also does not counter the claims of the people. Yahweh simply acknowledges the determination of the people to do what they have said they will do—fulfill their vows and make offerings to the Queen of Heaven. Yahweh brings the debate between the people and the prophet to an end by declaring to the devotees of the Queen of Heaven, **Go ahead then, do what you promised! Keep your vows!** (v 25). The responses of the prophet and Yahweh claim that offering incense and cakes to the Queen of Heaven will be of no avail, since it was doing these things that caused the people to be in this situation in the first place.

■ **26-30** For the most part, Yahweh's second oracle against the refugees duplicates the previous oracles in this chapter, specifically vv 11-14. There are a few differences, however. Whereas the first oracle asserts that Yahweh has turned his face against the refugees in Egypt for harmful (lit., "evil") purposes, the second claims that **no one from Judah living anywhere in Egypt will ever again**

invoke my name or swear, "As surely as the Sovereign LORD lives" (v 26). This is a bold statement, perhaps even more so than ultimately ascribing to Yahweh the evil that is about to happen to the people (v 11). According to this perspective, the people will no longer be able to commit the sin of using the name of Yahweh deceptively, for they will not be able to use his name at all! This may be understood as a ban on the use of Yahweh's name in oath-taking. More likely, this means that Yahweh's judgment will wipe out all the Jews who live in exile in Egypt (except a few refugees who escape; see vv 11, 14), and that there will be none left in Egypt to swear falsely by Yahweh's name (Lundbom 2004b, 166). Verse 27 seems to support this view.

Verse 27 makes explicit what was implied by v 11. Whereas the first oracle maintains that Yahweh is determined to bring "evil" upon the Judean refugees, here Yahweh is **watching over them for *evil*, not for good**. In both verses the MT utilizes the word *raʿ* ("evil") for Yahweh's purpose for the Judeans in Egypt.

Evil in the OT

Modern biblical translations shy away from ascribing "evil" (*raʿ*) to God, but the Hebrew Bible is not as reticent. A prominent example of this is Job 2:10: "Shall we accept good from God, and not trouble?" A more expressly theological version of this comes in Isa 45:7: "I form the light and create darkness, I bring prosperity and create disaster." These verses are sanitized by the translators of the NIV and most other English translations as well. The NASB renders *raʿ* as "adversity," in Job 2:10 and "calamity" in Isa 45:7, closer to the original but still not quite strong enough. The old King James Version, however, gets it right in both instances. Evil, as the word is used in these instances, refers to a wide variety of misfortunes. In the OT thinking all things—misfortunes as well as good—come from one God. The purpose of some misfortunes is left unexplained, as in the case of the book of Job, though the prologue connects it with God (Job 1—2). Others, like the disasters and destruction, the loss of the land, the exile, are also labeled "evil" that Yahweh sent as punishment on the people who have violated their covenant with him. In those contexts, it is clear that evil that God sends is the outcome of evil that people commit. The OT also entertains the idea of the disciplinary/instructive function of evil along with its punitive function (see Amos 4:6-11; Job 33:14-33). In conclusion, the OT does not view evil as the work of the devil or some other supernatural power. However, it should also be noted that the OT does not describe God as evil or as the source of evil. What this means is that the term "evil" in the OT does not have the connotation that the modern mind attaches to it; i.e., the work of a power that is diametrically opposed to and in conflict with God, who is the source of goodness and truth. It seems that the difficulty modern interpreters may have with the translation of *raʿ* lies less with the worldview of the text than with their own modern worldview informed by various perceptions of the origin and cause of evil.

The suggestion that Yahweh is now looking out for evil concerning these refugees directly contrasts with statements like 29:11. According to the logic of this oracle, however, it is the choice that these refugees have made to come to Egypt that has gotten them into this situation.

Verse 28 of ch 44 closely echoes v 14. This verse also reiterates the escape of some from the sword and their return to the land of Judah. A key element in this second oracle is the test of validity between the two opinions. The question is: will Yahweh's word or the people's word be proved correct? The time is coming that all the Jewish exiles in Egypt will come to recognize the truth that they now refuse to admit. The inescapable conclusion of this text, and that of the entire book, is that Yahweh's word, spoken through the mouth of the prophet, will prove to be correct. The Judeans are shown here to be grossly mistaken and lacking in foresight in the events following the assassination of Gedaliah. In the challenge between Yahweh's words and their own mistaken and misguided theological perspective, the judgment of Yahweh is final. There is no doubt whose words will stand the test of time and truth.

The second oracle against the refugees, as well as the public words of Jeremiah, ends with a prediction of destruction for Egypt (vv 29-30). This text is presented here as a **sign** to the Jews in Egypt, though the event mentioned here has to do with the history of Egypt. The question of the truthfulness of Yahweh's words or the words of the people will be made clear through this historical event. Pharaoh Hophra will be handed over to Nebuchadnezzar in just the same way as Zedekiah was handed over to him. In this way, the Judeans who feared retribution from Nebuchadnezzar, seeking to escape it in Egypt, will themselves suffer when the Babylonians invade Egypt. The Jews in Egypt will then know that this is their punishment and the fulfillment of Yahweh's words against them. Hophra, also known as Apries, was pharaoh from 589 to 570 B.C. Josephus mentions that Nebuchadnezzar invaded Egypt in his twenty-third year (582 B.C.), but Hophra's death is widely believed to have taken place during a palace revolt led by Amasis who ruled Egypt from 570 to 520 B.C. (Lundbom 2004b, 167). It is possible that the promised destruction of Egypt is due to the unfaithfulness of the Judeans, so that the Egyptians are suffering vicariously, as it were. More likely, however, is that the two events are unrelated except in the sense of demonstrating the truth of Yahweh's words regarding the Judean refugees. Further information regarding the downfall of Egypt may be found in the oracles against the nations, for Egypt is first on the list (see ch 46).

FROM THE TEXT

The refugees in Egypt come in for tremendous condemnation in chs 43—44. Yahweh's final word to the Judean exiles in Egypt seems to suggest that they have committed an unpardonable sin (44:26). While it is recognized that this term has a significant and rather mysterious theological weight attached to it, it seems appropriate to use it here. From this oracle there appears no hope left for the redemption of those who have gone to Egypt, except an undefined, small number of survivors.

Even for those survivors, their straggling return back to Judah cannot really be described as redemption, for the question easily presents itself concerning what prospects remained for them there. If it is true that they, along with their leaders, had irrevocably sinned against God, then how could they enter into relationship with him again? This should not be developed into a full-blown taxonomy of sin, ranging from fully pardonable to fully unpardonable. Such an exercise is beyond the point, and it is an expression of human pride to presume to know the mind of God in any case.

Chapter 44 preserves two ideologies and perspectives, one preserving the claim of true Yahwistic faith in Israel, and the other preserving the counterclaim of those who practiced syncretism. Both attempt to convey the theology of blessings and curses, but from the perspective of competing religious claims. It is important to note here that the book of Jeremiah preserves here the claims of a people who argued for an alternative to Yahwism and their theological perspective on the cause of the events of 587 and the exile. From the perspective of the devotees of the Queen of Heaven, Josiah's enforcement of Yahwism in Jerusalem has caused the devastation because it entailed abandonment of the queen. In short, it was not at all a question of Yahweh failing them; rather, they had failed the queen! Their argument is that Yahweh interfered with proper worship rather than demanding it, and so caused the queen to cease providing good things for her people. It is not clear how long this debate continued in Judaism; perhaps this was a debate that was confined to the Jewish exiles in various parts of Egypt. In reality, this theology was just like the majority opinion of the book of Jeremiah: Yahweh blesses those who are loyal to him, and his curses come upon the disobedient. Jeremiah's viewpoint is ultimately vindicated, however, in that Yahwism and not the worship of the Queen of Heaven ultimately achieved exclusive dominance in Israel. Moreover, the perspectives of this group on the cause of the exile never became the recognized view in the OT.

The argument that the people in exile in Egypt have made is "the argument that every religion seeks to make, that a god is judged by the gifts that are given" (Brueggemann 1998, 407). Interestingly enough, neither Jeremiah nor God enter into an argument about falsity of the claims of the worshippers of the Queen of Heaven. The text simply conveys the idea that the community in Egypt is not interested in a religion that does not profit them. They interpret history and come to the conclusion that what they have been doing, their worship of the God of Israel in the hope of good fortune, indeed did not yield its intended outcome. So they decide to be more pragmatic and go with a goddess whom they think has the capacity to fulfill what she promises to do for her worshippers. The counterclaim of this text, however, is that it is Israel's

God who is working in history, and that his words have the final say about what happens to the nations and the destiny of Israel that continues to reject his word. The text ends without settling the debate, but with a note about what will happen to the people who have questioned the credibility of the God of Israel. Events that will happen in Egypt's history will answer their question; then they will know whose words have power—Yahweh's or their god's. In that sense, the text ends with a challenge to the Judean audience that in the meantime, until they know for sure who has the power, what matters the most is unswerving loyalty and devotion to God even though they are faced with difficult circumstances in life. The book of Jeremiah's placement in the canon indicates that the perspective of Jeremiah had the last word.

The text is a reminder of the truth that if we expect only good things in life because of our worship of God, then the temptation will be to view every bad turn of events as the failure of God to do that which we hoped or expected him to do. What proves the correctness of our faith and trust in God is not events that have short-term impact on our personal lives, such as prosperity or misfortune, but rather the biblical narrative that is rooted in history, which provides the resource for the faith traditions of Israel and the Christian church. In the end, what is important for our faith is not gods who come and go, but the God who remains, the God who has an ongoing history and relationship with his people. The text very clearly reminds us that religious choices we make are not simply choices between gods that are equally credible, but choices between claims of faith that have deep historical rootedness and those that lack history or ongoing moral and communal claims. The text makes clear that it is the test of history that will eventually vindicate Jeremiah's claims. The God of Jeremiah who speaks in this text is holy; he is deeply concerned about the value of life and our relationship to him and our neighbor. The Queen of Heaven that the people claim to be the source of their well-being lacks holiness, history, and moral texture (see Brueggemann 1998, 410-13, for a detailed discussion of the theological issues of this text). The church confesses the truth that the God of Jeremiah, the sovereign Lord of history, who revealed himself in the person of Jesus of Nazareth is "the way and the truth and the life"; there are no other gods, and that those that claim to be gods are not gods at all (John 14:6; see Jer 10:1-16; Isa 40:18-20; 44:6-17).

"BUILD AND PLANT"

YAHWEH'S WORD TO BARUCH (45:1-5)

Like the oracle of comfort for Ebed-Melech the Ethiopian in 39:15-18, this short oracle of comfort for Baruch seems, at first glance, to interrupt the flow of the book. Verse 1 seems to suggest that the oracle would fit better in the context of the long narrative of ch 36, which deals with the dangerous conditions of life for Jeremiah and Baruch after the production of the scroll. However, even though the oracle is out of place where it stands, it may have proved an even greater interruption had it been placed in the context of ch 36, since that chapter ends with the account of the making of the second scroll. Since both chapters (36 and 45) refer to the same date (the fourth year of Jehoiakim) and Baruch as the scribe of Jeremiah, some scholars view ch 45 as the conclusion to the so-called Baruch document, which presumably begins in ch 36 (see Brueggemann 1998, 414). It is possible that this chapter is placed here to show that both the prophet and his trusted friend and scribe share in the suffering of the nation in spite of their faithfulness to communicate and preserve Yahweh's word to Judah. Brueggemann entertains the possibility that, though Baruch is a person, here in the text he stands as a representative of all those "right minded" people in Judah who saw along with Jeremiah Yahweh's plans and purposes for their nation through the instrumentality of Babylon (1998, 414). Lundbom sees an entirely different function for this chapter. He argues that, based on its content and location, this chapter presents a "colophon" of Baruch, which at one time may have served as the conclusion of an expanded edition of the book (2004b, 171-73). Yahweh's governance over the whole world is a theme in 45:5. This theme is unpacked in the oracles against the nations in chs 46—51. In the literary setting of the book, this chapter also provides a link to the next major literary unit (chs 46—51) in the book.

BEHIND THE TEXT

Baruch, as has been noted, was Jeremiah's scribe and part of a rather important Judean family. A supposed archaeological find in 1975 revealed a seal impression with the name "Baruch son of Neriah, the scribe," though this piece was included among several alleged forgeries in an ongoing Israeli criminal case (Shanks 2005, 64-65). Whether or not independent historical evidence for Baruch's existence could be found, his importance for the book of Jeremiah cannot be disputed. The close connection of Jeremiah to Baruch, and the overall encouraging message Jeremiah gave to those who aligned with him, contributed to the importance of this oracle in the book.

The text begins with a narrative introduction (v 1) that places the oracle in the fourth year of Jehoiakim (605 B.C.). This is followed by a messenger style speech that recounts Baruch's complaint/lament (vv 2-3). Yahweh then instructs Jeremiah to speak to Baruch and give him Yahweh's word (vv 4-5). In the LXX, this text is found in 51:31-35.

IN THE TEXT

■ **1** Verse 1 indicates that Jeremiah gave the oracle to Baruch **in the fourth year of Jehoiakim son of Josiah king of Judah, after Baruch had written on a scroll the words Jeremiah was then dictating.** It is not clear if the oracle was a response from the prophet to Baruch's lament made during the process of writing what the prophet was dictating to him as Yahweh's word, or if the lament and the response happened when the process of dictation and writing was completed. Perhaps the words of judgment that Jeremiah dictated, which he wrote on the scroll, made him realize that his future was also in jeopardy; the judgment when it comes will affect everyone in the nation, including those who remained loyal to God and the prophet.

■ **2-3** In typical fashion, the oracle begins by quoting words Baruch has said in his complaint. The oracle against Jehoiakim in the story of the two scrolls (36:29-31) also does this, quoting the king's words against him. An interesting point to note in v 4, which begins Yahweh's answer to Baruch's complaint, is the shift of address. Whereas v 2 has a direct address to Baruch, here one finds a command to the prophet. This emphasizes the intermediary function of the prophet. This emphasis is continued in the latter part of the verse when reference is made back to the substance of Jeremiah's call (see 1:10).

Baruch's lament begins with a typical lament formula (**woe to me**), which also comes from the mouth of Jeremiah in 10:19 and 15:10 (NRSV). Here **woe** is a personal cry or lament, though the prophet also utilizes this word to convey words of judgment and the utter ruin of his audience. The reason for the lament is given next. It is not clear what Baruch means by his complaint, **Yahweh has added sorrow to my pain.** Yahweh has not given him a direct word of judgment; what he considers as the cause of his sorrow are most likely the words of judgment he is writing at the dictation of Jeremiah. He experiences sorrow as he writes the judgment word; he does not detach himself from the pain and suffering that is coming upon the nation. He experiences it when he writes; he will again, along with the nation, experience it with its full intensity when the Babylonians invade the land. There is inner turmoil and anxiety over the coming disaster. Baruch finds **no rest,** which could mean rest from his weariness and anxiety or an actual place of rest, or both.

■ **4** Yahweh's response to Baruch proclaims his governance over the whole land and, indeed, over the whole world. This oracle utilizes verbs that are found in the commission given to Jeremiah (see 1:10; see also 12:14-17; 18:7-9; 24:6; 31:28; 38—40; 42:10). Yahweh is about to bring radical changes in the land; the language here anticipates military actions of the Babylonian army that will result in the uprooting of Judah from its land and breaking down of the nation that Yahweh built up. The placement of this oracle here thus affirms Yahweh's final word given to the Judean exiles in Egypt in 44:26-30. It is Yahweh who governs the world and determines the destinies of the nations. In this way, a very subtle move is made toward resolving the question of whose words will stand (see 44:28). Although this word would not be realized until a much later point, it can be seen here in a proleptic form.

The Oracles Against the Nations in the Septuagint

While the Greek and Hebrew texts place the oracles against the nations in different spots, the logic is nonetheless rather similar. For in the Greek text, the oracles against the nations appear right after Yahweh's declaration that "I will bring upon that land all the things I have spoken against it, all that are written in this book and prophesied by Jeremiah against all the nations" (25:13). This statement brings together the fates of Judah and the rest of the nations of the world under the governance of Yahweh.

■ **5** Finally, the last verse of the chapter contains both an injunction and a promise as well as Yahweh's word that he is bringing disaster upon all flesh. Though Baruch is certainly very important in the communication and preservation of Jeremiah's message, that does not mean that he is privileged to seek an important place for himself (see Luke 14:7-10). In the context of comforting Baruch, Yahweh says, through Jeremiah, that the disaster Baruch seems to be experiencing will soon fall on everyone. This includes not only Judah but also all the surrounding nations and Babylon (chs 46—51). The promise, however, is that Baruch will survive the horrors that are coming. That this promise recalls that given to Ebed-Melech the Ethiopian (39:15-18) indicates further the connection between these two people who assisted Jeremiah. That both of them are promised their lives **as a prize of war** indicates they will prevail over the enemies they fear, for it is the victors to whom the prizes of war go. Far from being mere payment for services rendered—in the one case rescue from a dangerous prison (38:7-13) and in the other case scribal skill (36:4-13)—these promises assume that Yahweh will not fail to bless those who remain faithful to him in trying times, which is a consistent witness throughout the Bible.

FROM THE TEXT

Life is the only sure promise that God gives to Baruch (and to the prophet; see 1:19; 15:20-21). When the nation Judah was given no hope for its survival, the one who remained faithful and loyal to the prophet received the promise of life. What God promised to the prophet, he also promises to his trusted friend (and also to Ebed-Melech), who came to rescue the prophet's life. Life that God gives as his gracious gift is worth far more than great things in life, though we may be tempted to think that such things are our reward because of our service to God. Jesus reminded James and John, when they asked him for a place at his right and left hand, that they did not know what they were asking. He went on to say to the disciples that he did not come "to be served but to serve, and to give his life a ransom for many" (Mark 10:45, NRSV; see vv 35-46). In our contemporary hearing, this text speaks to us more about life that is eternal than mere physical existence. Bonhoeffer, who found great comfort in Jer 45, writes in his reflections on the day of the baptism of Dietrich Bethge in May 1944: "It will be the task of our generation, not to 'seek great things,' but to save and preserve our souls out of the chaos, and to realize that it is the only thing that we can carry as a 'prize' from the burning building" (1971, 297). He wrote earlier, in a letter dated February 23, 1944, to his friend Eberhard Bethge: "I can never get away from Jeremiah 45 . . . Here too is a necessary fragment of life: 'but I will give you your life as a prize of war'" (1971, 219). Many in the world who faithfully follow God, though like Bonhoeffer, hold on to the promise of God for their physical life, continue to give up their life for the sake of the gospel, knowing that it is in losing that they gain eternal life. Like Bonhoeffer, they understand clearly what Jesus has said: "For what will it profit them if they gain the whole world but forfeit their life? Or what will they give in return for their life?" (Matt 16:26 NRSV).

Salvation is essentially cooperation between God and humanity. Such an idea lies at the very heart of the Wesleyan theology of salvation. God provides the way for humans to be saved and draws them along through prevenient grace. However, he neither compels them to walk on it nor does he determine in advance who will and who will not accept the offer. For those who do, sometimes they face troubling or dangerous circumstances. The enduring message of the oracle of comfort to Baruch is that, when these things happen, God will not fail those who do not fail him. Even if the situation one faces leads to death, as in the case of Dietrich Bonhoeffer, the promise of life in the age to come triumphs even over that.

The text also suggests that the future of the community of faith rests on individuals like Baruch who trusted in the words that Jeremiah spoke in the name of God. Brueggemann insightfully comments that Baruch in this text, like Joshua and Caleb who trusted in the promises of God and carried faith for the next generation, functions as "the means by which God will open a faithful way into the future" (1998, 417). Though the text speaks of death and destruction, it also speaks of God preserving life and thus making it possible for the community of faith to survive. The hope we find in this text in the promise of the preservation of the life of Baruch (also in the promise to Ebed-Melech) is the hope that sustains all those who put their trust in God in difficult and life-threatening circumstances of life.

In another way, Jeremiah here may also be passing on the torch to Baruch. Oracles of comfort like this one are common, especially when a seasoned leader approaches the end of career and/or life. Another biblical example of this is the endearing instructions of Paul to Timothy in 2 Tim 4. Faced with the prospect of death, Paul charges Timothy to continue the work and preach the message and carry the faith into the next generation. The community of faith can survive only when faithful generations pass on the mantle of faith and leadership to the coming generations. Jeremiah, Paul, and a host of other faithful leaders of God's people remind us of this truth and model for us what it means to be faithful members of the community of faith in our generation.

45:1-5

"BUILD AND PLANT"

ORACLES AGAINST THE NATIONS (46:1—51:64)

Overview

This lengthy section, found in the Septuagint after 25:13, is perhaps the most tedious of anything in the book of Jeremiah. Though it contains a substantial wealth of theologically significant material, it is also perhaps most susceptible to misreading and overreading than anything else one may encounter in the OT. To avoid this misreading, careful attention must be paid to the context of these oracles (as much as this can be recovered), even though their content is often stifling, repetitive, and banal.

For the most part, it is impossible to line up these oracles with specific events in the histories of the named peoples and their relationship with Judah. The central theological contribution of the oracles is to assert with a degree of forcefulness that Yahweh is not only God of Israel but God of the other nations as well. Thus, these oracles, for all of their tedium, advance the cause of monotheism in the development of Israelite religion. More than that, the oracles clearly show Jeremiah as Yahweh's "prophet to the nations" (see 1:5, 10).

The fact that the oracles against the nations in the MT begin with Egypt and end with Babylon may be an indication of the critical roles these nations played in the history of Israel. Egypt, the first nation to hold Israel in bondage, is treated first in the series of oracles in this section. The mere reference to Egypt conveys not only Israel's bondage but also Yahweh's redemption—the exodus story that remained as central to the faith traditions of Israel. The exiles in Babylon now hear words of judgment on Egypt, which would have conveyed to them hope in their restoration and freedom from Babylon, the nation that holds Israel in captivity at the present time. Similarly, the final oracle—words of judgment on Babylon—would have conveyed hope in the immediate freedom of the Jewish captives. In ch 29, in the letter to the exiles, the prophet communicated the word that Yahweh's visitation (in judgment) of Babylon would usher in the freedom of the exiles and their restoration to their homeland. Thus the end of Babylon (51:64) in a real sense is the announcement of the end of the exile and the beginning of a new exodus for the people of Israel.

BEHIND THE TEXT

Jeremiah is not the only prophetic book to contain oracles against the nations. Similar sections of oracles against the nations are found in Isa 13—23 and Ezek 25—32. Jeremiah's oracles against the nations are the longest in the prophetic literature; however, in terms of proportion to the whole, Jeremiah pales in comparison to Obadiah and Nahum. Both of these are completely consumed with oracles against nations—Edom in Obadiah and Nineveh/Assyria in Nahum. Among the rest of the twelve prophets, shorter versions are found in Joel (3:1-16), Amos (1:3—2:16), and Zephaniah (2:1—3:8). There are no significant collections of oracles against the nations in Hosea, Jonah, Micah, Habakkuk, Haggai, Zechariah, and Malachi.

Whereas in the MT, the section begins with oracle against Egypt and ends with Babylon, in the LXX, Egypt and Babylon, in that order, occupy the second and the third place in the list of the nations. In the LXX, the first nation addressed is Elam. The MT placement of Egypt at the beginning and Babylon at the end parallels 25:19-26 where nations are given the cup of Yahweh's wrath to drink. The reason for the shift in the order of the nations in the LXX is not clear. In the MT, the placement of Egypt as the first in the list provides continuity with the oracles against the Judean voluntary exiles in Egypt in chs 43—44. The placement of Babylon at the end is significant. Babylon, the world leader, a nation that Yahweh uses as an instrument of his judgment on Judah, does not receive immunity. Its judgment will be the ultimate display of Yahweh's sovereignty over the nations.

There is no consensus among scholars on the authenticity of the oracles against the nations in Jer 46—51. Nineteenth- and twentieth-century scholars have either entirely denied the authorship of these oracles to Jeremiah or only attributed some portions of these oracles to Jeremiah. More recent scholars, more or less, follow the same verdict. Some scholars like Carroll and McKane consider these oracles as non-Jeremianic, whereas others (Bright, Holladay, and Thompson) attribute some or most of these materials to Jeremiah. A final verdict on the issue of authorship is difficult to reach. It is very likely that most of the materials belong to the prophet, though one cannot dismiss the likelihood of additions by the editors of the book. These oracles follow a particular genre found in a number of OT prophets, as indicated above. Recent scholarship has also shown that this genre has its origin within Israelite prophetic tradition (see Lundbom 2004b, 182-83). These oracles generally address the issues of wickedness, pride, and idolatry of the nations addressed. Though these oracles show many literary parallels to the poetic oracles addressed to Judah, they lack specificity of issues and other elements found in the prophet's oracles addressed to Judah, such as specific acts of sin, calls to repentance, and salvation (Lundbom 2004b, 183).

The date of these materials is an equally difficult issue. Though there are some indications of a possible date in the oracles against Egypt (46:2), Kedar and Hazor (49:28), it is difficult to place the materials in any specific historical setting. Scholars who see these as the work of anonymous authors place them at a very late date. It is possible that the oracles were given at various times in the life of the prophet, some as early as 605/604 B.C. and some as late as the period of his sojourn in Egypt after the fall of Jerusalem. Considering the possibility of some anonymous materials in these chapters, we assume that these oracles would have been made part of the book within a couple of decades after 587 B.C. (see Thompson 1980, 687).

The basic worldview under which these oracles operate requires some explanation. Some modern governments and nations, particularly democratic ones, seem to believe that different nations, even those that historically have been distrustful or even openly hostile toward one another, may work together for a perceived common, transnational good. Such an idea would have been incomprehensible to Jeremiah and his oracles against the nations. For these oracles, the fortunes of the nations are a zero-sum game. That is, benefit or blessing for one nation requires an equivalent curse or calamity for another nation, or a cumulative series of them for several other nations. These oracles seem to suggest that though Judah is under the curse of Yahweh, the nations also are going to come under Yahweh's curse. However, Yahweh's judgment of the nations also means the reversal of the misfortunes of Judah. These oracles thus convey the idea that Judah will be the ultimate beneficiary of Yahweh's judgment of the nations. In the defeat and ultimate destruction of Babylon, the destroyer nation that Yahweh has used as his servant to carry out his purposes, the Judean exiles will find hope for deliverance and return to their homeland.

A single Behind the Text section will serve the purpose here for this whole section (chs 46—51) because much of the material in this section is similar in form and content in several oracles.

IN THE TEXT

1. Against Egypt (46:1-28; LXX 26:1-28)

■ 1 First in line for the wrath of Yahweh in these oracles against (the NIV's **concerning**, though a literal translation of the Hebrew preposition ʾal, is far too weak) the nations is Egypt, Israel's oldest nemesis, out from under whose oppression the nation of Israel was ultimately born. That these oracles would begin with Egypt and end with Babylon, moreover, says something important about the thematic role these two great world powers had in the history of Israel and Judah. The book of Jeremiah handles their roles a bit differently, however, going as far as to assert that the return from exile in Babylonia will supplant the exodus from Egypt as the primary historical event at the core of confession of faith in Yahweh (see 16:14-15; 23:7-8; and the commentary on 52:31-34).

■ 2 Here one finds a historical reference point, after a fashion, for the oracle to follow. Pharaoh Neco II was the Egyptian ruler who killed the Judean King Josiah in the battle of Megiddo in 609 B.C. (2 Kgs 23:29). Yet the armies of Egypt under Neco's command were themselves decisively defeated at the Battle of Carchemish, in the fourth year of Jehoiakim (605 B.C.). The Egyptians deposed Shallum/Jehoahaz who became king after the death of his father Josiah and gave the kingdom to his brother Jehoiakim (2 Kgs 23:31-35). It was also at Carchemish that a skillful Babylonian general earned his stripes—the crown prince Nebuchadnezzar.

■ 3-6 The following four verses begin the oracle poem properly. Here the reader finds a summons to battle. One might imagine a bard singing this tale, as it seems throughout a circumspective look back at the brave resolve of Egypt's mighty armies. There is almost a satirical, even cynical tone to these verses that is only made clear in v 5. For here the warriors of mighty Egypt **are terrified, they are retreating, their warriors are defeated.** They are giving ground rather than taking it. By saying this, the prophet/bard lays the greatest dishonor possible at the feet of the soldiers, essentially accusing them of cowardice. Not only have they been defeated, but they have been routed, and the survivors are running off in any direction, seeking relief from the advancing, victorious Babylonians. The phrase **terror on every side** recalls 6:25 and 20:10, where these same words are used to describe the impending fall of Jerusalem. Just as that event was momentous for the history of Judah, so the defeat of the Egyptian army was momentous for the history of Egypt and, indeed, for the entire face of the ancient Near East. For the defeat of Egypt cemented the rise of Babylonia, and even though the Neo-Babylonian Empire was only short-lived (see the commentary on 52:31-34) its effects were undeniably far-reaching. In v 6, the once-mighty, once-fearsome enemies of Judah are not able to escape from the sword of Babylon. All of them fall by the river Euphrates. This text seems to imply joy in the victory of the Babylonians, the nation that inflicted great terror on Judah. Yet, as will become clear a few verses further on, this is not a celebration of the military might of Babylon but rather of the supremacy of Yahweh over the events of human history. This text quietly but firmly asserts the lordship of Yahweh over all the peoples of the earth.

■ **7-9** The mocking song continues by quoting what may have been a common Egyptian war-chant (Brueggemann 1991, 219; Thompson 1980, 688-89; Jones 1992, 493). The reference is made to the mighty Nile, which at certain intervals would rise up above its banks and flood the surrounding countryside, enabling the crops to grow and turning otherwise inhabitable Egypt into a hospitable place. Similarly, when Egypt **rises like the Nile,** the image is one of overflowing the borders of Egypt to capture surrounding territory for the glory of Pharaoh and the glory of their gods (v 8). Again, though, this prideful chant is turned against those who make it (Holladay 1989, 320-21). At least on this day, the pride of Egypt, the enthusiasm of the cavalry, charioteers, infantry, shield bearers, and archers will come to naught.

■ **10** The claim being made here is that this day of battle belongs not to the Egyptians who rise up like the Nile—or even, for that matter, to the Babylonians who set them to flight. Rather, the prophet declares that the day of battle belongs to Yahweh. The title given here as **the Lord, the LORD Almighty,** is an expressly military one (*ʾadonāy yhwh ṣebāʾôt,* lit., **The Lord, Yahweh of Hosts**). By use of this phrase, the prophet indicates that Yahweh himself has joined the battle between Egypt and Babylon. While Yahweh's action here is not, as in former times, understood as being directly on behalf of his chosen people, nevertheless by using Babylon as his agent (see Jer 25:9; 27:6; 43:10; Hab 1:6) Yahweh is asserting his lordship over all the kingdoms of the earth, able to move them around like chess pieces according to his own design. By doing so, however, he does act for the benefit of Judah, at least in a roundabout way. For if Egypt should get its comeuppance—no matter the earthly power who delivers it—there would certainly not be much sympathy for Egypt among the Judeans. The oracle against Egypt thus flies in the face of attempts like Jehoiakim's to curry favor with one world power against another. In the historical sweep of things, this policy of allegiance to Egypt would result in yet another devastation for the Judean royal establishment, though admittedly not until after Jehoiakim's death. First Jehoiachin would be exiled and later Zedekiah would be taken off in chains and his sons murdered for trying to play Egypt off against Babylon. The overarching feature of this oracle, therefore, is that Egypt is yet another chess piece in Yahweh's hand, and he can use it or cast it aside as is his pleasure.

■ **11-12** The shamed, defeated Egypt is by and large ordered to put its shame and defeat on display before the world. In a phrase reminiscent of an oracle attacking Judah (30:12-17), the prophet counsels Egypt to go and find healing for its wounds. The balm from Gilead (8:22) was a famous healing ointment well known for its effectiveness. Alas, however, in this instance, no healing remains for Egypt. The mighty nation and its powerful army have been destroyed, and the news of it has traveled throughout all the earth. The warriors, known as an effective fighting force both individually and collectively, now stumble together off the field of defeat, barely able to keep themselves upright. The vivid picture painted by the prophet of a humiliated army captures the emotions, especially in light of the established history of on-again/off-again friendship and enmity between Egypt and Judah.

■ 13 Here the reader finds a new historical note, making the verses following, at least according to form, a second oracle against Egypt. This time, however, the battle that lies behind the words of the oracle takes place on Egyptian soil (Thompson 1980, 691). This is in contrast to the seeming last-ditch effort of Neco II, his Egyptian army, and his Assyrian allies to check the rising power of Babylon, an attempt that came to a decisively negative end at Carchemish, as previously noted. Holladay provides an alternative view, suggesting that this campaign of Nebuchadnezzar against Egypt was intended to punish Egypt's incursion into Palestine (1989, 328). Whatever the case may be, this second oracle reinforces the message of the first: proud Egypt will go down to an ignominious defeat, and just as there was before the Exodus, there will be a loud cry in all of Egypt (Exod 11:6).

■ 14 Like v 9 in the previous oracle, this verse issues a summons to battle that spreads throughout Egypt. In light of the fact that the battleground is now Egypt rather than Babylon, one would expect a bit fiercer resolve on the part of the Egyptian army. This is reinforced by the content of the message that is to go out in **Migdol, Memphis,** and **Tahpanhes.** These cities were all prominent at various times in the history of Egypt. **Migdol** was a city or a town in the east Delta region of Lower Egypt. **Memphis** (Hebrew *nōp*) was the capital of Lower Egypt, as well as of Upper Egypt from about 3100 B.C. to 2200 B.C. and sporadically thereafter. Its strategic placement near the center of the country contributed to its importance. Tahpanhes, also located in the east Delta region, was the place where Johanan and his group of Jewish exiles settled down (see 43:7). Furthermore, the geographical distribution of these cities is a clear indication that all of Egypt is to be included in this drastic warning. Finally, that ***the sword has devoured your surroundings*** makes the warning even direr.

■ 15-17 Even though the resolve of those defending the Egyptian homeland is probably stronger than the mighty warriors who went to fight on enemy territory, the result, unfortunately for Egypt, is the same. The reason for the failure of the Egyptians is the same as that given in the first oracle—Yahweh is fighting against them. His will in this battle is that the Babylonians succeed against Egypt, and once that will has been proclaimed it is unshakable.

Verse 16 continues the description of what Yahweh has done to Egypt. Along the way, the prophet proclaims that Yahweh caused confusion among the Egyptian ranks, so that he **made many stumble, and they fell over one another.** This is slightly different from the similar expression in the first poem. There, the warriors were stumbling together as they were leaving the field of battle after their defeat, wounded and unable to stand on their own. Here, the image is of warriors unable to organize themselves even before the battle begins, and deciding to return to their home, thus making the Babylonians, as it were, victors by default.

Verse 17 continues the taunt of Egypt, this time directing a personal attack against Pharaoh and giving him a mocking name (**loud noise, *who has wasted time***). The taunt is that the king of Egypt speaks in a loud voice but lets opportunity pass by. This seems to assume that there was a time when Egypt could have reasserted its dominance by defeating Babylon. Perhaps this is speculation from a retrospective standpoint, for otherwise it is unclear how Babylon's tremendous military might could have been checked by a waning Egypt and a crumbled Assyria. In any event, if as has been argued this second oracle is later than the first, then Babylon has already delivered the decisive blow to Egypt and Assyria. Alternatively, this phrase could reach back to the first oracle's celebration of Egypt's defeat at Carchemish, thus adding insult to injury, as it were. Either way, the essential point is that the pharaoh has miscalculated, wasting time on incidental pursuits rather than taking advantage of whatever opportunity may have been afforded him to reshape the history of the ancient Near East.

■ **18-26** These verses are marked off from the rest by a frame consisting of Yahweh's direct declaration that he will accomplish these things predicted (in v 18 the future tense is used; vv 25-26 again use the "prophetic perfect"). The English versions fail to recognize this frame, however, by translating the final word (*yābô'*) in v 18 as **one will come.** The text is ambiguous, however, as to the antecedent of *yābô'*. An alternative presents itself: ***As surely as Tabor is among the mountains and Carmel is by the sea, this will happen.*** This alternative is to be preferred for two reasons. First, it is more in harmony with the tenor of the verse. In other words, v 18 does not need to introduce a human subject (presumably Nebuchadnezzar) in order to have a complete thought. Second, this alternative is within the range of acceptable translations for the Hebrew verb *bô'* (meaning "to come," "to happen"). Yahweh is here affirming on his own existence that this promised end to Egypt will happen. Support for this is found in the Targums (Keown, Scalise, and Smothers 1995, 284).

Can God Swear by His Own Self?

Can God swear by his own self? Such a concept might catch the careful reader off-guard. A human swearing by the life of God is rather common in the OT, with thirty-seven instances in the NIV. Of course, this was not a matter taken lightly, and potential abuses of it were targeted by the third of the Ten Commandments. Yet Yahweh swears by his own life as well, though this is somewhat rarer: thirty-one instances in the NIV. Of these, nineteen are found in Isaiah (49:18), Jeremiah (22:24; 46:18), and Ezekiel (16 times). It is not surprising that Ezekiel would have the greatest number of these references, for in an exilic context there was a much greater need to assert the activity of Yahweh over against, for example, the gods and goddesses of Babylon who were said to be quite active and involved in their religious texts. The function of these texts in Isaiah, Jeremiah, and Ezekiel where Yahweh is said to swear by himself is similar in each instance—to remove all doubt as to the reliability of what Yahweh says he will do. A human could misuse the name of Yahweh and swear to something that would not happen, at the expense of not being held guiltless (Exod 20:7). But Yahweh could not swear falsely by his own name, since that would entail the blotting out of his own existence should that which was promised not come to pass (see Gen 15:7-21, which illustrates a similar point). So, then, can Yahweh swear by his own name? The answer from the prophetic literature is clear: yes, he can and, when he does, there cannot be any doubt that what he says is true and reliable, without exception.

The command of v 19 lends further support to this alternative translation suggested for v 18. For here again one does not find direct reference to the human figure of Nebuchadnezzar, but rather to the results that will follow upon Yahweh accomplishing the word that he swore by his own life to bring about. Egypt is told to pack its belongings for exile, **for Memphis will be laid waste and lie in ruins without inhabitant.** The strategic city at the center of the kingdom will be destroyed when Babylon comes calling, Yahweh promises, and so there is no more hope for Egypt (yet see v 26). This oracle has been looking at the destruction of Egypt from the vantage point of the future—for such is the implication of the mostly past-tense verbs. The tense of the verbs changes to future with v 19, however. This means that while the defeat of Egypt's army appears in the past as a reality already achieved, there is more yet to come in terms of punishment for Egypt: Egypt's fate is essentially the same as Judah's: exile with the cities lying in ruin, without inhabitant (Jer 9:11; 42:2).

46:18-26

Verses 20-24 of ch 46 heap up further metaphors for the disarray and chaos that are to come upon Egypt when Babylon's armies invade. The image of **a gadfly . . . coming against her from the north** (v 20) is reminiscent of the enemy from the north predictions in the early part of the book (see 1:14). The dual cattle metaphors, first for Egypt in 46:20 and then for its mercenary helpers in v 21, are interesting. For all of its beauty and its once vaunted power, Egypt will be left defenseless when the punishment comes, and even those who were paid to defend it will run off like defenseless cattle; even for these people punishment is surely coming. Again, this is neither a lament for Egypt's fall nor a celebration of Babylon's victory. It is ultimately an expression of confidence in the leadership of Yahweh over all the kingdoms of the earth. This short unit concludes with another reference to the foe from the north in v 24, which enforces the claim that Yahweh is handing Egypt over.

Verses 25-26 make explicit the theological dimension of this punishment. In v 25 **Amon god of Thebes** is said to receive punishment from Yahweh. **Thebes,** like Memphis, was a one-time capital of Egypt. Later in Egypt's history it was known as "the city of Amun," which provides a connection to the text under consideration. Furthermore, special punishment by Yahweh is called out not only for Amon but also *on Egypt, upon its gods, upon its kings, upon Pharaoh, and upon all who trust in him.* In this way, the prophet declares that the entirety of the nation is coming under punishment. Moreover, Yahweh is handing *them over to those who seek their lives, to Nebuchadnezzar king of Babylon and his officers.* Perhaps more unexpected, however, is the note of hope for Egypt expressed in the last part of v 26. Scattered throughout the oracles to the nations, typically near the end of the oracle of judgment, one finds an oracle of salvation, of sorts, for some of the peoples mentioned. Such a promise is also given in the oracles against Moab (48:47), Ammon (49:6), and Elam (49:39). The rest of the nations (Philistia, Edom, Damascus, Hazor and Kedar, and Babylon) are not given such a promise, which surely indicates something of a worse attitude toward those nations than the four whom Yahweh promises to restore.

■ **27-28** The promise to restore Egypt and its cities effectively ends the oracle of judgment. Attached to it, however, is a short note of comfort to Israel. Both verses begin with a *fear not* message of salvation addressed to *my servant Jacob*. The promise of salvation to Israel is explicit in these verses. The presence of this note of comfort in the oracle against Egypt contributes to the understanding developed above that Yahweh's action in judging Egypt benefits Judah in a roundabout way only. Judah is not involved in the promised destruction—or the promised restoration—of Egypt, but nevertheless it derives some benefit for it. This short oracle of comfort makes explicit a theme that is hidden in the long oracles that deal with Egypt's destruction. Judah would certainly not weep for Egypt but would rejoice that the wrath of Yahweh has at long last been turned against an ancient enemy. This is perhaps the overriding motif running throughout the oracles against the nations, namely, that Yahweh is Lord of all the nations and will rightly punish those who have mistreated his chosen people Judah.

Verse 28 may be a second oracle of comfort, for it begins with the same phrase as does the previous verse. The message of salvation also contains the assurance of Yahweh's presence with Israel. It also contains a well-worn promise to Judah, that Yahweh **will not completely destroy you.** Other examples of this phrase may be found in 4:27 and 5:18. This is doubtlessly related to the exile being not only punitive but also purgative. In other words, it is not the point to punish Judah merely for the sake of punishment. If Judah were completely wiped out, then there would be no one left to move on in the purged/purified relationship with Yahweh for which the prophets longed. The oracle ends with the declaration that Yahweh will not fail to punish his people but with the hidden promise that he will also not fail to redeem them.

2. Against Philistia (47:1-7; LXX 29:1-7)

■ 1 Coming next in line for an oracle of judgment is another historic enemy of Judah, the Philistines. Once the united kingdom was established under David, the Philistine threat largely dissipated, although during the reign of Saul and the early years of David's career it was not certain at all that the Philistines would ever be defeated. This short oracle of judgment against Philistia is unique among the oracles against the nations in Jeremiah, however. Its uniqueness comes in that the oracle is **the word of the LORD that came to Jeremiah the prophet *against* the Philistines before Pharaoh attacked Gaza.** Thus it is linked not to the action of the Babylonian army, as was the overwhelming amount of judgment material against Judah—and for that matter, against the other nations. That an unnamed pharaoh is involved in this attack further contributes to the mystery. The oracle against Egypt links back to the attack of Babylon (46:2), as does the oracle against Kedar and Hazor (49:28)—the latter much less specifically. The oracle against Elam suggests merely that it was delivered during "the reign of Zedekiah king of Judah" (49:34). No temporal references are given for the oracles against Moab (48:1), Ammon (49:1), Edom (49:7), Damascus (49:23), or Babylon (50:1).

Several factors must be borne in mind when attempting to describe the history behind this oracle. First, the LXX 29:1 eliminates the historical reference, lending credence to the suggestion that this was a secondary assertion. Thompson rightly maintains that "the rest need not for that reason be regarded as an erroneous interpolation. No doubt it was an editorial expansion, but it may be taken as factually correct" (1980, 696). Second, Carroll notes that the "phrase 'before Pharaoh smote Gaza' raises a problem because the poem speaks of the threat to the Philistines as coming from the north . . . rather than the south, whence an Egyptian campaign would come. It is arguable that the secondary introduction is . . . an indication that the poem refers to a defeat inflicted on the Philistines *before* the more recent Egyptian onslaught on Gaza" (1986, 774; emphasis original). Third, Harrison, following the main line of interpretation, suggests that the "chronological note . . . is obscure . . . The attack may have occurred when Necho was marching to Harran in 609 B.C." (1973, 172). It may be that the exact historical reference is not as important as the theological assertion that Yahweh is behind the events of world history. The oracle simply asserts the truth that "whoever the foe from the north may be, the LORD is the warrior" (Keown, Scalise, and Smothers 1995, 299).

■ 2-3 These verses naturally recall the enemy from the north motif found in various parts of the book. A key overturning of this motif will be found in the

46:27—
47:3

oracle against Babylon (chs 50—51), in which the one who formerly was the enemy from the north is now attacked from the north. Here, however, the motif also departs from its typical usage. The enemy being referred to is, by implication, Egypt, on the strength of information supplied from 47:1. However, the difficulty for this suggestion is that Egypt lies to the south of Philistine territory. The imagery of water surging forth is typical language of the Egyptian army massing for battle. In 46:9, this imagery is turned against Egypt. Carroll, who denies the Jeremianic authorship of the oracles against the nations, also admits that the flexibility of the images used throughout these poems mitigates the judgment that the oracles against the nations are little more than pedantic nationalism (see 1986, 751-59, for an excellent discussion of the critical issues).

The skillful use of imagery continues in the next verse, describing the wailing that will be heard throughout Philistia on the day that Egypt comes to call. The word **galloping** (*šaʿaṭat*) is certainly onomatopoeic. The sounds of war and destruction contribute to the chaotic, helpless feeling of the people. This helplessness is characterized in two different ways in the oracle. Here **fathers will not turn to help their children; their hands will hang limp**. The verse could also be translated so as to reflect the fathers' shame and not being able to protect the children: *fathers will not look to their children because of their inability to act.* The warriors are unable to defend the land; the fathers are unable to save their children; Philistia is unable to withstand the onslaught.

■ **4-7** The theme of promised help not being delivered is picked up again in v 4. The despair is on a wider level now, for now the invaders will **cut off all survivors who could help Tyre and Sidon**. This recalls judgment against Judah throughout the book in not looking toward shaky international alliances (see 37:7). Yet again, the imagery is turned over for a new use. Whereas, with reference to Judah, it is Egypt that is considered to be a broken reed, here with reference to Philistia they are leaning on broken reeds against the threat of Egypt. Moreover, Egypt is a tool in Yahweh's hand, just as Babylon is so described elsewhere. The synonymous parallelism at the end of v 4, **the Philistines, the remnant from the coasts of Caphtor,** recognizes the Philistine background as a seafaring people. **Caphtor** refers to the island of Crete. In this way, the imagery of water running over the banks and creating chaos in the land gathers even more power, for water running over the bow of a ship has always been of great concern to sailors.

The last three verses of the oracle against Philistia continue the themes of chaos and mourning in the face of a great military defeat. In addition, two different uses of the metaphor of cutting are put to use. First, in v 5, the poet asks how long the **remnant on the plain** (surely another oblique reference to Philistia) will continue to gash themselves in mourning. The origins of this metaphor are in some kind of "funerary ritual" (Carroll 1986, 777), though the precise meaning is uncertain. With poetry, however, locating reference for the images employed is somewhat beside the point; rather, the artfulness should instead be enjoyed—although it certainly was not enjoyed by the Philistines! The second usage of cutting is in reference to the sword of Yahweh. In v 6, the poet calls for the sword to *rest and be still.* Yet, as v 7 maintains, there can be no **rest when the LORD has commanded it.** The NIV of v 6 lessens the power of the term **rest** by translating *herāgě'î* as **cease.** The sword of Yahweh cannot indeed rest until it accomplishes Yahweh's command—the complete destruction of the Philistine cities.

3. Against Moab (48:1-47; LXX 31:1-44)

■ **1-2** With the exception of the oracle against Babylon (chs 50—51), this is the longest of the oracles against the nations. In addition, as noted above, there is no temporal reference for this oracle. While it is certainly more than a mere attack on Moab for the sake of attacking an old enemy, the specific occasion that engendered it is lacking. Stulman sees the generally confused, repetitive nature of this oracle as reflecting a variety of different hands in the composition (2005, 360-66). This suggestion may be strengthened by the lack of a temporal reference, although such lack does not necessarily mean that many people have contributed to an oracle. This chapter mentions a number of cities in Moab. Several of the cities mentioned here have been excavated in part, but the locations of a number of cities are not known (Thompson 1980, 701-2). Verse 1 announces the destruction and shame that will come upon some of the principal cities of Moab, the fame of which was once lauded throughout the region. **Nebo** is most likely a city near Mount Nebo from which Moses saw the Promised Land (Deut 34:1). The location of **Kiriathaim** is not known, though some scholars identify it as a city near Nebo. Both Nebo and Kiriathaim are mentioned in the Moabit stone (Lundbom 2004b, 246-47). Verse 2 speaks of the enemies of Moab consulting together in Heshbon on how to bring it down. Heshbon is identified today with Tell Hesban, about 12 miles south of Amman, and not too far from Mount Nebo. The text also mentions the silencing of **Madmen,** an unknown city in Moab. The focus of these two verses is on the complete destruction of Moab and its removal from the list of nations in the world.

■ **3-10** According to this oracle, the celebratory shouts in praise of Moab will be turned into the weeping of Moab's citizens. The location of Horonaim is not known. Moab **will be broken** (v 4), a phrase that could mean many different things: broken bones; broken pride; broken temples, altars, and cultic images. The **little ones will cry out** (v 4) refers not just to little children crying for the pain they themselves face but also to general wailing for Moab's destruction that is sure to be swift and complete. The next few verses utilize in various ways the metaphor of leaving. **Luhith** (v 5) is another town whose location is not precisely known. Scholars think that **the way to Luhith** is a road from the Moabite highlands down to the Jordan Valley. The people are described as **weeping bitterly as they go,** which indicates clearly that the Moabites are being chased from town to town, always fleeing to "safe ground" in the face of the attacking army—whoever it may be. The people will become like a **bush** (ʿărôʿēr) or "Juniper" (Holladay 1989, 341) in the desert; the meaning of ʿărôʿēr is not known. Some translations follow the LXX and translate this as "wild ass" (NRSV). Lundbom thinks that Aroer refers to a city that was destroyed like the cities of Sodom and Gomorrah (2004b, 253). Verse 7 indicates self-sufficiency, self-trust, and pride in its wealth as the reasons for the judgment on Moab. **Chemosh will go into exile** (v 7) conveys a specific theological claim. **Chemosh** was the principal god of the Moabite pantheon. This verse demonstrates Yahweh's power to put even the gods of Moab as well the priests and officials of Moab to shame and send them away into exile. Babylon is most likely the **destroyer** nation mentioned in v 8. No city or town or valley or plateau region in Moab will escape destruction (v 8). Verse 9a is difficult to translate; most translations translate the noun ṣiṣ as **salt** and interpret v 9a to mean that the land of Moab will be scattered with salt and thus make it an uninhabitable place. Verse 10 indicates that the destruction of Moab is the work of Yahweh. The phrase, **curse on *the one* who is lax in doing the LORD'S work,** encourages the enemies of Moab not to spare the sword from any of the Moabites; this may cause sensitive readers difficulty. If this seems to ascribe too much violence to Yahweh, the reader should bear in mind that the mind-set operating in a general way across cultures in this time period is one of the gods being intimately involved in the affairs of humanity, and warfare in particular.

In addition, the **curse on *the one* who keeps *the* sword from bloodshed** (v 10) may hearken back to the oracle against Philistia, where it was noted that Yahweh's sword is never satisfied until it has completely consumed his enemies. Though this language may be striking, perhaps even jarring, to postmodern readers, nevertheless it should be taken with due recourse to and understanding of the prevailing worldview expressed in the oracles against the nations, that the fortunes of the nations are a zero-sum game. That Yahweh is mentioned as the one directing the events indicates that Israel and Judah may just be the ones who derive the most benefit from Moab's downfall.

■ **11-13** Whereas before the celebration of Moab's glory had been turned into weeping, now it is time for a change to come to Moab's history of **rest** from exile, which other nations have experienced in their history. **Moab has been at rest from youth** (v 11) means that it has enjoyed a quiet life; the analogy that follows **(like wine that is left on its dregs, not poured from one jar to another)** conveys the settled state of life Moab enjoyed in its history. **She has not gone into exile** makes clear the meaning of the above analogy. Verse 12 announces that this condition is about to change and that Yahweh is about to send "decanters to decant Moab" (Lundbom 2004b, 268). Moab will be emptied and it will be broken into pieces. Yahweh's judgment on Moab will be a demonstration of his power and at the same a display of the total worthlessness of Chemosh, the chief god of the Moabites. Moab will then recognize the truth about their god and will be ashamed of this god in whom they trusted, just as the northern Israelites were ashamed of the calf at Bethel in which they trusted for their security and well-being (v 13).

■ **14-18** Verse 14 mocks at the boasting of Moabite soldiers; they claim to be warriors and valiant men in battle, but they cannot protect their country from being destroyed by the enemy. Verse 15 again asserts Yahweh's dominance over Moab and all the other kingdoms of the earth. While up to this point the Moabite army may have been claiming its prowess, now it has met in Yahweh an enemy that it cannot withstand. Once the destruction, promised to **come quickly** (v 16), does arrive, then the summons goes out to all the nations to mourn for Moab's loss (v 17). Previously, they had all extolled Moab as being among the greatest of the nations; now they stare in horror over its destruction. Verse 18 addresses the city of Dibon, the Iron Age capital of Moab, located on two hills, about forty miles south of Amman (Lundbom 2004b, 275). The city is here personified as a woman; she is being asked to come down from her place of glory and splendor and sit like a captive, because the enemy is about to come and destroy her fortified places.

■ **19-25** Verse 19 calls the people of Aroer to stand by the road and ask the fleeing men and women **"What has happened?"** But there is no answer from the people, but only the announcement from the prophet that Moab is disgraced and destroyed, and a summons to the people to announce as they are heading toward the Arnon River that **Moab is destroyed** (v 20). Verses 21-24 list the names of the cities of Moab that are under the judgment of Yahweh. Verse 21 identifies the plateau region as the location of the cities listed here. Verse 24 also mentions judgment on **all the towns of Moab.** This section concludes with an announcement from Yahweh that the strength of Moab (**Moab's horn; her arm**) has been cut off and broken (v 25).

■ **26-27** Verse 26 begins with a summons to Yahweh's agency of judgment (Babylon) to make Moab drink from Yahweh's cup of wrath. The goal of it is to induce drunkenness that will result in vomiting and disgraceful acts and thus to make Moab an object of ridicule among other nations. Verse 27 makes clear that Moab's destruction is in response to or is avenging Moab's former treatment of Israel. This verse lacks reference to the particular time at which Moab made Israel **the object of your ridicule** (v 27). Yet whenever this was done, the same treatment is to be given back to Moab, and this again highlights the implicit suggestion that it is Israel and Judah who are most going to benefit from Moab's downfall. Jeremiah's oracles against the nations do not take into account what benefit other nations may reap from the downfall of Egypt, Moab, or Babylonia—to mention only the longest three—so, as far as the book is concerned, they do not take any sort of benefit. All of the benefit is reserved for Israel and Judah, for they are the ones who were most affected by the arrogance of Moab.

■ **28-34** Verse 28 is a summons to the citizens of Moab to leave their cities and take up their dwellings among the **rocks**. The reference here is perhaps to the "rocky gorge of the Arnon" (Lundbom 2004b, 286). They are to live **like a dove that makes its nest at the mouth of a cave**. The homeless fugitives will be like doves looking for a place of safety from predatory animals that pursue them. Verses 29-31 follow the pattern of a dialogue between an unspecified group of people and Yahweh. The people who speak in v 29 report that they have heard of the **pride** and **arrogance** and the **haughtiness** of Moab. Yahweh responds by saying that he also knows of Moab's futile pride and boasting that accomplishes **nothing** (v 30) and that he will weep and lament over Moab and the people of ***Kirheres*** (in the MT, "for the men of Kirheres he will weep"). The NIV **Kir Hareseth** is based on the spelling in 2 Kgs 3:25. ***Kirheres,*** which was probably a capital of ancient Moab, is commonly identified with modern Kerak, located about 17 miles south of the Arnon and 10 miles east of the Dead Sea (Lundbom 2004b, 289).

Yahweh's speech continues in vv 32-33. The NIV **I weep for you, as Jazer weeps** follows the LXX reading. The MT reads, ***More than the weeping for Jazer, I weep for you O vine of Sibmah!*** Yahweh will weep more for Sibmah than for Jazer. Jazer, located near the Ammonite border, may have once been a Moabite city (Lundbom 2004b, 292). Sibmah, a Moabite town known for its high quality grapes and raisins, was located somewhere near Heshbon, though the actual site is unknown to us (Lundbom 2004b, 292). Verse 32 describes the destruction of the vineyards and fruit of Sibmah as the **destroyer** has descended on Moab from the northern border. This destruction has put an end to the sound of rejoicing **from the orchards and fields of Moab** (v 33). Verse 33 also makes clear it is Yahweh who stopped the **flow of wine** and put an end to the **shouts of joy** in the land. Instead of shouts of rejoicing, what is being heard throughout the land, from **Elealeh** in the north to **Jahaz** in the south is sound of the cry of the people that originates in **Heshbon**. This cry is also heard in **Zoar** and **Horonaim**, located in southern Moab. The location of **Eglath Shelishiyah** is not known. The terrible effect of judgment is that it even dries up **the waters of Nimrim** (v 34). Scholars consider the location of this source of water in southern Moab, and some identify it with Wadi en-Numeirah, which flows into the Dead Sea (Lundbom 2004b, 295).

▪ **35-39** Yahweh continues his speech in vv 35-38. The focus here is on the end of religious rituals. He threatens to **put an end** to offerings and sacrifices to the gods of Moab (v 35). In v 36, Yahweh's speech turns into a lament; he says that he **laments for Moab** and for ***the people of Kirheres*** like a flute; this may indicate a low-pitched moaning sound, in contrast to the loud noise of shouts of joy that were once heard in Moab. The reason for this lament is Moab's loss of its wealth. The people of Moab also show signs of their grief; they have shaved their heads, cut their beards off, slashed their hands, and put sackcloth on their waist (v 37). The roofs of houses and public squares, which were once places of rejoicing, have become places of mourning because Yahweh has broken Moab like an unwanted and useless jar (v 38). Yahweh's wailing for Moab continues in v 39. Moab is shattered; it has become an object of shame and ridicule, a sight of horror to all the surrounding nations.

■ **40-46** Verses 40-46 describe the scene of an invading army coming down upon Moab and the terrible impact of invasion. The enemy (Babylon) will come down upon it like an eagle with its wings spread out to capture its prey. The whole land of Moab will be covered by the spread-out wings of Babylon (v 40). Every city of Moab will fall victim to the enemy's attack, and the soldiers of Moab will have their hearts pound like that of **a woman in labor** (v 41). Again, the text makes clear that it is Yahweh who is the real enemy of Moab; the cause of his wrath on Moab is that Moab has **defied Yahweh** (v 42). There will be no escape for the people of Moab from the enemy; wherever they turn for refuge, they will find only **pit** and **snare,** because they are in the **year of** their **punishment**—the time of Yahweh's visitation of Moab in judgment (v 44). The LXX lacks vv 45-47. The fire of judgment on Moab will be experienced by everyone in Moab; it will burn the heads of everyone for their pride. The fugitives who try to escape will find no help anywhere in the land (v 45). This long section of judgment on Moab ends with a final woe oracle. What awaits the people of Moab and their god Chemosh is their destruction and exile into the lands of their enemy (v 46).

■ **47** An interesting element in the oracle against Moab, however, comes in the last verse. At the end of the judgment speech, Yahweh speaks a word of comfort to Moab: **I will restore the fortunes of Moab in days to come** (v 47). This very thing is also said of Ammon (49:6) and Elam (49:39). Yet the unique thing is the almost liturgically styled ending of the oracle (**Here ends the judgment on Moab;** v 47). A similar statement will be made at the end of the long oracle against Babylon, though not specifically related to the punishment on that nation. It is ultimately unclear why this note is included, though it may also be related to the confused pile of seemingly disparate sources going into the oracle against Moab. The comment **here ends the judgment on Moab** may not mean that the judgment itself is ending, but that what precedes the comment has exhausted the poetic reserves of anti-Moabite material. Wherever the explanation is to be found, it is interesting that Israel's old enemy is given a promise of hope following closely on a lengthy promise of God's wrath.

4. Against Ammon (49:1-6; LXX 30:17-21)

■ **1** The lengthy oracle against Moab is followed by a much shorter one against another of Israel and Judah's old traditional enemies, Ammon. It should be remembered that Gen 19:30-38 is an Israelite-friendly legend about the questionable circumstances surrounding the origins of Ammon and Moab. If the Ammonites and Moabites knew that this legend was current in Israel, then it is not surprising that some animosity would be generated because of it. The frequency with which these bad relations boiled up into violence was certainly not lost on the editors of the book of Jeremiah. In fact, Ammon also played a role in the assassination of Gedaliah by Ishmael (see 40:13—41:18 above). The oracle against Ammon itself opens up in a way reminiscent of lament psalms. More directly, verse 1 recalls Jer 2:14, "Is Israel a servant, a slave by birth? Why then has he become plunder?" It is further interesting that the deity **Milcom** is cited as having **taken possession of Gad**. **Milcom** was the principal deity of Ammon, but it seems odd that a Hebrew writer would give credence in this way to the gods of another nation. Carroll (1986, 798) suggests that this is reminiscent of the language of ch 48 with Chemosh going into exile from Moab, and therein lies the solution to this apparent quandary. The notion that **Milcom** is the one who moved the Gadites out of their territory is used to set up the condemnation of Ammon and **Milcom** that will come throughout the remainder of the oracle.

■ **2** This verse specifically reverses the complaint in v 1. That this is so is in keeping with the genre of a lament psalm. First the complaint is addressed, whether to Yahweh specifically or to a more general audience. Then the oracle comes and Yahweh vows to exact judgment on the enemy, in this case Ammon. Now Yahweh **will sound the battle cry against Rabbah of the Ammonites**. Whereas in v 1 the chief deity of Ammon was cited as representative of the people, here the capital city plays that role. This is again a mere convention, like using "Washington" or "London" as a representative of, respectively, the governments—and by extension, the people—of the United States and the United Kingdom. The reversal of the specific occasion that engendered this complaint comes at the end of the verse: **Then Israel will drive out those who drove her out**. The reader will notice that this call is not, at this point, for an attack on the Ammonite heartland; it is merely a call for the restoration of how things were before the Ammonites invaded Gad.

■ **3** Typical of the oracles against the nations, this verse is a call for the target of the oracle to mourn and wail for the conditions that come to it when Yahweh exacts revenge for Israel. The city names in this oracle—**Heshbon, Ai, Rabbah**—are more recognizable than the cities mentioned in the oracle against Moab. Perhaps this is because Ammon has a little more involvement with the history of Israel than does Moab. In any event, that **Milcom is going into exile** surely recalls the same judgment leveled against Chemosh in 48:7. In this way, the prophet overturns the seeming validation of **Milcom** in v 1 by declaring that the god of the Ammonites—and, by extension, the Ammonites themselves—will go off into exile. Presumably, the agent of the Ammonite exile will be the Babylonians, though this is not stated. It is clear, however, that the oracle has advanced beyond restoring the previous condition of the territory of Gad; now the call goes out for the territory of Ammon itself to be invaded and destroyed.

■ **4-6** After the prediction of judgment is laid out, Ammon is then attacked for its prideful arrogance. Just like every nation that achieves a more or less secure existence, Ammon apparently had boasted in what belonged to it. Yahweh warns through the prophet that such arrogance will not go unpunished. So, while there is not a discernable benefit for Israel and Judah to gain from the downfall of Ammon, other than the restoration of the territory of Gad, nevertheless an oracle calling for the destruction of a long-hated enemy could not have failed to earn appreciation. The oracle against Ammon ends in v 6 with a note promising restoration (see 48:47 and 49:39). Verse 6 is lacking in the LXX.

5. Against Edom (49:7-22; LXX 30:1-16)

■ **7-11** A slightly longer oracle follows against Edom, another of the nations with whom Israel has had long-standing, if relatively minor, ill relations. Of course, Edom and Israel were cousins in their respective ancestries, having come from the brothers Esau and Jacob. What traditions might have been current in Edom concerning the origins of Israel is unknown. Alternatively, it may be likely that at least some in Edom would have considered the negative portrayal of their ancestor Esau by the Israelites as a biased tradition that favors Yahweh's election of Jacob the ancestor of Israel. Yet, apparently Edom rose above the simple-mindedness of its patriarch and developed a rather strong wisdom tradition. Such a tradition is assumed by the critique of v 7. Whatever there was in Edom in the way of sage ability has now departed.

Verses 8-11 describe the degree of devastation that is about to come upon Edom. Even though grape pickers would leave a few grapes, and even though robbers would only steal what they wanted, Yahweh **will strip Esau bare** (v 10). This is a vision of total annihilation for Edom, such that there can be no promised hope of restoration as was suggested for Moab, Ammon, and Elam. The animosity between the Edomites and Israelites is clearly deep-seated, on the basis of this poem. This means that the Israelite partisanship coming to expression here will not be satisfied until every grape on Edom's vine is plucked, every possession it has stolen, and every item of clothing stripped off. Yet some kind of hope is sounded for Edom, for v 11 suggests that Edom's orphans and widows **can trust in me.** This phrase strikes a curious note after the destruction scenario established in the preceding verses. However, just like the notes of restoration for Moab, Ammon, and Elam, this may serve as a testimony to Yahweh's faithfulness to care for those who are outcast in society. Even when the society itself comes under the wrathful gaze of Yahweh, those who cannot fend for themselves find a caretaker in the very one who has destroyed the rest of society.

■ **12-18** This note of ambiguous hope in the form of care for the orphans and the widows is itself tempered by a return to the language of judgment in the next few verses. First, vv 12-13 attack Edom's implicit view of its own inviolability. Even those nations who **do not deserve to drink the cup must drink it,** and so how can Edom be exempted? The clear implication of this is that

Edom does in fact deserve to drink of the cup of Yahweh's wrath (see 25:15). Presumably, as in all the other cases with the exception of Philistia and Babylonia, the tool for the delivery of Yahweh's wrath is to be the Babylonians. Later on in v 19 a key metaphor makes that identification all the clearer. Here, though, the pride of Edom is mocked again. The one who placed itself on a high rock will be taken down from that lofty place and destroyed, even though it trusted in its own inviolability. The destruction of Edom will be such that **all who pass by will be appalled and will scoff because of all its wounds** (v 17).

■ **19-22** The simile of a lion in v 19, though immediately linked to Yahweh, also bears marks of an allusion to Nebuchadnezzar.

This is perhaps yet another expression of the idea that Nebuchadnezzar is a tool in Yahweh's hand. When this statement is made of the Babylonian king, it most often refers to the destruction of Israel. However, it also serves to trivialize the power of the colonizer. The world powers, even relatively minor ones like Edom, are called to account for their arrogance and pride, especially as this affects Judah and Israel directly. Yahweh will surely pay back the nations for the harm they have caused, so the argument runs in this material and by doing so he will vindicate the righteousness of his people and restore their fortunes. Again, the oracles against the nations are not at all concerned with what benefit other nations might reap from the downfall of any one or more of these that are called out for special mention. Rather, the book of Jeremiah is concerned, as it should be, only with Israel and what will happen to Israel as a result of the punishment of the other nations.

6. Against Damascus (49:23-27; LXX 30:29-33)

■ **23-27** The shortest of Jeremiah's oracles against the nations contains many similar themes that are woven throughout this section of the book. It is also unique in that it is the only one that uses the name of a city as an eponym for its land (Carroll 1986, 808). A possible exception to this is 49:2 with reference to Ammon, as noted above. Yet this oracle against Damascus fits in nicely with the genre in that Israel's traditional enemies are brought under a curse. Even before being the capital of the Syrian empire, whose involvement with (then called) Judea ultimately brought about the Maccabean revolt, Damascus was the capital of the old Aramean empire, with which both the northern kingdom of Israel and the southern kingdom of Judah were involved from time to time (see 1 Kgs 19:15-18).

There is not much new as far as the content of the oracle against Damascus is concerned. The reader finds here two typical motifs. First the city is said to be crying like a woman in labor. Second, other, nearby cities having been thrown into a state of panic and fear because of what is happening to Damascus. The NIV of v 25 reads as a question: **Why has the city of renown not been abandoned, the town in which I delight?** It is better, however, to follow a textual emendation and read *How the glorious city has been deserted, my fa-*

vorite town! The future-sounding prediction that the **young men will fall in the streets** (v 26) is surely linked thematically to Yahweh's declaration that he **will set fire to the walls of Damascus; it will consume the fortresses of Ben-Hadad** (v 27). The interplay of past and future tenses highlights, in a way, the chaos that surrounds the fall of the city, ostensibly to the Babylonians. From another viewpoint, however, the theological thrust of this oracle is that because Yahweh has sworn to do these things, then they can be profitably spoken of as having already occurred in the past. In other words, this is an expression of the so-called prophetic perfect tense, speaking of future events as is if they were already in the past.

7. Against Kedar and Hazor (49:28-33; LXX 30:23-28)

■ **28-33** The identities of Kedar and Hazor are matters of some conjecture. **Kedar** may refer to a nomadic Arabian tribe that had dealings with Israel during the time of the united monarchy. **Hazor** relates to an old Canaanite stronghold, and also one of the principal cities that was fortified by Solomon during the consolidation of his reign. Others were Gezer, Jerusalem, and Megiddo (1 Kgs 9:15). Perhaps some kind of Canaanite population remained around this area even up to the time of Jeremiah. While such questions as the identity of these two kingdoms may be irresolvable at present, this does not mean that they should be ignored. The short length of this oracle in which two "nations" are the target tends to lead the reader into just such neglect, a tragic outcome to be sure.

Though Kedar and Hazor were not as important as were nations like Edom, Moab, Egypt, and Babylon in the history of Israel and Judah, nevertheless that they are included in Jeremiah's oracles against the nations should indicate something of their involvement with Israel. The oracle against Kedar apparently only consists of two verses, for the mention of Hazor in vv 30 and 33 form a nice frame for the oracle against that kingdom. This may also reflect the unsettled existence of Kedar, if in fact the term refers to the nomadic tribe mentioned in Ps 120:5; Song 1:5; Isa 21:16-17; 42:11; 60:7; Jer 2:10; and Ezek 27:21. These various references to the tribe or tribes of Kedar indicate some kind of importance, or at least awareness, of their existence.

As for Hazor, the oracle against it in Jer 49:30-33 mentions themes similar to those found in the oracle against Edom (vv 7-22). In particular, Hazor is attacked for complacency and pride, particularly in v 31. According to the oracle, Hazor is so confident in its own security that it **has neither gates nor bars; its people live alone.** Living in an unfortified city during a time in which great empires are battling for control of the region is unwise at best, suicidal at worst. However, apparently Hazor was unconcerned with these wider developments. This lack of concern prompted Yahweh to stir up his old tool Nebuchadnezzar and move against the complacent kingdom. The scattering of the people and the desolation of their flocks and herds are emblems of the total destruction Yahweh intends to wreak upon Hazor. Again, while it is uncertain how Hazor had been negatively involved in Israel's history, nevertheless they are not to be spared when the cup of Yahweh's wrath (25:15) is poured out for all the nations, and they are forced to drink it to the dregs.

8. Against Elam (49:34-39; LXX 25:14-20)

■ **34-39** In the LXX, this oracle begins the oracles against the foreign nations. The oracle against Elam is the only one with a temporal reference mentioning a Judean king (the beginning of the reign of Zedekiah). No specific attack is mentioned as with the oracles against Egypt and Philistia. Further, there is no reference to either the nebulous "enemy from the north" or to Nebuchadnezzar, as in the oracles against Kedar and Hazor, Philistia, Moab, and Babylon. The oracle against Damascus also lacks reference to a specific attack. That such variation should be found in a genre that exhibits many characteristic features could be taken as evidence of the involvement of different hands in the final form of the oracles against the nations.

Elam, located in the area east of the Tigris River, was an ancient country (Gen 14:1, 9); the OT lists Elam as one of the sons of Shem (Gen 10:22). The Elamites and the Medes occupied the area of modern Iran (ancient Persia). Jeremiah is the only OT prophet who pronounces judgment oracles against Elam (see Elam and Media in Jer 25:25). It is not certain why Elam became the object of attack by Jeremiah. Perhaps it serves the purpose of Jeremiah's assignment as a prophet to the nations (1:10). The mention of Elam here indicates its existence during the Neo-Babylonian period. As is typical of the shifting international relations both in ancient times and in modern, it may be assumed that the oracle predicts the Babylonian destruction of Elam. If this assumption is correct, then it represents a change in Babylonian policy toward Elam, who had once upon a time aided Babylon in its quest to be liberated from Assyrian domination. That Yahweh swears to **break the bow of Elam, the mainstay of their might** (49:35) alludes to the center of Elamite prowess in wartime and also a source of their pride. The power of the bow will not be able to save Elam in the time when Yahweh comes against them, however.

Furthermore, the suggestion that Yahweh **will scatter them to the four winds** may reflect some degree of historical knowledge. Elamite power became decentralized in the Neo-Babylonian period, and later it was incorporated into the Persian Empire by Cyrus the Great in 539 B.C., the same year as Babylon was overrun. The destruction of Elam is to be total, for **there will not be a nation where Elam's exiles do not go** (v 36). Further, v 37 maintains that Yahweh **will pursue them with the sword until I have made an end of them.** These statements are tempered by the promise of restoration to Elam in v 39. Yet, in this case—as opposed to the others in which restoration is promised—the restoration may be connected to the same event with which Judah's restoration is said to be connected: the takeover of Babylonia by Cyrus. This was considered a momentous event for Judah (Isa 45:1; 2 Chr 36:22-23; Ezra 1:1-4; 6:1-5). The suggestion may therefore be reasonable that Elam thought similar things about the activity of Cyrus. Such a perception would be given further credence by the general Persian policy of restoring peoples to the lands from which they had been exiled and the support of local cultic practices. Both of these policies were designed to generate and ensure loyalty to the Persian hierarchy over the region. It is interesting to note that Isa 11:11 mentions a remnant of Judah from Elam; Acts 2:9 mentions Elamites among those who were present in Jerusalem on the Day of Pentecost.

9. Against Babylon (50:1—51:64; LXX 27:1—28:64)

■ 1 In the oracles against the nations, the book of Jeremiah saves the best, as it were, for last. If the Babylonian exile is the chief event lying behind the production of and theology informing the book of Jeremiah, then Babylon itself would surely have been the greatest enemy that could be imagined, at least up to that time. Carroll is correct when he writes: "These [chapters] are almost as long (110 verses) as the material against the other nations in 46-49 (121 verses). Their length indicates the obsessional antagonism felt toward Babylon as the national enemy which had destroyed Jerusalem and ruined the nation" (1986, 814). As will be noted below, Babylon and Nebuchadnezzar came to be known, singly and collectively, as the paradigm of evil in Jewish imagination. This synecdoche of evil spills over into Christianity as well, with "Babylon the Great" serving as a cipher for Rome, most notably in the book of Revelation (Rev 14:8; 16:19; 17:5; 18:2, 10, 21). In a passage not quite so polemical, 1 Peter brings to its readers the greetings of the believers "who [are] in Babylon" (1 Pet 5:13).

As to form, it also has one unique feature in comparison with the other oracles against the nations. Here we have the formula **This is the word the LORD spoke through Jeremiah the prophet concerning Babylon and the land of the Babylonians.** In only two other oracles is Jeremiah specifically mentioned at the beginning. Yet even these statements are not quite as elaborate. The first reads, ***That which Yahweh spoke to Jeremiah the prophet concerning the Philistines*** (47:1). The second reads, ***This is the word that Yahweh spoke to Jeremiah the prophet concerning Elam*** (49:34). One might not be able to say more than that this distinction is interesting. However, it may yet speak to an even further significance for the oracle against Babylon, perhaps especially so in light of the declaration in 51:64 at the end of this lengthy oracle of judgment: ***Thus far the words of Jeremiah.*** In this way, the note that this oracle was spoken by Yahweh ***through the agency of Jeremiah the prophet,*** together with the note that Jeremiah's words end after this, form a nice frame for the oracle against Babylon.

■ 2 The oracle proper begins here with an exhortation to spread the news throughout all the world of Babylon's coming defeat. This verse exhibits nice examples of synonymous parallelism. The first two lines (**Announce and proclaim among the nations, lift up a banner and proclaim it**) are parallel commands to make the news known. The next two lines, respectively, end one synthetic parallel chain and start another. That is, **keep nothing back, but say** goes with **lift up a banner and proclaim it** while **Babylon will be captured** is further explicated in the next two lines. **Bel will be put to shame, Marduk filled with terror** is another example of synonymous parallelism, for Bel is a later name for Marduk, the titulary deity of the city of Babylon and, by extension, the entire land of Babylonia. The verse ends with another synonymous parallel chain. Moreover, the four lines after **Babylon will be captured** form a nice extended synonymous parallel chain: the sequence runs **put to shame ... filled with terror,** and the elements traded out from the beginning of the lines are **Bel ... Marduk** and *her cultic images ... her idols.* This verse thus demonstrates some of the best of the poetry in the book of Jeremiah.

■ **3** The prediction comes that **a nation from the north will attack her** surely reminds the reader of the "enemy from the north" motif earlier in the book (see 1:14-15; 4:5-6; 6:1, 22; 10:22; 13:20; 25:9). Elsewhere, the imagery of an enemy coming from the north was used as a threat to Judah or other nations. The "enemy from the north" presumably referred to Babylon, as it did elsewhere in the oracles against the nations (see above on Egypt and Philistia), for to attack this area the army had to march up the Euphrates and cross the Jordan before sweeping down into the Jezreel valley from the north. The target of such a march could surely be Judah, but it could also be Philistia or Egypt. Yet here, the motif of the enemy from the north is turned around and it is Babylon that is now in the sights of the enemy. The result after the enemy from the north sweeps down into Babylon will be devastation, just as was predicted with regard to Judah, Egypt, and Philistia.

■ **4-10** The following seven verses seem at first glance to be an interruption in the oracle of judgment against Babylon. This text deals with two issues: (1) The return and reunification of Israel and Judah; (2) The downfall of Babylon. These issues do not present an interruption to the oracle against Babylon but simply demonstrate the nature of Yahweh-Israel-Babylon relationship and Yahweh's role in the upcoming reversal of the present conditions of Babylon and Judah. The claims of this text are as follows: though Babylon was the orchestrator (at the behest of Yahweh; see 25:9; 27:6) of the downfall of Jerusalem and Judah, it is about to experience its own downfall. The demise of Babylon will come through the agency of other nations or a nation that will rise to be a world power. The beneficiaries of these geopolitical changes are Israel and Judah; though they were destroyed and deported into various parts of the Assyrian and Babylonian empires because of their sin against Yahweh (50:6-7), they will be restored and reunited as one nation and they will come together to seek Yahweh in Zion and to be united with him in an everlasting covenant (vv 4-5). Thus perception in this text is that the present situation is about to be reversed—for both Babylon the great empire and Israel and Judah that live in exile. The text anticipates the imminent downfall of Babylon and directs its audience with an urgent imperative to go out of Babylon, like goats pushing their way to be in front of the flock (v 8).

This text thus proposes a solution to a very old problem—the split between Israel and Judah. The idea behind this poem is that this division serves as an emblem, if not a cause, for many of the nation's principal ills, and thus the reunification of Judah and Israel could serve as a hallmark of the promised future under the rule of Yahweh. The reunification of Israel and Judah is a theme also found in 3:18; 30:3; 31:7-9, 27; 33:7; see also Hos 1:11; Ezek 37:21-22.

■ **11-13** The next set of verses makes clear the revenge-seeking aspect of the oracle against Babylon. This will become even more clear in vv 17 and following, but here it is stated in terms not only accusing the Babylonians of ravaging Judah but for laughing and rejoicing as they did so. The first of these claims is indisputable. The second probably utilizes a bit of rhetorical flourish in the midst of a reflection upon the tragedy brought to bear upon Judah by Babylon and its mighty armies. This poem shows evidence of great literary artistry, and compares Babylon to a stamping heifer and a neighing steed that rejoices at an appalling devastation. The essential thought is that Babylon will get what it deserves for having done all that it did to Judah and to Jerusalem, those who **pillage my inheritance** (v 11). By a statement like this, Yahweh reaffirms that his covenant with Judah still can be reestablished. Even in the face of all the destruction that he has either caused or allowed to happen, Yahweh still has a heart for Jerusalem and still longs to reestablish relationship with Judah.

■ **14-16** Next comes a summons to other nations, and their armies in particular, to enact Yahweh's vengeance upon Babylon. A summons like this is surely related to the idea that Yahweh has in his hand all the nations of the earth. In several places, the book of Jeremiah calls Nebuchadnezzar Yahweh's servant for the purpose of punishing Judah (25:9), all of the nations (27:6), or Egypt (43:10). This oracle indirectly uses the same sentiment here to call upon various unnamed servants of Yahweh to enact vengeance on Babylon. In this way, Yahweh proclaims his superiority over all the other nations of the world, and Babylon in particular. The thrust of this small section comes in v 15: **Since this is the vengeance of the LORD, take vengeance on her; do to her as she has done to others.** Now has come the time for Babylon to suffer as it has made others to suffer, and it is all at the command of Yahweh.

■ **17-20** On first glance, an oracle of salvation for Israel seems out of place in the middle of an extended oracle of judgment against Babylon. Again, as we have seen before, curse pronounced on one nation necessarily entails blessing for another; thus judgment on Babylon means salvation to Israel. As the book of Jeremiah is mainly concerned with the fortunes of Judah, the one set to benefit from the blessings that correspond to the curses that are heaped upon Babylonia is, naturally, Judah.

It is interesting, however, that just as in the earlier passage from this chapter (vv 4-5), both Israel and Judah are mentioned as beneficiaries of the favor that corresponds to the judgment upon Babylon. Verse 17 summarizes the exilic experiences of the chosen people by naming first Assyria and then Babylon in a historical retrospective. Israel in v 17 refers to the covenant nation as a whole. This verse melts away a key distinction when it reads that **the first to devour him was the king of Assyria, *and afterwards Nebuchadnezzar king of Babylon broke his bones.*** The northern kingdom of Israel, and not Judah, was the target of Assyria's devouring; the southern kingdom of Judah, and not Israel, was the target of Babylonia's bone-crushing. However, this verse links the two experiences of defeat and exile, each belonging to a separate member of the divided kingdoms, as the combined experience of the whole nation. Thus once again the text affirms what has already been a theme in this chapter; the curse heaped on Babylon means blessing to the covenant nation and the healing of the old fracture between Israel and Judah. Not only this, but in declaring *I am bringing punishment upon the king of Babylon and his land, just as I punished the king of Assyria* Yahweh is answering the older complaint of Habakkuk. Habakkuk wanted to know how the evil Babylonians could be used to punish the evil Assyrians and Judah as well, and Yahweh reassured him that everything was in his power (see Hab 1:5-17).

50:17-32   Along with this, Yahweh declares that the sin of both Israel and Judah will be wiped clean, and that he **will forgive the remnant.** Use of the term **remnant** carries with it all the theological freight of that term from elsewhere in the prophetic literature. Jeremiah develops on the theme by saying repeatedly that God ***will not completely destroy*** Judah (see 5:18, among others). Negatively, the remnant also comes under judgment (for example, in 44:12 the community that has gone off in voluntary exile to Egypt in defiance of Yahweh's command). For the most part, however, use of the term **remnant** goes along with oracles of salvation for Judah and Israel, as it does here.

■ **21-32** In this next long poem, the focus again shifts back to Babylon as the particular target of Yahweh's wrath. In v 21, the reader finds two alternative names for Babylon, **Merathaim** and **Pekod.** According to medieval Jewish exegetes, **Merathaim,** which literally means "double rebellion," is here a disparaging name given to Babylon (Lundbom 2004b, 403). It may also mean something like "bitter waters," and thus it may refer to the name of a Babylonian district near what is now known as the Persian Gulf (Carroll 1986, 827). If this is the case, then this district functions as a synecdoche for the entire land of Babylon, in the same way as saying "Washington" or "London" may refer, respectively, to the entirety of the United States or Great Britain (see above on Rabbah of the Ammonites, 49:2). Similarly, **Pekod** may refer to a tribe and region in southeastern Babylon, many of whose members served in the Babylonian army. According to Stulman, this "play on two regions in Babylon . . . highlights Babylon's wrongdoing and its impending fate" (2005, 374). Both of these districts, as representative of the entire nation of Babylon, are the prey of those who **kill and completely destroy,** which itself is reminiscent of the old commands given to the people of Israel going in to take possession of the land of Canaan.

The next four verses (vv 22-25) turn the earlier proclamation that Babylon was a tool in Yahweh's hand to punish Israel against Babylon itself. Verse 22 describes the land of Babylon as the place where the noise of the battle is being heard as well as the place that experiences great destruction. Verse 23 introduces another metaphor for Babylon **(the hammer of the whole earth)**, but also quite effectively demonstrates that, even for all its power, not even Babylon is immune from destruction. Throughout all of this, the poems assert Yahweh's governance over the world, and it is Yahweh who moves the nations around as he chooses, rather than their military might (or, in the case of Judah, apparent lack thereof). In 23:29, the metaphor of a hammer also appears, there describing the "equally destructive power of Yahweh's word" (Carroll 1986, 827). Yahweh declares to Babylon in 50:24 that it was **caught before you knew it,** which is clearly a shot at imperial boastfulness. Empires that boast often fall when they least expect it; pride of the nations is often the cause of their fall and the agent of their collapse is usually an emerging power either they ignored or considered insignificant. The snare of Babylon is its pride, and it has fallen into its own trap. Babylon has no place to hide; it has been found and caught by Yahweh. The reason for its fall is its arrogance and defiance of Yahweh (v 24).

Verses 25-32 continue the assault upon Babylon, the empire who thought, like all others before and after it, that it was impervious to attack and collapse. Verse 25 describes Yahweh as a warrior who has **opened his arsenal and brought out** his **weapons** to execute **his wrath** in the land of the Babylonians. Verses 26-27 contain a command from Yahweh to the enemies of Babylon to enter the land from ***every quarter,*** break open the granaries, pile up dead bodies, and leave no one alive in Babylon. It is not clear what the command to **kill all her young bulls** means in v 27. Commentators understand it as Yahweh's command to destroy the mighty warriors of the Babylonian army or its top officials. They are to be slaughtered like animals. It is possible that v 27 conveys a command to the enemies of Babylon who act as Yahweh's agents to slaughter the army of Babylon or its high-ranking officials as sacrifice to Yahweh. Babylon the destroyer has finally come to the day of its own punishment and destruction. These verses clearly anticipate that the fall of the once great and mighty Babylonian empire will happen at the command of Yahweh and not due to natural forces, internal corruption, or military defeat. In history, though these may have been contributing factors for the fall of Babylon, texts like these understand such events as Yahweh's work to bring about his ultimate purpose for Israel and Judah. Verse 28 seems to be the center of this small section; this verse summons the readers to hear the undoubtedly joyful reports of the **fugitives and refugees** coming **from Babylon.** In Zion they will announce that Yahweh has vindicated Zion and his temple. Yahweh's wrath has been poured out on Babylon, and he has completed his task. Again, the point of all of this is not just the destruction of Babylon, but the benefit this destruction would entail for Judah and Israel reunited as one nation.

■ **33-34** These verses continue the by now familiar theme of curse for Babylon resulting in blessing for Israel and Judah, with an added note on rest that will come to the earth. As far as Jeremiah and this oracle against Babylonia are concerned, Israel and Judah are the primary beneficiaries of the fall of Babylon. Yahweh is acting here to liberate his people who have been oppressed by those who have held them in captivity and have refused to let them go. Yahweh comes into the midst of the affliction of his people as their strong **Redeemer** to rescue them from their captors. The text echoes Yahweh's rescue of Israel from the Egyptian bondage. The one who comes to defend the cause of Israel is *Yahweh Sebaoth* (Yahweh of hosts). The outcome of Yahweh's intervention on behalf of his people is **rest** to the *earth.* The inhabitants of the earth will enjoy peace when Yahweh brings the power of Babylon to an end. However, there will be no rest to the inhabitants of Babylon, the nation that caused much unrest in the world through its war and conquest.

■ **35-46** This section utilizes traditional motifs in service of new ends. The first unit (vv 35-38) depicts what will happen to various groups of people, military forces, the wealth of Babylon, and to the waters of Babylon. Yahweh summons **a sword** against various inhabitants of Babylon, officials, wise men, prophets, warriors, horses, chariots, mercenary soldiers, and the treasures of Babylon. The sword will be wielded against the people, the officials, and the wise men of Babylon. It will make the prophets **fools,** destroy the warriors, make mercenary soldiers weak and ineffective (**become women**), and plunder and carry away the treasures of Babylon. **Sword** is repeated five times, most likely to create the image of this weapon thrusting into various parts of the body of its victim repeatedly, to inflict deep pain and ensure death. The curse upon the waters that they **will dry up** (v 38) is directed to the rivers of Babylon that provide water for the inhabitants to keep the land fertile and productive. A severe drought is pronounced on the land because it is a land filled with idols that cause such fear among the people who worship them. Oracles like these would certainly have communicated hope to the Jewish people living in exile; the more insult and curse the text lavished on Babylon, the more hope and blessing it promised to the exiles.

The prose oracle in vv 39-40 utilizes the traditional image of wild animals and ostriches inhabiting the land (see Isa 13:20-21). This short saying has continuity with the preceding poem. The land from which the population is cut off by the sword of judgment will become a desolate place fit only for wild animals.

The curse of desolation is extended for all generations to come. The severity of judgment is intensified by comparing the fate of Babylon to that of Sodom and Gomorrah, the cities overthrown and destroyed by God's judgment.

Verses 41-43 repeat the language of 6:22-24. In 6:22-24 the foe from the north is Babylon and the people living in fear are the people of Judah. The poem here recycles the earlier poem to announce the coming of a foe from the north against Babylon. The invader in 6:22-24 is here the victim; the nation that caused fear is now living in fear. The fearsomeness of the enemy coming from the north (50:42) surely recalls what was said about Babylon in 6:23. Whereas the victim of attack in 6:23 is the "Daughter of Zion," the victim here is the **Daughter of Babylon** (50:42). In 6:24, fear has overtaken the people of Judah and they are made weak and helpless and they are in agony like **a woman in labor.** In 50:43, it is the king of Babylon who experiences fear, anguish, and helplessness **like . . . a woman in labor.** The reference here may be to the last king of Babylon or, more precisely, the regent ruling in place of the last king, Belshazzar the son of Nabonidus. Belshazzar was a very weak king, and it was only a matter of time before Cyrus II of Persia took over the Babylonian Empire. Such a victory was made complete in 539 B.C., ultimately fulfilling the words of Jeremiah's great and lengthy oracle against Babylon.

Verses 44-46 duplicate 49:19-21 (oracle against Edom) with minor variations. References to Edom and Teman in 49:19-21 are replaced here with **Babylon** and **Babylonians.** Though no one is specifically addressed, it is likely that here we have a summons to the whole earth to hear of Babylon's downfall and Yahweh's plans and purposes for that nation. Yahweh is depicted here as a **lion** coming out of **Jordan's thickets** (see 4:7 where this imagery is used to describe the impending Babylonian invasion of Judah). The main thrust of the message is in the incomparable power of Yahweh over world affairs; he will choose a nation that will rule over Babylon. The enemy that Yahweh will bring against Babylon will drag away **the young of the flock** of Babylon. When the news of the capture of Babylon is announced, there will be much rejoicing among the nations that have been victims of the oppressive rule of Babylon during its relatively short period of dominance in the ancient Near East.

■ **51:1-5** The second chapter of the oracle against Babylon continues by-now familiar themes: the summoning of enemies to destroy the one previously so summoned and the benefits to be reaped by a potentially reunified Israel and Judah through the downgrading of Babylon. The oracle begins with an announcement that Yahweh is about to stir up a ***destroying wind*** (*rûaḥ mašḥît*), an enemy that will cause the destruction of Babylon. Verse 1 also introduces a new cipher, or "code name," for Babylon. **Babylon and the people of Leb Kamai** here function as a kind of parallel chain within the same poetic line, so here the cipher is not quite as cryptic as Sheshach in 25:26. However, **Leb Kamai** and Sheshach are created in the same way, through *atbash* coding. This coding substitutes the first letter of the Hebrew alphabet, '*aleph*, for the last, *tav;* the second, *bet,* for the second-to-last, *shin,* and so on. So, **Leb Kamai** is a cryptic name for *kasdîm,* "Chaldeans," the principal tribe ruling Babylonia at the time of the exile of the Judeans.

The next four verses indicate, first, the total devastation that will come upon Babylon. The winnowing metaphor in v 2 indicates the complete dispersion of the Babylonian population and emptying of the land. Enemies will surround Babylon, and the Babylonians will not be able to defend themselves. The call further goes out to utterly destroy the Babylonian army (v 3). The word used is a form of *ḥerem,* the word typically used to describe the ultimate dedication of the spoils of war to Yahweh. Such dedication was carried out through unsparing destruction, and in fact the failure to carry out this command caused Israel a great deal of tragedy (for example, the defeat at Ai and the rejection of Saul as the first king). Verse 4 speaks of the dead and the wounded of Babylon fallen in the land and lying in the streets. Verse 5 turns attention to Israel and Judah. Though terrible tragedies have come upon these nations of Yahweh and **though their land is full of guilt,** they have not been forsaken by **the Holy One of Israel** before whom the people stand as guilty of covenant breaking.

■ **6-10** These verses turn the prediction of Babylon's fall into a lament, calling for foreigners who live in Babylon to flee the time of its destruction. This language is reminiscent of the call to flee Jerusalem in its own calamity—which was wrought by Babylon at Yahweh's command (see 4:6). Yahweh is here punishing Babylon because of its sins; the oracle urges its audience not to perish in Babylon when Yahweh brings his judgment on Babylon. Even though **Babylon was a gold cup in** Yahweh's **hand** who **made the whole earth drunk** (v 7; see ch 25 for a similar image of a cup of wrath), it is apparent now that Babylon has overstepped the bounds that Yahweh established for it and has therefore called Yahweh's righteous indignation down on its own head. The one who made the whole earth drunk with its violent power will now **fall and be broken** (v 8), having itself become drunk on its own power. The operating principle behind this metaphor is that the lust for power corrupts nations both ancient and modern. The success of Babylon and its ascendancy over the region at that time would surely have caused it to grow arrogant, to believe that its power could not be questioned. However, the experience of history is that empires always fall; it is just a matter of time.

Verses 9-10 indicate that the wound of Babylon is incurable, which recalls a similar judgment placed on Judah earlier in the book (30:12). While it may strike the reader as odd that an attempt was made to cure Babylon's wound, nevertheless because of the futility of this attempt the call goes out to **leave *it* and . . . go *back* to *our* own land** (v 9). It is not clear who is speaking here; the speakers (***we tried to heal***) here could be the foreigners who were urged to leave Babylon (Lundbom 2004b, 441). They recognize that the condition of Babylon is beyond cure; its evil was as high as heaven, so it is now the judgment that is on Babylon. So they decide to forsake Babylon and to depart for their respective countries. Upon leaving, the people (Jewish exiles) will **tell in Zion what the LORD our God has done** (v 10). The testimony to Yahweh's action in bringing about the destruction of Babylon and the consequent benefit for **Zion** is surely related to the new confession of faith in Yahweh that is created out of the return from exile. *No longer shall it be said, as Yahweh lives who brought us out from the land of Egypt, but as Yahweh lives who brought us back from the land of the north, and from all the nations to which he had exiled us* (16:14-15; 23:7-8). A great victory is about to be won over Babylon; but again, it is not a victory by Judah, even though it is for Judah's benefit. It is a victory achieved solely by Yahweh, and for that reason Yahweh is to be glorified and the people of Judah are to tell the story in Judah of what Yahweh has done on their behalf.

■ **11-14** The militaristic theme of this oracle against Babylon continues in v 11a. Even though Jeremiah does not know that it is King Cyrus who will destroy Babylon, the comment that Yahweh **has stirred up the kings of the Medes, because his purpose is to destroy Babylon** indicates something of an awareness of the geopolitical/military situation at the decline of the Babylonian period and the rise of the Medo-Persian period (v 11). Keown, Scalise, and Smothers summarize arguments for and against the authenticity of this note (1995, 361-62). The most important line comes in v 12: **The LORD will carry out his purpose, his decree against the people of Babylon.** This is, beginning to end, the work of Yahweh; no human might is primary. Again, this is consistent with the testimony of the book of Jeremiah throughout. Just as it was not merely by Babylonian military might that Judah and the other nations were defeated, so it is also not merely by military might that Babylon will be defeated. Regardless of whether the prediction of the Median takeover was original to Jeremiah, the book is correct that Babylon's ascendancy, though total over the ancient Near East, was short-lived. Very quickly the reins of power were transferred to the Medes and the Persians, whose empire is prominent in the OT in the books of Esther and Ezra-Nehemiah. Incidentally, this note about power being transferred to **the kings of the Medes** might be an indication of a later date of composition than 560 B.C., the thirty-seventh year of the exile of King Jehoiachin (see 52:31). At the least, this note about the Medes as the successors to the Babylonians on the stage of power may be an insertion from a later time. In any event, the text conveys some limited awareness about to whom power will be transferred after Babylon's inherent weaknesses come to light. Again, the text conveys the idea that it is Yahweh as the Lord of history who directs all of the nations of the world (see Isa 40:15).

■ **15-19** The focus now shifts slightly away from an oracle against Babylon to a hymn in praise of Yahweh. This hymn with minor variations is a duplicate of 10:12-16. See commentary on 10:12-16 (Varughese 2008, 145-46). Something like this should be expected in an extended declaration of Yahweh's power over the nations and in particular over the mighty, now falling, nation of Babylon. The authority Yahweh has over the nations is rooted, as is traditional, in the fact of Yahweh's creation of the world (v 15). Further, v 16 notes that Yahweh's command stretches over the "natural" elements: thunder, lightning, rain, and wind. This is also an expected statement in the light of the ascription of naturally occurring "celestial" events in antiquity to the activity of the gods. It serves here, however, to bolster the claim that Yahweh is able to move the nations as he wills; there is nothing and no one who is able to challenge the power of Israel and Judah's God. Verses 17-19 contain a polemic against idolatrous worship of divine cult images. The contrast is set up between Yahweh, a living god, and the idols, dead gods, the work of human hands. Thus these verses contribute to the hymn of praise to Yahweh. The contrast being set up here is between those idols that are the creation of human hands and the living God, **the Portion of Jacob** (v 19) who created not only the world but also the human hands who created the idols. By thus setting Yahweh above everything, the oracle forever sets idolatry aside as not a worthy practice for giving proper honor and glory to Yahweh.

■ **20-24** These next verses contrast the place Babylon once held and the place it holds now in Yahweh's eyes. Previously, as has been noted, Babylon was a tool in Yahweh's hand, sent out to destroy the nations of the world, and in particular Judah, for their sins. The imagery of this section makes this even clearer in strikingly militaristic terms. Here Babylon is Yahweh's **war club, [his] weapon for battle** (v 20). The next three verses lay out in tremendous detail the targets of Babylon's smashing. Yet v 24 starts the contrast. Now the standing Babylon has in the eyes of Yahweh is much different. It is reasonable to assume that lying behind this is the belief that Babylon has overstepped its bounds in being Yahweh's chosen instrument for the punishment of the nations. That this is so is demonstrated by Yahweh's declaration that he will repay Babylon for everything it has done. Moreover, the fact that Babylon is being specifically repaid **for all the wrong they have done in Zion** (v 24) makes explicit yet again that Israel and Judah are to be the primary beneficiaries of the blessing-turned-curse upon Babylon.

■ **25-26** Yahweh turns his address to Babylon, declaring that he is now **against you, O destroying mountain, you who destroy the whole earth** (v 25). Calling Babylon the **destroying mountain** may perhaps be an oblique reference to the Akkadian phrase "go beyond the mountain," which means to disappear forever. Leaving the mountain that is Babylon is death, but here Yahweh pronounces a death sentence on the mountain itself. Thus the prophet asserts again Yahweh's dominance over all the nations of the world; not even mighty and now crumbling Babylon is able to stand up to the power of Yahweh. Verse 26 proclaims utter destruction for the destroyer. The language is reminiscent of Jesus'—in the eyes of his opponents—prediction of the total destruction of the temple without leaving one stone upon another (Matt 24:2). Verse 26 states that not even one stone will be taken or kept from the destroyer nation as a corner or foundation stone for the future building of Babylon. The land will remain desolate and ruined forever.

■ **27-33** In this oracle Yahweh gives order to a coalition of nations, their kings and other leaders, led by the Medes to join in a holy war and make preparations to attack Babylon (v 27). These nations include **Ararat,** ancient Urartu (modern Armenia), located north of Assyria; **Minni,** a small kingdom located north of Assyria, the home of Manneans; and **Ashkenaz,** located north of Ararat and Minni, the home of Scythians. These nations came under the power of the Medes in the early part of the sixth century B.C. **The kings of the Medes** in v 28 probably means the kings of the coalition nations. The leader of this coalition is Media, an ancient kingdom located in the northwest part of modern Iran. Media became a major power in the late seventh century and joined forces with Babylon to bring about the collapse of the Assyrian Empire in 612 B.C. Cyrus the Great of Persia later incorporated Media into the Persian Empire in 549 B.C., some years after the latest date (560 B.C.) explicitly mentioned in the book of Jeremiah (52:31). In 51:27-28, the text describes the stirring up of the Medes against Babylon. The text thus recognizes the increasing influence of the Medes over the region. Again, these details are not as important as the overall declaration that Babylon's fall will come not by the power of the Medes but by Yahweh's might. The strength of the world empires is irrelevant, for it is only by Yahweh's direction that they move and are able to do anything. Verse 29 makes it clear that Yahweh's purpose against Babylon is firm and that his plan is to make Babylon a desolate place without inhabitants. One messenger follows after another, announcing the news of the destruction of Babylon's defense systems and the burning of the marshes by the advancing coalition forces, which creates panic among the soldiers (vv 30-32). Commentators think that the burning of the marsh grass in the swamps surrounding Babylon was either an offensive action or a defensive move to cut off escape routes from the city of Babylon (Lundbom 2004b, 467). The language of vv 31-32 sounds very much like that of Job 1:6-22 where the messengers come one after another to inform Job of the tragedies done to his family and possessions. It is only a matter of time before final destruction is achieved; regardless of the human empire that carries it out, ultimately it is the fulfillment of Yahweh's plans and purposes.

Many different metaphors and similes are mixed together beginning with v 33. **Daughter Babylon** is called **a threshing floor** and a crop to be harvested (v 33), a ***dragon*** (v 34), **a heap of ruins** and **a haunt of jackals** (v 37), **lion cubs** (v 38), **lambs *for* slaughter** (v 40), **the praise *of the whole earth*** (v 41), and a ***desolation*** (v 43). Though there are some positive images of Babylon in this material, they clearly carry here a sarcastic connotation. This array of images surely speaks to the importance of Babylon's fall and the implications it has for Israel and Judah within the ideology of the book of Jeremiah.

Daughter Babylon, the powerful and glorious city of Babylon, will be a threshing floor when the armies of the nations come through it (v 33). Babylon's boasts are used against it to make the point resound that Babylon's power, glory, and might are not at the level the empire claimed for itself. Yahweh has now turned his former blessing of Babylon into a curse against it, and when once this turn has been made Yahweh is relentless in his destruction of the old destroyer.

■ **34-35** Here Jerusalem laments and cries out for vengeance. The language is similar to the imprecatory psalms that contain Israel's urgent call to Yahweh to take vengeance upon its enemies. In v 34 Jerusalem laments about being devoured, crushed, and swallowed up and then spewed out by Babylon. This is followed by the curse on Babylon and its inhabitants; the inhabitants of Jerusalem call upon Yahweh to carry out his vengeance against Babylon with the same kind of violence done to them by the Babylonians (v 35). If the principal enemy in Jeremiah's time is the Babylonian Empire, then it is only natural to see something like this included in a lengthy prediction of the empire's fall.

■ **36-40** These verses contain the answer to the plea for vengeance. The entire group of verses is couched in the language of a promise to Israel and Judah. **I will defend your cause and avenge you,** says Yahweh (v 36). Verses 36*b*-40 give vivid expression to the desolation that is promised for Babylon. The land of Babylon, known for its water resources, will become a dry place, a heap of ruins without human inhabitants, and a home for jackals. Though Babylon will roar and growl like young lions, and show its arrogance and pride, Yahweh will make it drink from his cup of wrath (v 39). The text conveys in vv 39-40 two images to describe the end of Babylon: the perpetual sleep from which there is no waking up, and lambs being led to their slaughter. The image of drinking and making merry and falling asleep, though it is a judgment word here, also implies that the people of Babylon and their leaders had become drunk on their own success and they were too ignorant of the teetering foundation on which that success was built. Just as quickly as Babylon rose to power, its influence waned and was ultimately swallowed up by the Persian Empire which became the next major power in the region.

■ **41-53** The judgment on Babylon continues in vv 41-53. Verse 41 utilizes the cipher **Sheshach** to refer to Babylon (see also 25:26). Under the *atbash* system of letter substitution (see above on 51:1), **Sheshach** becomes *babel*; this is a reference to the city of Babylon or the nation/empire Babylon. In v 41 Babylon appears in the second part in poetic parallelism (like Leb Kamai in 51:1); so Sheshach here is not cryptic as in 25:26. The focus of v 41 is on the fall of Babylon, the once mighty and powerful nation on the whole earth, to a detestable and horrific place among the nations.

Verses 42-44 continue to pile on description of the destruction of Babylon. Like the oracle against Moab (48:1-47), the language becomes almost pedantic. At the same time, there is an inescapable note of joy in these verses. The joy is founded precisely on Babylon getting what it deserves for what it has done to the world, and to Judah in particular. Verse 44 makes a direct attack upon the gods of Babylon, predicting the shaming of the god Bel, which was another name for Marduk. Yahweh's judgment will bring an end to the streaming of nations to Babylon to pay tribute to Bel. It is easy to understand the prophet's critique of religious systems that accepted or encouraged the use of images because Israel's traditional faith expressly forbade idol making and idol worship (see vv 17-19). Attacking Bel by name elevates this critique to a higher and more sophisticated level; there is nothing and no power in Babylon that escapes the judgment of Yahweh. The famous walls of Babylon also will be destroyed (see also v 58).

Verse 45 is addressed to the Judean exiles. Yahweh summons his people to go out and save their lives from Yahweh's judgment on the city of Babylon. Yahweh also encourages the Judean exiles not to become dispirited and give up hope because of rumors that circulate in the land about violence and struggle for power among rival rulers in the land. After the death of Nebuchadnezzar in 562 B.C. there were at least two violent takeovers of the throne, including the one by Nabonidus in 556 B.C. Commentators think that v 46 reflects the period of instability from 562 to 556 B.C. (Lundbom 2004b, 485). Verses 47 and 48 reiterate the previous words of Yahweh's judgment; the destroyers will come from the north as Yahweh's agents of the destruction of Babylon and its idols. The whole land of Babylon will be put to shame by Yahweh's judgment, which will bring great joy to the whole of creation. The fall of Babylon is the just retribution from Yahweh for slaying the people of Israel and other nations (v 49).

In vv 50-51, Yahweh's people are encouraged to leave Babylon and return to their native land. These verses exhibit some of the characteristics of communal laments in the book of Psalms with the promise of divine deliverance given by Yahweh himself. The people cry out that they **are disgraced** (v 51) by what Babylon has done in the land of Judah, **because foreigners have entered the holy places of the LORD's house.** The problem of foreigners entering into the temple of Yahweh recurred throughout the later history, eventually touching off the Maccabean revolt when the Seleucid king Antiochus Epiphanes IV ordered a pig statue to be set up in the holy of holies. This is the "abomination that desolates" spoken of in the book of Daniel (Dan 9:27; 12:11 NRSV; see also 11:31). Here, however, Yahweh delivers a promise that the horrible situation in which the people now find themselves will soon enough be reversed, and they will be empowered to once again take control of their own lives and live faithfully before Yahweh.

The theme of the judgment on the idols continues in v 52. Judgment on Babylon is thus first and foremost judgment on the gods of Babylon, to whom the Babylonians gave credit to their victory over Judah. The Babylonians perhaps claimed their victory as the victory of their gods over Yahweh the God of Israel. Yahweh's plan is to send destroyers to destroy Babylon though it aspires to reach the heaven and builds fortified places in the heights (v 53). These verses do not give any hope to the proud and arrogant nation that gives credit to idols for their glory for its survival. It is likely that Yahweh's judgment on the idols of Babylon (see vv 44, 47, 52) could also be understood as his just retribution for the violence done to his house by those who worship these idols (see v 47).

■ **54-58** This unit makes up the final segment of the oracle against Babylon. The destruction of Babylon is treated here as if it is already happening. A cry of despair and anguish is being heard in the land of Babylon as the destroyers are carrying out the task of destruction. Again, it is Yahweh who is at the center of this historical event of bringing down the mighty empire of Babylon. It is the day of Yahweh's recompense, and he intends to pay back in full for all of Babylon's evil deeds. The image of drunkenness and perpetual sleep of all powerful people in Babylon is repeated in v 57. The city with its gates and walls will be leveled. The end of the mighty empire includes the destruction of every symbol of its greatness. The oracle ends with what seems to be a wisdom statement about people and nations exhausting themselves and spending energy for nothing, because in the end, an enemy may set fire to everything they have built up.

■ **59-64** This prose narrative describes a symbolic action against Babylon that was to be carried out by Zedekiah's official Seraiah son of Neriah, the son of Mahseiah, the brother of Jeremiah's scribe Baruch (see 32:12). While some commentators question the authenticity of these verses, others think that this is an authentic account of Jeremiah's instruction to Seraiah son of Neriah. Seraiah was among those who accompanied Zedekiah on a royal mission to Babylon in the fourth year of Zedekiah (594/3 B.C.). Though the Hebrew text seems to convey the idea that Seraiah went **with Zedekiah,** some commentators follow the LXX reading ("from Zedekiah") and assume that the king himself did not make the trip and that Seraiah was sent by the king to Babylon. The text does not indicate the purpose of this mission. If Zedekiah himself went, as the MT suggests, he perhaps did so in response to a summons from Nebuchadnezzar or to affirm his loyalty to Nebuchadnezzar or to pay tribute to the Babylonian king or for some official business.

Verse 60 indicates that Jeremiah wrote on a scroll **all the disasters that would come upon Babylon,** meaning perhaps the words of 50:1—51:58. Lundbom, who labels 51:59-64 as "Seraiah's colophon," thinks that Seraiah wrote the words concerning Babylon at the dictation of Jeremiah (2004b, 507). Jeremiah then gives instruction to Seraiah to read the words of the prophecy when he arrives in Babylon (v 61). Thus the instruction given to Seraiah here is very similar to that which Jeremiah gave to his scribe Baruch, Seraiah's brother, in 36:6. From a literary standpoint, the commands to both of the sons of Neriah to read words of judgment against a land written on a scroll form a nice narrative frame for this entire section of the book of Jeremiah running from chs 36 to 51.

Verse 62 contains the words Seraiah was to say as a prayer before reading the words on the scroll. This prayer affirms in a summary fashion Yahweh's judgment on Babylon, to make it a desolate place forever without any human or animal life. Jeremiah instructed Seraiah to tie a stone to the scroll after he finished the reading of the words on the scroll and throw it into the middle of the Euphrates. Seraiah's final act would be the pronouncement of a curse on Babylon. The curse comes from Yahweh. The disasters that Yahweh is about to bring upon Babylon would cause it to sink, like the sinking of the scroll with a stone tied to it in the Euphrates. It will never rise again to be a nation, a power in the world, and a place for the dwelling of humans and animals. We do not know if Seraiah performed this symbolic act following the instructions given to him by Jeremiah. It is likely that he did.

The narrative of 51:59-64 ends with an editorial statement that **the words of Jeremiah end here** (v 64). This conclusion, however, does not formally end the book; the book ends with a somewhat anomalous retelling of the fall of Jerusalem in ch 52. There are two ways to deal with this issue. First, the commentary on the last chapter demonstrates that it is an expanded version of ch 39 in which the same story is told. The destruction of Jerusalem and the Judean exile to Babylon is a central theme in the book of Jeremiah. The two accounts in chs 39 and 52 appear as repetitions of that theme to show its central place in the book. The second way of dealing with the problem of chapter 52 is provided in the text itself at 51:64. This verse has rightly caused some confusion among interpreters, for it seems that the editors are prejudicing the reading in some way by suggesting that v 64 is the formal ending of the book of Jeremiah. While such a suggestion may make sense in light of the almost complete duplication of 2 Kgs 25 in ch 52, it may have the unintended consequence of relegating the second telling of the fall of Jerusalem to a kind of secondary status when compared with ch 39. That is, by accepting what the editors suggest in 51:64, the reader is thereby forced to accept ch 52 as a copy of 2 Kgs 25. If, however, the reader does accept 51:64 as the formal ending of the book, then it opens up other avenues for interpreting ch 52 and the way in which the book formally ends.

FROM THE TEXT

These oracles against the nations serve a very simple function. They bring home the point in a convincing, albeit somewhat ponderous, way that the God of Israel is the God of the entire world. Further, because God controls the world, all the nations are to him "like a drop in a bucket" (Isa 40:15). An assertion like this would have been rather bold in the context of domination by Babylon. For one of the key religious rituals in Babylon was the reading of the Tablet of Destinies during the New Year festival. According to Babylonian theology, the Tablets of Destiny established the fortunes of everyone in Babylon from the king to the lowest slave, and also every nation, from the great Babylon to the lowest nation. However, according to the book of Jeremiah (and other places where oracles against the nations are found), the God of Israel determines the fates of all the nations of the world, not merely once a year as a part of the renewal of the world, but for all time. Thus these oracles move in the direction of establishing God's sovereignty over the world. He is not only the sovereign God but also the sovereign Judge of all nations. Thus God is concerned about sin not only among his own covenant nation but also among nations in the world. These oracles indicate his strong determination to bring all sinful people to his righteous judgment.

In preaching or teaching these oracles, however, one should avoid a great temptation. Judah was a small vassal state, really a colonized power without independent existence at the time these oracles were put into writing. The context of these oracles is God's covenant relationship with Israel and the place of Israel in the world in the sixth century B.C. situation of the rise and fall of major world powers. In this context of changing political realities, it was natural and legitimate for Jeremiah to perceive Yahweh the God of Israel whom he worshipped as the sovereign Judge of the nations that have been enemies of the land of Israel and have taken the people into captivity. The idea of God's sovereignty over the world and his intimate involvement in the affairs of the world as the sovereign Lord and Judge of all nations is a valid theological claim of these oracles when we hear them today. It is, however, a grave error, and perhaps even a sinful misuse of Scripture, to equate any particular people or lands as enemies of the people of God and thus enemies of God, and object of his wrath, just because they receive mention in these oracles. These oracles do not permit any nation to be the judge of other nations. No nation is called a righteous nation that has the divine commission to carry out a holy war against other nations. The destroyer nations in these oracles remain as destroyers who simply fulfill God's plans and purposes for the world. In the end, they also face God's judgment because of their evil, pride, and arrogance. It is thus important to read and interpret these oracles in the political realities of the sixth century and resist the temptation to import them wholesale into our situation nearly two and a half millennia later.

"BUILD AND PLANT"

THE FALL OF JERUSALEM—REPRISE (52:1-34)

Overview

Like a musical theme encountered throughout a symphony, the exile always lies at the heart of the book of Jeremiah. Naturally, a key part of the exile is the destruction of Jerusalem. The reader meets in Jer 52 a narration of Jerusalem's fall slightly different from that found in ch 39. In the main, however, the two stories are parallel, such that we may feel justified to stay with the image of music and consider ch 52 a reprise of ch 39, a conclusion that, characteristically, is alternately thunderous and melodic, echoing perhaps the jumbled feelings that would be expected in a society undergoing such momentous changes as was Judah in the early sixth century B.C. This final chapter has often been treated as a much later addition, due largely to its close affinity to the ending to 2 Kings. That may be so, but this is no reason to relegate it to the discard pile. It is important to consider this chapter as a genuine part of the book of Jeremiah that reflects the thought patterns and experiences of a people in turmoil.

BEHIND THE TEXT

The description of the siege, fall, and destruction of Jerusalem in ch 52 may be compared, on the one hand, with Jer 39; and, on the other, with 2 Kgs 25. What has been called the "reprise" has much more detail than the original appearance of the theme, but nevertheless both of them together constitute the heart of the book of Jeremiah. Comparisons with 2 Kgs 25 reveal a few more differences in detail, with Jer 52 being a bit more expansive in its reporting. That the account here has more detail than its counterpart in the Deuteronomistic History may well indicate that it is a later production, though it calls into question literary dependence of Jeremiah upon 2 Kings. Either the compilers of Jeremiah had access to a different source that is now lost (like the Synoptic Gospels and "Q" in the NT), or else both Jeremiah and 2 Kings are emphasizing different things in the common stock of tradition in service of their own distinctive theological themes.

IN THE TEXT

1. (Re-)Introduction of Zedekiah (52:1-3)

In contrast to the summary introduction that Zedekiah receives in 39:1-2, the introduction of Zedekiah in 52:1-3 is a bit more expansive. This version is much more like 2 Kgs 24:18-20. This coupled with the statement in 51:64 that the words of Jeremiah have ended seem to indicate that all or part of ch 52 may come from a different hand. Even if it does, however, it does not affect the meaning or importance of the passage in more than negligible ways.

■ 1 Here one finds the details of Zedekiah's age at accession and the length of his reign. His eleven-year reign lasted from 598/7 B.C. to 587/6 B.C. Verse 1 concludes by noting the identity of Zedekiah's mother. This was a common practice in the ancient Near East, for kings often had multiple wives in the desperate attempt to produce an heir and secure the line. This was further important because of the honored position given to the queen mother. Although the introduction of Zedekiah is more expansive here, however, the narration of the events of his reign is more truncated than that found in chs 37—39. Here in ch 52, the text moves right to what was naturally thought to be the most significant event occurring during his reign, the fall of Jerusalem.

■ 2 The succinct judgment upon Zedekiah's quality as a ruler speaks volumes. Verse 2 notes that Zedekiah followed the example of Jehoiakim, which was enough to declare him as a wicked ruler. The longer treatment of Zedekiah in chs 37—39 shows several instances where Zedekiah might have repented of his sins, but ch 52 presents him as nearly irredeemable.

■ 3 This exclusively negative judgment upon Zedekiah is reinforced. In effect, the entirety of the blame for Jerusalem's collapse is here placed on

Zedekiah. This move is made even though the claim was made in v 2 that Zedekiah has done evil in the sight of Yahweh just like Jehoiakim. Yet it is somewhat common to hold a leader on whose watch something catastrophic happens as culpable, even if the event in question has its background in actions of the leaders' predecessors. Therefore, the point of this completely negative judgment upon Zedekiah is that he did, in fact, have a chance to stave off the results that might have come from what Jehoiakim had begun. But because he did not avail himself of this opportunity, Yahweh's anger burned hot against Jerusalem, and the city wherein he had caused his name to dwell fell to the army of the Babylonians. This reprise of Jerusalem's fall—and, perhaps, justification for blaming Zedekiah—has its beginning in the simple statement of v 3*b* that **Zedekiah rebelled against the king of Babylon.**

2. Siege, Fall, and Destruction of Jerusalem (52:4-27)

■ **4-5** The first two verses give a summary of the scene, much like what one finds in the shorter version of the fall of Jerusalem in 38:28*b*—39:3. It is unfortunate, as has been mentioned, that the portion of the Babylonian chronicles having to do with the siege and destruction of Jerusalem have been lost. Comparison between the Judean perspectives or, at least, *a* Judean perspective presented here in ch 52 and the perspective of the conquerors would be most fruitful. The point of such an exercise is not to judge one accurate and the other not or one affected by ideological concerns and the other objective, but instead to gain as full a picture as possible of the events in question. Though the events were certainly more momentous for the history of Judah than for Babylon, nevertheless the capture of Judah and the resulting access to strategic military and trade routes would certainly have been significant for the empire's continuing aspirations for growth and domination. As in ch 39, the narrative of ch 52 is unconcerned with how Babylon's capturing of Judah impacted the geopolitical scene. Instead, its focus is on interpreting the events of 587 B.C. as Yahweh's punishment on the nation's sinfulness.

■ **6-11** The siege lasts until "the eleventh year of King Zedekiah" (v 5). As is typical of siege warfare, soon enough **there was no food for the people to eat** (v 6). This note recalls the actions of Ebed-Melech the Cushite taken on behalf of Jeremiah. Had Jeremiah stayed in the cistern into which he had been thrown up until the time narrated in this story, he would have starved to death (39:8). When food runs out in the city, despair sets in, and surrender is near. An analogous situation is reported during the Assyrian siege of Jerusalem about 130 years earlier (see 2 Kgs 18 and its parallel in Isa 36). Verse 7 says that surrender was not necessary, however, for **the city wall was broken through, and the whole army fled.** The army fleeing certain defeat captures in a vivid image the songs celebrating the downfall of the other nations, particularly Egypt (see 46:5). Apparently the king also abandoned the city in its time of need; ironically, the king himself was abandoned by the soldiers who were sworn to protect him (52:8). That this would happen demonstrates the utter despair of the situation. The king, supposed to be Yahweh's choice to defend the city and, especially, the temple from encroachment by foreign invaders, is not even able to stay in the city and fight. Instead, even his attempt to escape with his life (see 38:17) was thwarted; the Babylonian army caught up with him and put him on "trial," surely a military-style tribunal put on only for show (52:9). Truly the prospects for life in Judah have become grim by this point in the text.

What happens to Zedekiah is a cruel fulfillment of the prophecy given him in 32:4 that he will "see him [the king of Babylon] with his own eyes." Zedekiah does in fact see his conqueror, if only briefly. The last image entering the king's eyes, and one that was certainly intended to be burned onto his mind, is the slaughtering of his sons (52:10). The fact that this practice was common and, therefore, perhaps even expected of Nebuchadnezzar, does not lessen its gruesomeness. It is to be expected, again, that Nebuchadnezzar would have slaughtered anyone around whom resistance could be built. So all the Judean officials were executed just like Zedekiah's sons (v 10). It is clear that the Babylonians did not wish to come back to Judah to quell another rebellion, so they, in typically violent fashion, sought to settle the Judean question once and for all. Although genocide was not necessarily on the agenda—as it was during the Shoah—the devastation wrought by the Babylonians was near total, at least in terms of psychological impact. Even though the reader is instructed not to like Zedekiah by 2 Kgs 24:19; Jer 37:2; and 52:2, nevertheless only the most vindictive of readers will take a perverse joy in what happens to the last king to sit on David's throne. Blinded and in fetters, Zedekiah makes his journey as a prisoner of war to spend the rest of his life in prison in Babylon (v 11).

In the commentary on ch 42 above, it was shown that the conversation there centered on whether the Babylonians would indeed return after the assassination of Gedaliah to completely wipe out the remaining Judeans. There Jeremiah was convinced that they would not, that the siege and destruction of Jerusalem had satisfied the Babylonians' thirst for blood (and that Johanan's pursuit of Ishmael was enough of an effective response to the threat of rebellion).

■ **12-16** These verses describe the destruction of Jerusalem and the exile proper. Nebuzaradan, the captain of the guard who had an important role in Jeremiah's fate (39:13-14; 40:1-6), burned the temple of Yahweh and all the great houses of the city. The referent of the latter phrase is uncertain, though it may perhaps refer to the houses belonging to the city officials who supported the revolt of Zedekiah or who may have supported (or even led) future revolts. If this is the case, then it is but another way that the vengeance of the Babylonians is brought to bear not only on the land as a whole but on individual inhabitants of it as well. Verse 14 of ch 52 mentions the destruction of the walls, the defense system of Jerusalem. It is no longer a protected and safe place for anyone. After the text explained what happened to the city, the next two verses (vv 15-16) detail what happened to the people. In the case of one of the groups mentioned, a powerful link can be drawn to the literary context. The people taken to exile include **those who had gone over to the king of Babylon.** During the initial account of the siege, Jeremiah told Zedekiah, "If you surrender to the officers of the king of Babylon, your life will be spared and this city will not be burned down" (38:17). Here, however, those who voluntarily surrendered to the Babylonians are also included among the exiles. This may indicate a change in Babylonian foreign policy, and perhaps those who surrendered would have rather gone to Babylon than stay in a ruined Jerusalem (see 24:1-10). Nevertheless, it is significant that even those who voluntarily surrendered are deported (see 39:9). The only ones who remained in the land were the poorest inhabitants, given fields and vineyards to tend, presumably for the benefit of the empire (see 39:10).

■ **17-23** In contrast to vv 13-16, the verses in this subsection recount in great detail the furnishings taken from the temple of Yahweh and carried off to Babylon. There is no reference to this in ch 39. Such an elaborate description not only of the implements but also of the temple itself seems woefully out of place in this story of the siege and fall of Jerusalem. However, these verses still find their counterparts in 2 Kgs 25:13-16. As has been indicated, the account here is more elaborate. One example is the slightly expanded list of articles in Jer 52:18 ("sprinkling bowls" do not appear in 2 Kgs 25:14). In addition, Jer 52:19 has many more articles not found in the complementary verse in 2 Kgs 25:15. Jeremiah 52:20, like v 18, has one detail lacking in 2 Kgs 25:16. Jeremiah 52:21 and 2 Kgs 25:17 are nearly identical (though for some reason the NIV translators chose to convert the Hebrew measurements into feet in 2 Kings), with the only detail not in 2 Kings having to do with the thickness of the bronze pillars. The divergence between Jer 52:22 and 2 Kgs 25:17 is rather significant: whereas the former suggests **the bronze capital on top of the one pillar was five cubits high,** the latter records the height of the capital as "four and a half feet high," or three cubits. Finally Jer 52:23 does not have a counterpart in 2 Kgs 25.

We are surprised to find in the text detailed description of the furnishings of the temple that were taken away to Babylon. Especially in light of the sparser description of Jerusalem's fall in ch 39, these details seem ponderous at best and overbearing at worst. At the same time, however, these verses may yield a glimpse into the intense psychological pain wrought on the community by the destruction of the temple. The elaborate and costly implements dedicated to Yahweh's service may well have been a point of pride for Judah, and at least for the priests in charge of regulating temple service. While this in no way serves as definitive evidence for a priestly background for the Prophet Jeremiah, it is plausible that a priest, or one with priestly lineage at any rate (see 1:1), would be so concerned about the loss of the temple implements to leave behind a description of what they looked like in order to educate readers should they never be returned.

■ **24-27** The final four verses of the reprise account of Jerusalem's fall return once again to a description of people involved in the exile. In the same way as vv 17-23 are more elaborate than the summary statement in vv 13-14, so these verses include more detail than the summary statement in v 10. The earlier verse reported merely that "all the officials of Judah" were executed. By contrast, here we have two specific names, the high priest Seraiah and his second-in-command Zephaniah, plus a host of other people identified by title or function rather than name. All of these people summarized in v 10 and given in detail here were the principal leaders of the community in the absence of one king (Jehoiachin) and the incapacity of another (Zedekiah). If, as was suggested above, the policy of the Babylonians was to exterminate all those who could generate support for or lead a further rebellion against their authority in Judah, then an act such as this would be understandable. However, again, just because the act of a nation is understandable does not make it less barbaric. Furthermore, the book of Jeremiah is convinced of two things. First, even the heinously violent activity of the Babylonian Empire is under the control of Yahweh (see Jer 27; Hab 1). Second, the punishment of the people of Judah at the hands of the Babylonians would not result in their final destruction (4:27; 5:10, 18; 30:11; 46:28).

FROM THE TEXT

The great amount of detail to which this account of the fall of Jerusalem goes surely indicates something of the significance of these events for the self-understanding of the community. Moreover, that three roughly parallel accounts exist between Jeremiah and 2 Kings reinforces this significance. Even in the almost ponderous detail to which the book goes in describing the furnishings and the decorations of God's temple contributes to the profound sense of loss that the fall of Jerusalem must have instilled in the people, both elites and nonelites, religious establishment, government workers, tradespeople, farmers, and laborers. The theological implications of this passage, and the memory it enforced, can be summed up in the following ways.

This narrative shows the importance of remembering, even in a dire situation, where we have come from, even if the past circumstances involve painful memories. Just as it is important to remember past victories and gain strength from them, it is also important to learn from past mistakes so that they will not be repeated. God, through the Prophet Jeremiah, persistently warned that just the kinds of things described in ch 52 would come about if they refused to repent and return to God. Now that they found themselves in the situation of exile, that was not the end of their story. It was important, instead, to write down in great detail what had happened to them, thus preserving it for all time, as both a record of the past and a warning for the future. Included in this is the idea that God had chosen the people of Judah and Israel to be his most treasured possession out of all the peoples of the earth (Exod 19:5). If that was the case, then even after the trauma of exile, God's Spirit would move to restore that relationship that had been broken down through the sinfulness of the people.

The text also reminds us that memory can be a powerful tool but also a dangerous weapon. It is possible to imprison oneself in memory, so that one fails to live authentically in the moment. This happens with good memories just as much as with the kind of bad memories preserved in this passage. In this way, memory is a weapon used on oneself. Yet memory can also be used as a weapon against other people. By lording knowledge of past failures over someone else, a person can take an inordinate amount of power over someone and effectively enslave the other by what he or she knows about him or her. The more positive uses of memory are, as shown, to demonstrate the good points to be celebrated and the bad points to be avoided, without treating either as more than they ought to be treated.

God who is the primary actor in the events narrated in this text rules even over our memory of past failures, guilt of sin, and the destructive consequences of our sinful actions. One of the best-loved hymns by Charles Wesley says, in part, "He breaks the power of canceled sin, / he sets the pris'ner free! / His blood can make the foulest clean, / his blood availed for me!" The power of canceled sin is nothing other than guilt over the past. One may indeed wallow in the guilty feelings one has over past wrongs. But the enduring promise of the Bible is that God, through the sacrifice of Jesus, has removed our sin from us "as far as the east is from the west" (Ps 103:12). The pervasive power of God's forgiveness waits on those who believe in him and in his Son to claim it as their own. When they do, they find that even their remorse over what they have done fades from memory, for God actively purges from his memory all the wrong that humans have done once they surrender control of their lives to him.

3. Counting the Cost (52:28-30)

BEHIND THE TEXT

The book of Jeremiah ends with specific details—the number of Judean people taken to Babylon as exiles during various stages of deportation and details of the favorable treatment Jehoiachin, the exiled Judean king, received in Babylon. If the exile of the Jews by the Babylonian Empire is the loom upon which is woven the tapestry that is the book of Jeremiah, then these matters of detail are significant in two respects. First, these details allow readers to compare the biblical material to available external sources that may have information about the exile. The point of this exercise is not to test the historicity of the biblical witness, judging it unreliable when it diverges from the external evidence or reliable when the two correspond to each other; such an approach only serves to privilege the external sources over the Bible in terms of historical reliability. It is certain that both the biblical accounts and nonbiblical sources have their respective concerns and interests and one can expect to find such interests and concerns in both sources. Both sources are needed, however, to construct a more complete, and by-and-large more accurate, picture of the history of the sixth century B.C.

The second reason why the details of the exile are significant has more directly to do with study of the book of Jeremiah itself. The somewhat cold calculation of numbers in vv 28-30 anchors the prophecies of judgment in real life, by recognizing the tremendous impact the exile had on the life of Judah. This text implies that the land was never quite emptied of inhabitants (see also 39:10). Nevertheless, the number of the deported was significant enough to have persisted in the memory of Judah and to have been preserved in the Bible as part of the record of God's dealings with the people. In the same way, the text acknowledges Nebuchadnezzar's role in the exile; however, other statements in the book (especially 27:6 and 43:10) make clear that the Babylonian king is Yahweh's servant. The text thus effectively calls into question the potential claim of Babylon that the exile of Judah is evidence of its superior military status and political domination in the first half of the sixth century B.C.

IN THE TEXT

■ **28-30** The statistics of the three exiles include the number of deportees and the dates of their removal from the land. This summary of the number of prisoners taken by Babylon is lacking in 2 Kings. As is typical of the period, the dates are given with reference to the reigning monarch. At first glance, one might be surprised that the dates given all reference the Babylonian emperor Nebuchadnezzar, for this seems to give implicit assent to the legitimacy of the empire's claims for domination. Several instances in the book of Jeremiah, by contrast, reference the years of Judean kings and ignore Nebuchadnezzar (36:1, 9; 39:1-2). On deeper reflection, however, dating the exiles exclusively with reference to Nebuchadnezzar's reign avoids a particular difficulty. Each of these events took place during the reign of a different Judean monarch. In fact, the third exile took place when no Judean sat on David's throne. Hence, dating all of these in the years of Nebuchadnezzar provides consistent historical references.

The list begins with the number of prisoners taken during the seventh year of Nebuchadnezzar's reign (597 B.C.). The number given in 52:28 (3,023) is significantly less than the number given in 2 Kgs 24:14, 16 (10,000 according to Jer 52:14 and 8,000 according to v 16). Some think that Jeremiah's list counts only the adult males; others think that Jeremiah's count is perhaps more accurate and that the figures in Kings are inflated. Jeremiah 52:29 gives 832 as the number of prisoners taken into exile in the eighteenth year of Nebuchadnezzar (587/6 B.C.). Verse 30 lists a third deportation of 745 Judeans in the twenty-third year of Nebuchadnezzar (582 B.C.). Verse 30 also gives 4,600 as the sum total of all three deportations.

As for the numbers of exiles given, one may consider three points. First, these numbers fall outside the realm of verifiable data, and thus once again the comparison between the biblical record and external sources becomes important in order to construct as full a picture as possible of the events in question. Second, these statistical reports yield a collection of numbers that one might find somewhat incredible because of their precision. This is further complicated by the fact that the number of deportees in 597/6 here does not correlate with the numbers in 2 Kgs 24 and by the fact that 2 Kgs 25 does not give a number of the deportees of 587 and 532. However, the numbers involved in each of the separate deportations—3,023, 832, and 745—seem more realistic and believable. As Albertz maintains, "the brief Jeremiah list seems clearly preferable... Its precise numbers (3,023; 832; 745) give the impression of being more trustworthy, even if their round sum (4,600) does raise some doubts" (2003, 85-86). Third, the relatively small number of exiles raises questions about the severity of the exile for the history of Judah. If the total number was actually 4,600, then the exile seems rather insignificant when this number is compared to a relatively large population of Judah (Albertz 2003, 86). This raises the possibility that the number must have been larger than 4,600 for the exile to have caused such a great impact on the collective consciousness of Judah. Though the report that the land was completely emptied of inhabitants (2 Chr 36:21) may be a bit of exaggeration, it is likely that exile drained from the land all potential sources of leadership necessary for an orderly existence of those who were left in the land. In summary, the discrepancies between 2 Kings and Jeremiah make it difficult to come to a reasonable conclusion about the actual number of those who have been exiled to Babylon. One possibility is that 52:28-30 comes from an independent source, perhaps based on the actual number who finally arrived in Babylon. One final thing bears mention. The third exile mentioned in v 3, dated to the twenty-third year of Nebuchadnezzar (582 B.C.) is not mentioned anywhere else in the Bible. It is further significant that this deportation is attributed not specifically to Nebuchadnezzar but to **Nebuzaradan the commander of the imperial guard,** who would have acted on behalf of Nebuchadnezzar, his sovereign. Incidentally, Nebuzaradan is said to be the agent of the second exile in both chs 39 and 52. It is difficult, also, to suggest what might have triggered this final exile. No ready candidates from the book of Jeremiah present themselves. One possibility is that this happened as a response to the assassination of Gedaliah the governor (see ch 41). However, there is no other biblical account of this exile or the possible cause of a third wave of Babylonian invasion of Judah.

FROM THE TEXT

In three brief summary statements, the narrator gives us the number of deportations to Babylon and the number of Judeans deported each time. The text sums up in these three verses the ultimate price Judah paid for breaking its covenant with Yahweh. The text does not mention the casualties of various Babylonian military actions, but only the number of people taken into exile, which again shows the central role of the exile in the book. These verses seem to suggest that the ultimate price of Judah's sin is paid by the living, by those who are forced to leave their homeland to begin their lives in exile in a foreign land. The focus of this text is thus on God's expulsion of a people to whom he had given the land of promise as a gift in faithful keeping of his promise to their ancestors. They alienated themselves from God; now they are alienated from the land of promise, and thereby from the presence of God. They are sentenced to live and suffer the emotional and psychological and spiritual effect of the sin of their nation. We assume that perhaps the most painful thought of the exiled people was the question of God's presence. They were part of a religious tradition that promoted the idea that life in the promised land was necessary to experience the reality of God's presence. Would they ever be able to experience the reality of God's presence? Do they have to wait until the day of their restoration to be reunited with God? It seems that the vision of God that Ezekiel saw while in Babylon was God's answer to their agonizing questions about the possibility of experiencing God in the land of their exile (Ezek 1—2). Just as ch 52 ends with a ray of hope for the exiled people for their eventual release and freedom, Ezekiel gives them hope in the possibility of experiencing God even in the land of exile. Both Jeremiah and Ezekiel assure us that sin may separate us from the presence of God, but God is never so far away from sinners that he cannot be found by those who wish to experience his forgiving and saving grace.

4. The Ending That Does Not End (52:31-34)

BEHIND THE TEXT

The rejuvenated Babylonian Empire under Nabopolassar and his son Nebuchadnezzar II (also known as "Nebuchadnezzar the Great") was relatively short-lived. For after the death of Nebuchadnezzar II in 562 B.C., the empire saw a quick succession of ineffective rulers over the next two decades. **Amel-Marduk** was the first of these rulers. A short two years later, in 560 B.C., Amel-Marduk was killed in a violent coup led by the next king, Nergal-Sharezer, who held the throne until 556 B.C. Two other kings would reign in that year: Nergal-Sharezer's young son Labashi-Marduk, assassinated about nine months into his reign; and the final principal king of Babylon, Nabonidus. On this last king, opinions are divided, though it is clear that he moved the capital to the city of Teima in the Arabian desert for a time, leaving his son Belshazzar ruling in his place. This is reported in Dan 5, though there Belshazzar's father is named as the better-known Nebuchadnezzar rather than Nabonidus.

At the same time as Babylon was on the decline as an empire, a rising military superstar from Persia by the name of Cyrus II (also known, like Nebuchadnezzar II, as "Cyrus the Great") was gaining momentum, winning more and more territory for his homeland. Soon enough, Cyrus the Great would capture the Median kingdom ruled over by his grandfather Aystages and set the stage for the next grand shift in the ancient Near East. Cyrus would defeat Babylon in 539 B.C., an event that would prove important for the history of Israel as well, as can be seen in such places as 2 Chr 36:22-23; Ezek 1:1-8; and Isa 45:1-8.

IN THE TEXT

■ **31** The release of Jehoiachin from prison is dated to the thirty-seventh year of his exile, a date cross-referenced to the first year of Amel-Marduk. This relatively firm date of 562-561 B.C. thus establishes the beginning of Jehoiachin's exile, and the first attack on Jerusalem that came with it, in 598-597 B.C. The text here makes an important shift in reckoning historical events; it includes a key reference to the exile of Jehoiachin, which may have been important for the people in exile, especially to those who may have been looking forward to the exile lasting only for seventy years (29:10). One may find here the anticipation that in less than thirty-seven years the exile would come to an end. The new Babylonian king is called **Evil-Merodach**, a Hebrew transliteration of the king's name. The name means "Marduk's Man," rendered in the Old Babylonian tongue as "Awil-Marduk," perhaps a little closer to what appears in the Hebrew text. Although Amel-Marduk was not considered important by and for the Babylonians, he was rather significant for the Israelites, as seen in this brief glimpse into his concern for the exiled King Jehoiachin.

It is of interest, though not central to the meaning of the passage, that the specific day and month of the release are given. What is important to note is that these verses essentially duplicate those found at the end of 2 Kings, with an ever-so-slight difference in detail. Whereas Jer 52:31 says the release came on the twenty-fifth day of the month (twenty-fourth day, in the Septuagint), 2 Kgs 25:27 says it was on the twenty-seventh day. The specific dating might have served to bolster the credibility of the passage as part of a larger document bearing historical witness to the events of the mid-sixth century B.C., but this is uncertain.

■ **32-34** What is more certain is the note of hope that a story like this might have sounded to a community living in exile. However, this hope was at best ambiguous because it does not say anything about the condition of the exiled people and the way Babylon treated them. It is possible that the Judean exiles would have seen the release of Jehoiachin from prison as the harbinger of their own freedom that is soon coming. It certainly is plausible that Amel-Marduk, as new king of Babylon, could have reevaluated the treatment of imprisoned kings. There is therefore no reason to suspect this text as inventing history.

The book ends with a description of the favor shown to Jehoiachin by Amel-Marduk. He spoke kindly to Jehoiachin and gave him a place above other kings in captivity (v 32). The text indicates that Amel-Marduk honored Jehoiachin by having him dress, assumedly, in garments appropriate to his former position as king of conquered Judah and that Jehoiachin ate regularly at the king's table (v 33). In addition, the king granted daily allotment of food to the Judean king (v 34).

One further point bears mentioning. If this honoring of Jehoiachin took place in the accession year of Amel-Marduk, then it builds on the assumption that all relationships of power are subject to renegotiation when a new power comes to the throne. Yet a problem for interpretation arises, it seems, precisely on the antecedents of the phrases **as long as he lived** and **till the day of his death**. It is usual to read these as referring to Jehoiachin, with the resulting interpretation that so long as Jehoiachin lived he received an allotment of food from the king's table and was seated at the position of highest prominence among all the other exiled kings (vv 32-33). However, the fact that Amel-Marduk only reigned two years, as noted above in the history of Neo-Babylonian rulers, it could rather be that the arrangement beneficial to Jehoiachin only pertained so long as Amel-Marduk lived. The NIV word order actually seems to lend itself to this interpretation. On the other hand, that this passage makes no reference to what Nergal-Sharezer did with regard to Jehoiachin leads to two possibilities. If the way Amel-Marduk treated Jehoiachin was continued by Nergal-Sharezer, then once again the pronouns refer to Jehoiachin as according to the traditional reading. Alternatively, if the relationships between the Babylonian throne and the subjugated kings were reevaluated once more by Nergal-Sharezer, then it is also possible that the latter were put back into prison by the new ruler of Babylon. The resolution of this question will have to await more sustained investigation of Neo-Babylonian policy regarding the treatment of the rulers of subjugated states who had been exiled to Babylon.

FROM THE TEXT

As noted above, these four verses essentially say the same thing as 2 Kgs 25:27-30. That both the Deuteronomistic History and the book of Jeremiah end with a note regarding the fate of King Jehoiachin in exile seems to indicate the central importance of the exile not only for these two pieces of literature but also for the nation as a whole. While this repetition has been marshaled as further evidence for Deuteronomistic influence over the book of Jeremiah, it could be alternatively explained by the supposition that both the

Deuteronomists and Jeremiah are drawing on a common theological stock to make a similar point about the hoped-for-but-unrealized future dawning in God's promises to the people.

The reader must recognize, however, that in spite of the hopeful tone on which the book ends, Jehoiachin remains in exile after the last verse. So, at best, the hope is ambiguous, longing for a new, restored future in the land but still lamenting the situation of exile. A few significant theological lessons can be drawn from this.

Though the text recounts God's punishment of Judah for its covenant violations, this punishment does not mean the end of God's relationship with Judah. This text needs to be heard in tandem with the texts that speak of God's offer of forgiveness and restoration (see 29:10-14; chs 30—31). There are no sins for which God does not offer forgiveness, except for final rejection of his offer of salvation. No sin is greater than any other sin, and thus there is no one thing humans can do to make it impossible to return to God. Even the most vehement rebels against the will of God can be redeemed if they turn away from their sinful ways and return to him.

Though Jeremiah is absent from the final words of this book, the text reflects his thoughts, his hopes, and his visions for Judah. The complexity of the structure of the book makes it difficult to determine the location of the "last words" of the prophet in the book. It is likely that the oracle of comfort to Baruch may have been his final words (45:1-5). Nevertheless, the thought pattern expressed in 52:28-32 is consistent with that ascribed to Jeremiah throughout the book. The prophet suffered a great deal of anguish for his people, and he did not want to see them suffer just for the sake of suffering. Rather, he longed for the restoration of the relationship between the people and God. The narrative of Jehoiachin's release from prison reflects the optimism and the hope that the prophet maintained for the future of Judah. Jeremiah was convinced that though Judah destroyed its relationship with God through acts of disobedience, it could always be restored through a renewed faithfulness. What makes this restoration of sinners possible is the grace of God that reaches out to those in exile. It is possible to say, in keeping with the overall theology of God's sovereignty over the nations in Jeremiah, that Jehoiachin's release is not the outcome of the goodwill of a new ruler of Babylon, but evidence of God's gracious work on behalf of his exiled people. The Babylonian king is simply an instrument through which this grace comes to the exiled king of Judah, and by extension, to the exiled people of Judah.

The emphasis on the exile of Judah in this chapter is intentional in that the book and its editors (and Jeremiah himself) seem to present it as a turning point in Israel's history. The fact that the book ends with the description of the exile points the readers to the question, "What next?" The aim of this chapter is not necessarily to reiterate the punitive aspect of judgment (which has been told in several places in the book), but to turn the attention of the readers to the purgative aspect of judgment. It seems clear throughout the OT that the threat of exile was never meant to represent a condition from which the people could never return. The life in exile, most likely, offered the exiled people the opportunity to reflect on what they have lost—not only their land but also their relationship with God. It would not be unreasonable to assume that the exiled people longed for their return to their land and their God. The return from exile in Babylon, though it happened many years later, and though most of the first generation Judean exiles in Babylon and those who lived in the land of Judah who witnessed the collapse of their nation were not alive to see it, meant renewed relationship with God and his covenant promises. The return also introduced for the restored community a new historical reference for its confession of faith in the God who brought them out of the land of their exile (see 16:14-15; 23:7-8).

The strange way in which the book of Jeremiah ends implicitly conveys something significant about the strange way God acts in human history and in the lives of individuals to give hope to the sinful world. There is only a tiny ray of hope in the last words of the book—a slim chance for a future for the exiled Judah. Hidden in this somewhat ambiguous note of hope is the enduring conviction of the Scriptures that God is not only in the promise-making business but in the promise-keeping business as well. The hope at the end of Jeremiah is only proleptic. Though it is not offered in concrete terms, and though its fulfillment may be delayed, it will not be denied. Hill, commenting on the importance of the exile for the book of Jeremiah, notes: "While there are promises about an end of the exile, this is not yet in sight" (1999, 17). The book ends with the end of the exile not yet in sight; nonetheless, it ends with an optimistic note about new possibilities with God. The hope this text conveys is grounded in the very character of God who is faithful to his promises. This is the nature of hope in the Scriptures; it is the anticipation of something promised, the fulfillment of which is a certainty. That is why hope is linked with faith in the Scriptures (Heb 11:1). The Apostle Paul writes: "Hope does not disappoint us, because God has poured out his love into our hearts by the Holy Spirit, whom he has given us" (Rom 5:5). For Christians, the certainty of hope is grounded in the resurrection of Jesus Christ. Hope is indeed "a living hope" and this Christian hope is, first and foremost, hope in the coming of Jesus Christ, the object of our love and faith, and the source of our joy and salvation (see 1 Pet 1:3-9).